Spreading... Crocodiles in a ring...

Crocodiles expressing appreciation.

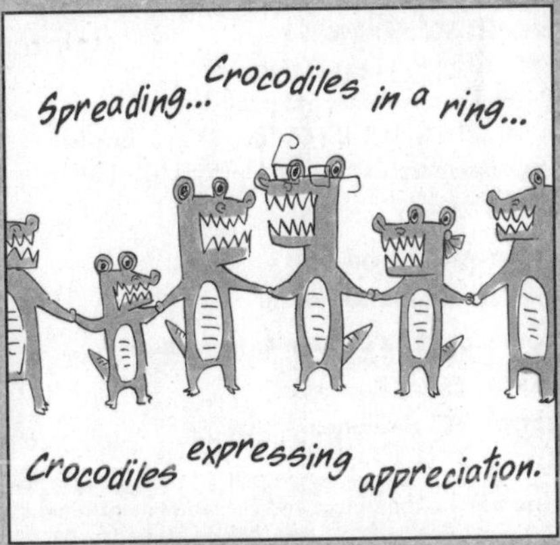

KOYOHARU GOTOUGE

I'm Gotouge. This is volume 11! Thank you for spreading this meager ring of crocodiles! I can never fully express my gratitude to everyone for spending their precious time on this manga. Perhaps we were comrades in arms in our former lives. Even when I feel like running away naked, some people still read it! When I realize I'm not alone, I can hang in there. I will work like mad so everyone can enjoy the series more!

DEMON SLAYER:
KIMETSU NO YAIBA
VOLUME 11
Shonen Jump Edition

Story and Art by
KOYOHARU GOTOUGE

KIMETSU NO YAIBA
© 2016 by Koyoharu Gotouge
All rights reserved. First published in Japan
in 2016 by SHUEISHA Inc., Tokyo. English
translation rights arranged by SHUEISHA Inc.

TRANSLATION John Werry
ENGLISH ADAPTATION Stan!
TOUCH-UP ART & LETTERING John Hunt
DESIGN Jimmy Presler
EDITOR Mike Montesa

Printed in Italy

Published by VIZ Media, LLC
P.O. Box 77010
San Francisco, CA 94107

11
First printing, March 2020
Eleventh printing, April 2022

viz.com

DEMON SLAYER
KIMETSU NO YAIBA

A CLOSE FIGHT

KOYOHARU GOTOUGE

CHARACTERS

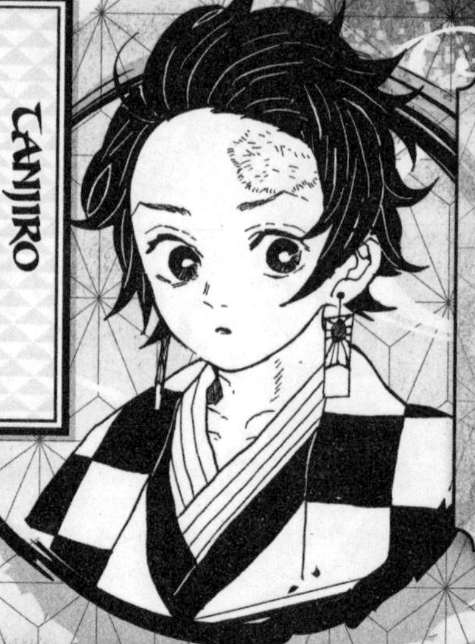

TANJIRO KAMADO

A kind boy who saved his sister and now aims to avenge his family. He can smell the scent of demons and an opponent's weakness.

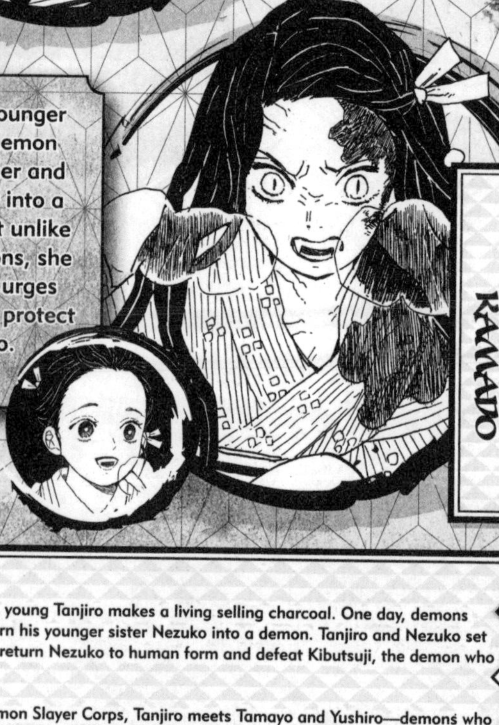

NEZUKO KAMADO

Tanjiro's younger sister. A demon attacked her and turned her into a demon. But unlike other demons, she fights her urges and tries to protect Tanjiro.

STORY

In Taisho-era Japan, young Tanjiro makes a living selling charcoal. One day, demons kill his family and turn his younger sister Nezuko into a demon. Tanjiro and Nezuko set out to find a way to return Nezuko to human form and defeat Kibutsuji, the demon who killed their family!

After joining the Demon Slayer Corps, Tanjiro meets Tamayo and Yushiro—demons who oppose Kibutsuji—who provide a clue to how Nezuko may regain her humanity. On a new mission, Tanjiro and the others work with the Sound Hashira, Uzui. They go to the Hanamachi entertainment district to confront the Upper Rank 6 demon Daki, who engages Tanjiro and Nezuko in a desperate fight. Uzui cuts off Daki's head, but from within her body appears her older brother, Gyutaro, wielding poisonous Blood Sickles. How can they defeat these two demons?!

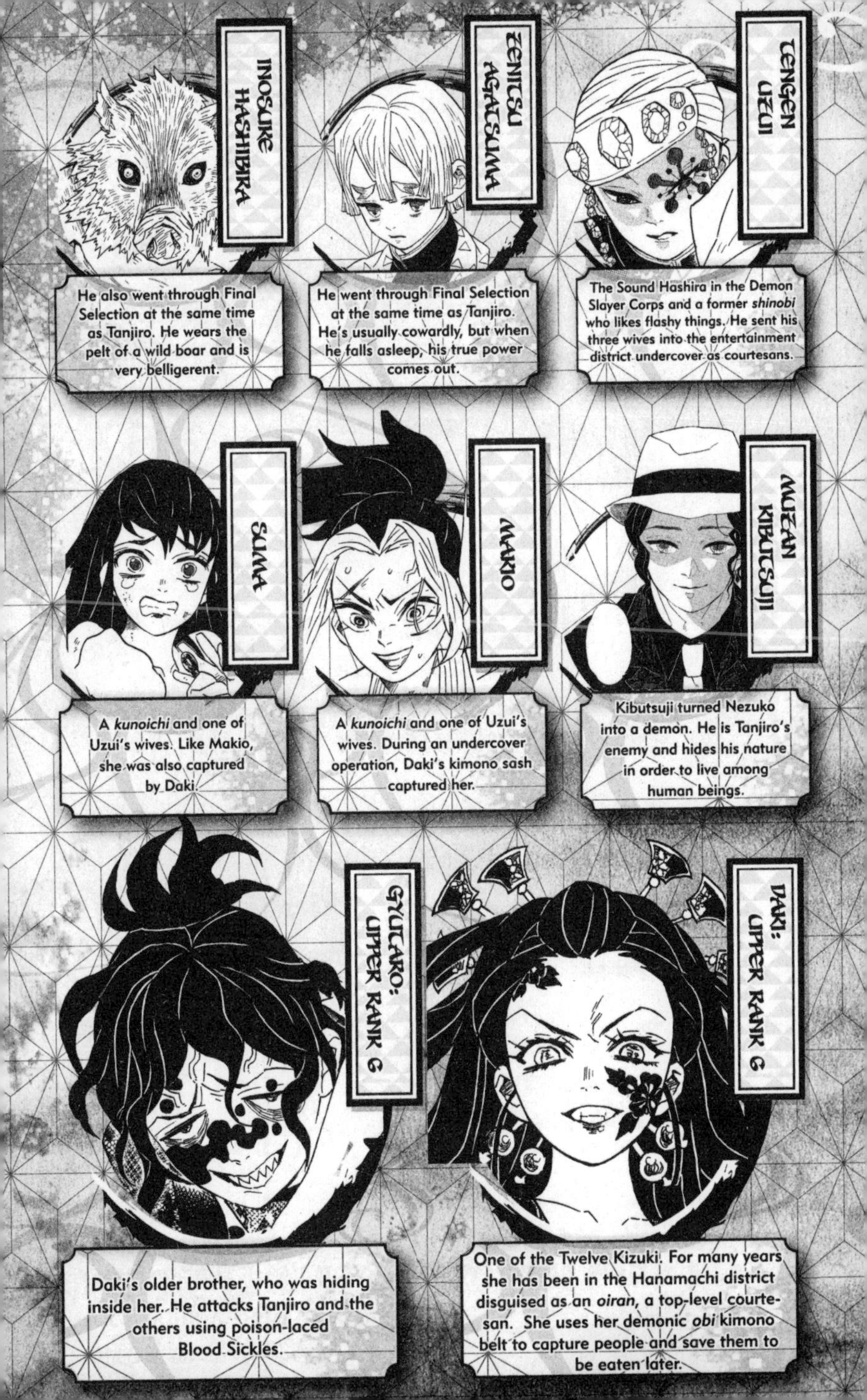
TENGEN UZUI
The Sound Hashira in the Demon Slayer Corps and a former *shinobi* who likes flashy things. He sent his three wives into the entertainment district undercover as courtesans.
ZENITSU AGATSUMA
He went through Final Selection at the same time as Tanjiro. He's usually cowardly, but when he falls asleep, his true power comes out.
INOSUKE HASHIBIRA
He also went through Final Selection at the same time as Tanjiro. He wears the pelt of a wild boar and is very belligerent.
MUZAN KIBUTSUJI
Kibutsuji turned Nezuko into a demon. He is Tanjiro's enemy and hides his nature in order to live among human beings.
MAKIO
A *kunoichi* and one of Uzui's wives. During an undercover operation, Daki's kimono sash captured her.
SUMA
A *kunoichi* and one of Uzui's wives. Like Makio, she was also captured by Daki.
DAKI: UPPER RANK 6
One of the Twelve Kizuki. For many years she has been in the Hanamachi district disguised as an *oiran*, a top-level courtesan. She uses her demonic *obi* kimono belt to capture people and save them to be eaten later.
GYUTARO: UPPER RANK 6
Daki's older brother, who was hiding inside her. He attacks Tanjiro and the others using poison-laced Blood Sickles.

CONTENTS

DEMON SLAYER
KIMETSU NO YAIBA

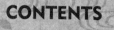

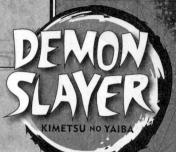

11

A CLOSE FIGHT

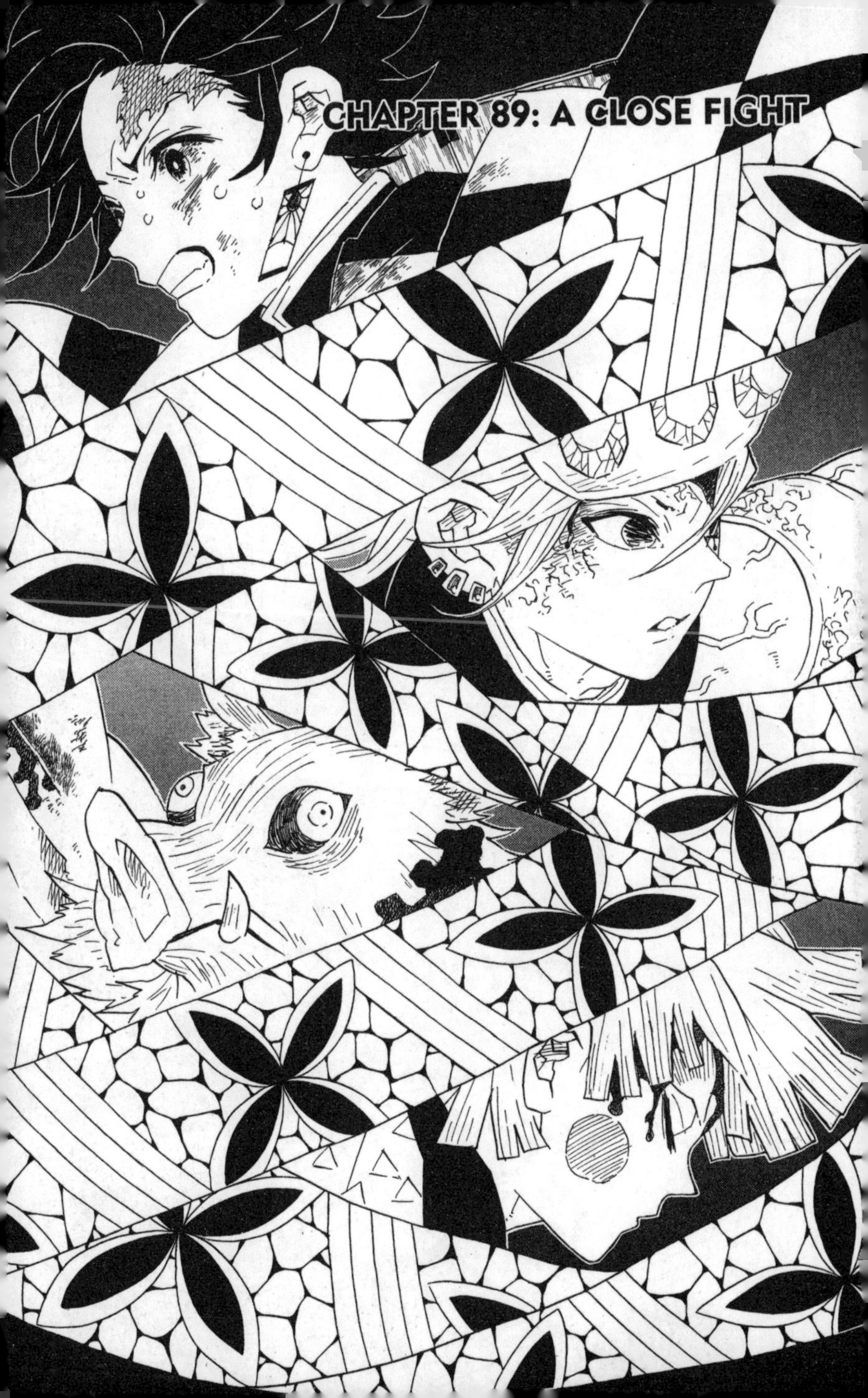
CHAPTER 89: A CLOSE FIGHT

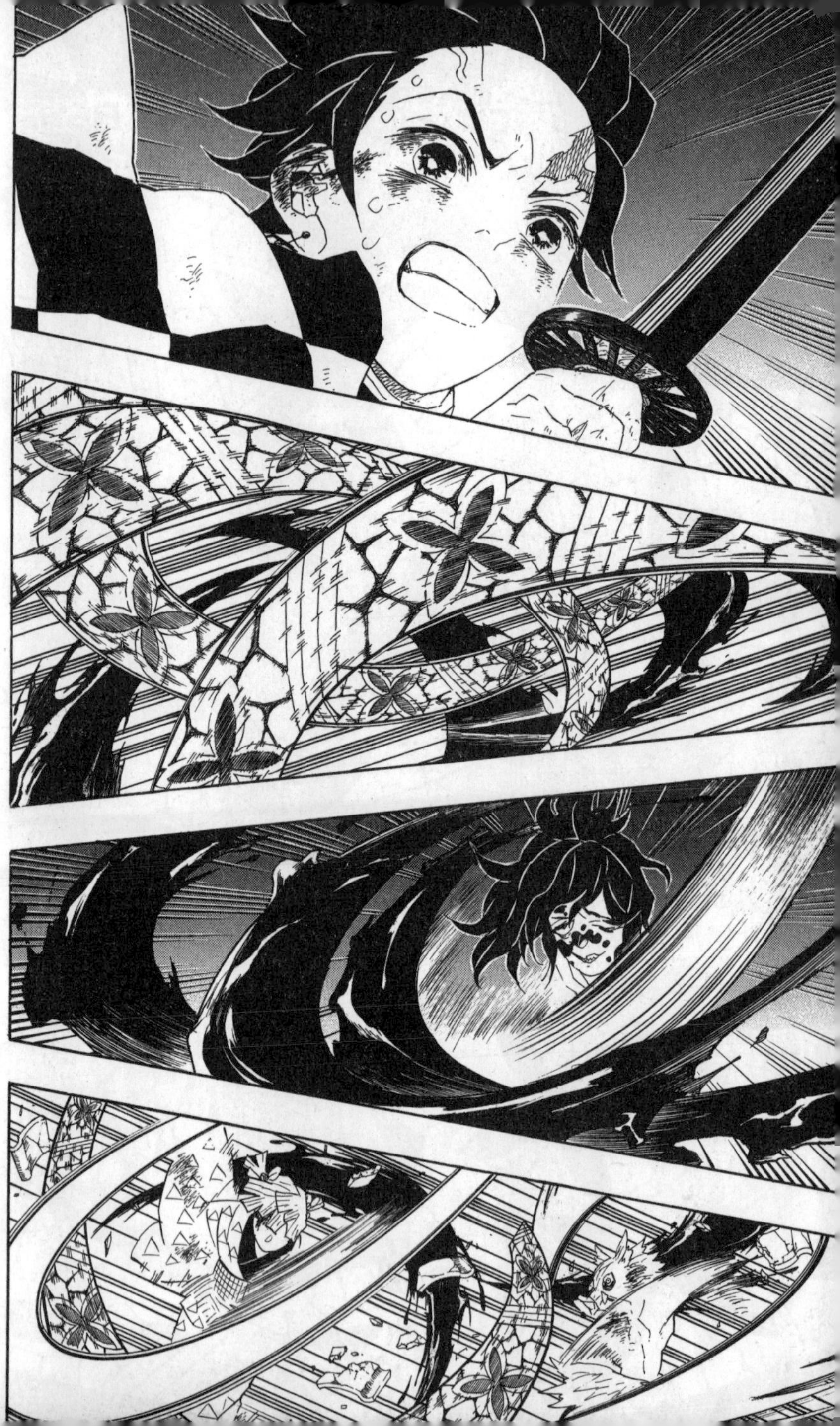

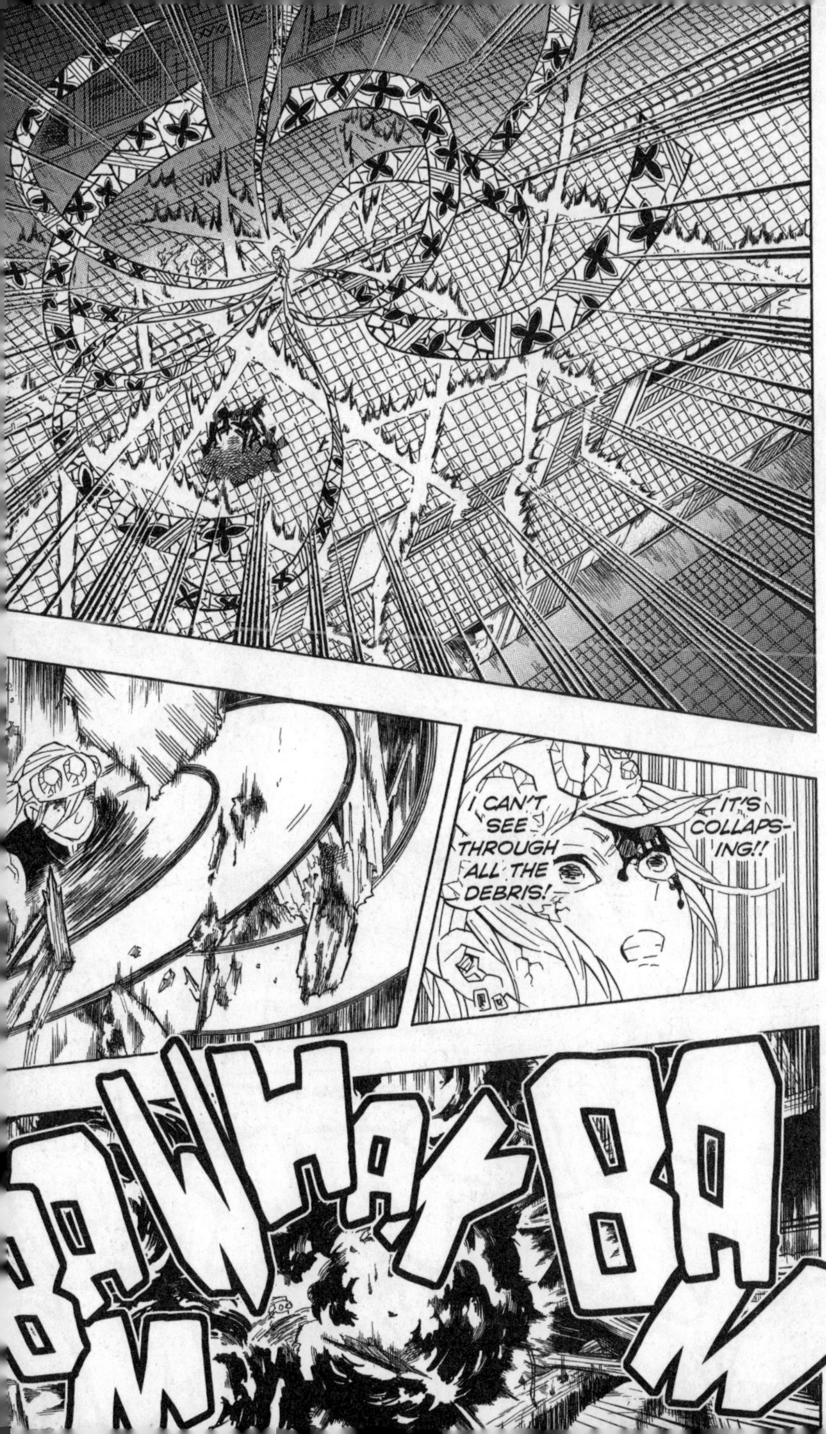
IT'S COLLAPS-ING!!
I CAN'T SEE THROUGH ALL THE DEBRIS!

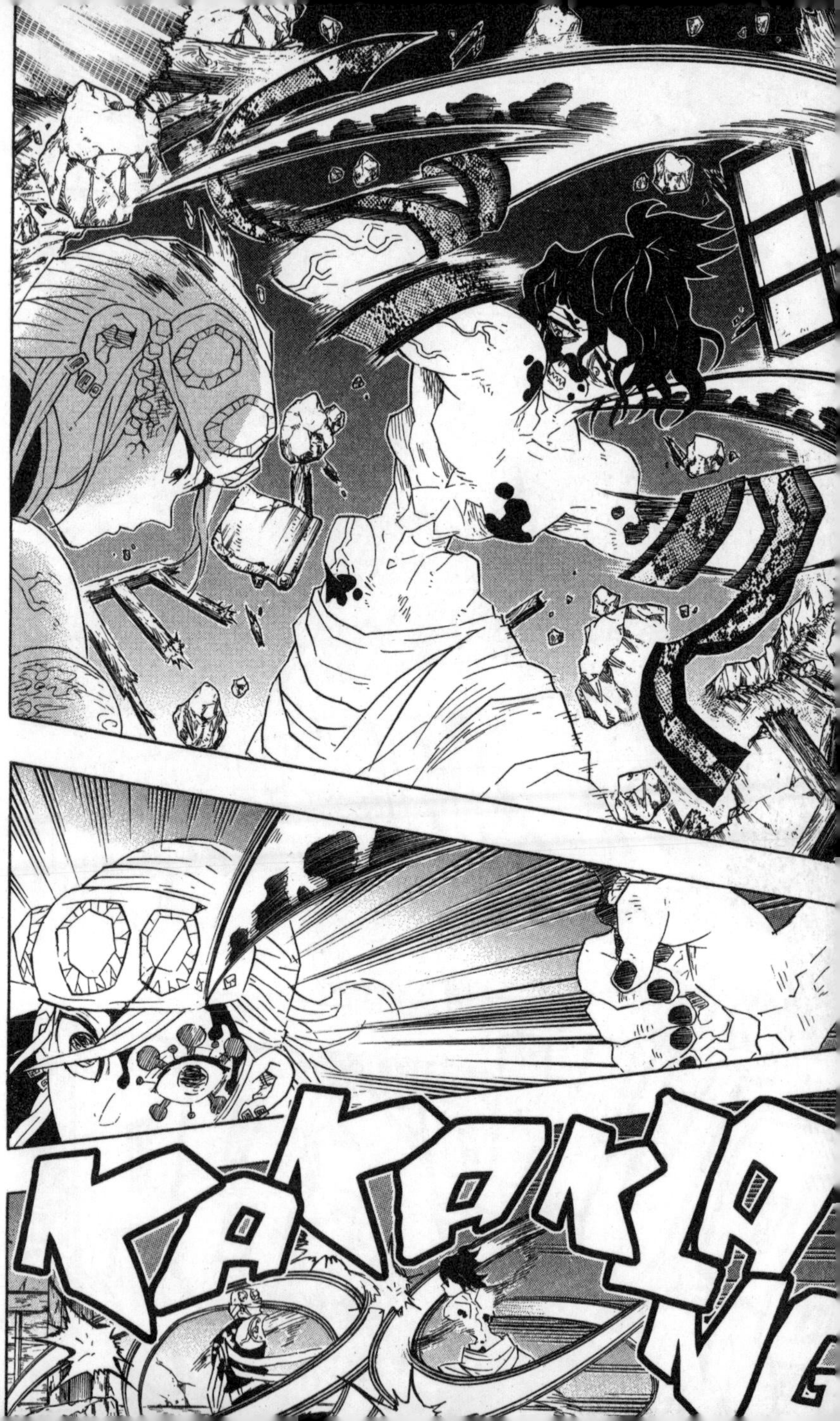

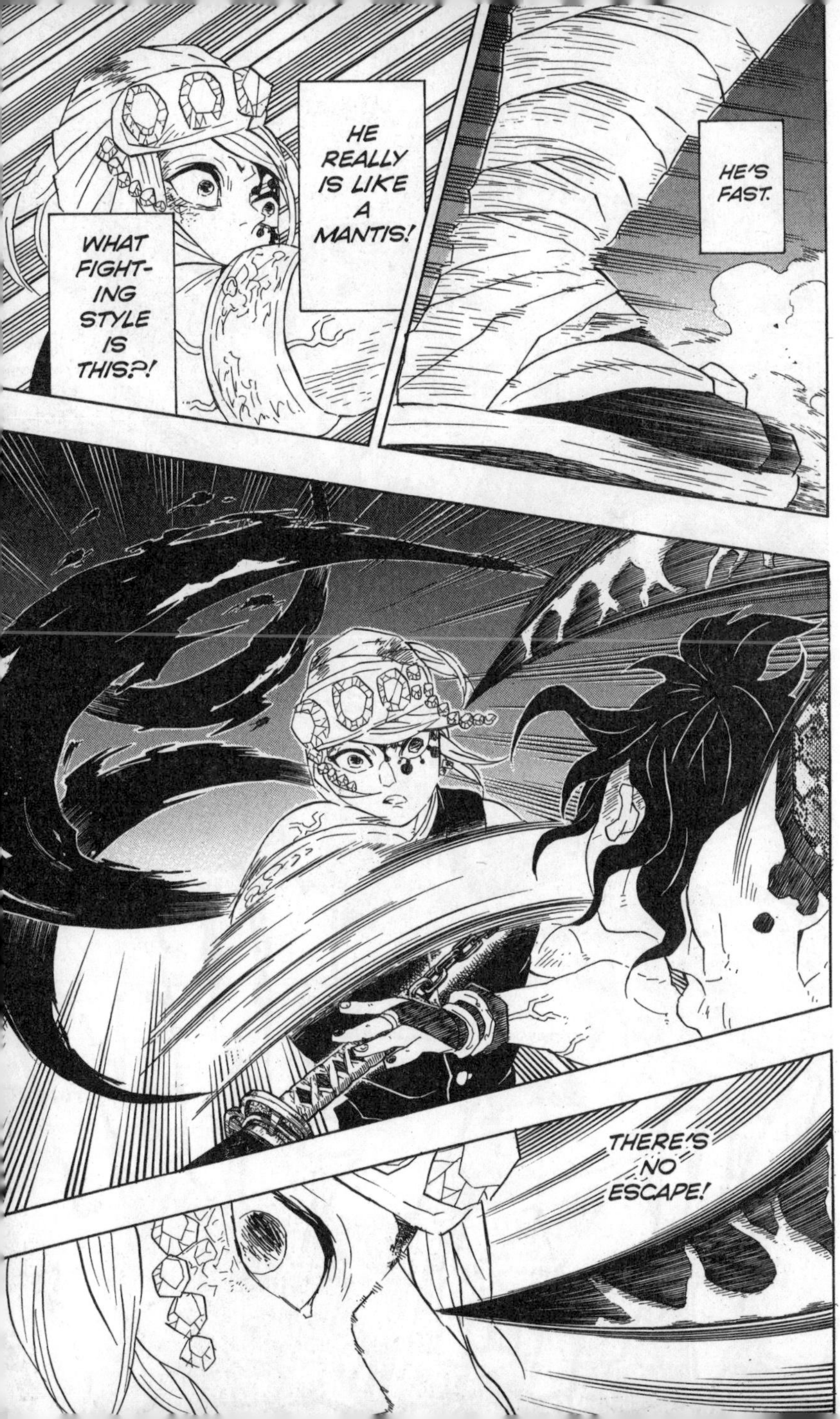
HE'S FAST.
HE REALLY IS LIKE A MANTIS!
WHAT FIGHTING STYLE IS THIS?!
THERE'S NO ESCAPE!

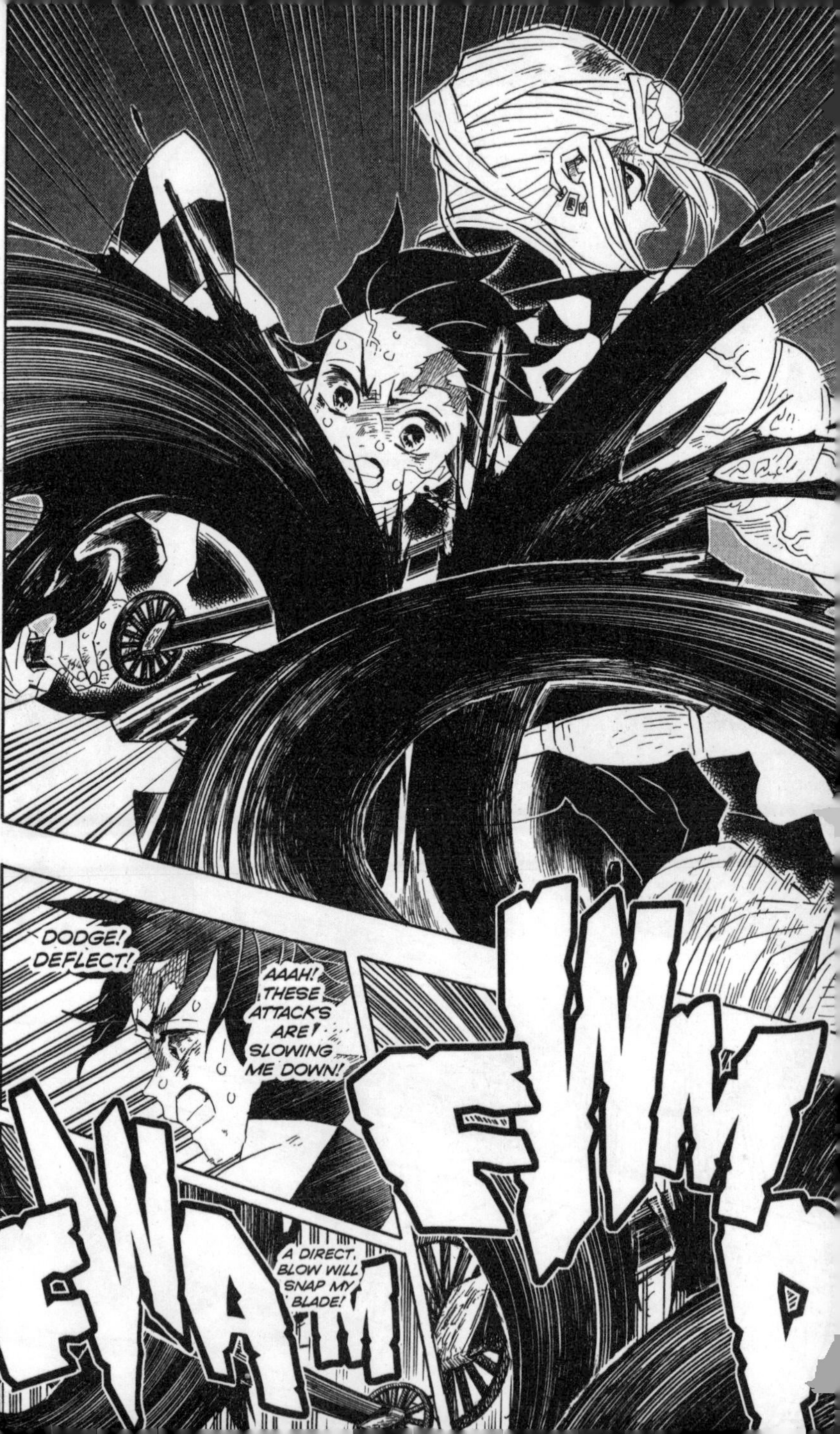
AAAH! THESE ATTACKS ARE SLOWING ME DOWN!
DODGE! DEFLECT!
A DIRECT BLOW WILL SNAP MY BLADE!

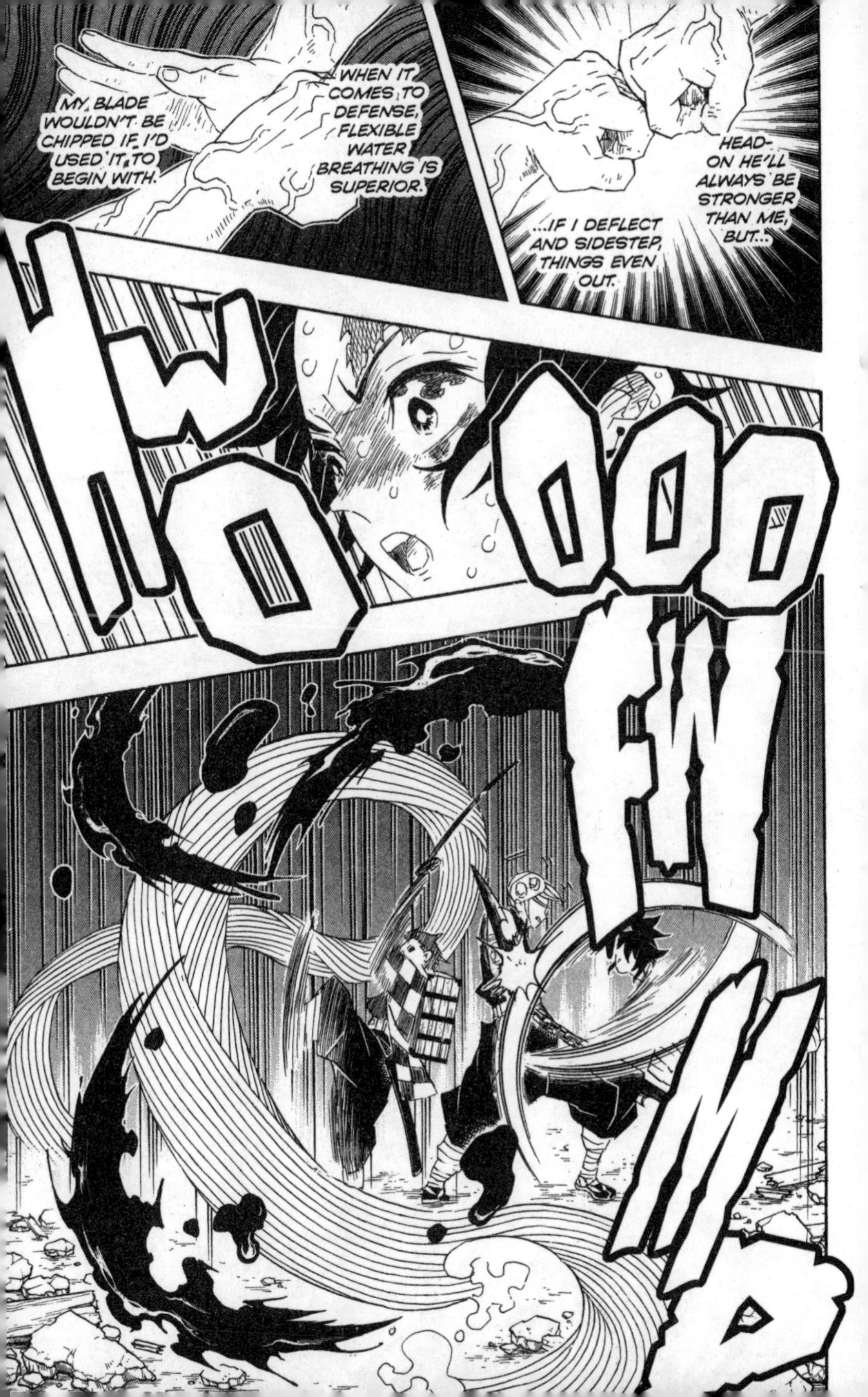
HEAD-ON HE'LL ALWAYS BE STRONGER THAN ME, BUT...
...IF I DEFLECT AND SIDESTEP, THINGS EVEN OUT.
WHEN IT COMES TO DEFENSE, FLEXIBLE WATER BREATHING IS SUPERIOR.
MY BLADE WOULDN'T BE CHIPPED IF I'D USED IT TO BEGIN WITH.

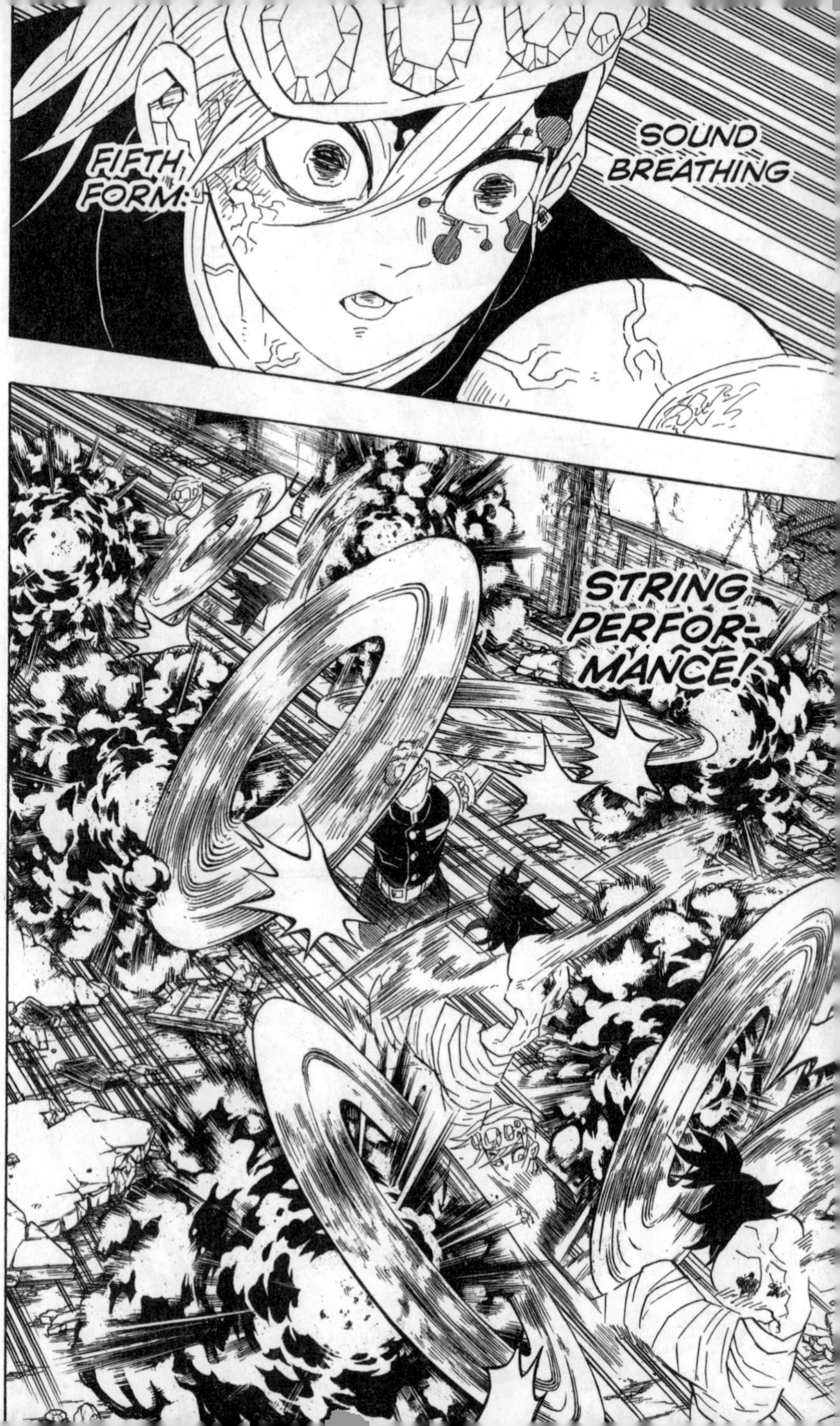
SOUND BREATHING
FIFTH FORM:
STRING PERFOR-MANCE!

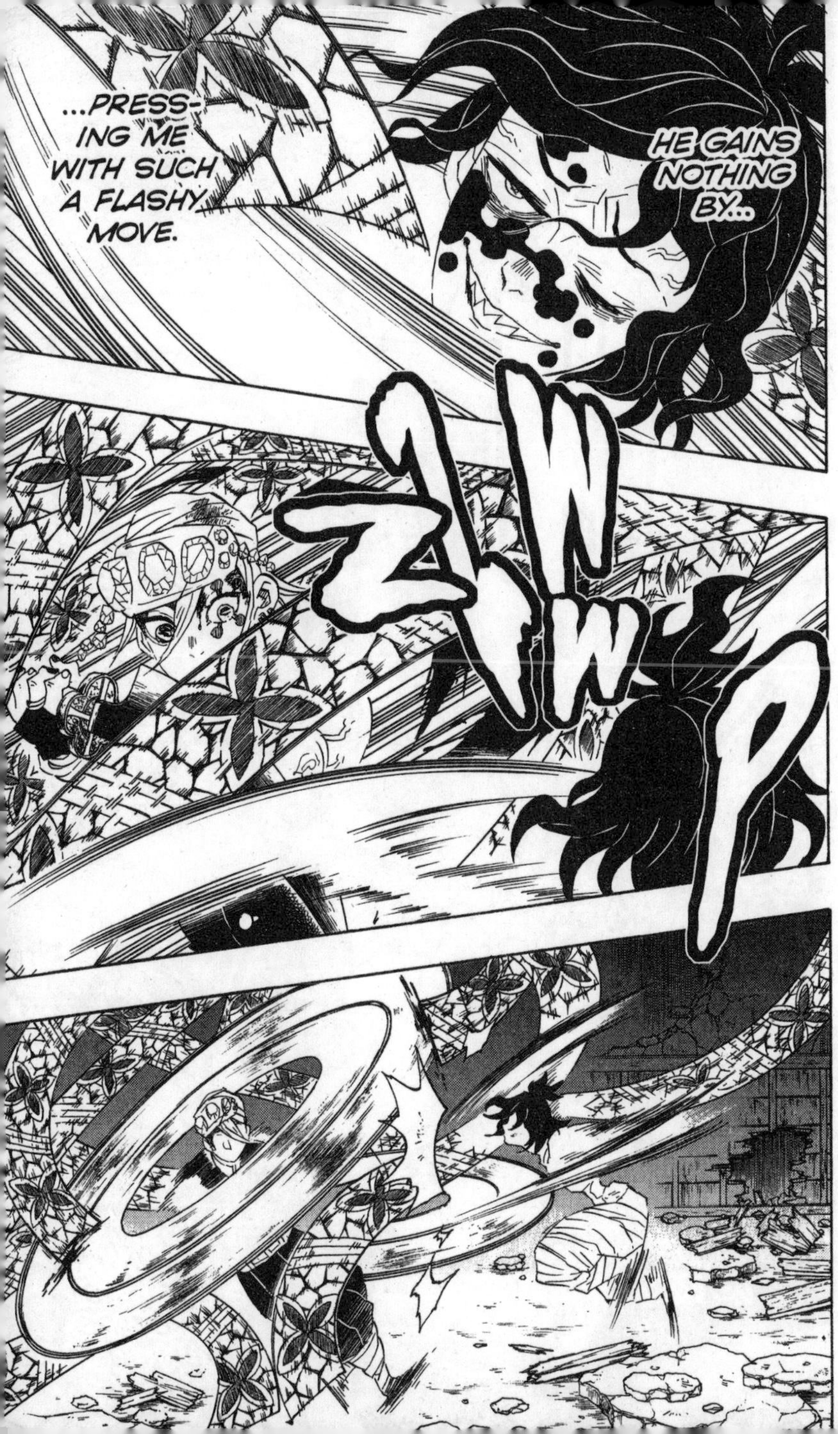
HE GAINS NOTHING BY...
...PRESS-ING ME WITH SUCH A FLASHY MOVE.
ZWWP

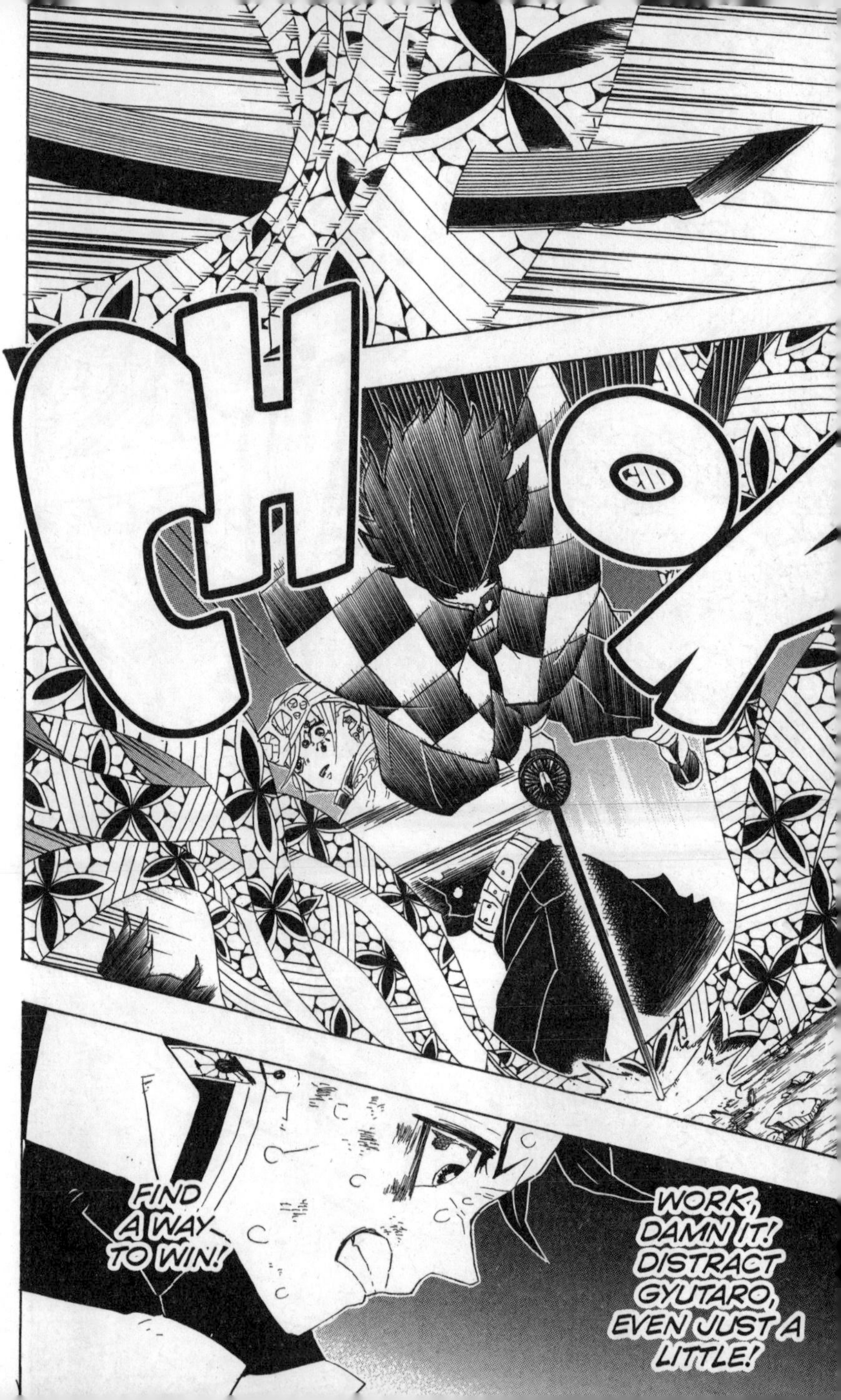
CHOM
WORK, DAMN IT! DISTRACT GYUTARO, EVEN JUST A LITTLE!
FIND A WAY TO WIN!

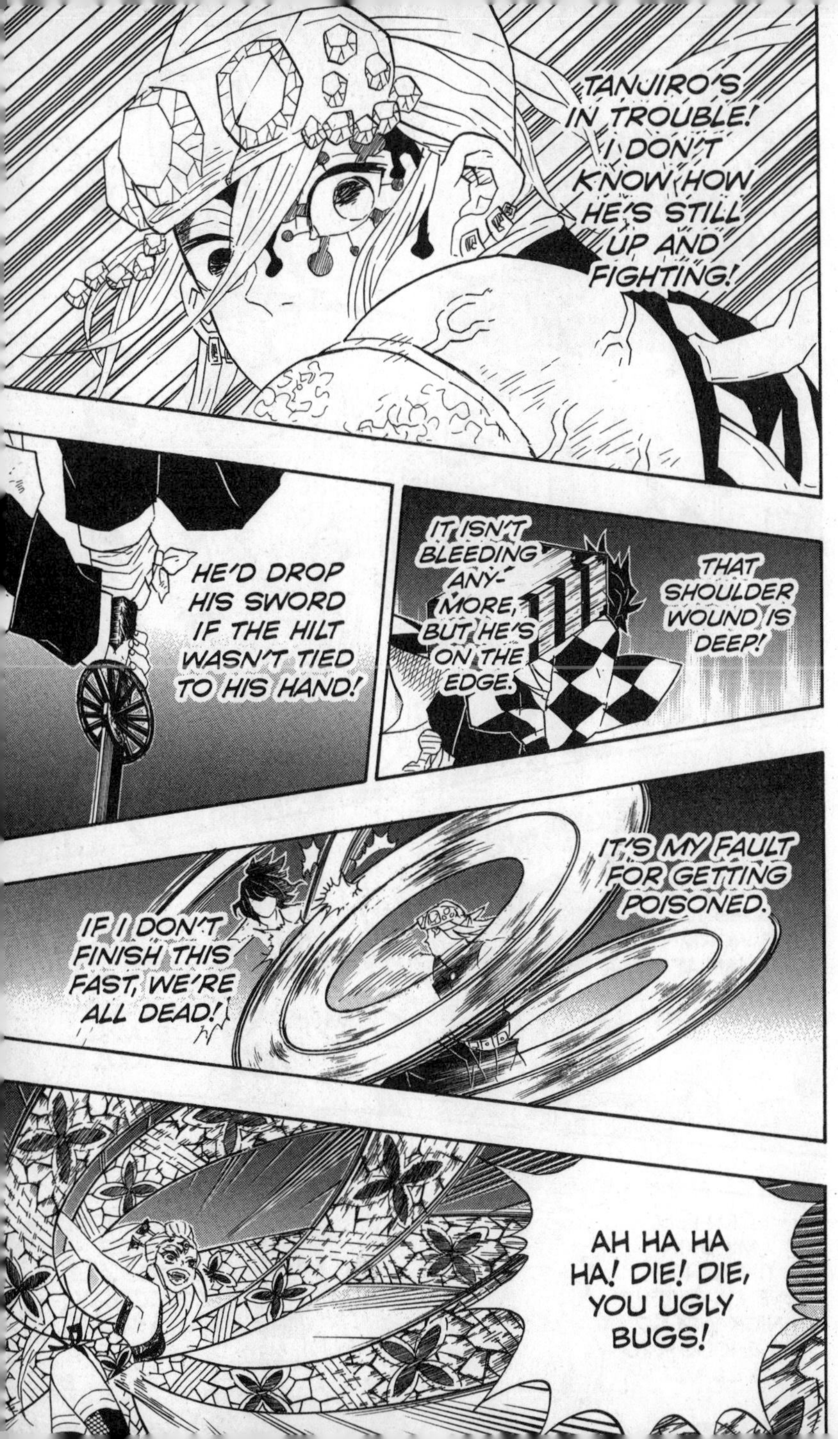
TANJIRO'S IN TROUBLE! I DON'T KNOW HOW HE'S STILL UP AND FIGHTING!
THAT SHOULDER WOUND IS DEEP!
IT ISN'T BLEEDING ANY-MORE, BUT HE'S ON THE EDGE.
HE'D DROP HIS SWORD IF THE HILT WASN'T TIED TO HIS HAND!
IT'S MY FAULT FOR GETTING POISONED.
IF I DON'T FINISH THIS FAST, WE'RE ALL DEAD!
AH HA HA HA! DIE! DIE, YOU UGLY BUGS!

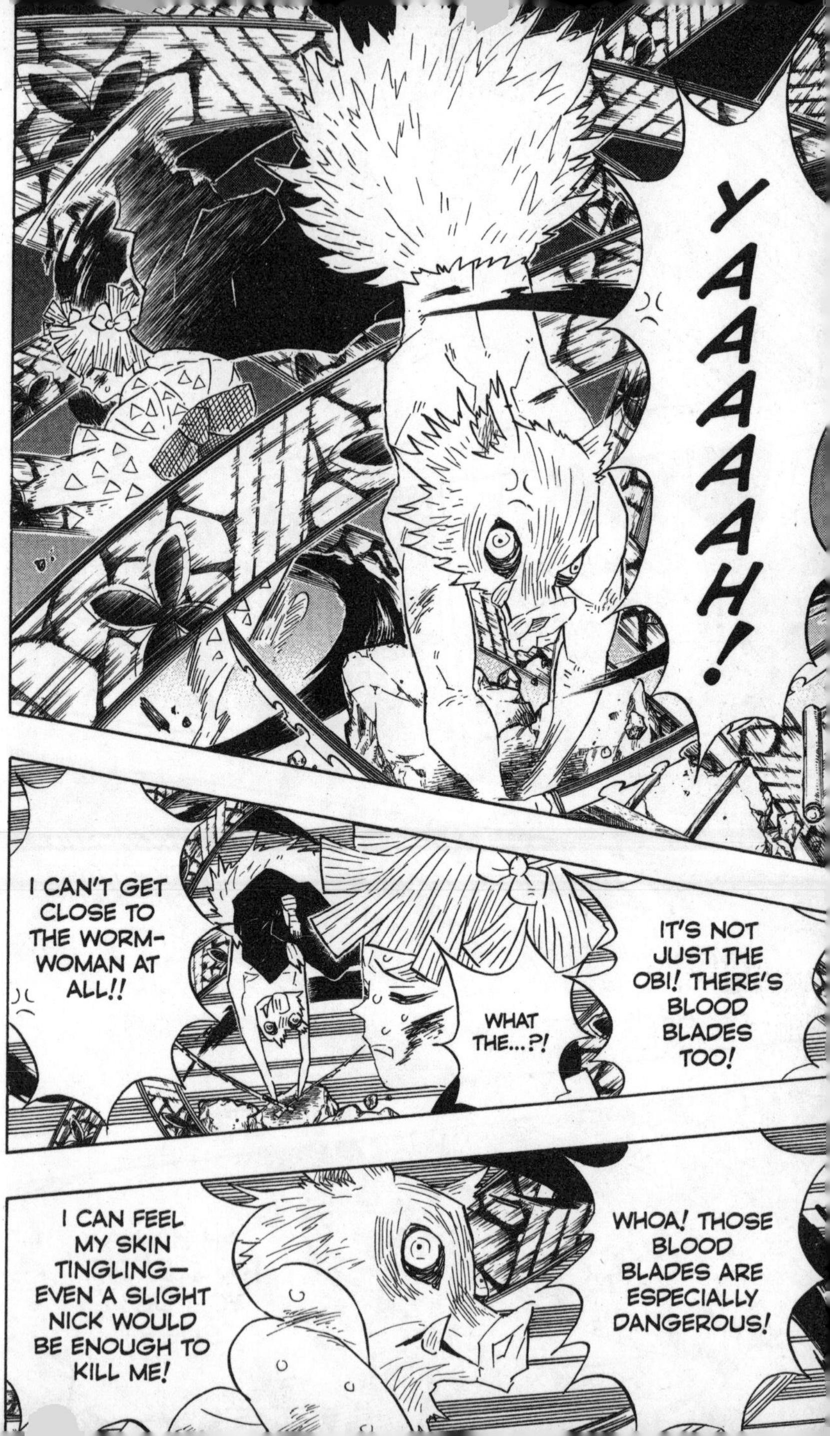
YAAAAAH!
IT'S NOT JUST THE OBI! THERE'S BLOOD BLADES TOO!
WHAT THE...?!
I CAN'T GET CLOSE TO THE WORM-WOMAN AT ALL!!
WHOA! THOSE BLOOD BLADES ARE ESPECIALLY DANGEROUS!
I CAN FEEL MY SKIN TINGLING— EVEN A SLIGHT NICK WOULD BE ENOUGH TO KILL ME!

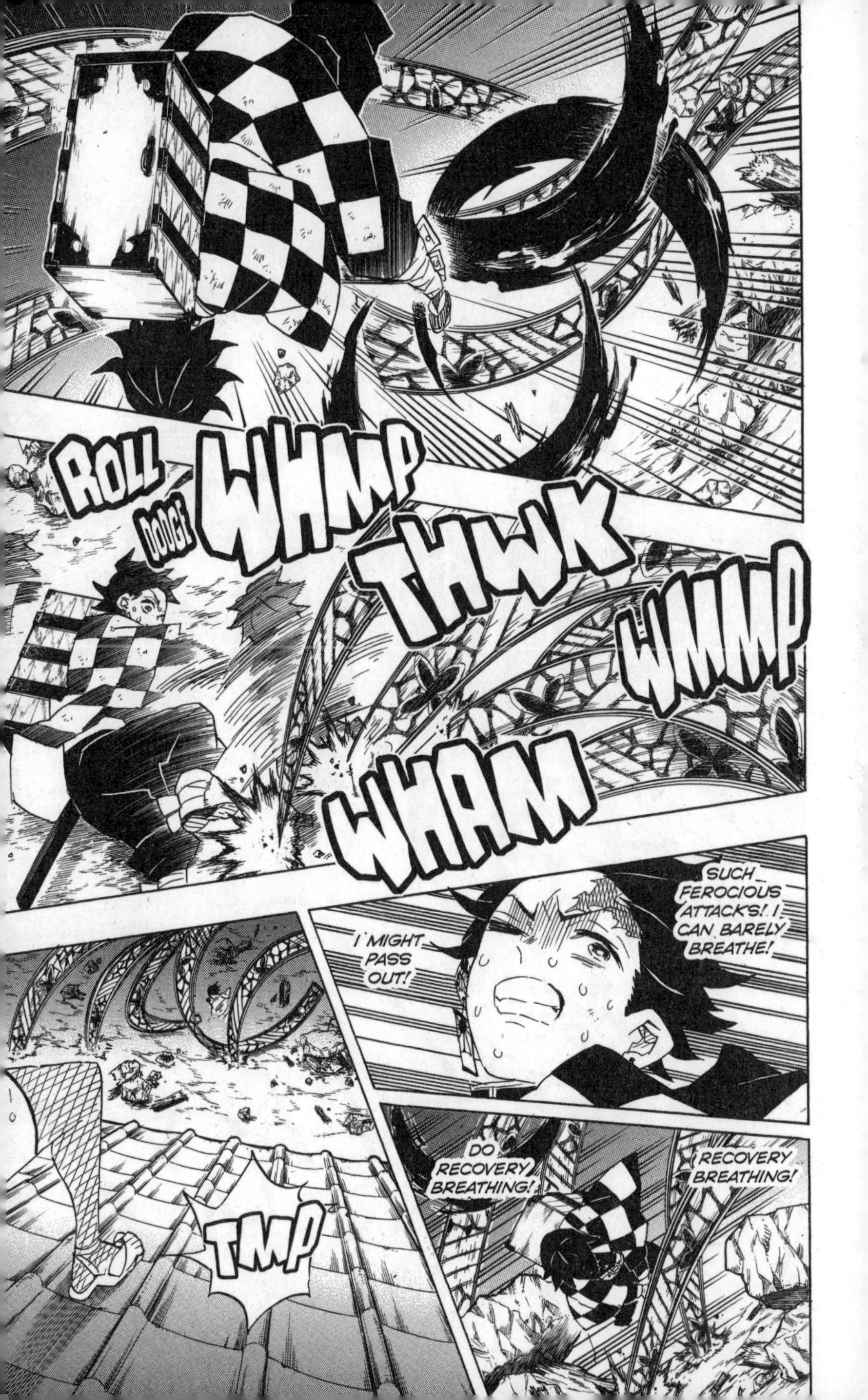
WHAMP
ROLL
DODGE
THWK
WMMP
WHAM
SUCH FEROCIOUS ATTACKS! I CAN BARELY BREATHE!
I MIGHT PASS OUT!
RECOVERY BREATHING!
DO RECOVERY BREATHING!
TMP

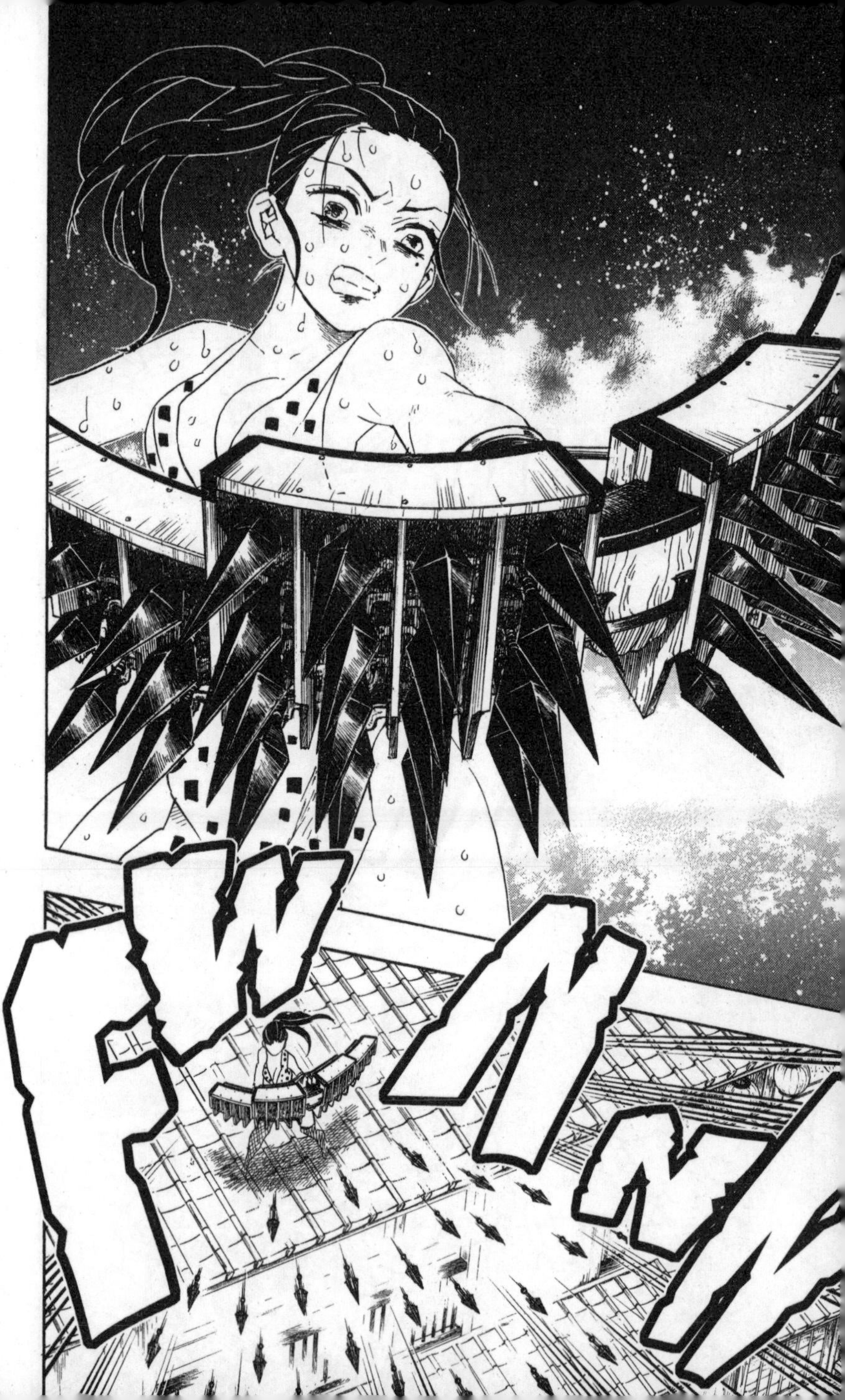

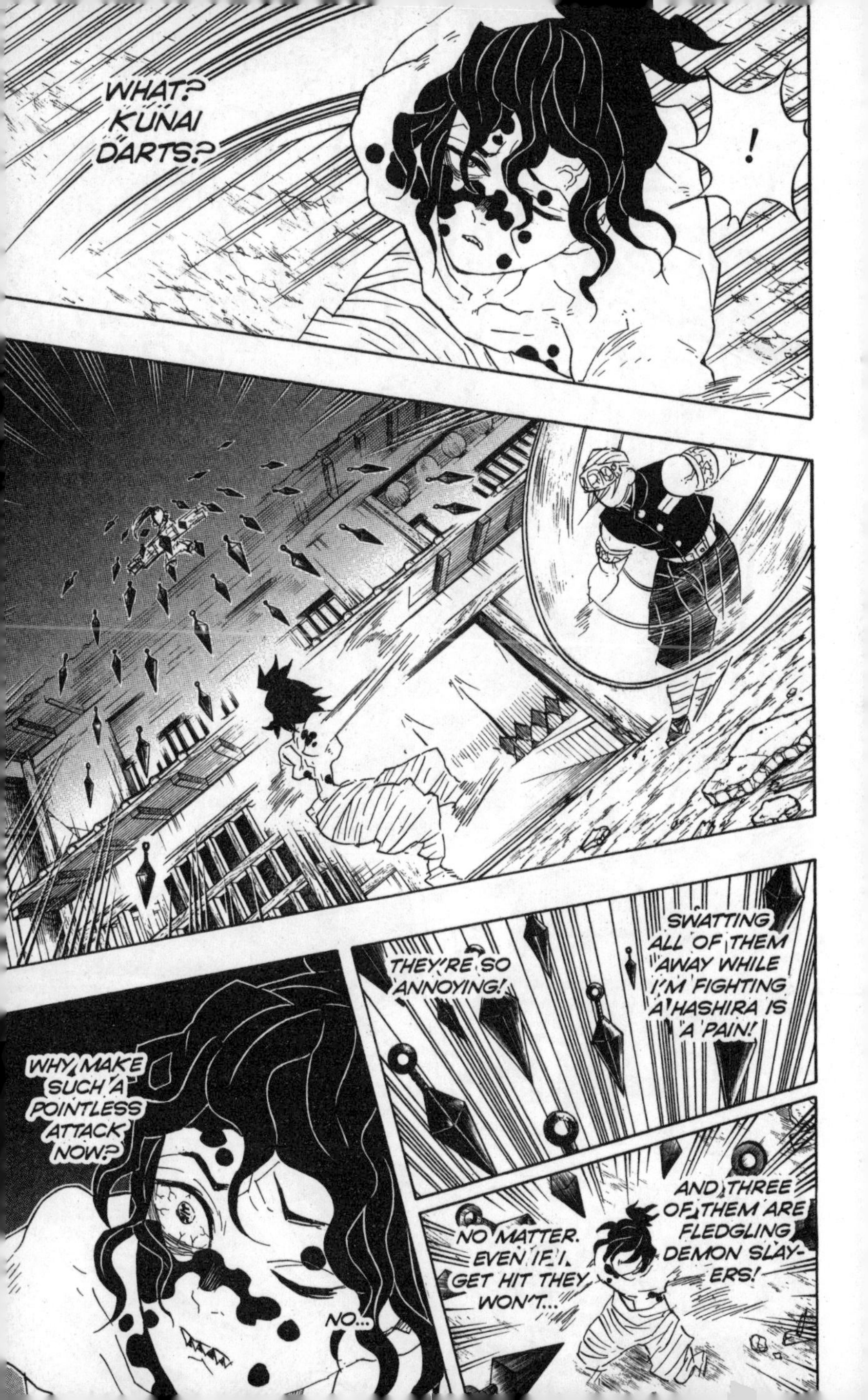
!
WHAT? KUNAI DARTS?
SWATTING ALL OF THEM AWAY WHILE I'M FIGHTING A HASHIRA IS A PAIN!
THEY'RE SO ANNOYING!
AND THREE OF THEM ARE FLEDGLING DEMON SLAY-ERS!
NO MATTER. EVEN IF I GET HIT THEY WON'T...
WHY MAKE SUCH A POINTLESS ATTACK NOW?
NO...

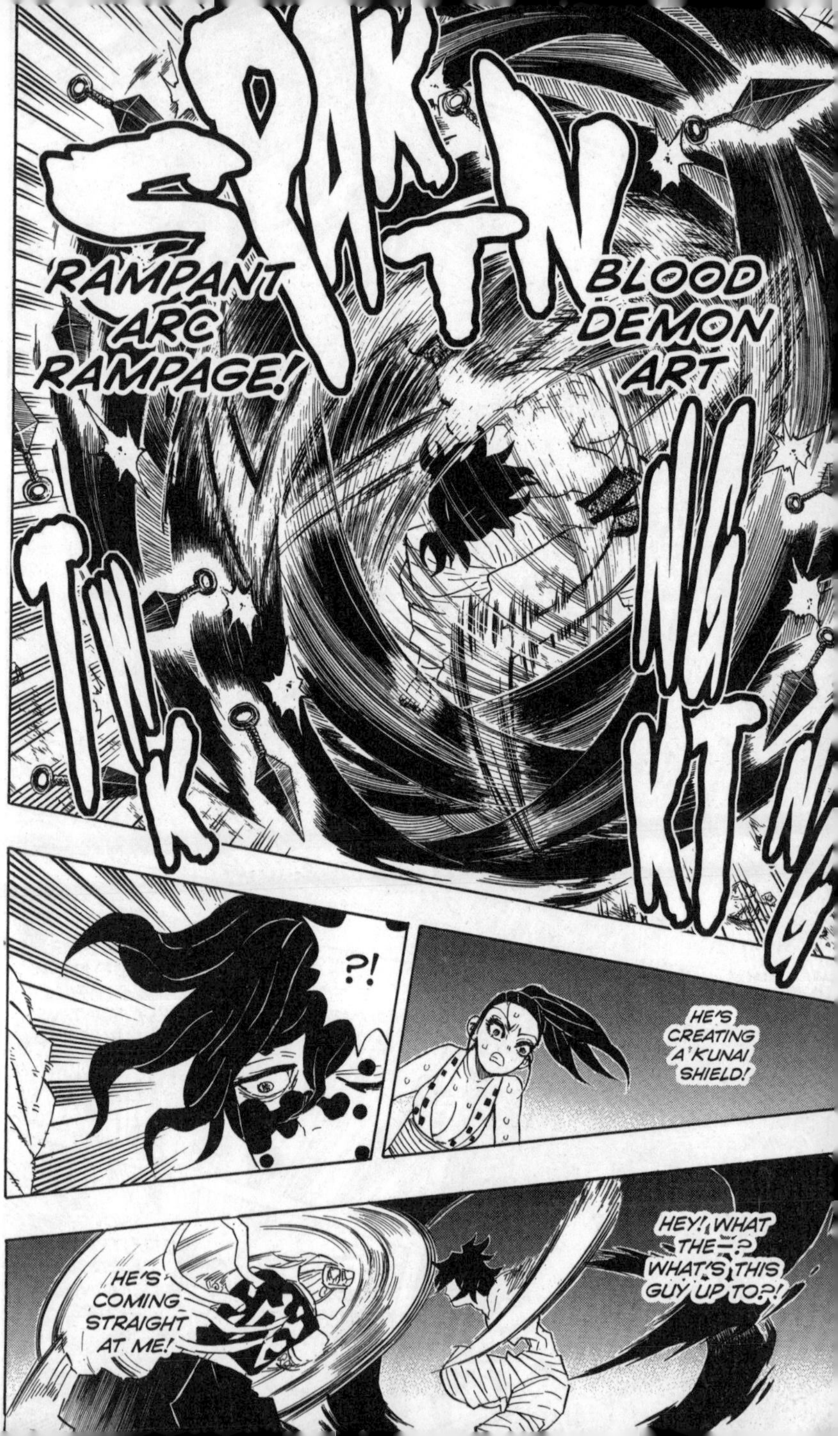
BLOOD DEMON ART
RAMPANT ARC RAMPAGE!
HE'S CREATING A KUNAI SHIELD!
?!
HEY! WHAT THE—? WHAT'S THIS GUY UP TO?!
HE'S COMING STRAIGHT AT ME!

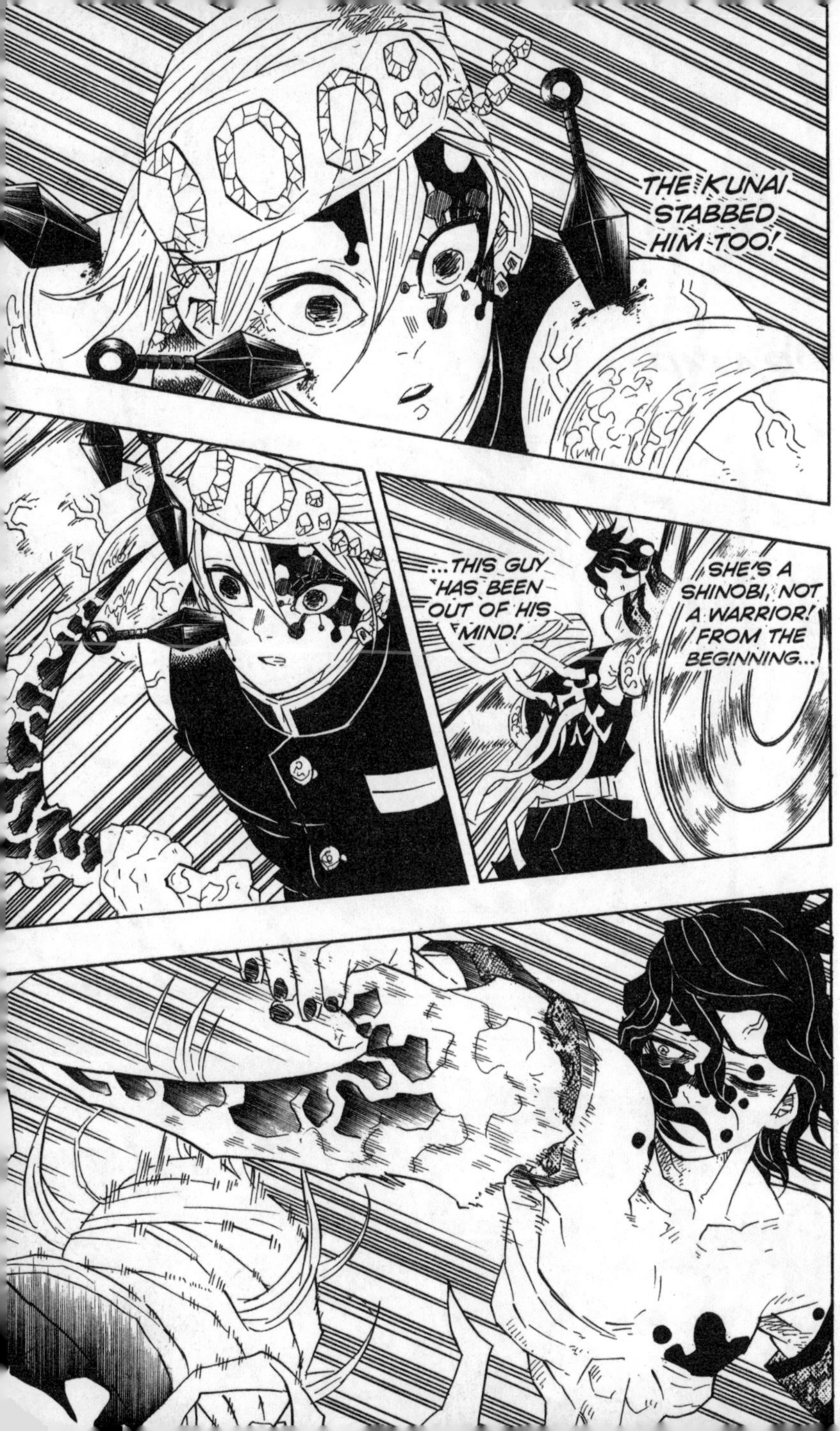
THE KUNAI STABBED HIM TOO!
SHE'S A SHINOBI, NOT A WARRIOR! FROM THE BEGINNING...
...THIS GUY HAS BEEN OUT OF HIS MIND!

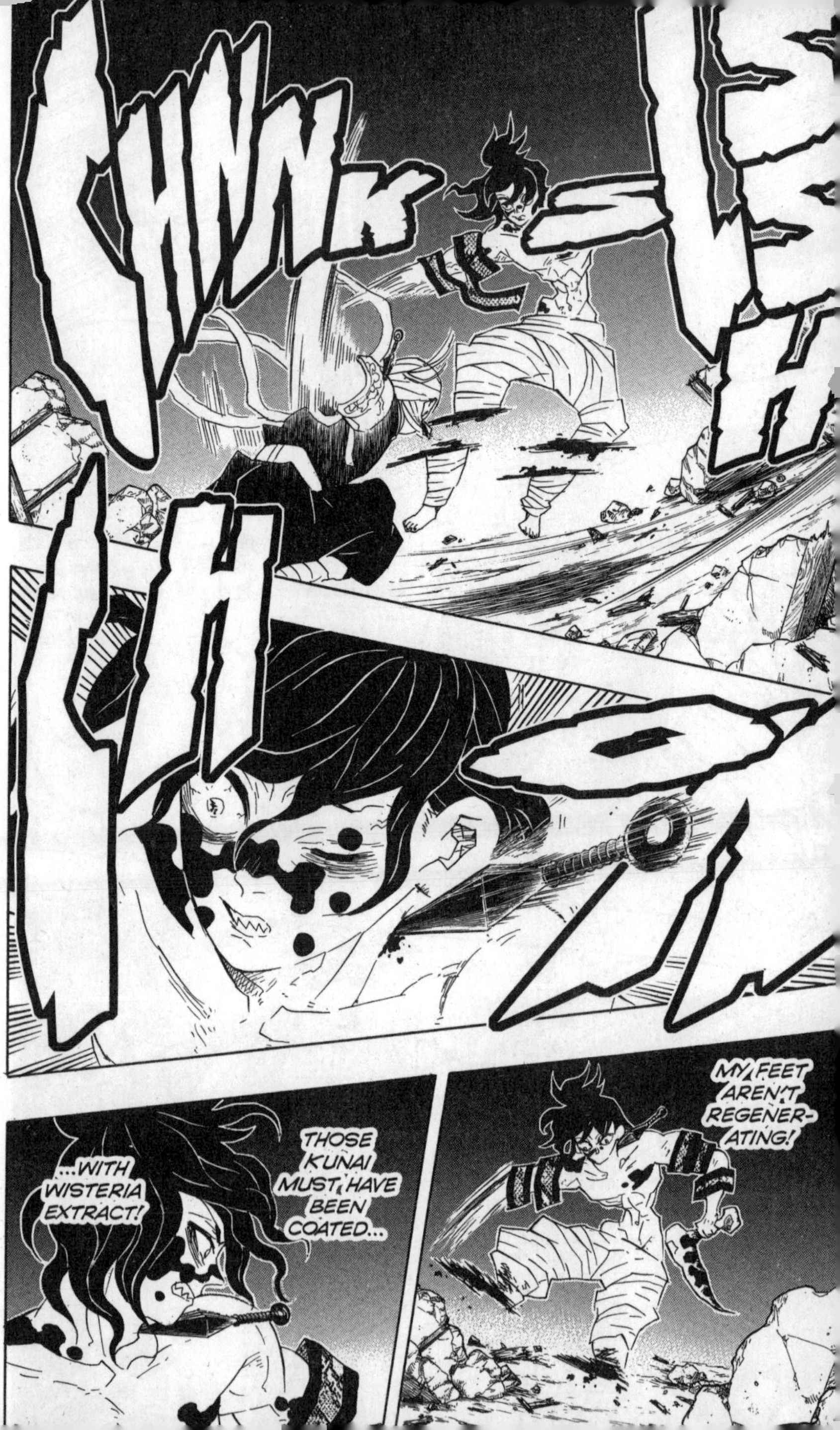
CHNK
MY FEET AREN'T REGENER-ATING!
THOSE KUNAI MUST HAVE BEEN COATED...
...WITH WISTERIA EXTRACT!

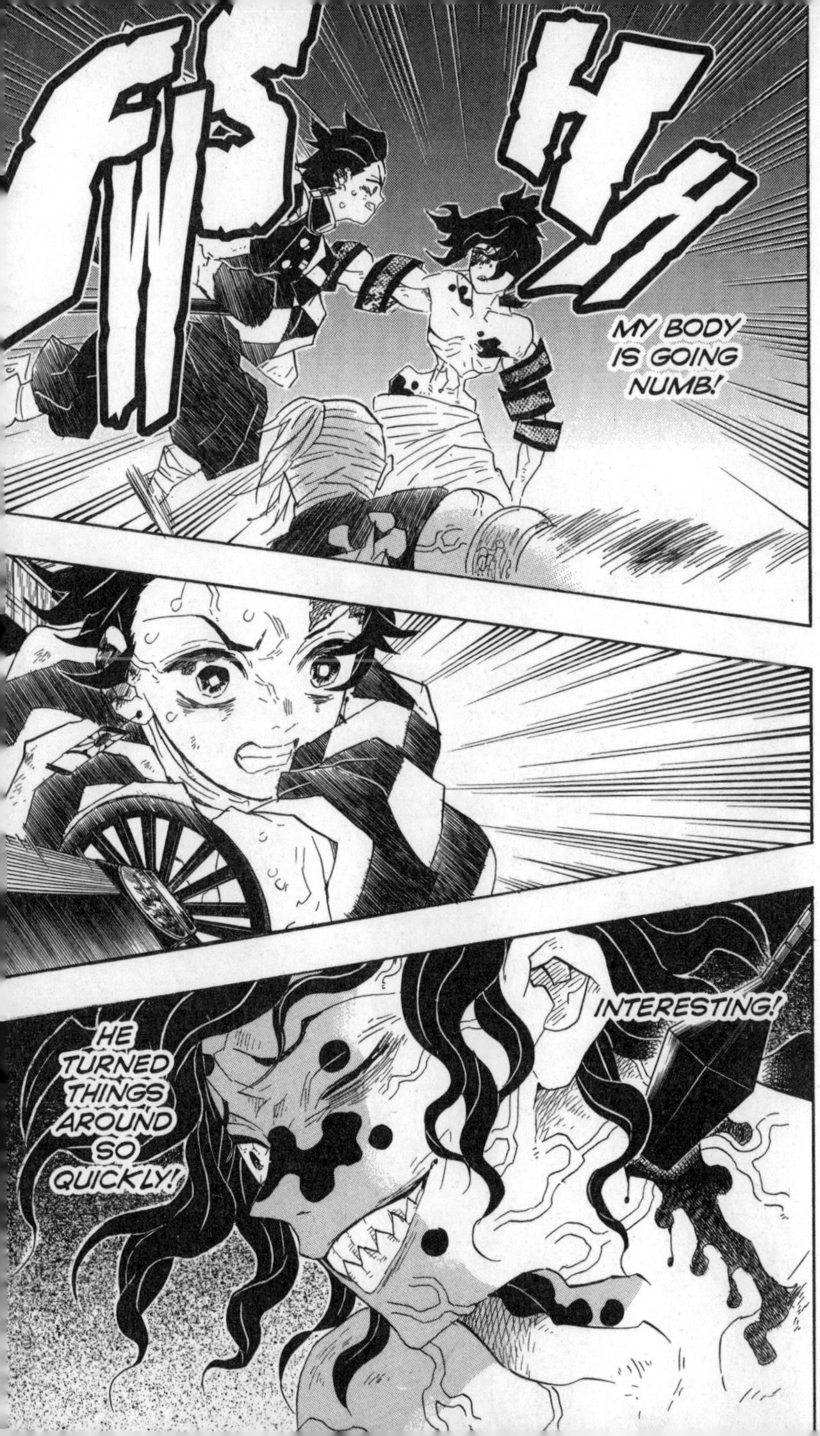
MY BODY IS GOING NUMB!
INTERESTING!
HE TURNED THINGS AROUND SO QUICKLY!

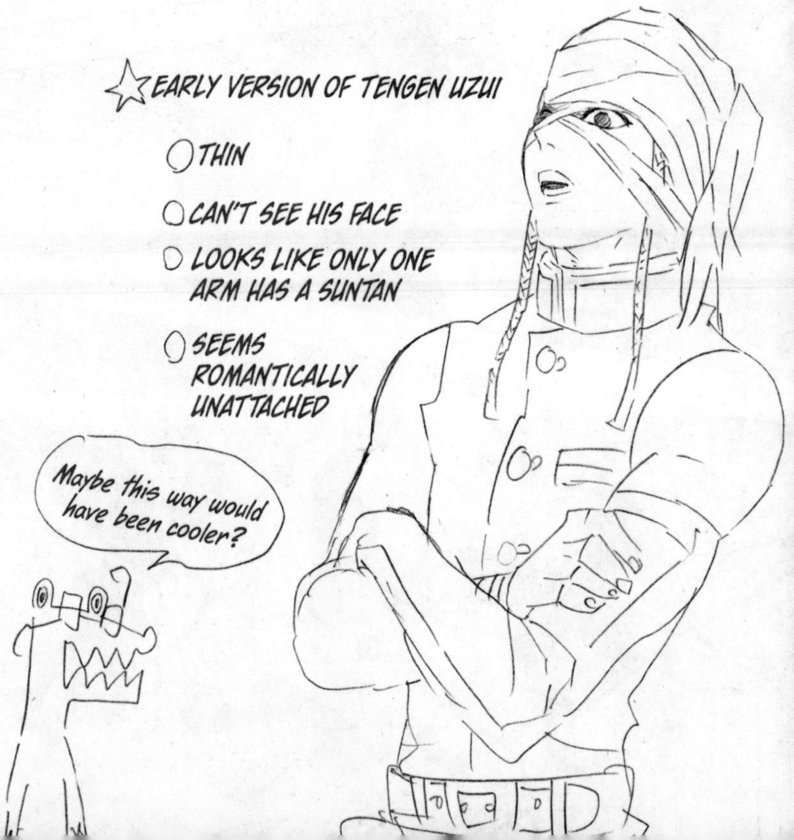

☆ EARLY VERSION OF TENGEN UZUI
○ THIN
○ CAN'T SEE HIS FACE
○ LOOKS LIKE ONLY ONE ARM HAS A SUNTAN
○ SEEMS ROMANTICALLY UNATTACHED
Maybe this way would have been cooler?

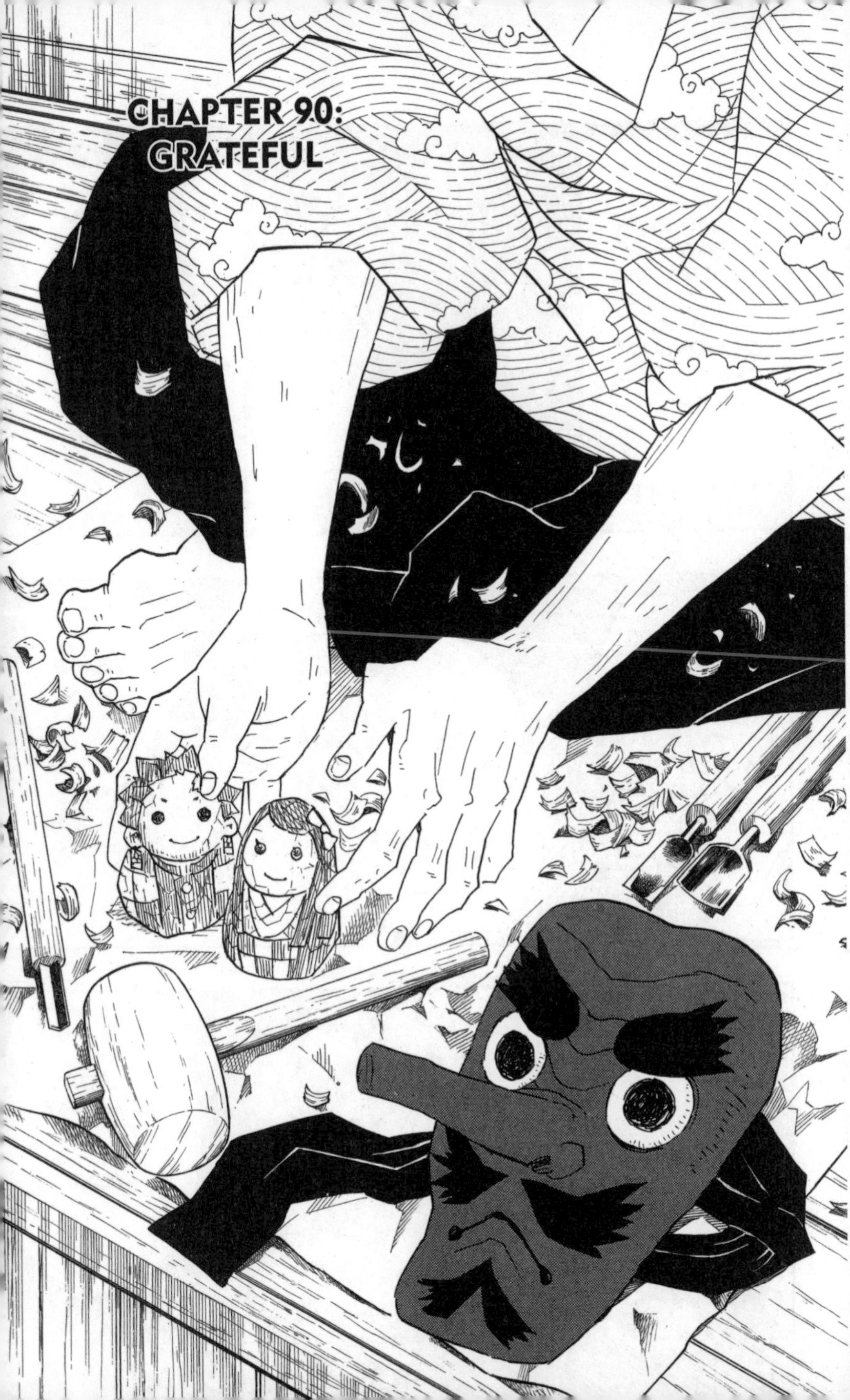
CHAPTER 90:
GRATEFUL

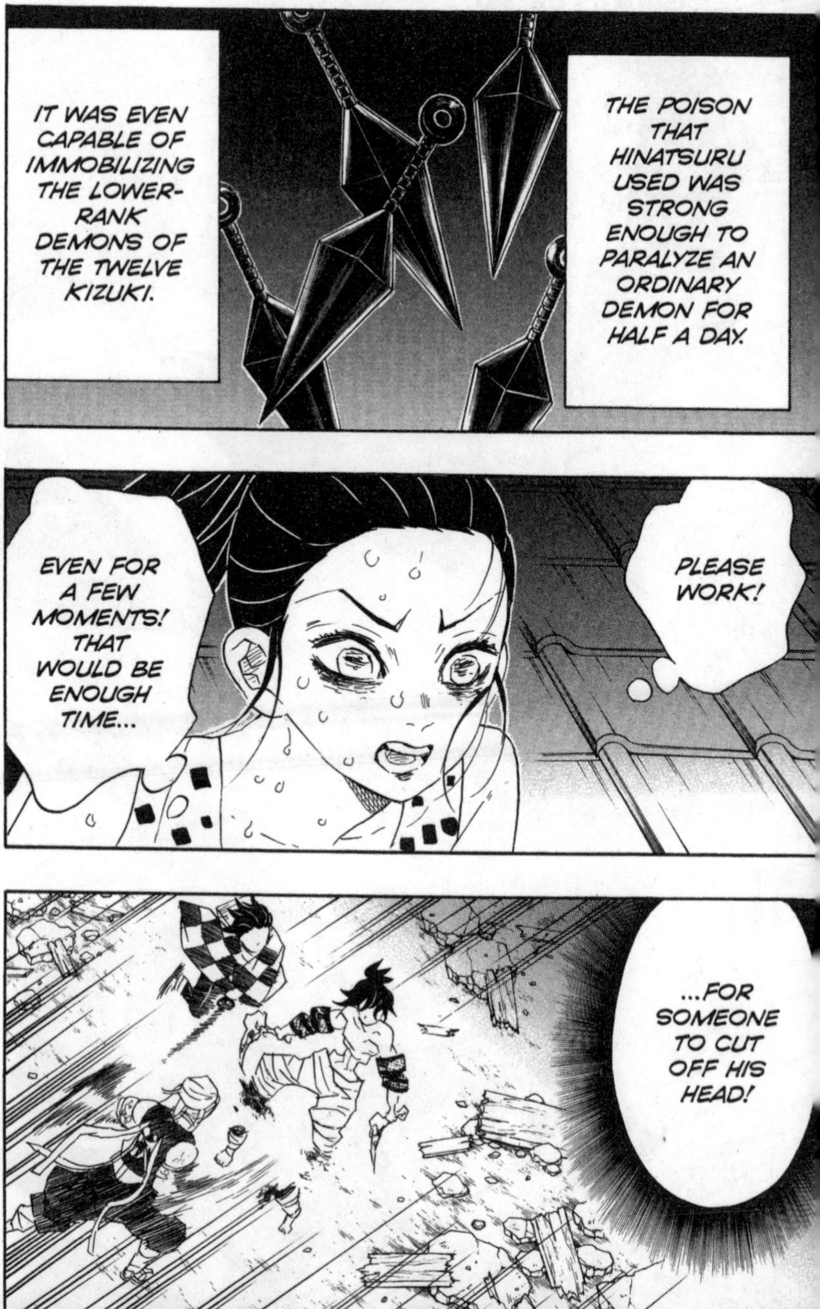
THE POISON THAT HINATSURU USED WAS STRONG ENOUGH TO PARALYZE AN ORDINARY DEMON FOR HALF A DAY.
IT WAS EVEN CAPABLE OF IMMOBILIZING THE LOWER-RANK DEMONS OF THE TWELVE KIZUKI.
PLEASE WORK!
EVEN FOR A FEW MOMENTS! THAT WOULD BE ENOUGH TIME...
...FOR SOMEONE TO CUT OFF HIS HEAD!

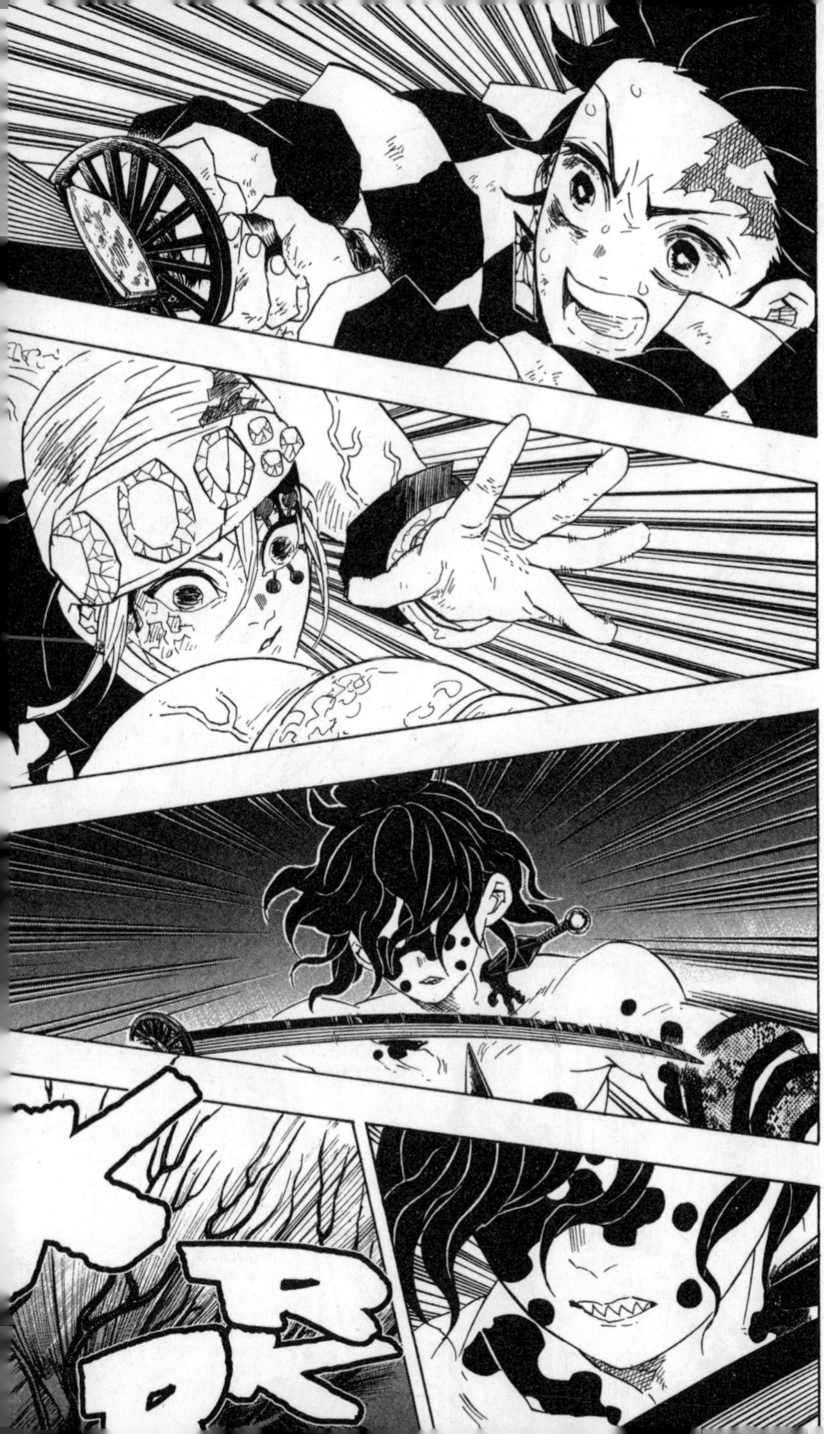

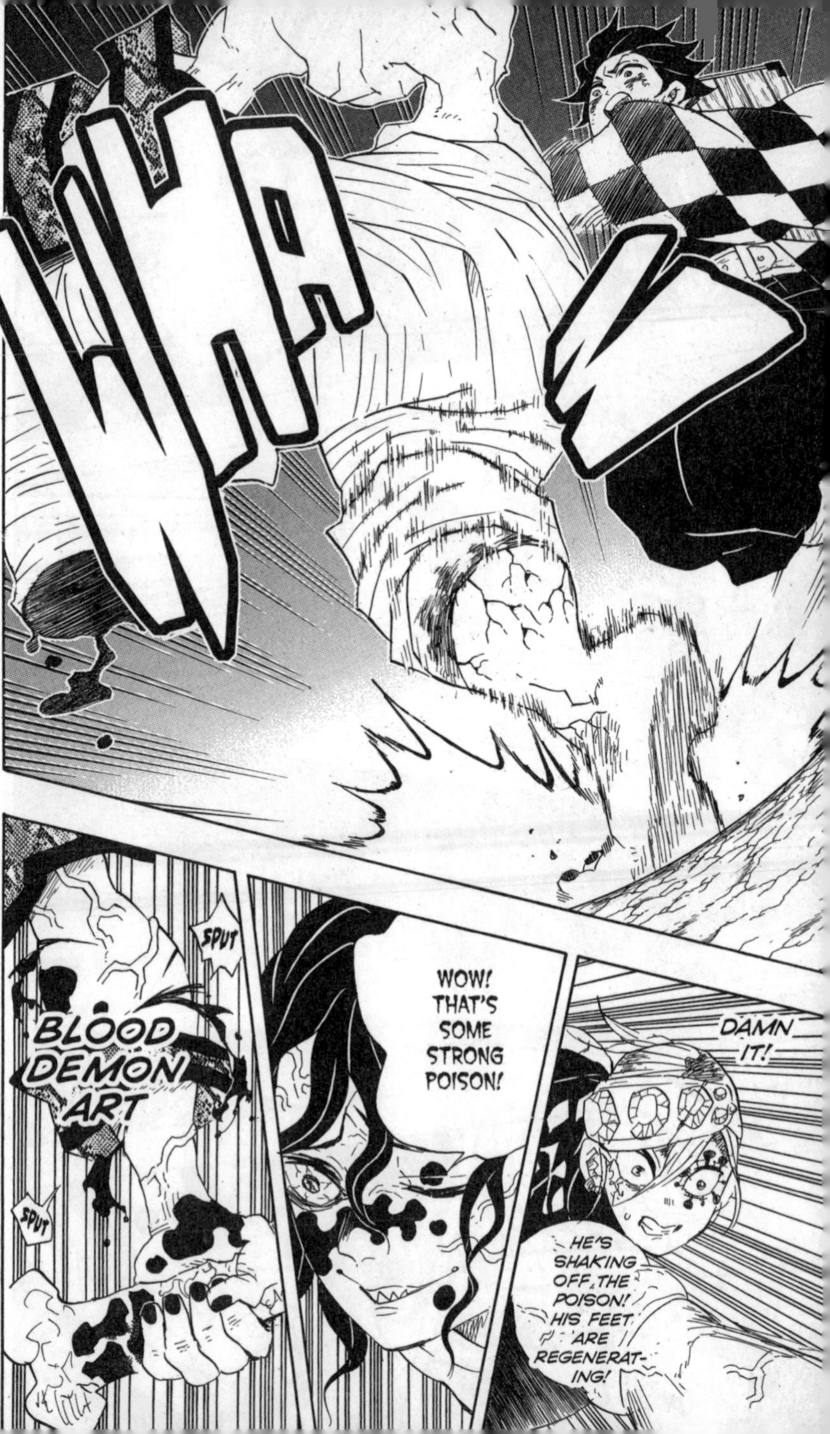
DAMN IT!
HE'S SHAKING OFF THE POISON! HIS FEET ARE REGENERATING!
WOW! THAT'S SOME STRONG POISON!
SPUT
BLOOD DEMON ART
SPUT

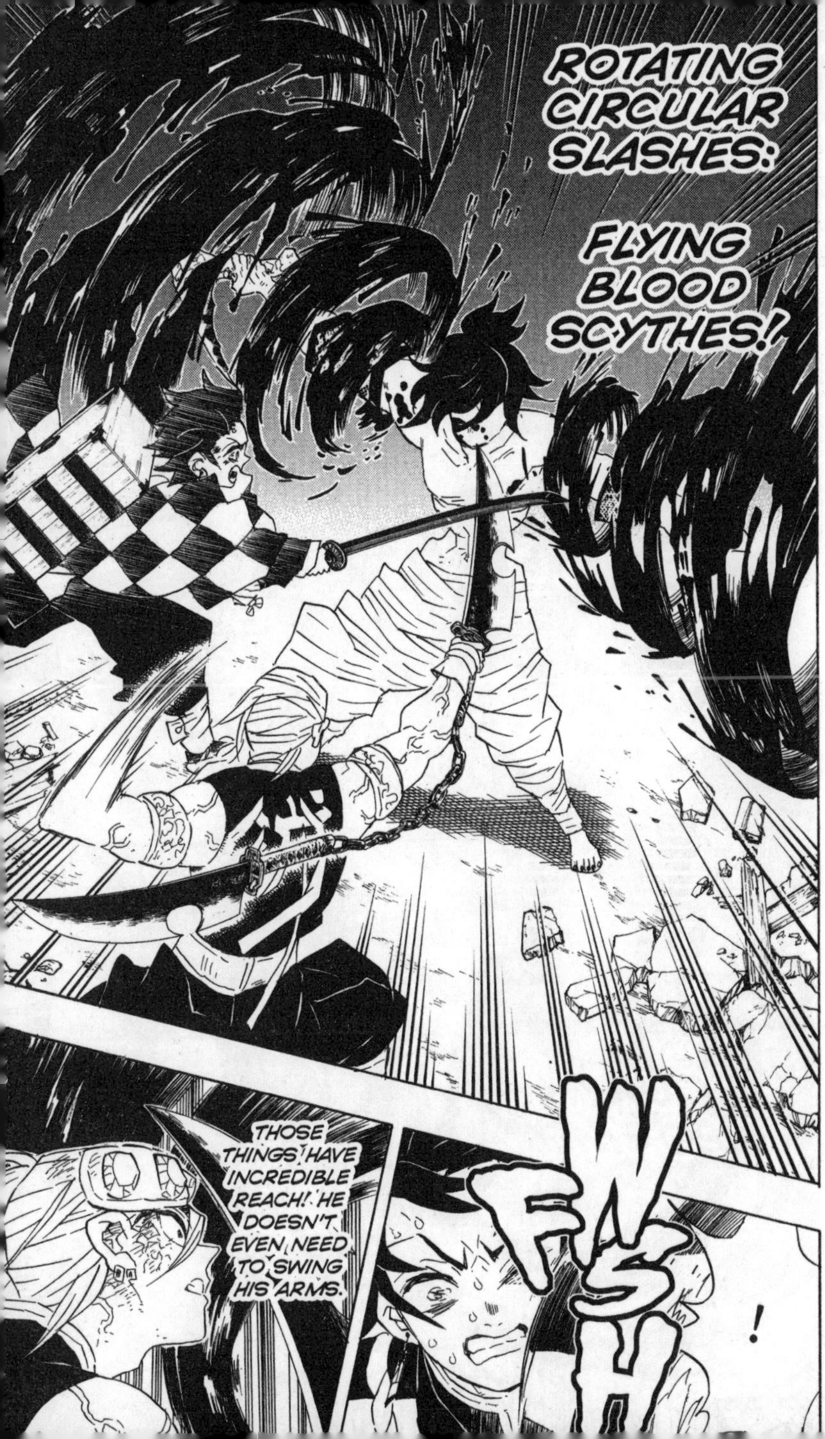
ROTATING CIRCULAR SLASHES:
FLYING BLOOD SCYTHES!
WHSH
THOSE THINGS HAVE INCREDIBLE REACH! HE DOESN'T EVEN NEED TO SWING HIS ARMS.
!

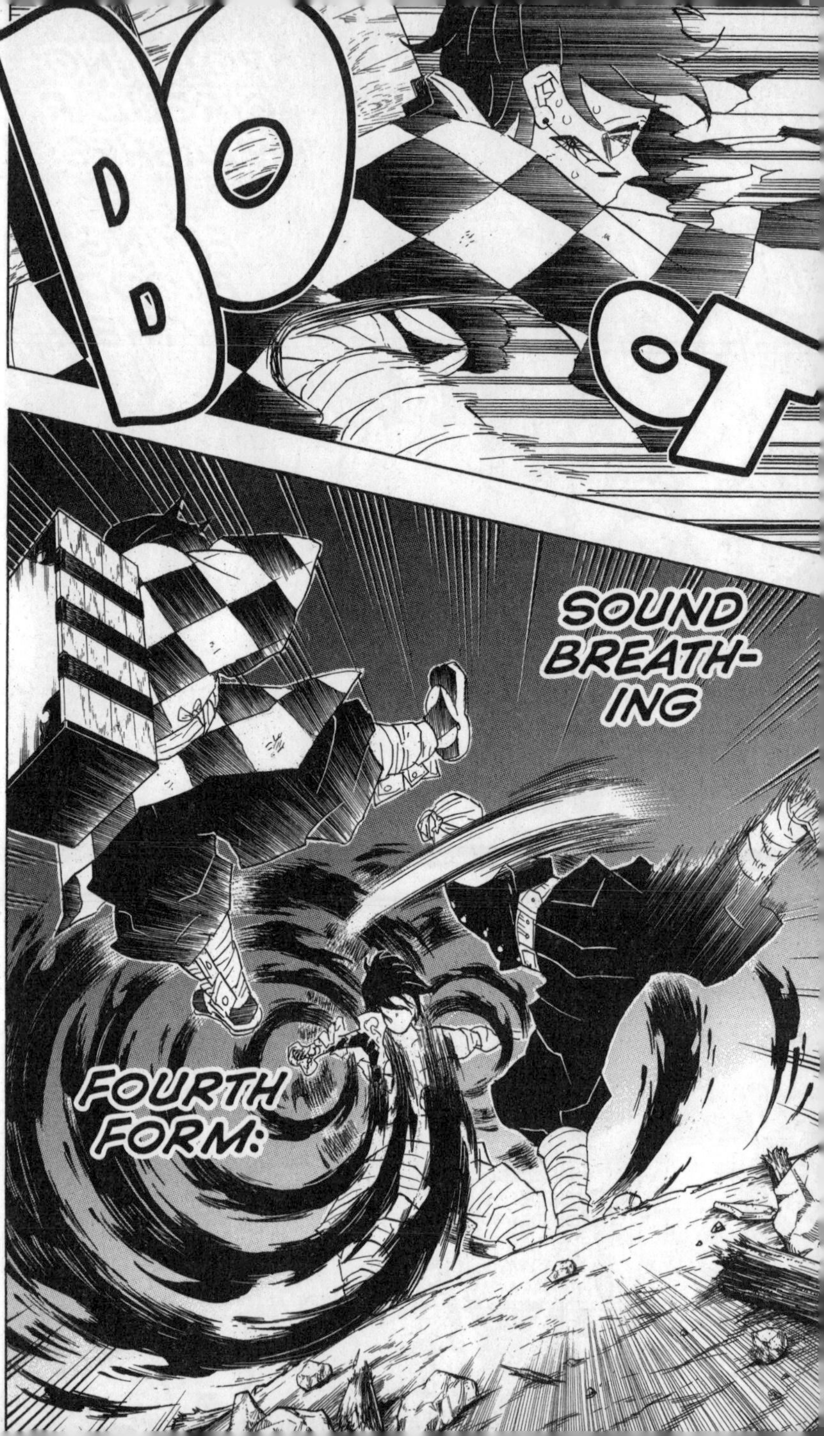
BOOT
SOUND BREATH-ING
FOURTH FORM:

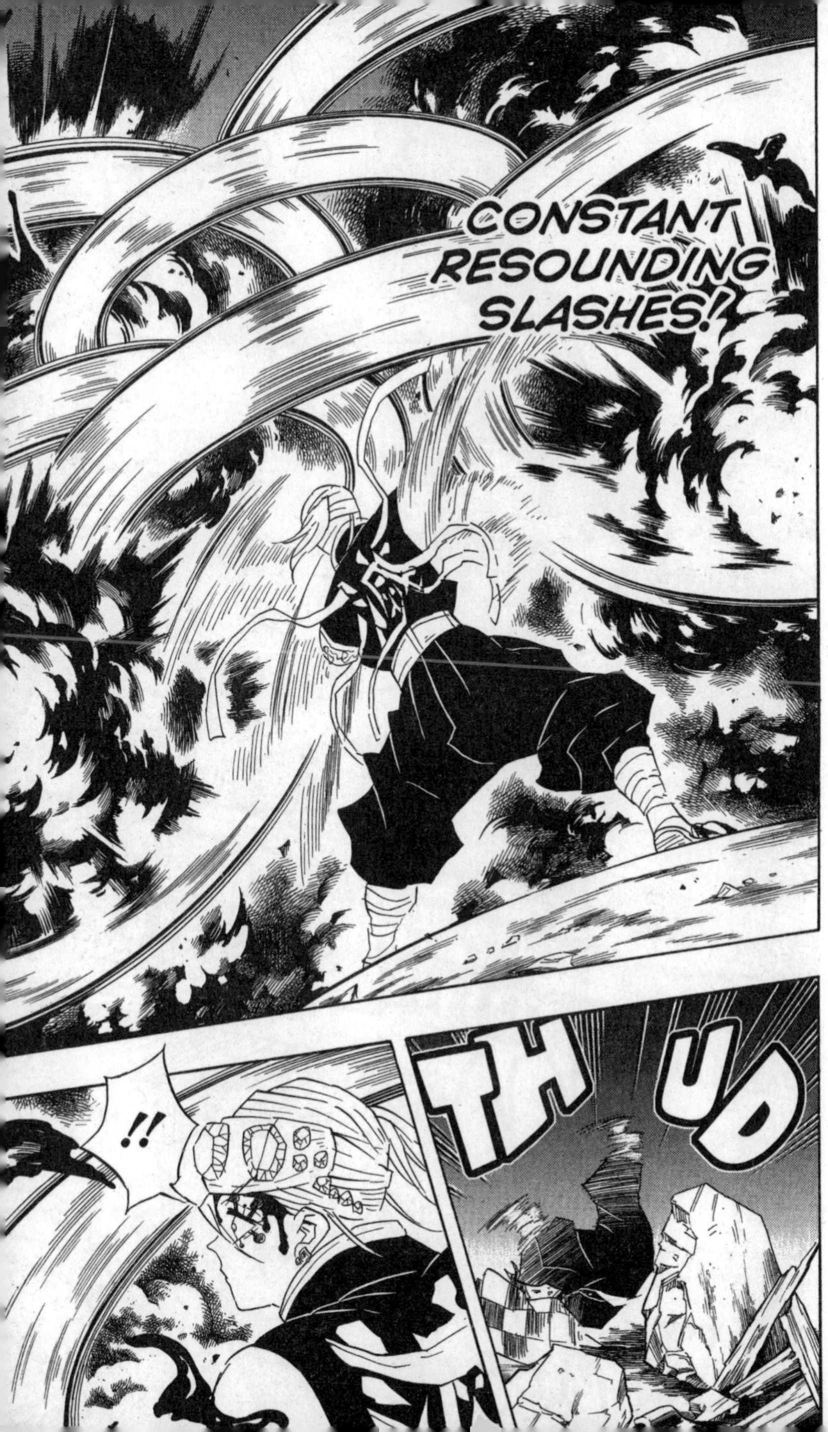
CONSTANT RESOUNDING SLASHES!
THUD
!!

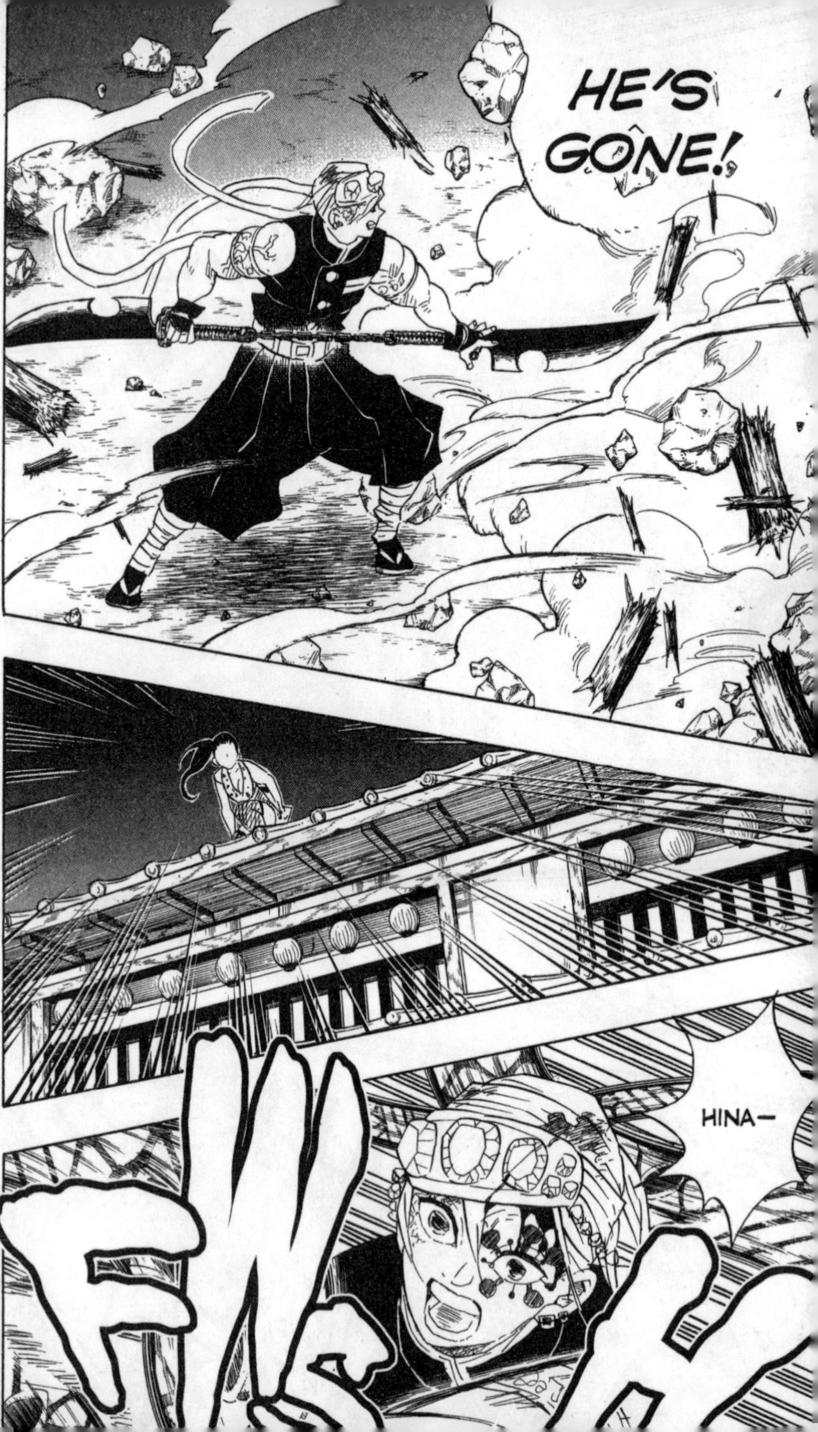

HE'S GONE!
HINA—

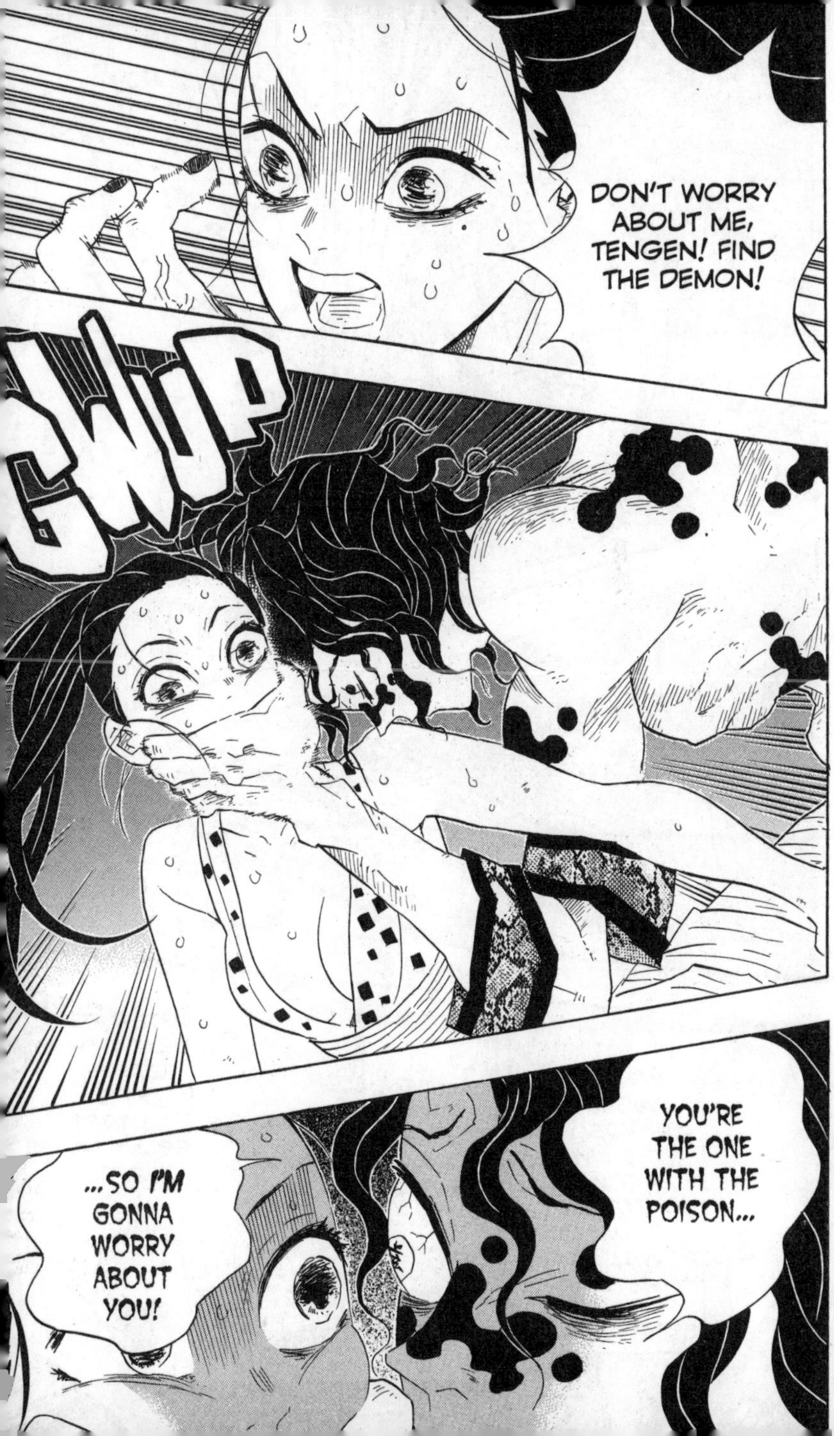
DON'T WORRY ABOUT ME, TENGEN! FIND THE DEMON!
GWUP
YOU'RE THE ONE WITH THE POISON...
...SO I'M GONNA WORRY ABOUT YOU!

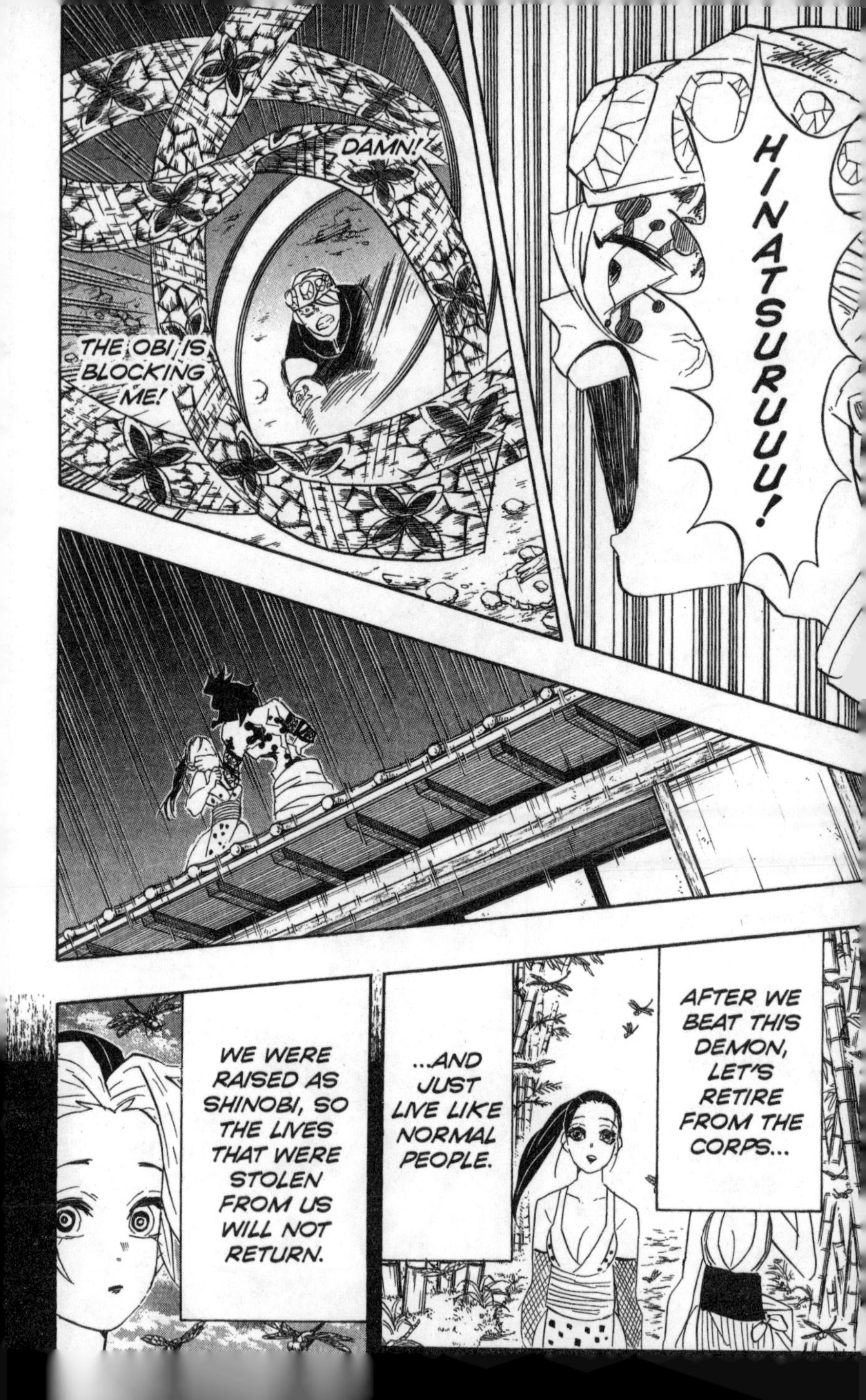
HINATSURUUUU!
DAMN!
THE OBI IS BLOCKING ME!
AFTER WE BEAT THIS DEMON, LET'S RETIRE FROM THE CORPS...
...AND JUST LIVE LIKE NORMAL PEOPLE.
WE WERE RAISED AS SHINOBI, SO THE LIVES THAT WERE STOLEN FROM US WILL NOT RETURN.

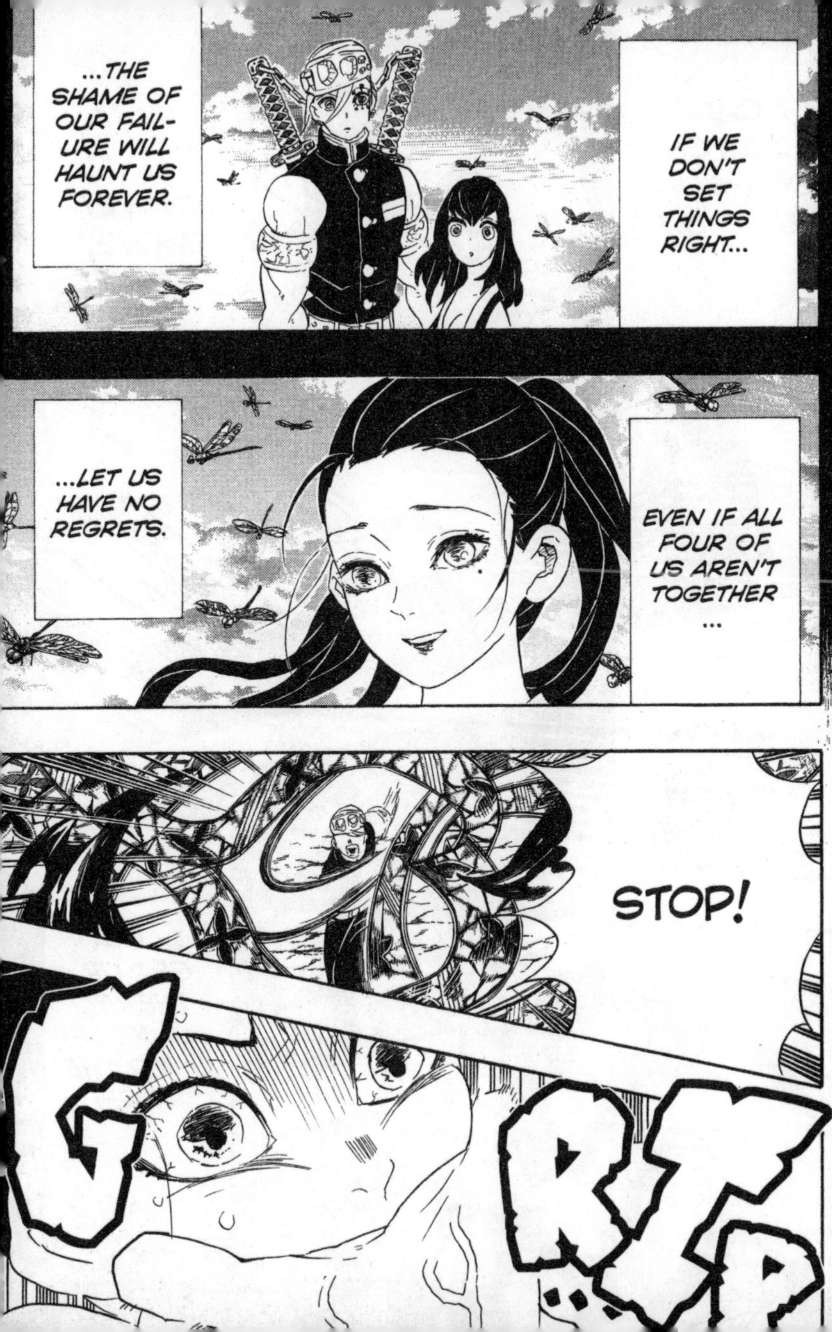
IF WE DON'T SET THINGS RIGHT...
...THE SHAME OF OUR FAIL-URE WILL HAUNT US FOREVER.
EVEN IF ALL FOUR OF US AREN'T TOGETHER...
...LET US HAVE NO REGRETS.
STOP!
GRIP

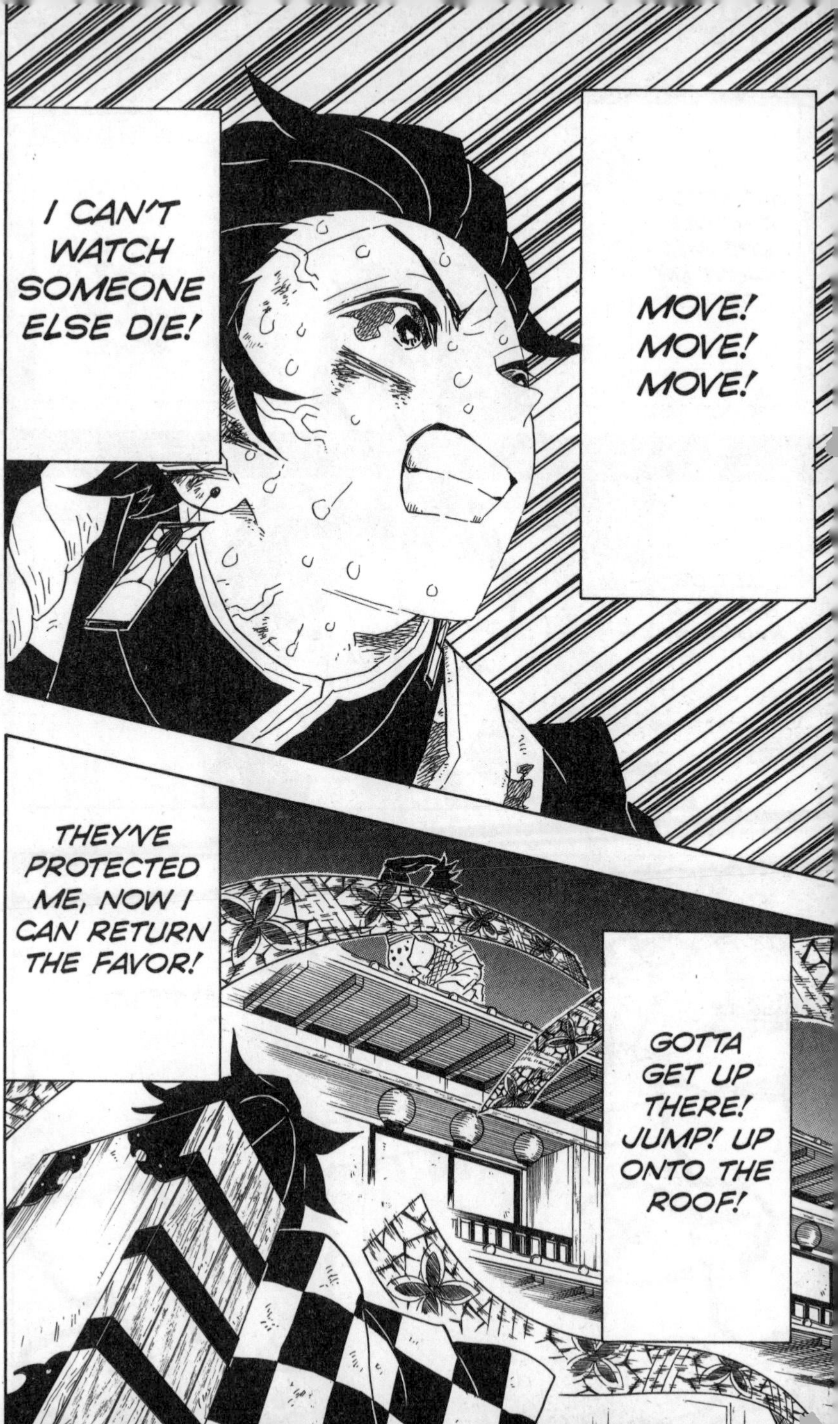
MOVE! MOVE! MOVE!
I CAN'T WATCH SOMEONE ELSE DIE!
THEY'VE PROTECTED ME, NOW I CAN RETURN THE FAVOR!
GOTTA GET UP THERE! JUMP! UP ONTO THE ROOF!

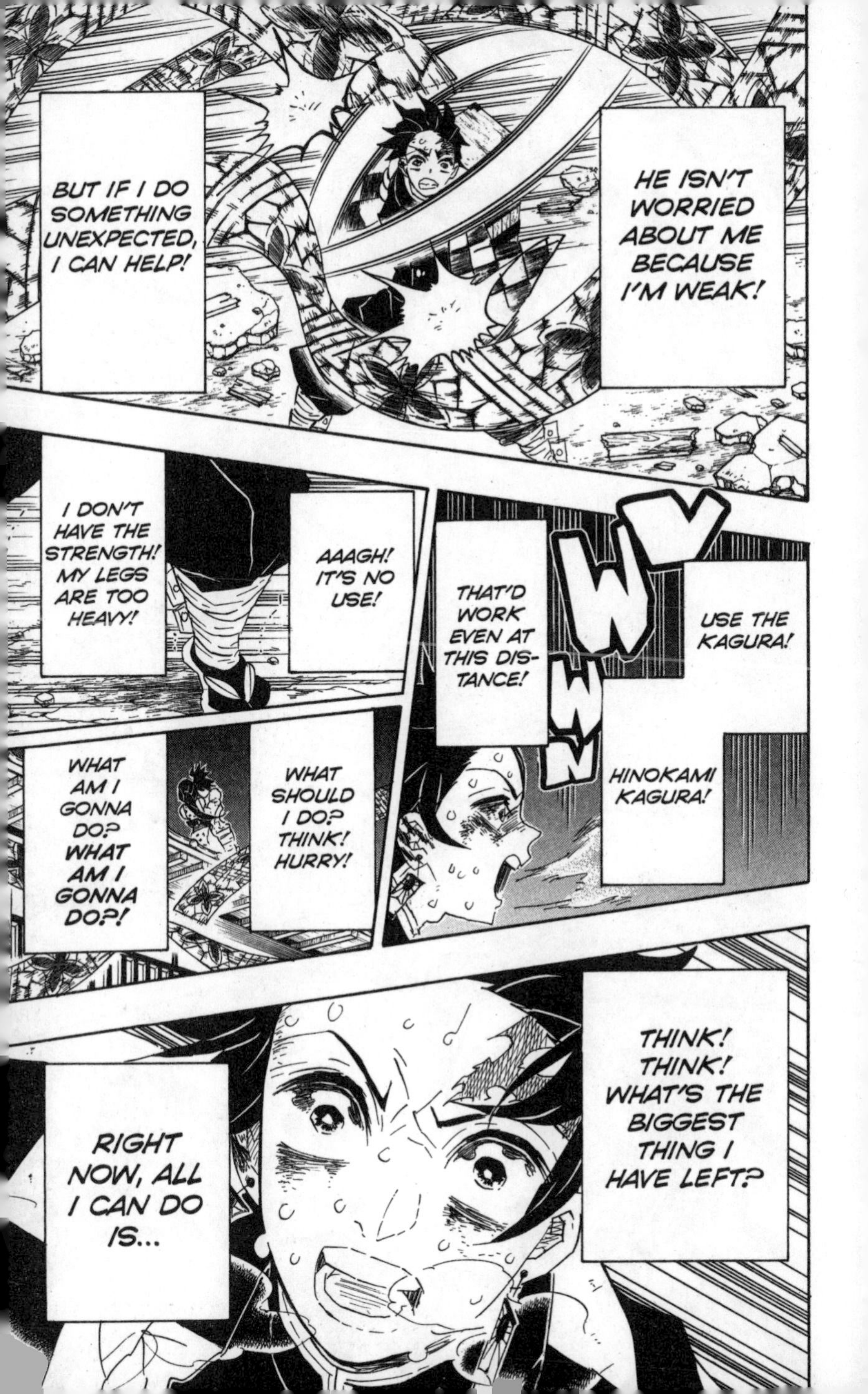
HE ISN'T WORRIED ABOUT ME BECAUSE I'M WEAK!
BUT IF I DO SOMETHING UNEXPECTED, I CAN HELP!
USE THE KAGURA!
THAT'D WORK EVEN AT THIS DIS-TANCE!
HINOKAMI KAGURA!
AAAGH! IT'S NO USE!
I DON'T HAVE THE STRENGTH! MY LEGS ARE TOO HEAVY!
WHAT SHOULD I DO? THINK! HURRY!
WHAT AM I GONNA DO? WHAT AM I GONNA DO?!
THINK! THINK! WHAT'S THE BIGGEST THING I HAVE LEFT?
RIGHT NOW, ALL I CAN DO IS...

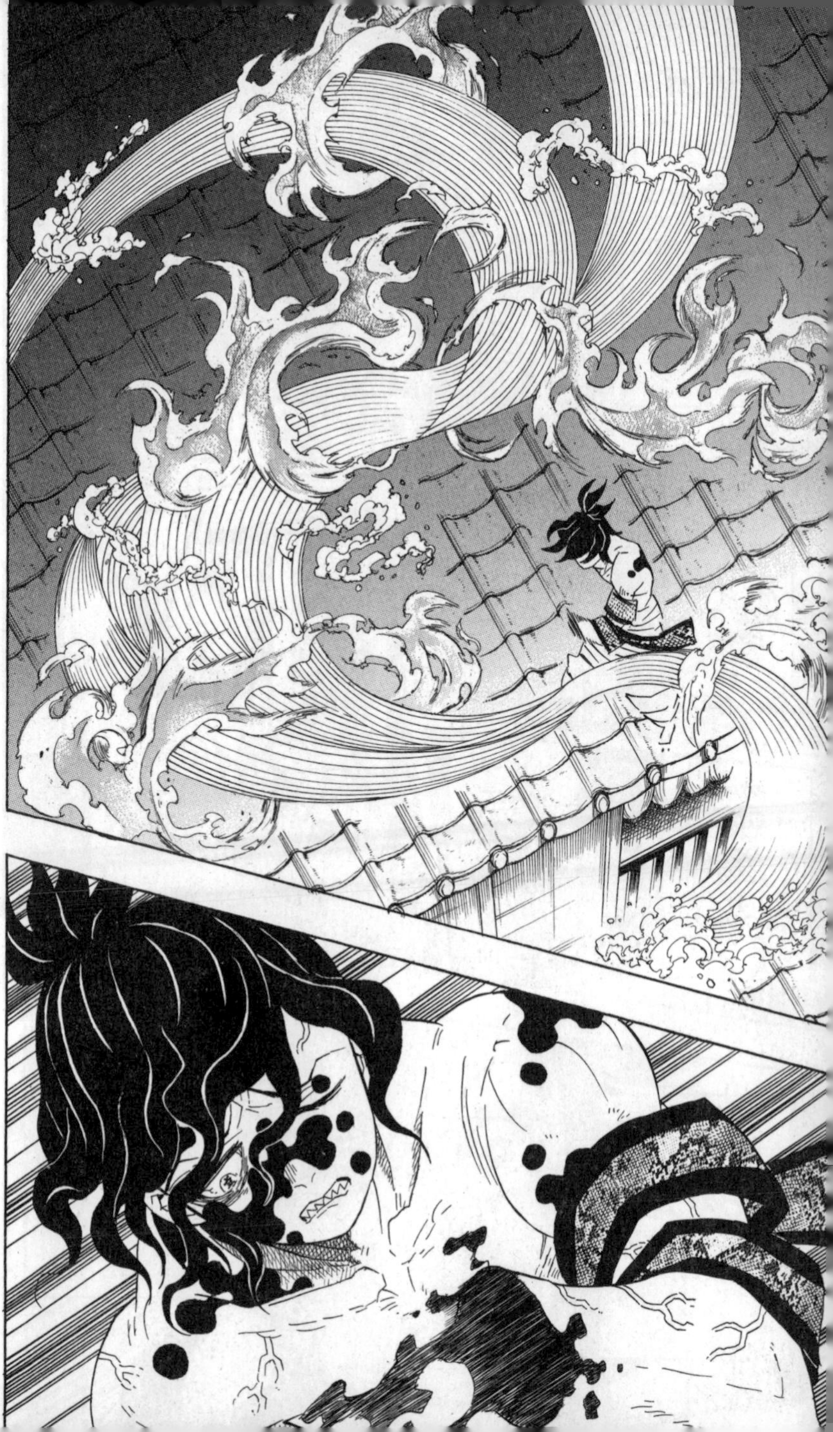

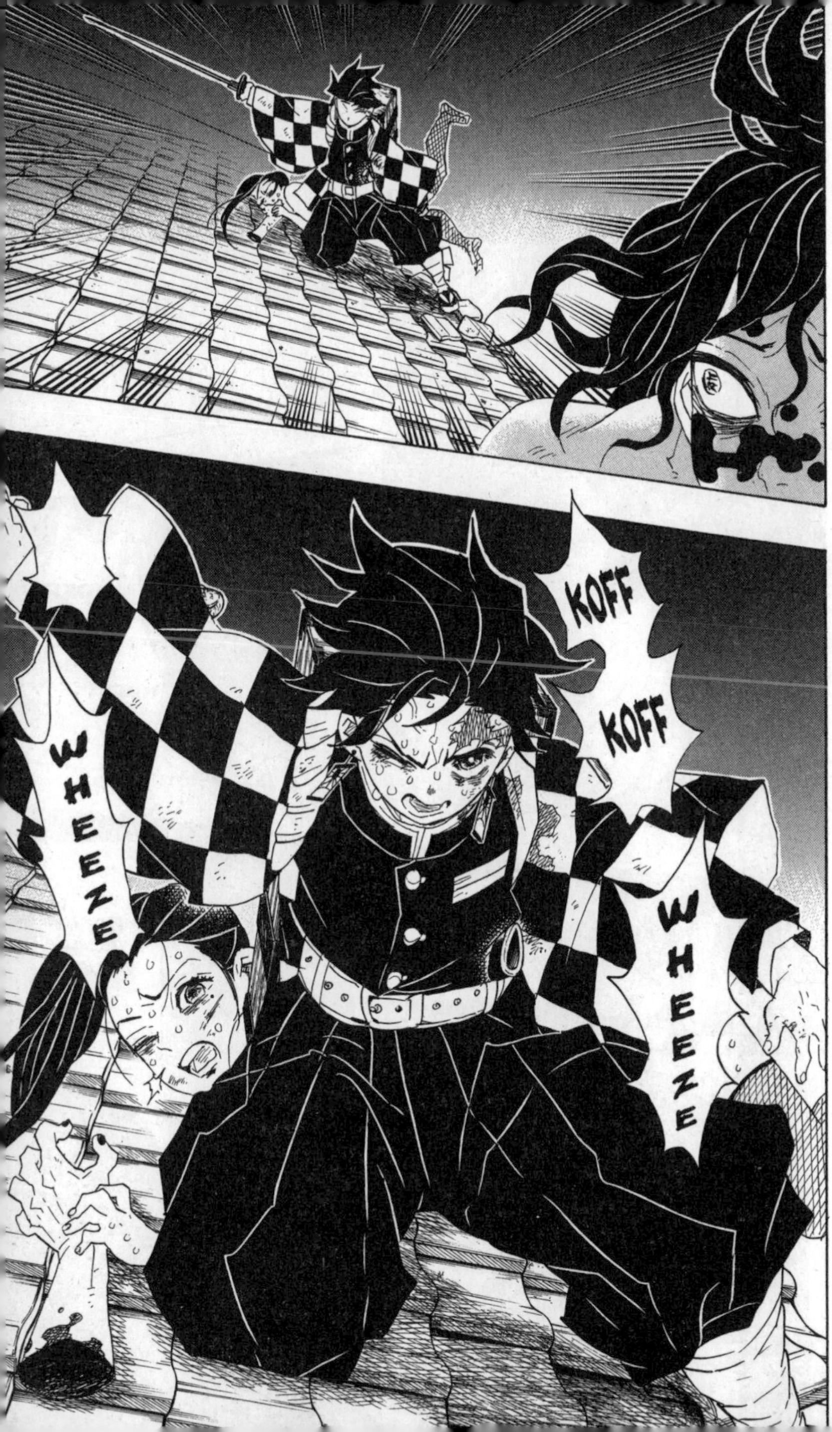
KOFF
KOFF
WHEEZE
WHEEZE

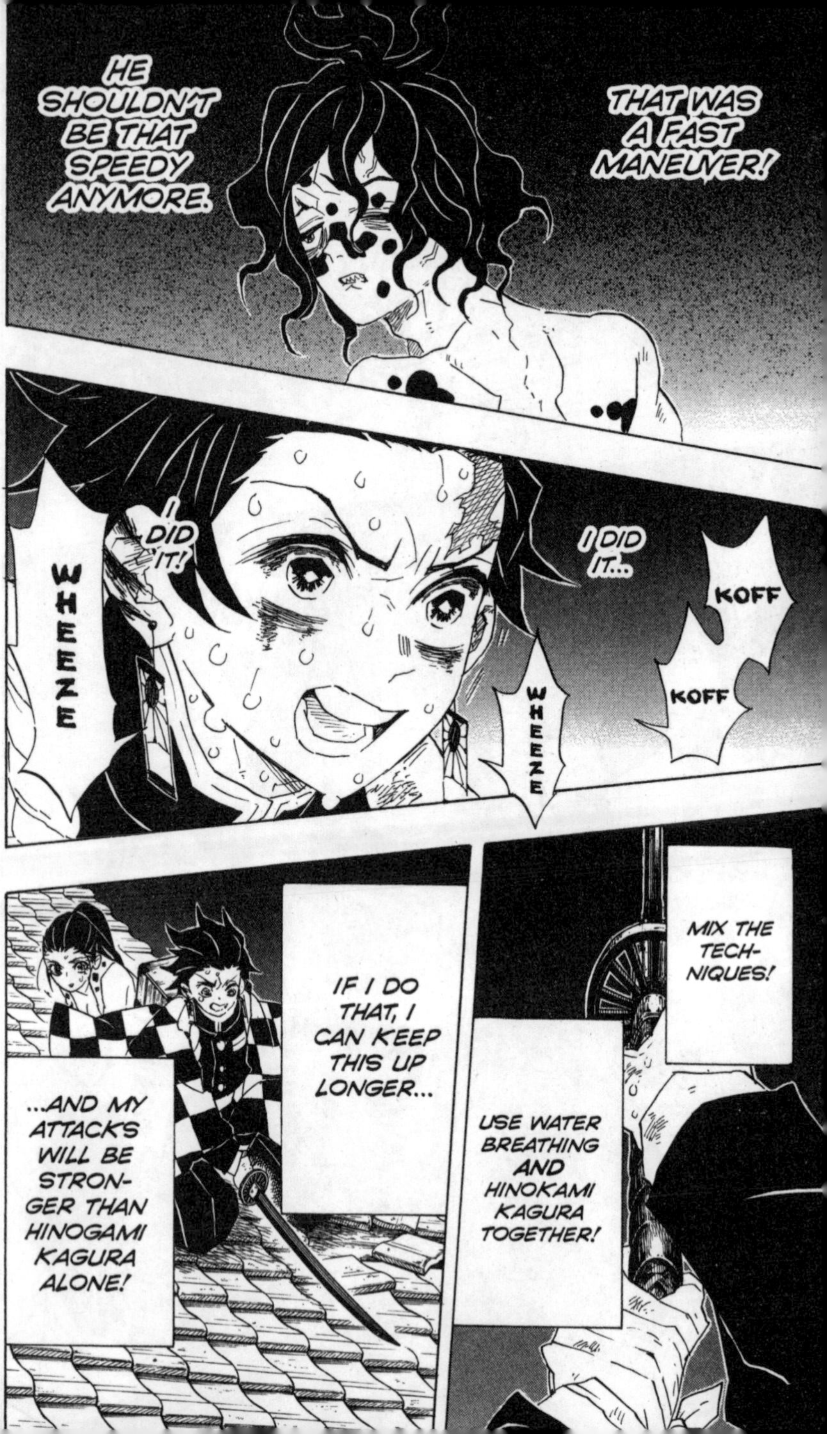
THAT WAS A FAST MANEUVER!
HE SHOULDN'T BE THAT SPEEDY ANYMORE.
KOFF
KOFF
I DID IT...
WHEEZE
I DID IT!
WHEEZE
MIX THE TECH-NIQUES!
USE WATER BREATHING AND HINOKAMI KAGURA TOGETHER!
IF I DO THAT, I CAN KEEP THIS UP LONGER...
...AND MY ATTACKS WILL BE STRON-GER THAN HINOGAMI KAGURA ALONE!

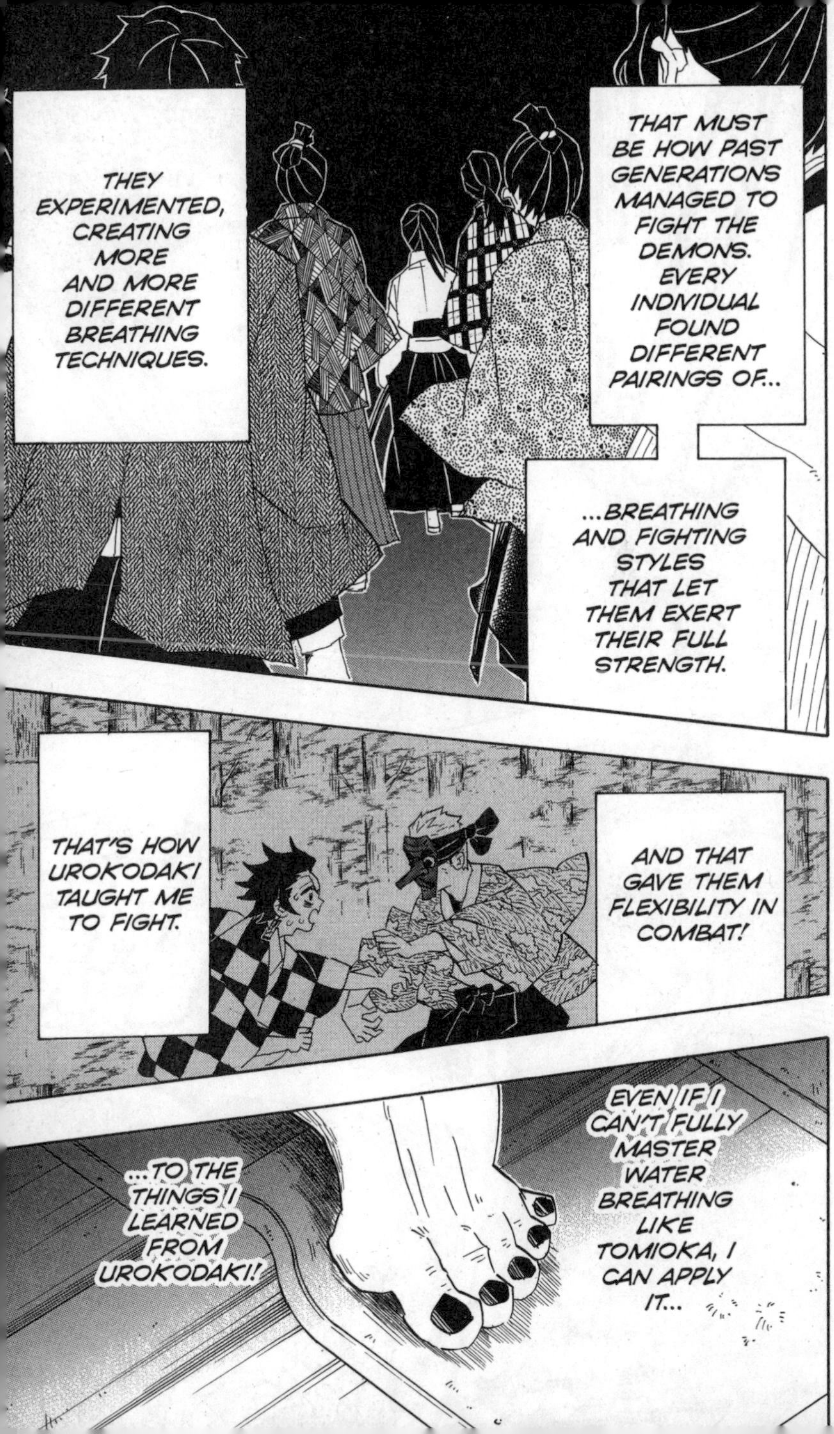
THAT MUST BE HOW PAST GENERATIONS MANAGED TO FIGHT THE DEMONS. EVERY INDIVIDUAL FOUND DIFFERENT PAIRINGS OF...
...BREATHING AND FIGHTING STYLES THAT LET THEM EXERT THEIR FULL STRENGTH.
THEY EXPERIMENTED, CREATING MORE AND MORE DIFFERENT BREATHING TECHNIQUES.
AND THAT GAVE THEM FLEXIBILITY IN COMBAT!
THAT'S HOW UROKODAKI TAUGHT ME TO FIGHT.
EVEN IF I CAN'T FULLY MASTER WATER BREATHING LIKE TOMIOKA, I CAN APPLY IT...
...TO THE THINGS I LEARNED FROM UROKODAKI!

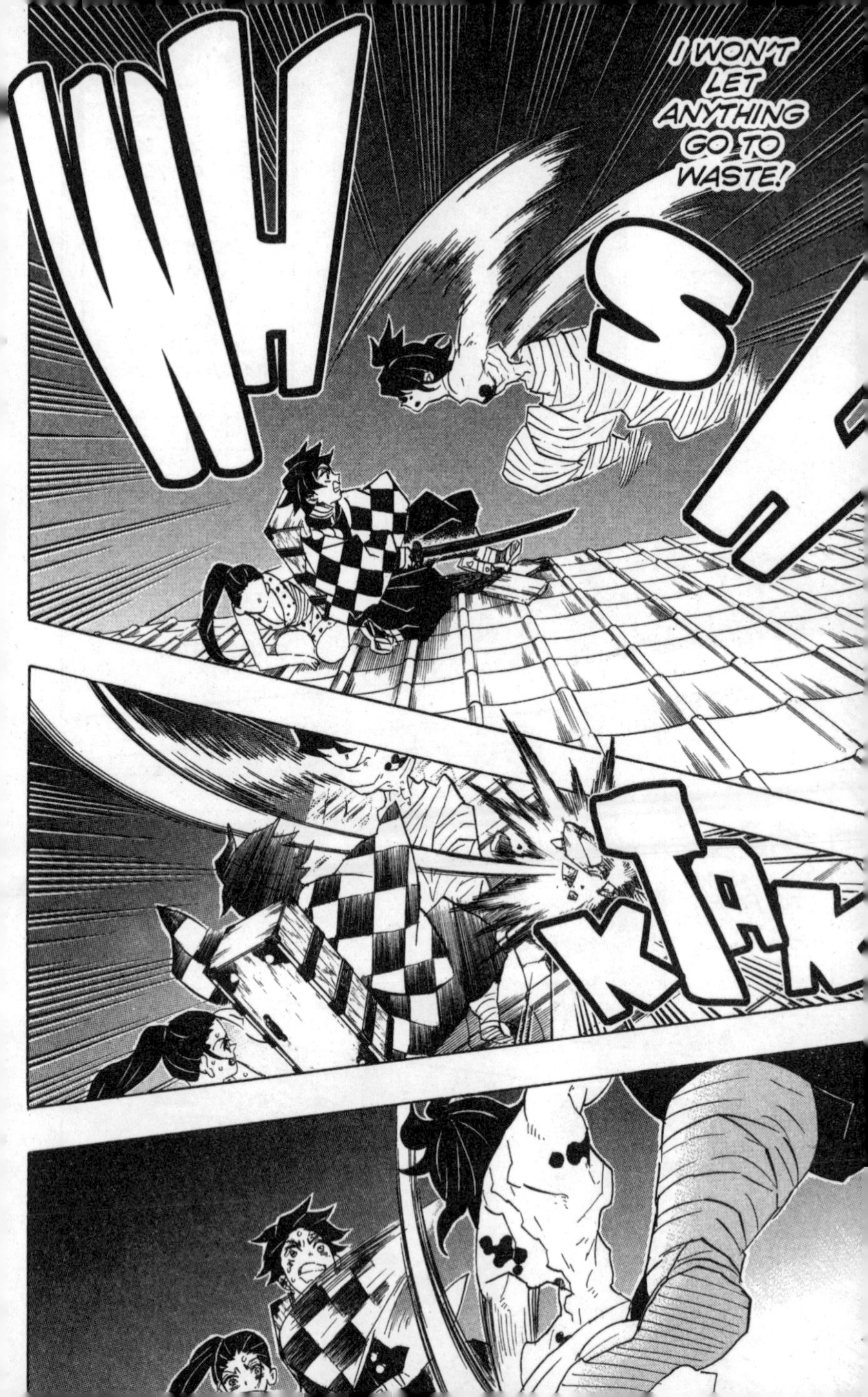
I WON'T LET ANYTHING GO TO WASTE!
WHSH
KLANK

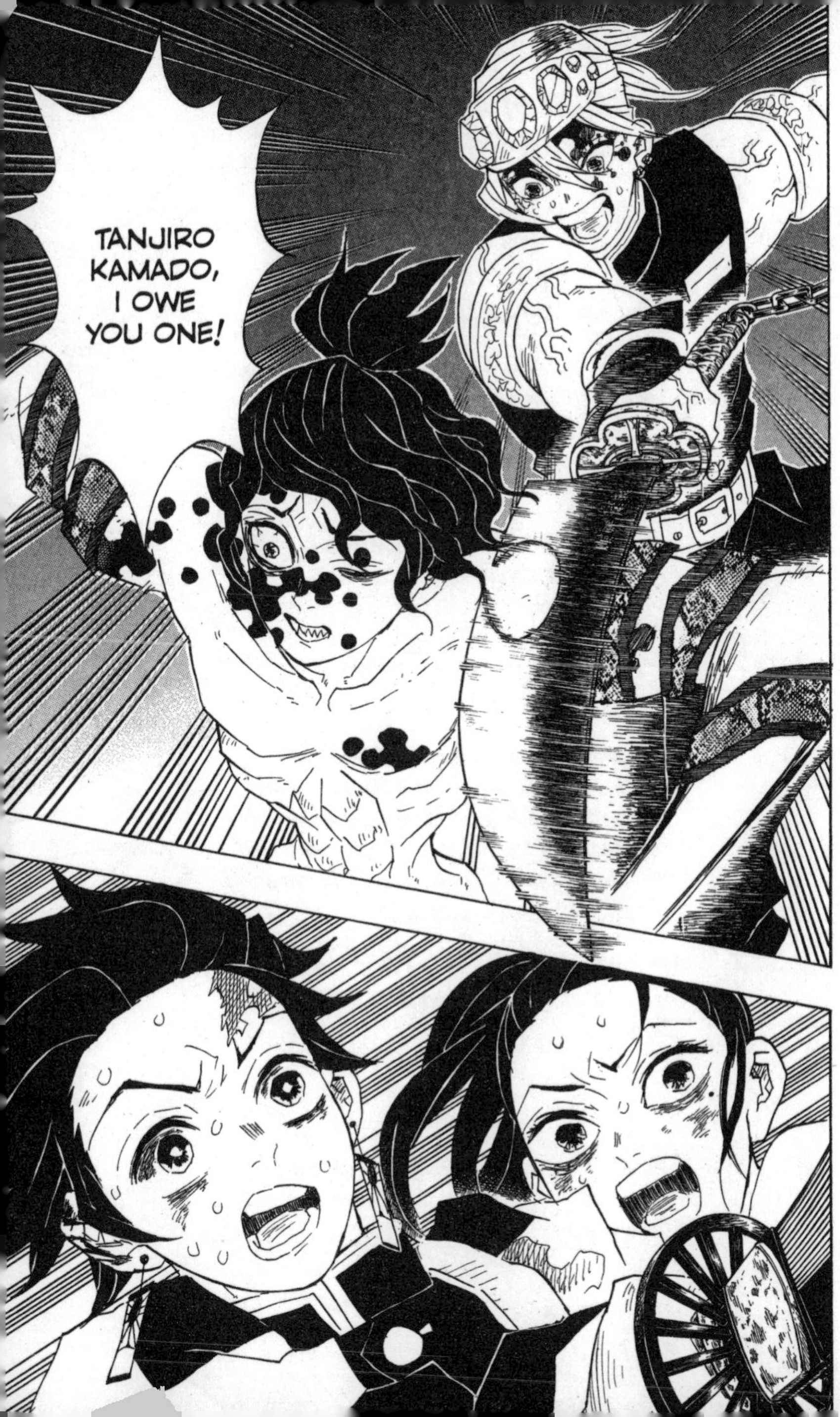
TANJIRO KAMADO, I OWE YOU ONE!

DEMON SLAYER CORPS Q&A

Nobuo-kun

About how long does it take to become a Hashira?

Normally it takes about five years, but quick learners can do it in two.

Croc

Nobuo-kun

How does one become a Hashira?

Defeat one of the Twelve Kizuki or 50 regular demons.

Croc

Nobuo-kun

How does one become a Tsuguko?

Croc

You apply to the Hashira and he or she decides to accept you. Or a Hashira might invite you. It's helpful to use the same style of breathing technique as the Hashira, but you can become a Tsuguko even if you don't.

Nobuo-kun

If I stole a Nichirin Sword that already had a color, would it change to my color?

First, don't ever do that! But once a blade has a color it won't change, even if it gets a new owner.

Nobuo-kun?

Rats!

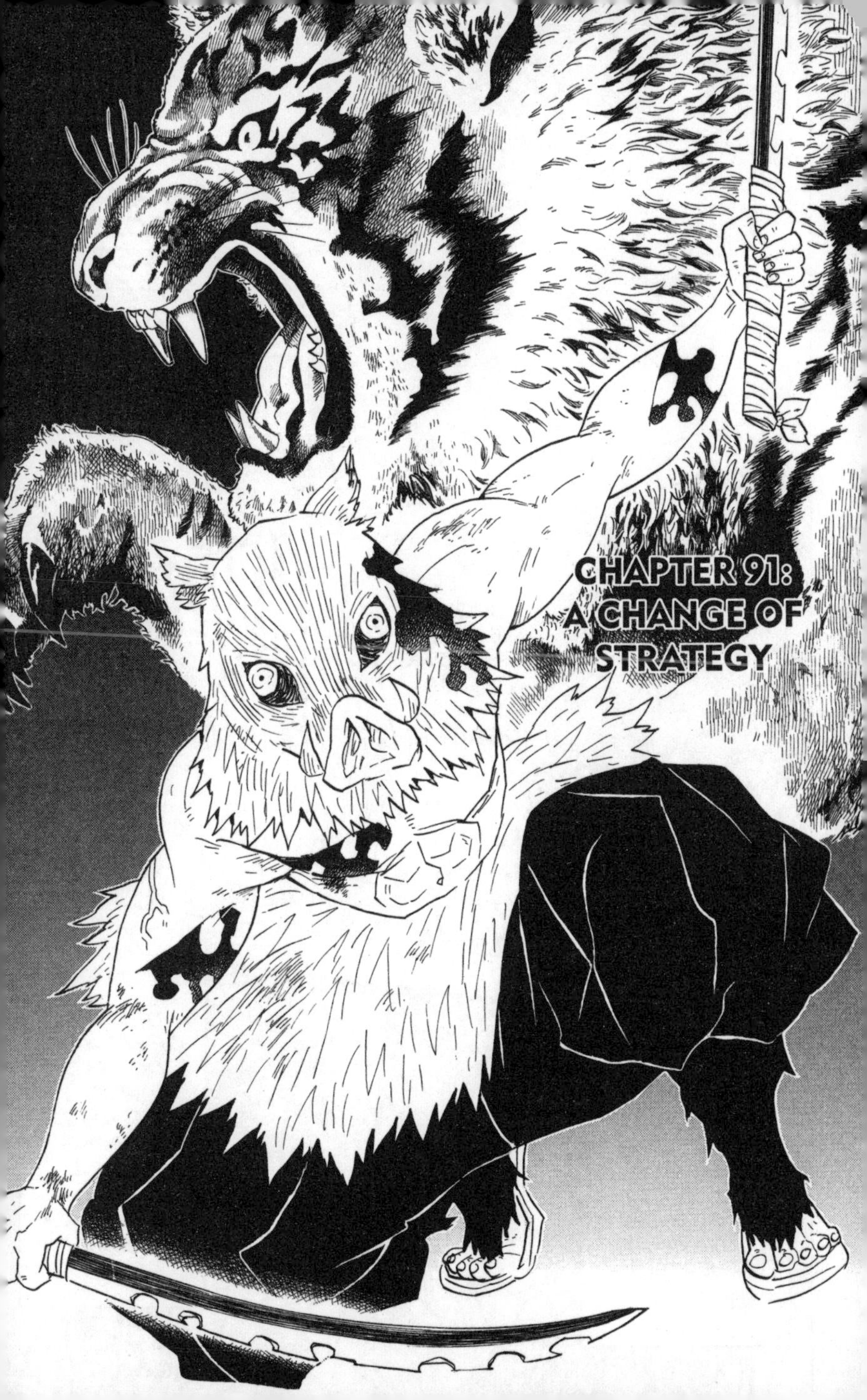
CHAPTER 91:
A CHANGE OF
STRATEGY

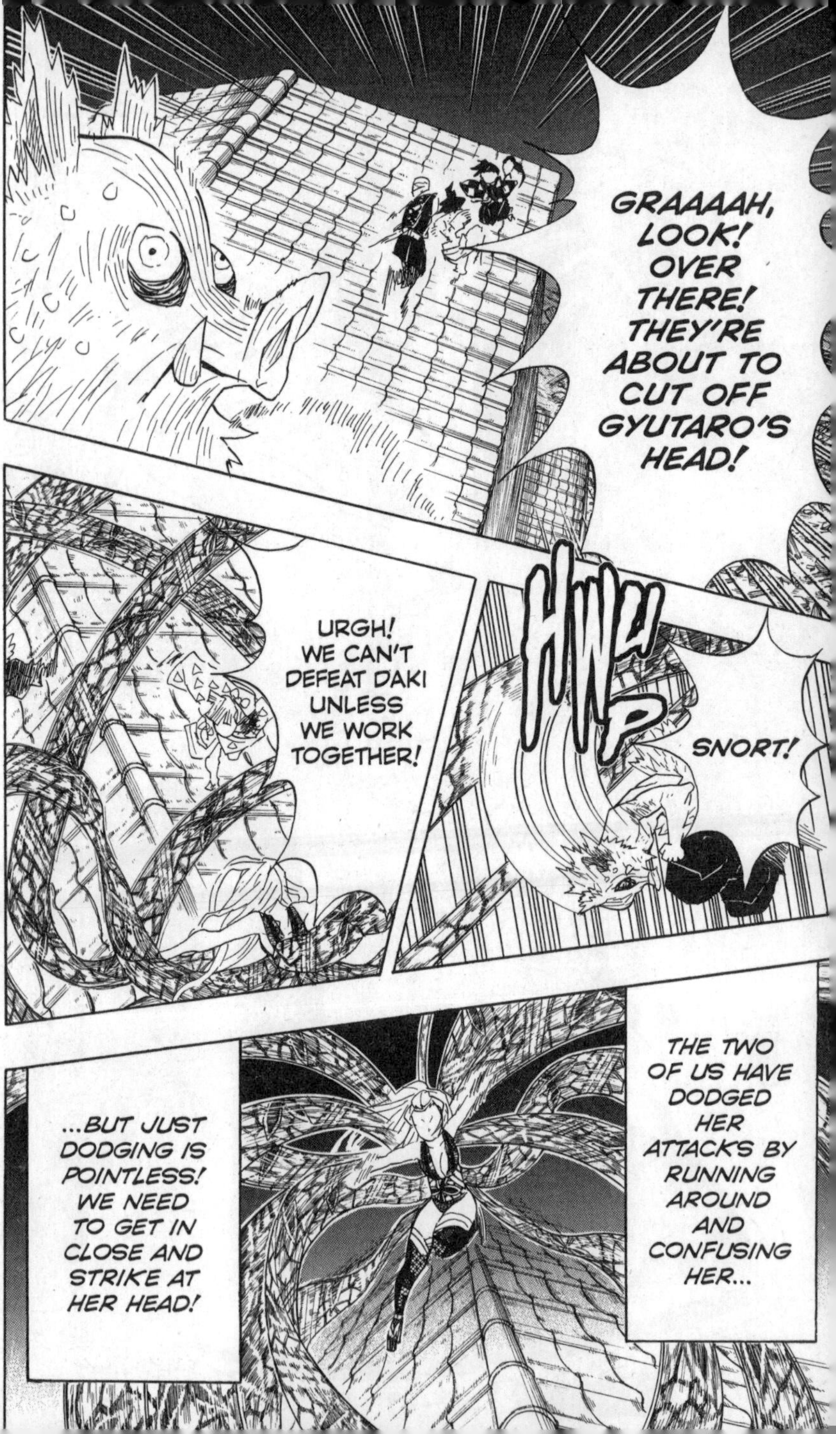
GRAAAAH, LOOK! OVER THERE! THEY'RE ABOUT TO CUT OFF GYUTARO'S HEAD!
HWUMP
SNORT!
URGH! WE CAN'T DEFEAT DAKI UNLESS WE WORK TOGETHER!
THE TWO OF US HAVE DODGED HER ATTACKS BY RUNNING AROUND AND CONFUSING HER...
...BUT JUST DODGING IS POINTLESS! WE NEED TO GET IN CLOSE AND STRIKE AT HER HEAD!

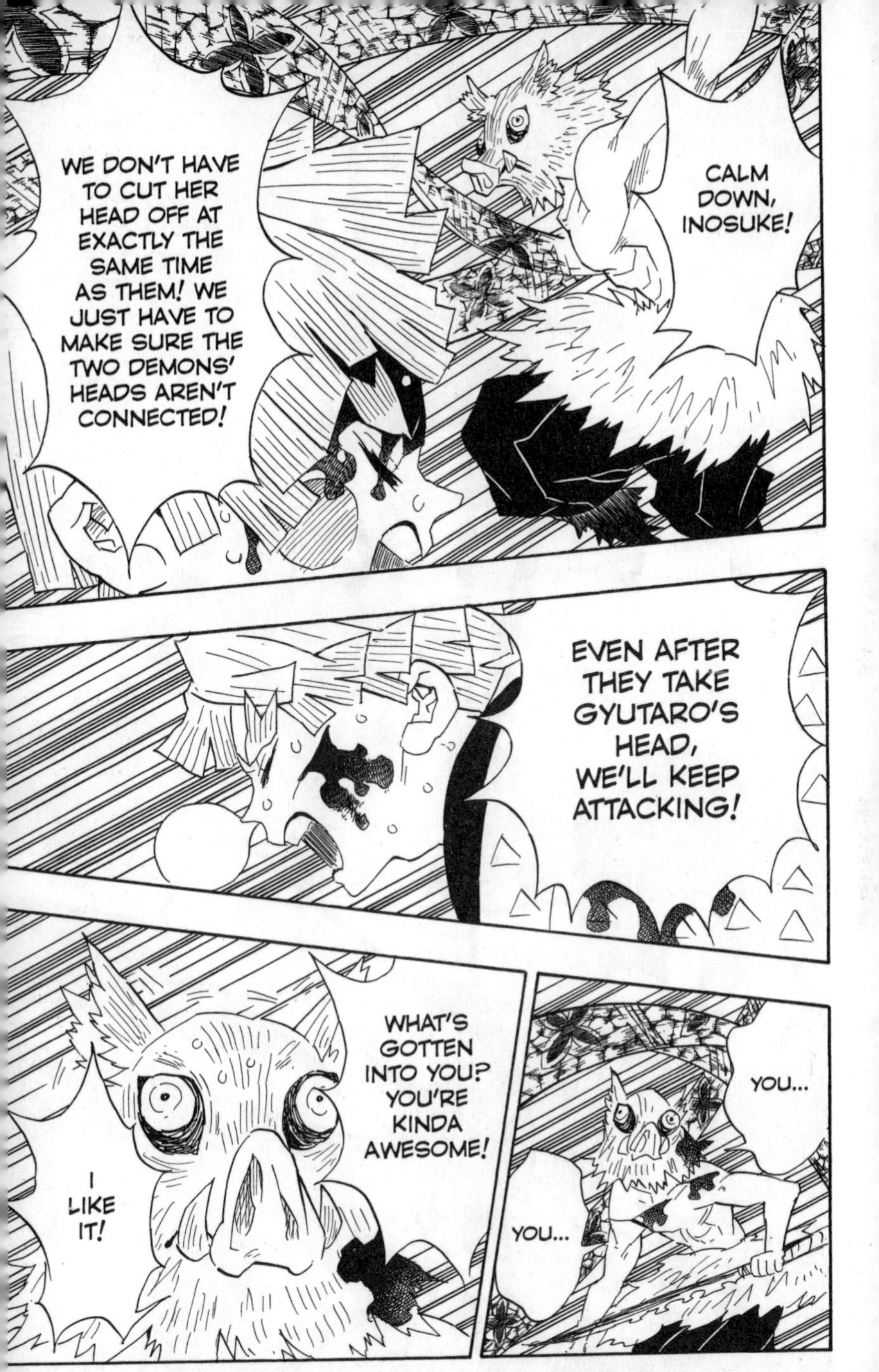
CALM DOWN, INOSUKE!
WE DON'T HAVE TO CUT HER HEAD OFF AT EXACTLY THE SAME TIME AS THEM! WE JUST HAVE TO MAKE SURE THE TWO DEMONS' HEADS AREN'T CONNECTED!
EVEN AFTER THEY TAKE GYUTARO'S HEAD, WE'LL KEEP ATTACKING!
YOU...
YOU...
WHAT'S GOTTEN INTO YOU? YOU'RE KINDA AWESOME!
I LIKE IT!

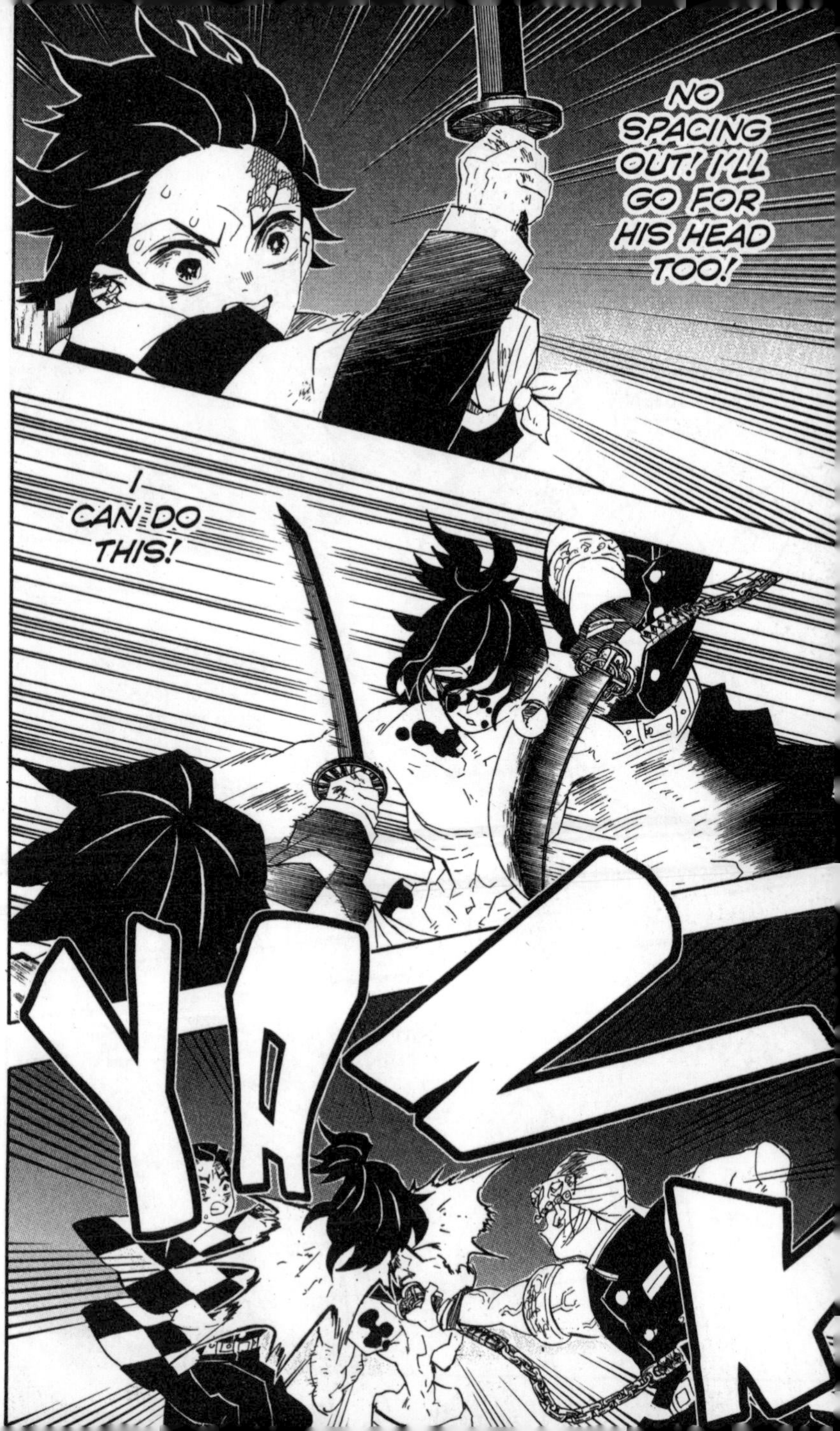
NO SPACING OUT! I'LL GO FOR HIS HEAD TOO!
I CAN DO THIS!
YANK

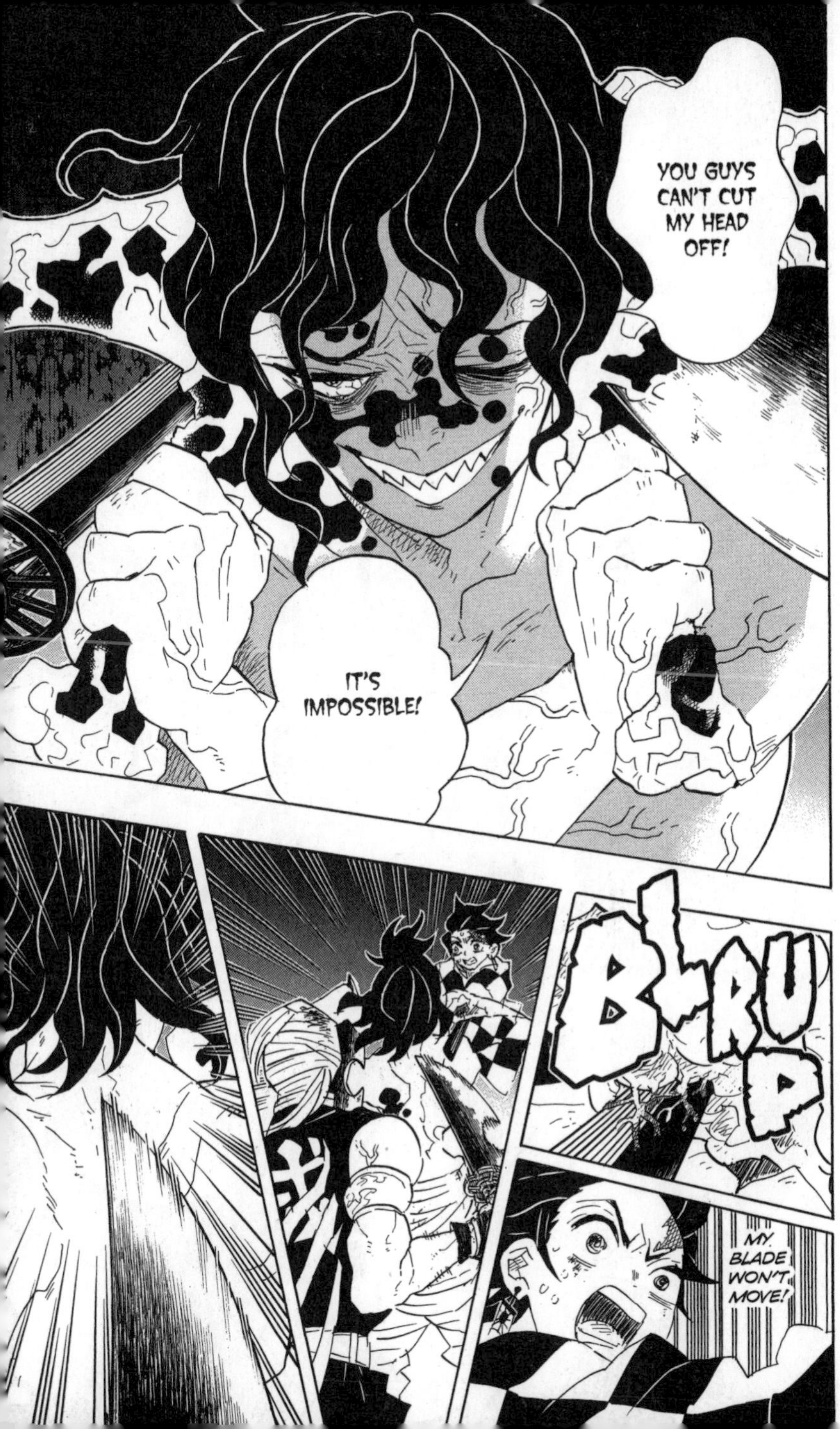
YOU GUYS CAN'T CUT MY HEAD OFF!
IT'S IMPOSSIBLE!
BLRUP
MY BLADE WON'T MOVE!

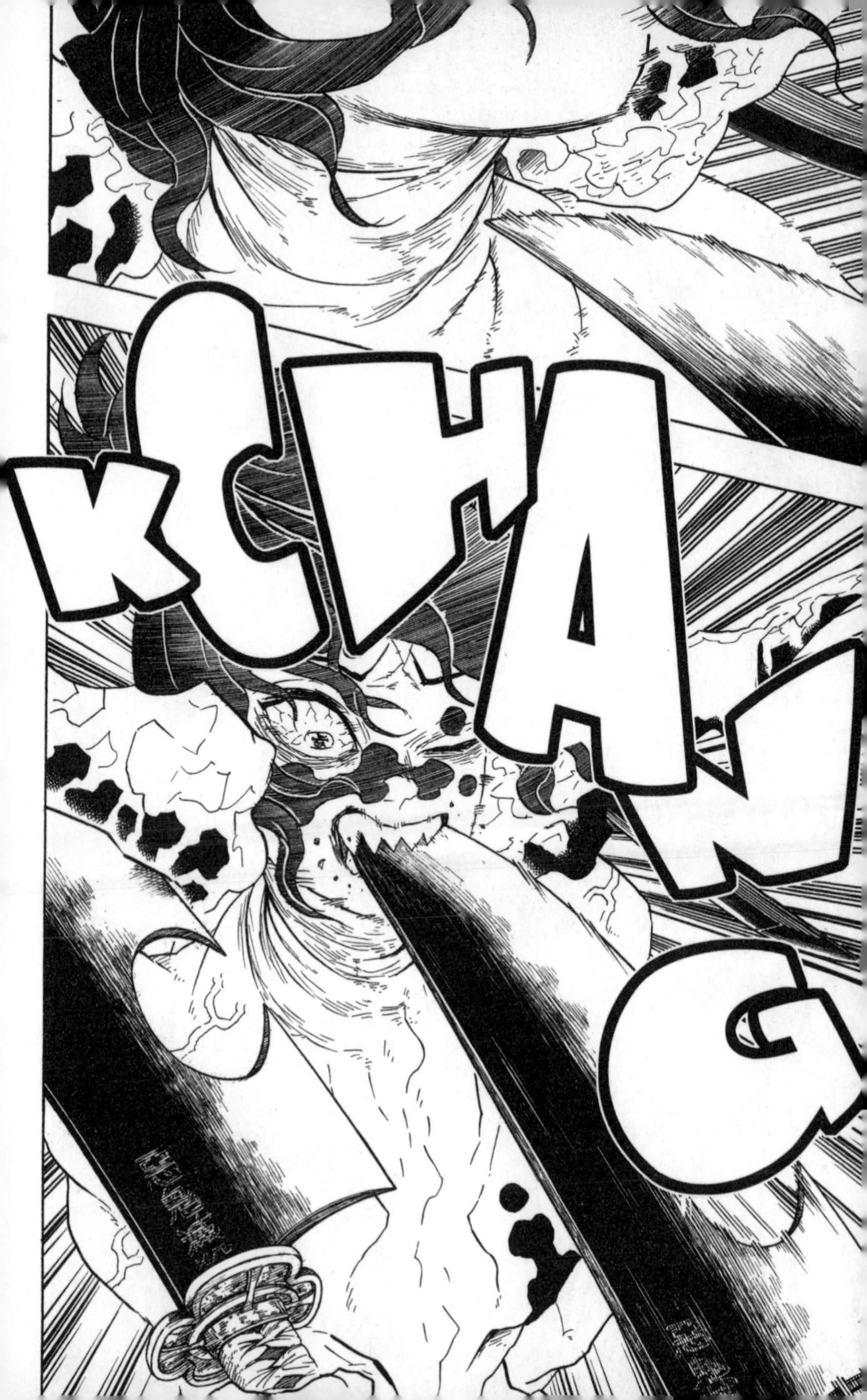
KCHANG

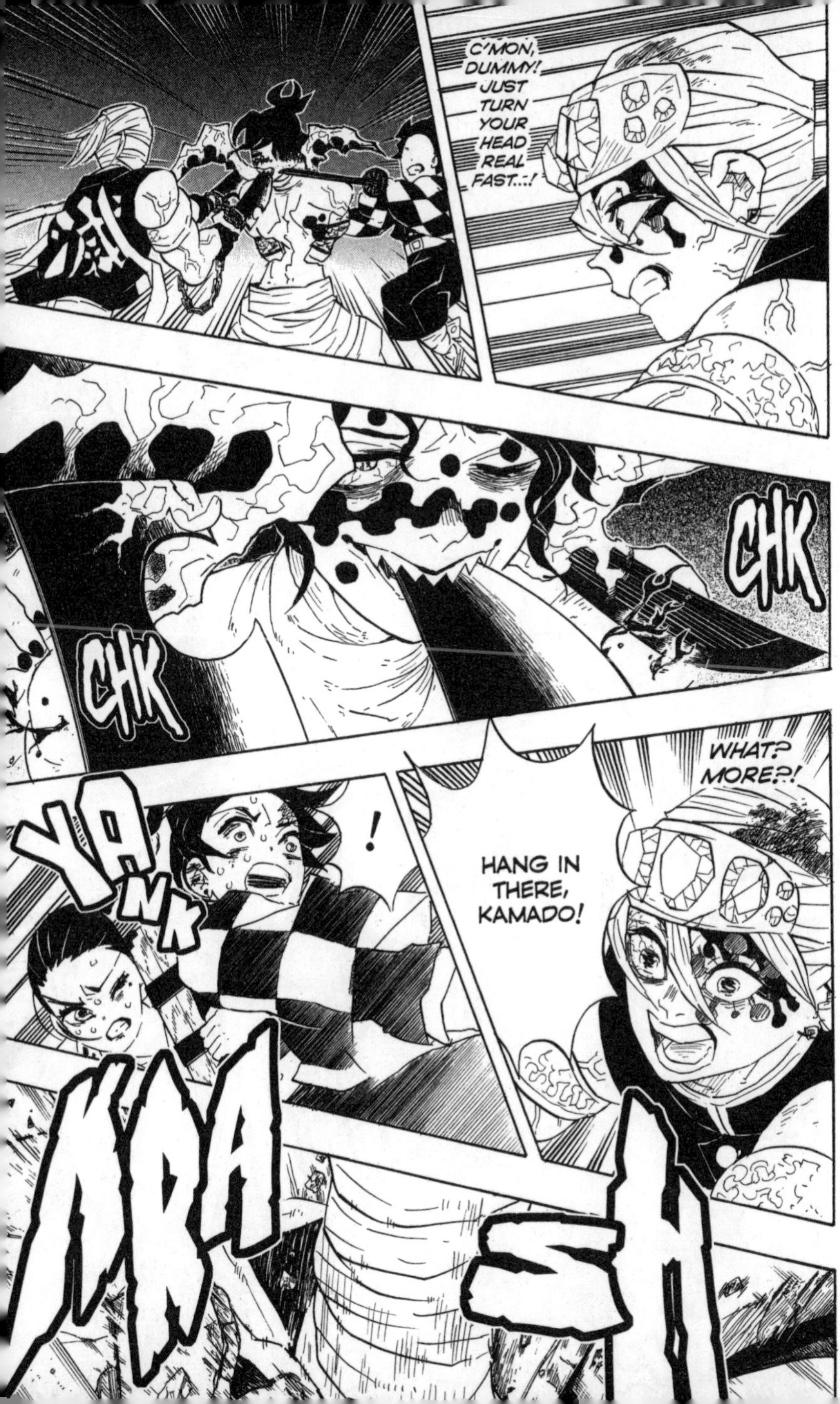
C'MON, DUMMY! JUST TURN YOUR HEAD REAL FAST...!
CHK
CHK
WHAT? MORE?!
HANG IN THERE, KAMADO!
!
YANK

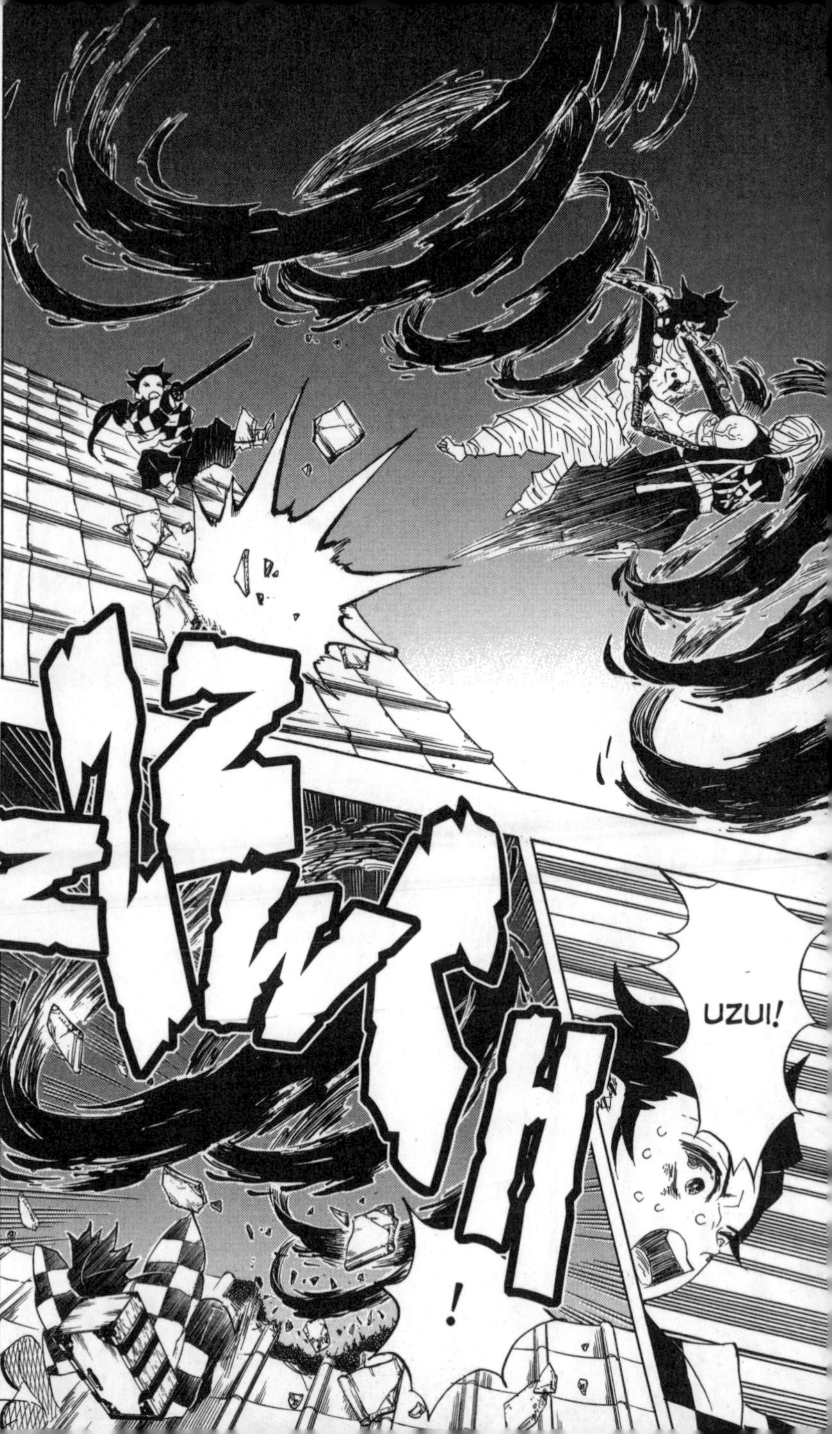
UZUI!
ZWAM
!

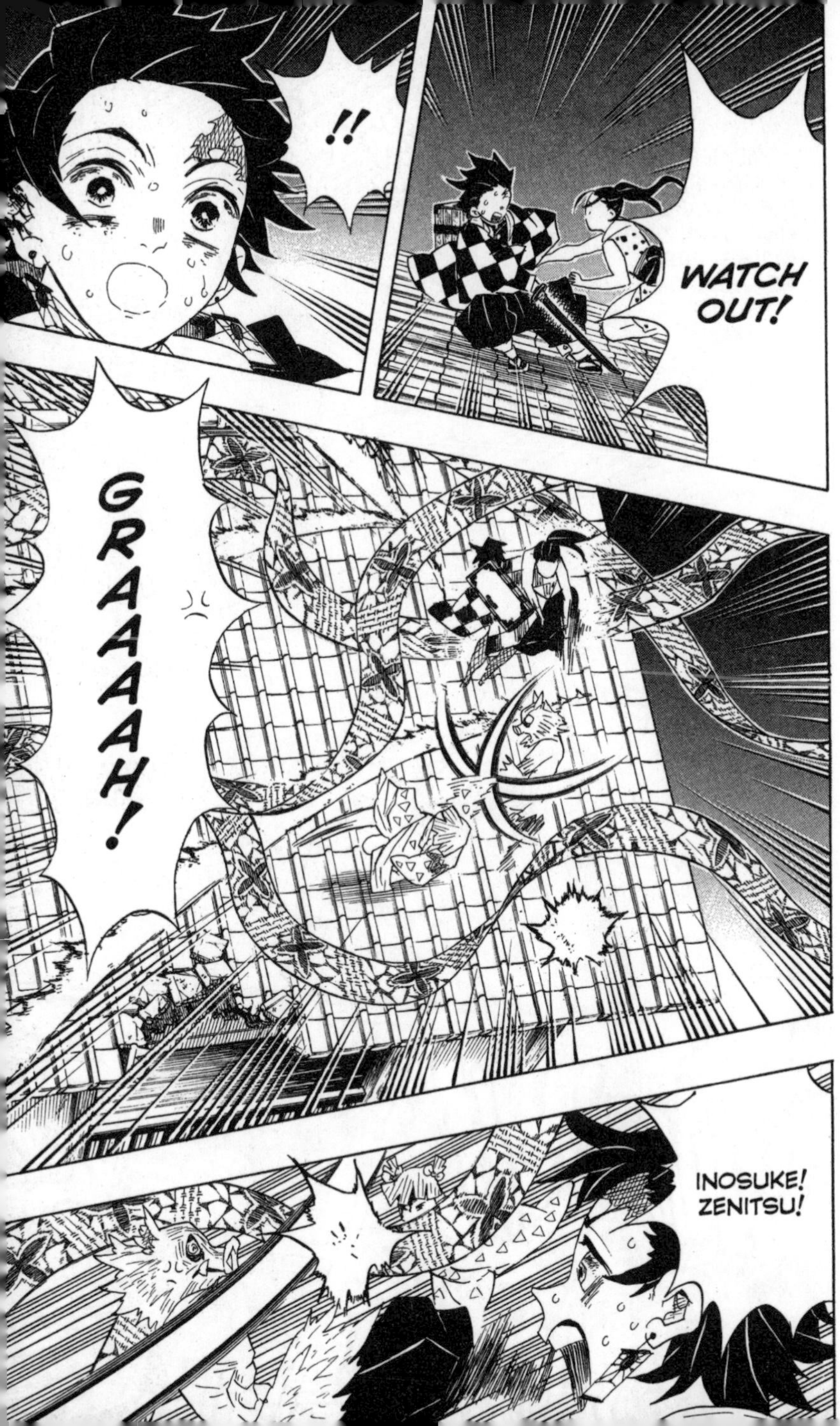
WATCH OUT!
!!
GRAAAAAH!
INOSUKE! ZENITSU!

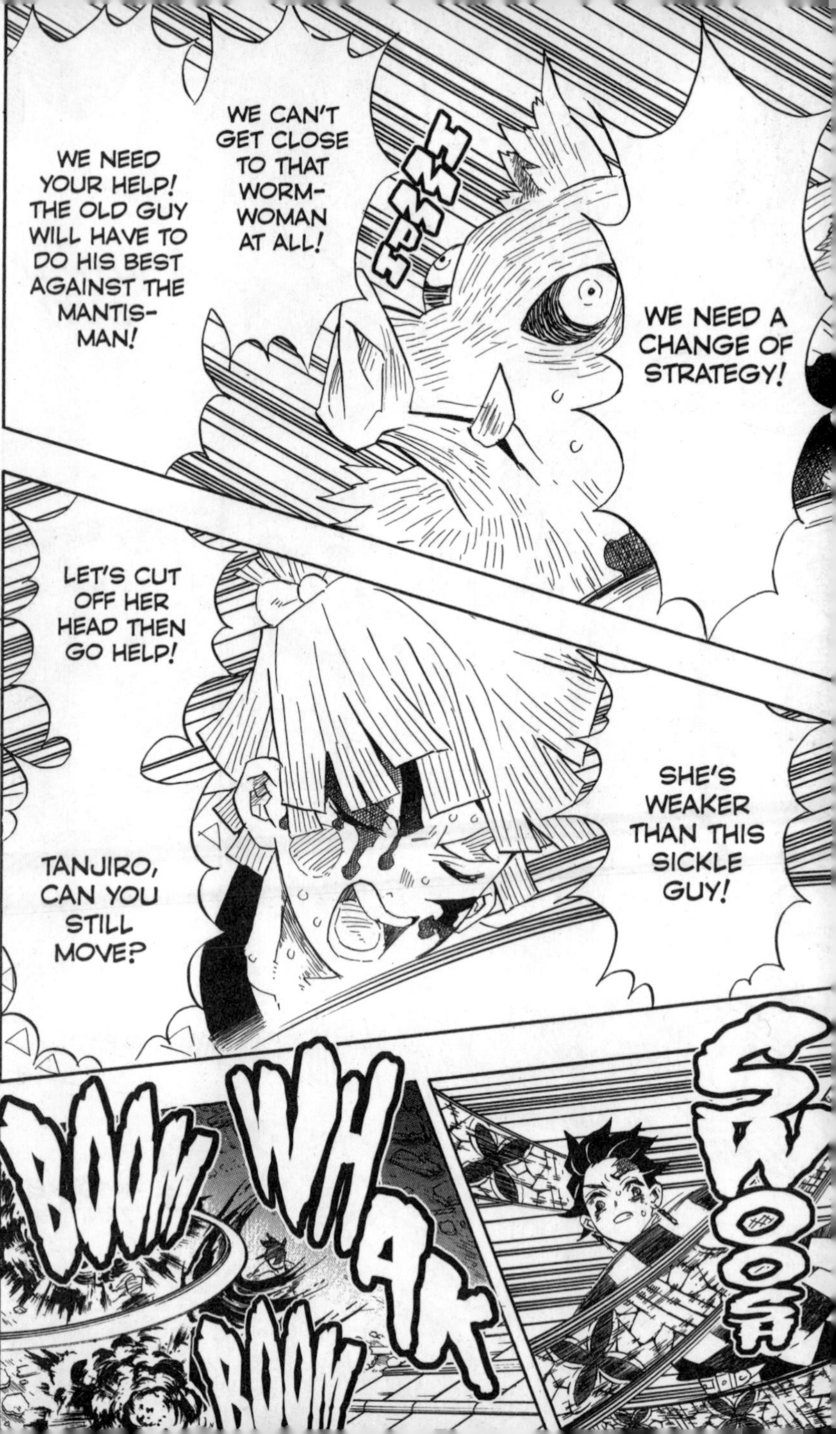
WE NEED A CHANGE OF STRATEGY!
HMMPH
WE CAN'T GET CLOSE TO THAT WORM-WOMAN AT ALL!
WE NEED YOUR HELP! THE OLD GUY WILL HAVE TO DO HIS BEST AGAINST THE MANTIS-MAN!
SHE'S WEAKER THAN THIS SICKLE GUY!
LET'S CUT OFF HER HEAD THEN GO HELP!
TANJIRO, CAN YOU STILL MOVE?
SWOOO
WHACK
BOOM
BOOM

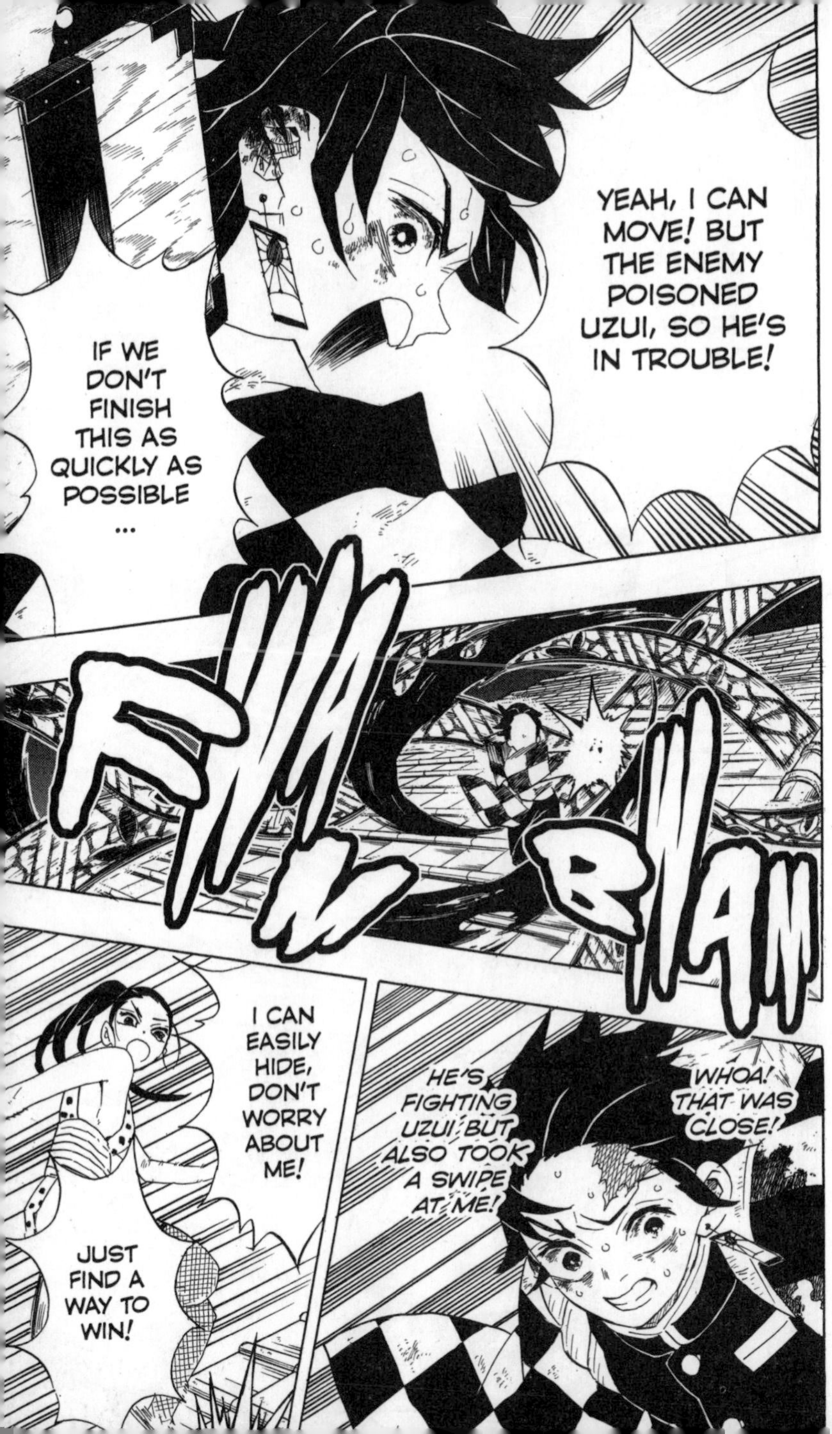
YEAH, I CAN MOVE! BUT THE ENEMY POISONED UZUI, SO HE'S IN TROUBLE!
IF WE DON'T FINISH THIS AS QUICKLY AS POSSIBLE ...
FWA
BLAM
WHOA! THAT WAS CLOSE!
HE'S FIGHTING UZUI BUT ALSO TOOK A SWIPE AT ME!
I CAN EASILY HIDE, DON'T WORRY ABOUT ME!
JUST FIND A WAY TO WIN!

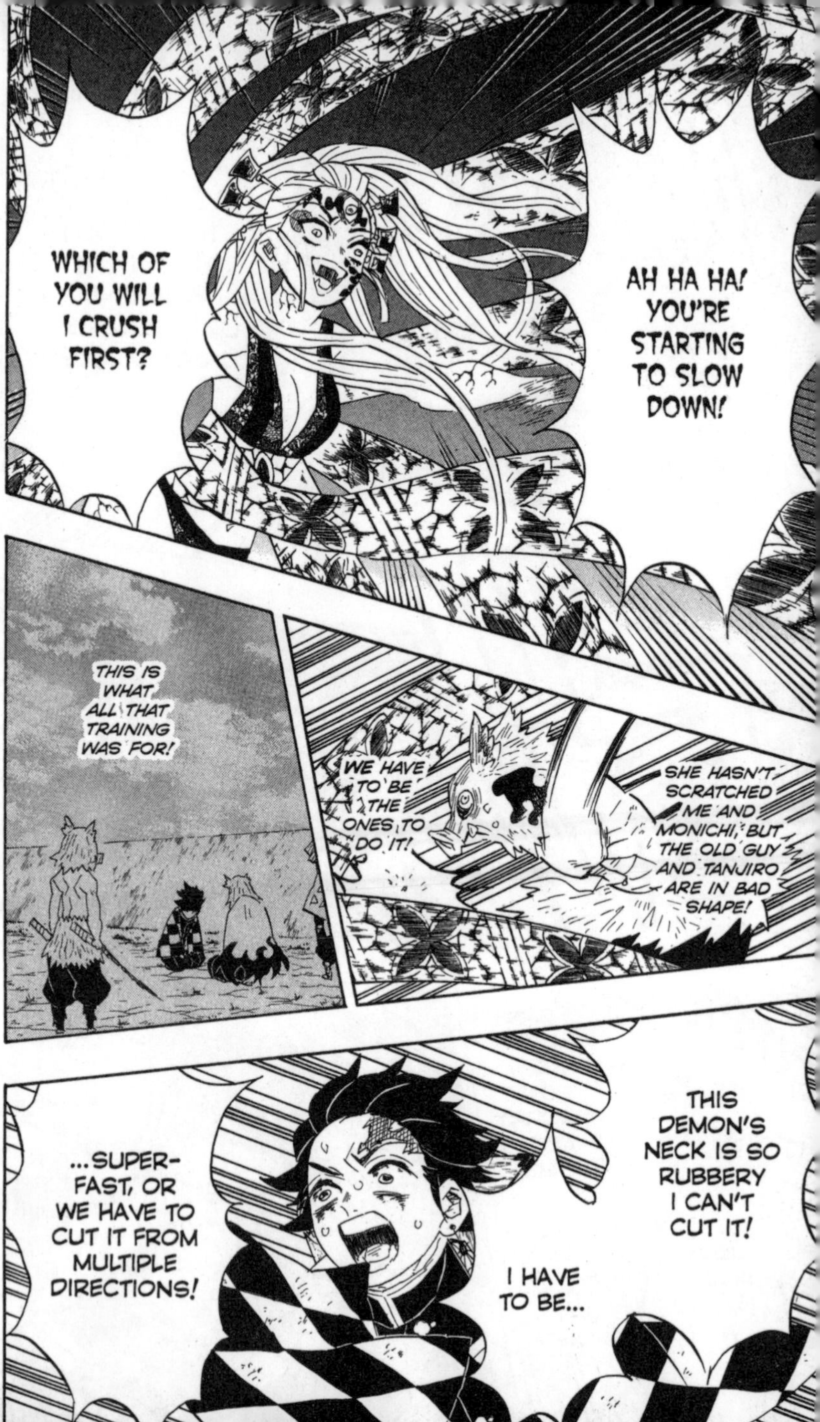
AH HA HA! YOU'RE STARTING TO SLOW DOWN!
WHICH OF YOU WILL I CRUSH FIRST?
SHE HASN'T SCRATCHED ME AND MONICHI, BUT THE OLD GUY AND TANJIRO ARE IN BAD SHAPE!
WE HAVE TO BE THE ONES TO DO IT!
THIS IS WHAT ALL THAT TRAINING WAS FOR!
THIS DEMON'S NECK IS SO RUBBERY I CAN'T CUT IT!
I HAVE TO BE...
...SUPER-FAST, OR WE HAVE TO CUT IT FROM MULTIPLE DIRECTIONS!

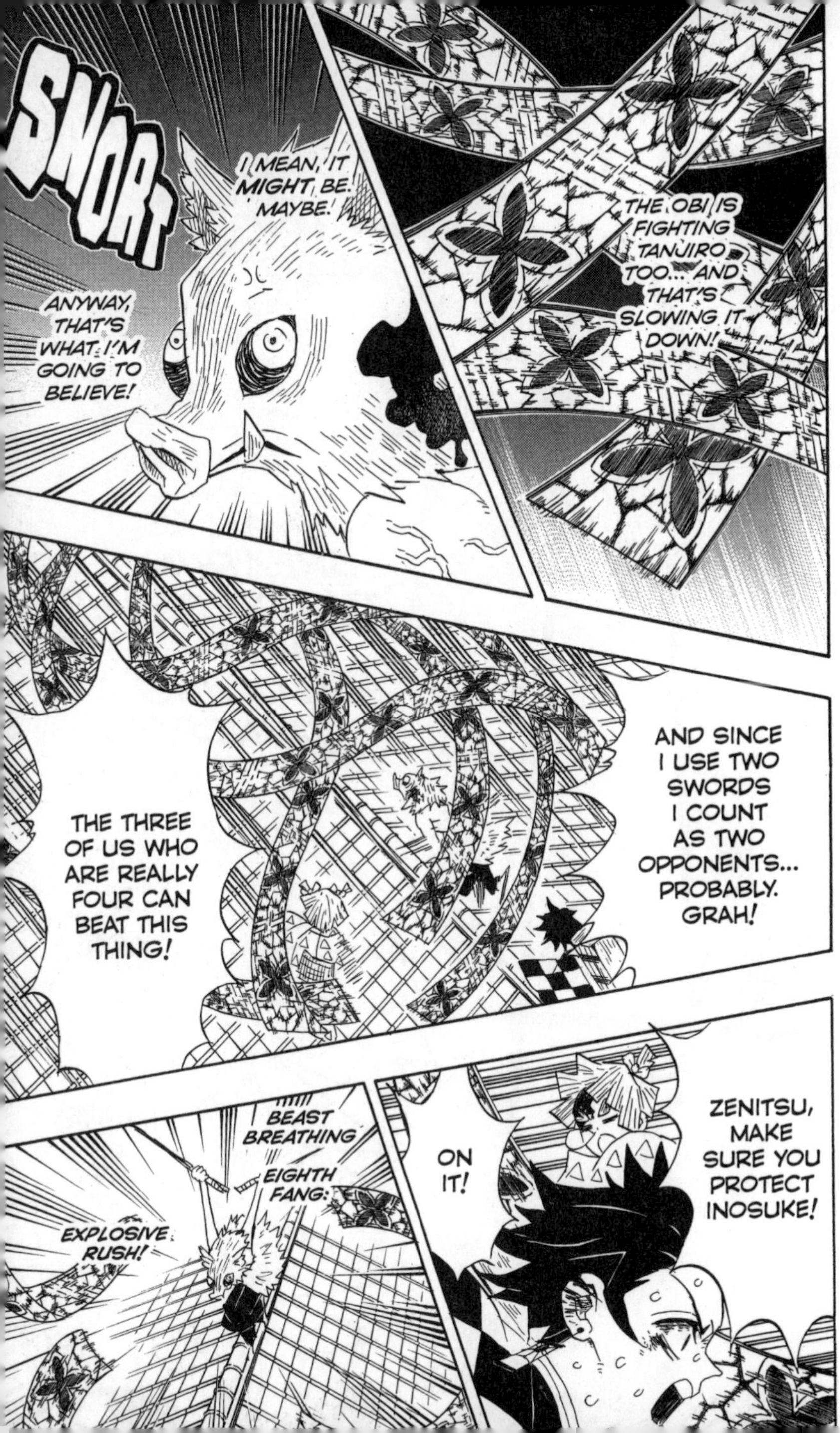
THE OBI IS FIGHTING TANJIRO TOO... AND THAT'S SLOWING IT DOWN!
I MEAN, IT MIGHT BE. MAYBE.
SNORT
ANYWAY, THAT'S WHAT I'M GOING TO BELIEVE!
AND SINCE I USE TWO SWORDS I COUNT AS TWO OPPONENTS... PROBABLY. GRAH!
THE THREE OF US WHO ARE REALLY FOUR CAN BEAT THIS THING!
ZENITSU, MAKE SURE YOU PROTECT INOSUKE!
ON IT!
BEAST BREATHING
EIGHTH FANG:
EXPLOSIVE RUSH!

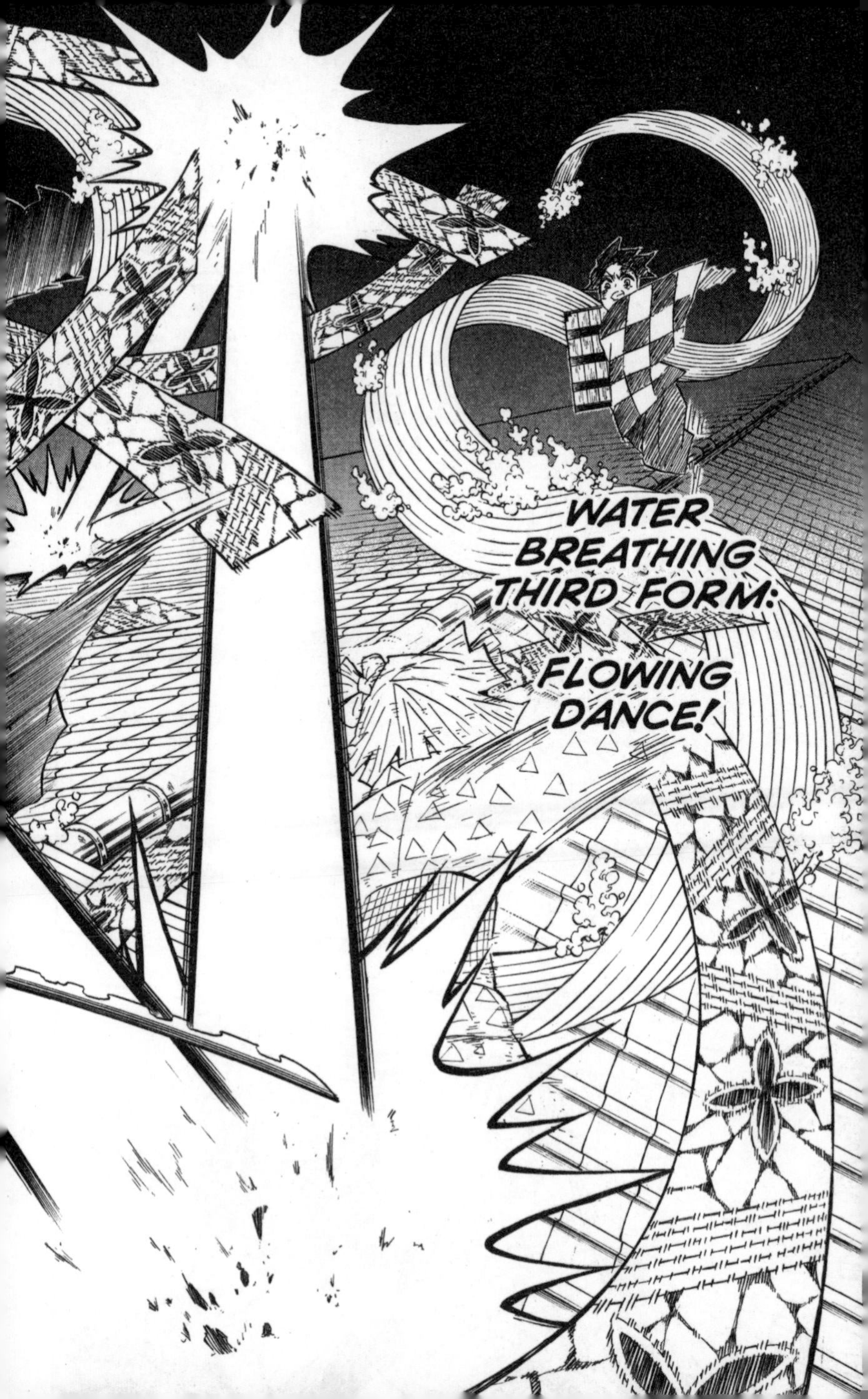
WATER BREATHING THIRD FORM:
FLOWING DANCE!

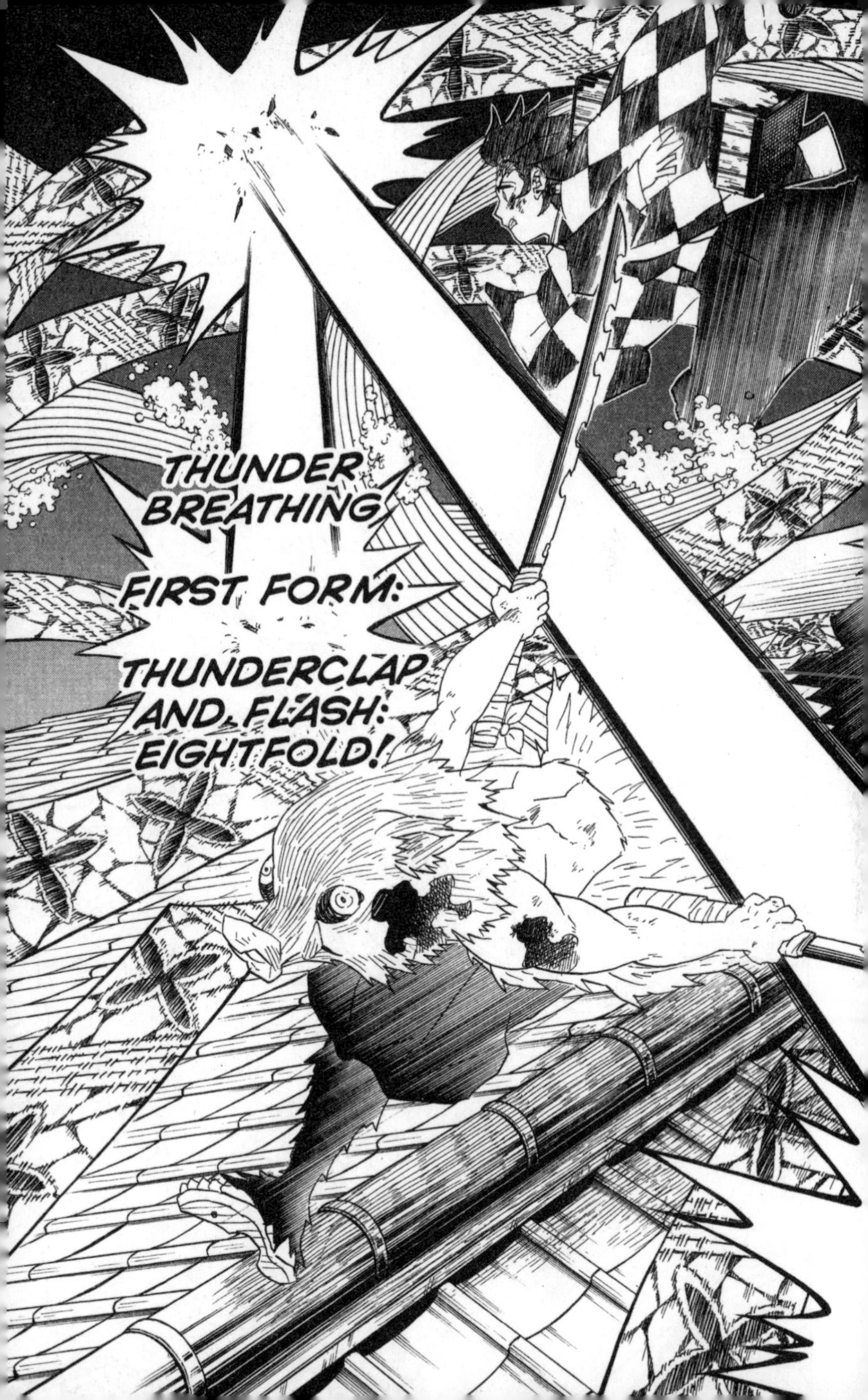
THUNDER BREATHING
FIRST FORM:
THUNDERCLAP AND FLASH: EIGHTFOLD!

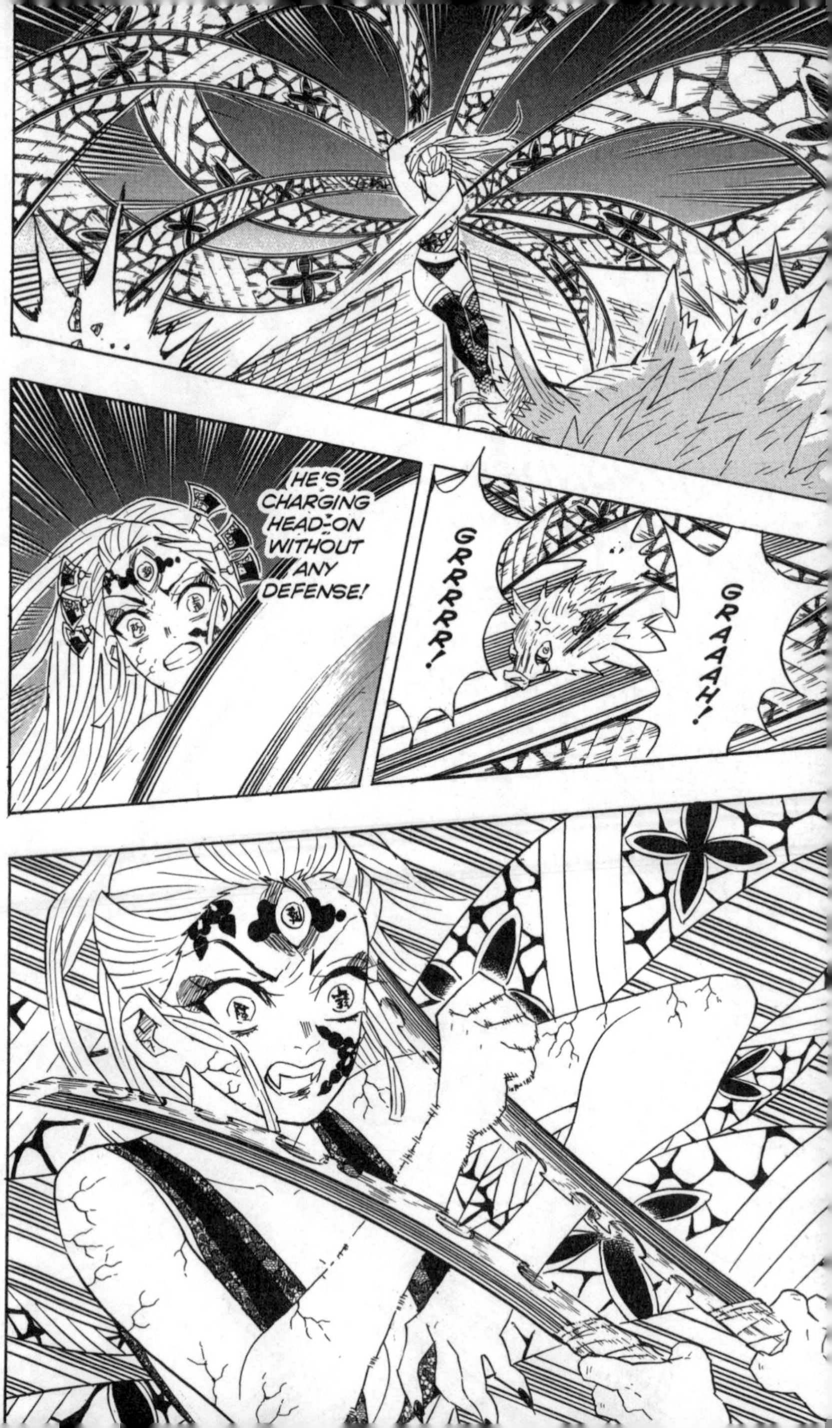
GRRRRRR!
GRAAAAH!
HE'S CHARGING HEAD-ON WITHOUT ANY DEFENSE!

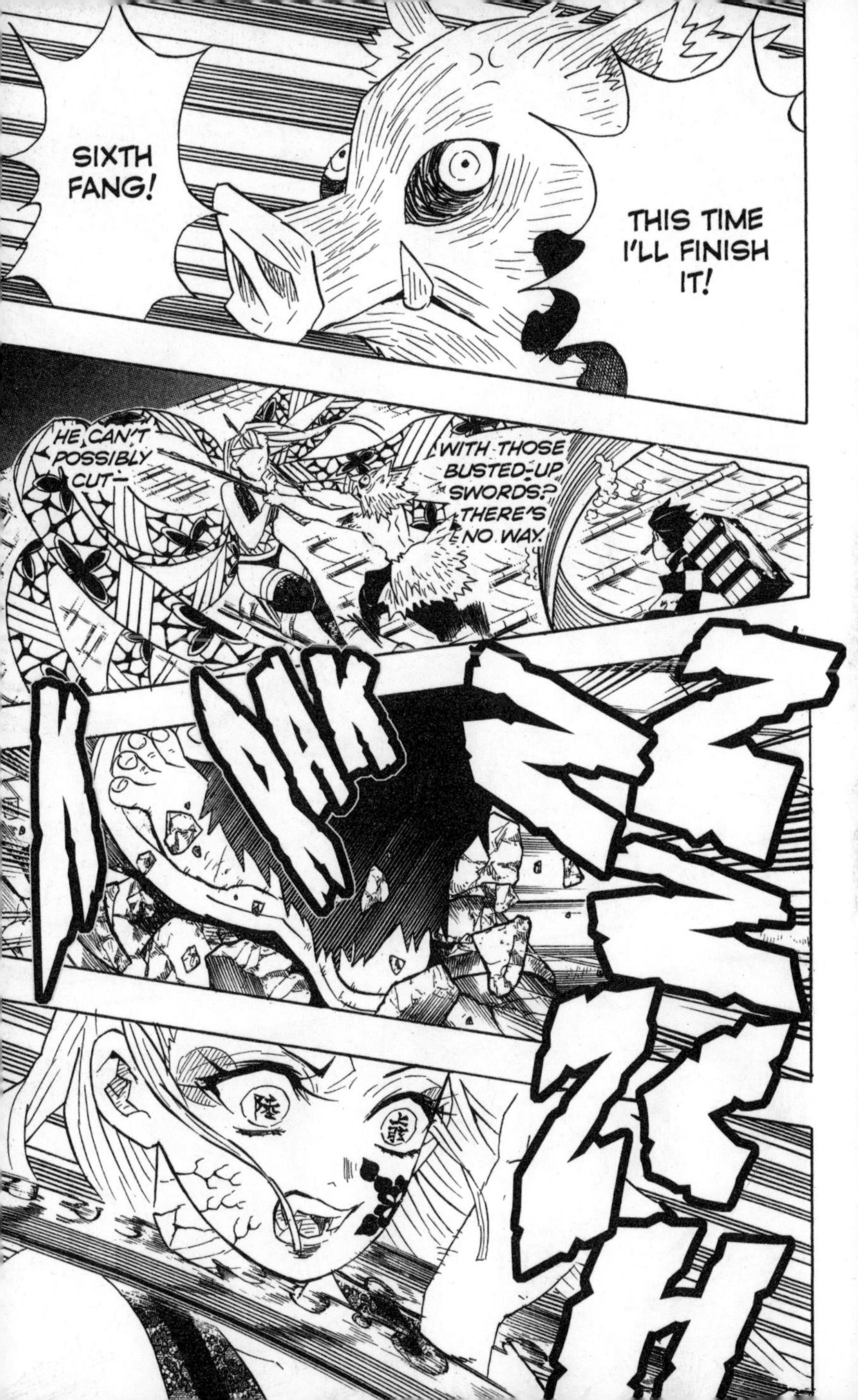
THIS TIME I'LL FINISH IT!
SIXTH FANG!
WITH THOSE BUSTED-UP SWORDS? THERE'S NO WAY.
HE CAN'T POSSIBLY CUT—

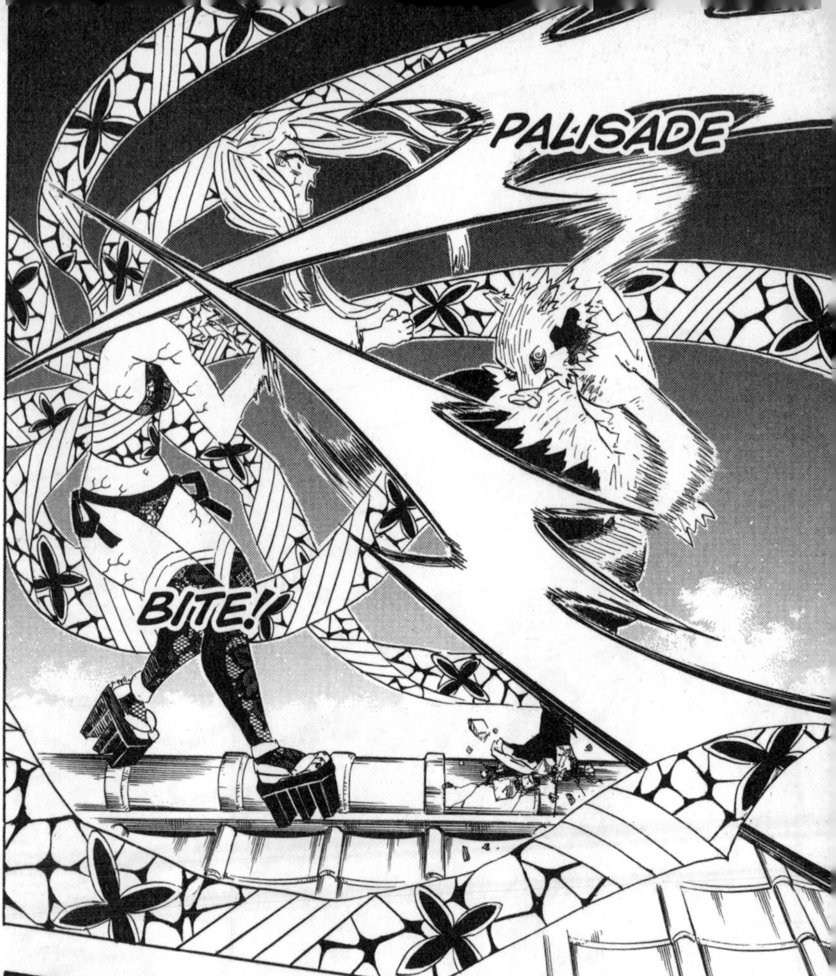
PALISADE
BITE!
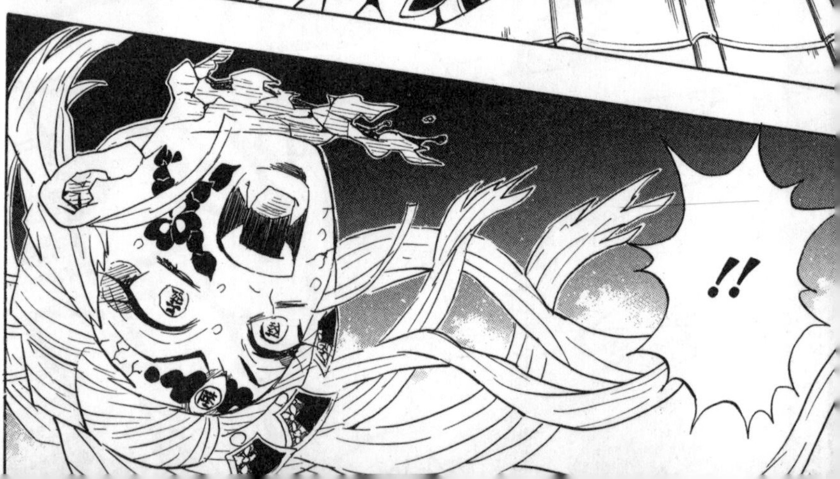
!!

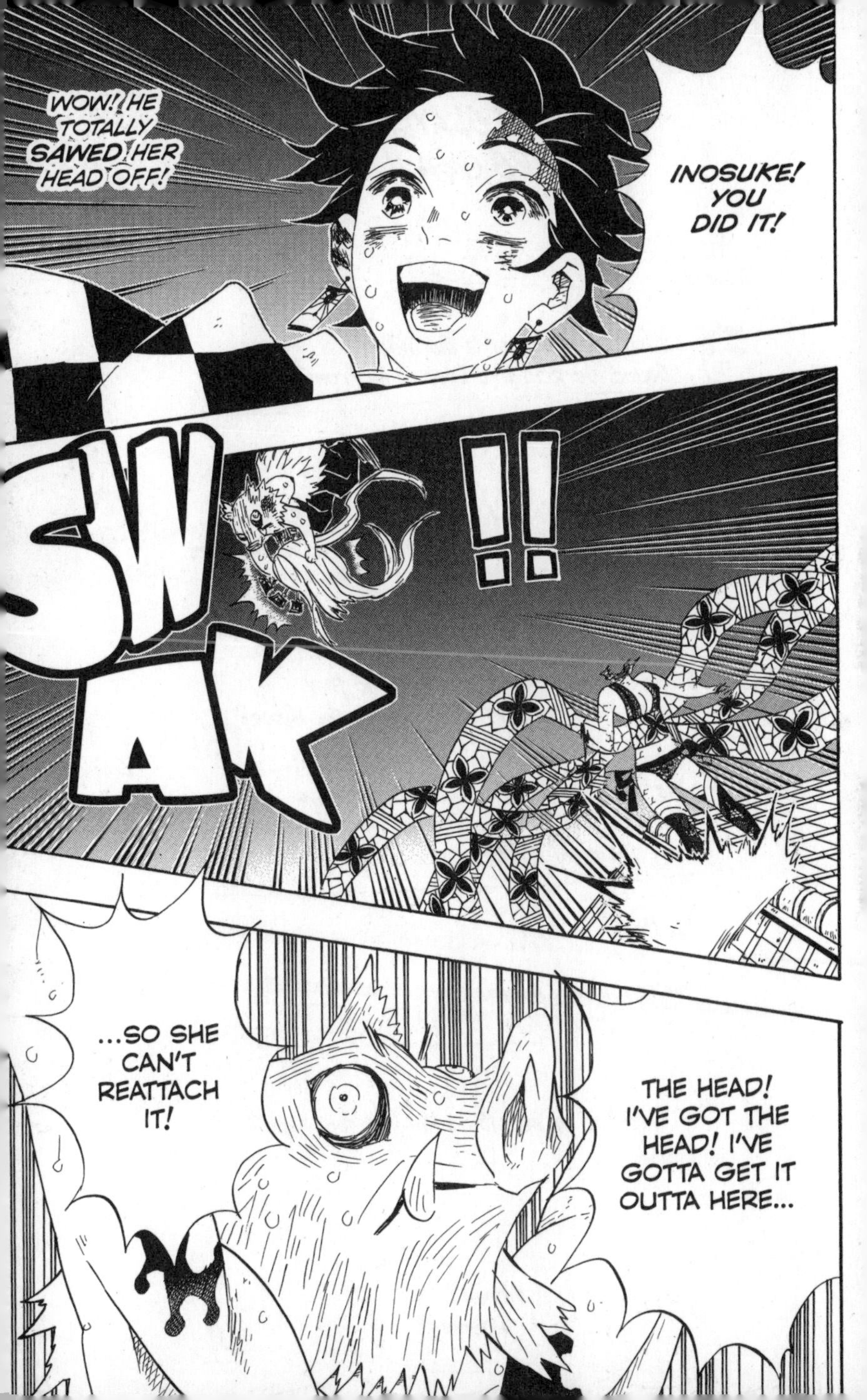
INOSUKE! YOU DID IT!
WOW! HE TOTALLY SAWED HER HEAD OFF!
SWAK!!
THE HEAD! I'VE GOT THE HEAD! I'VE GOTTA GET IT OUTTA HERE...
...SO SHE CAN'T REATTACH IT!

DEMON SLAYER CORPS Q&A II

Nobuo-kun

What breathing style did Insect, Sound, Serpent and Love come from?

Croc

Insect came from Flower, Flower and Serpent came from Water, and Sound came from Thunder.

Nobuo?

When a Hashira seat opens up, do they choose a replacement from among the Kinoe?

Croc

That's right. But as you might expect, a candidate can't take a Hashira spot unless they have the right powers.

That's all.

Thank you very much.

So as of now I'm a Hashira too, right?

Weren't you listening?

CHAPTER 92: WORM, SIMPLETON, STUPID COWARD

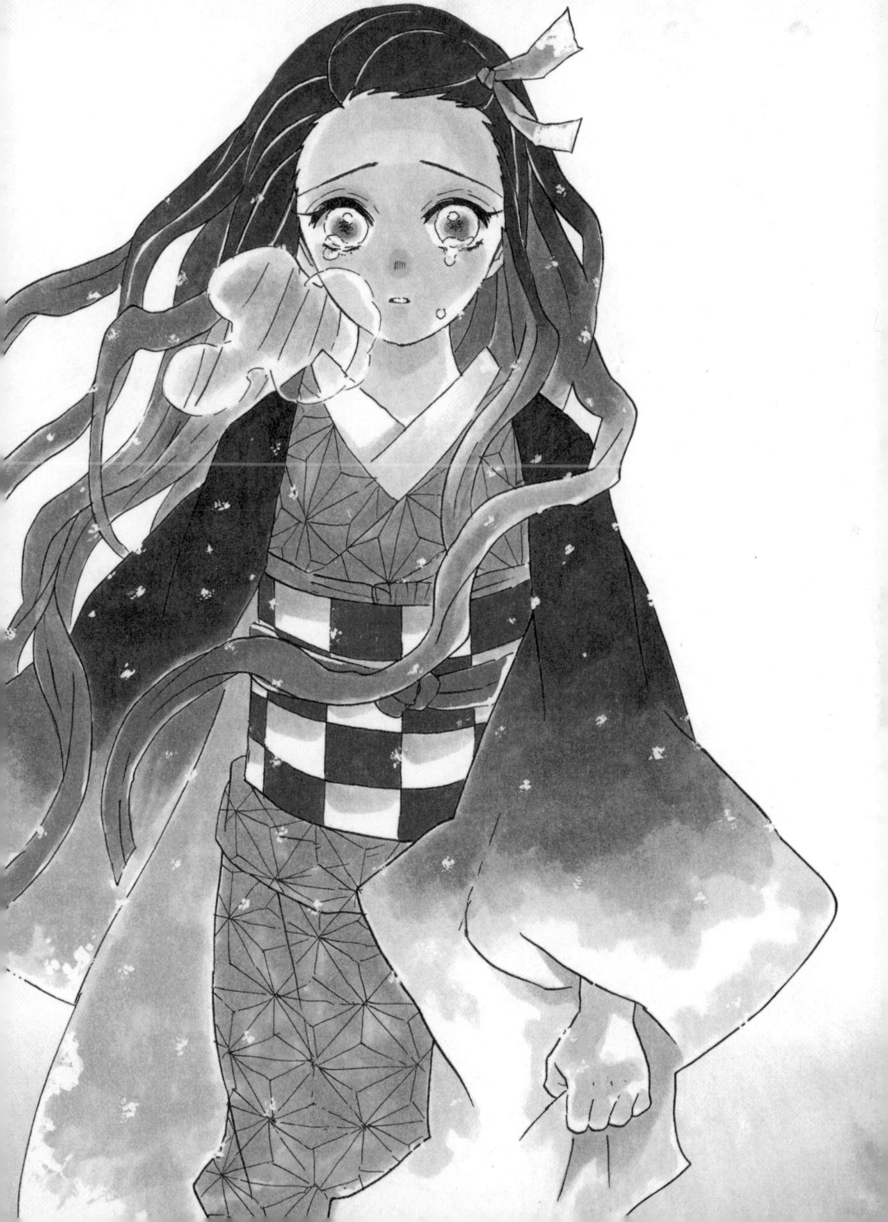

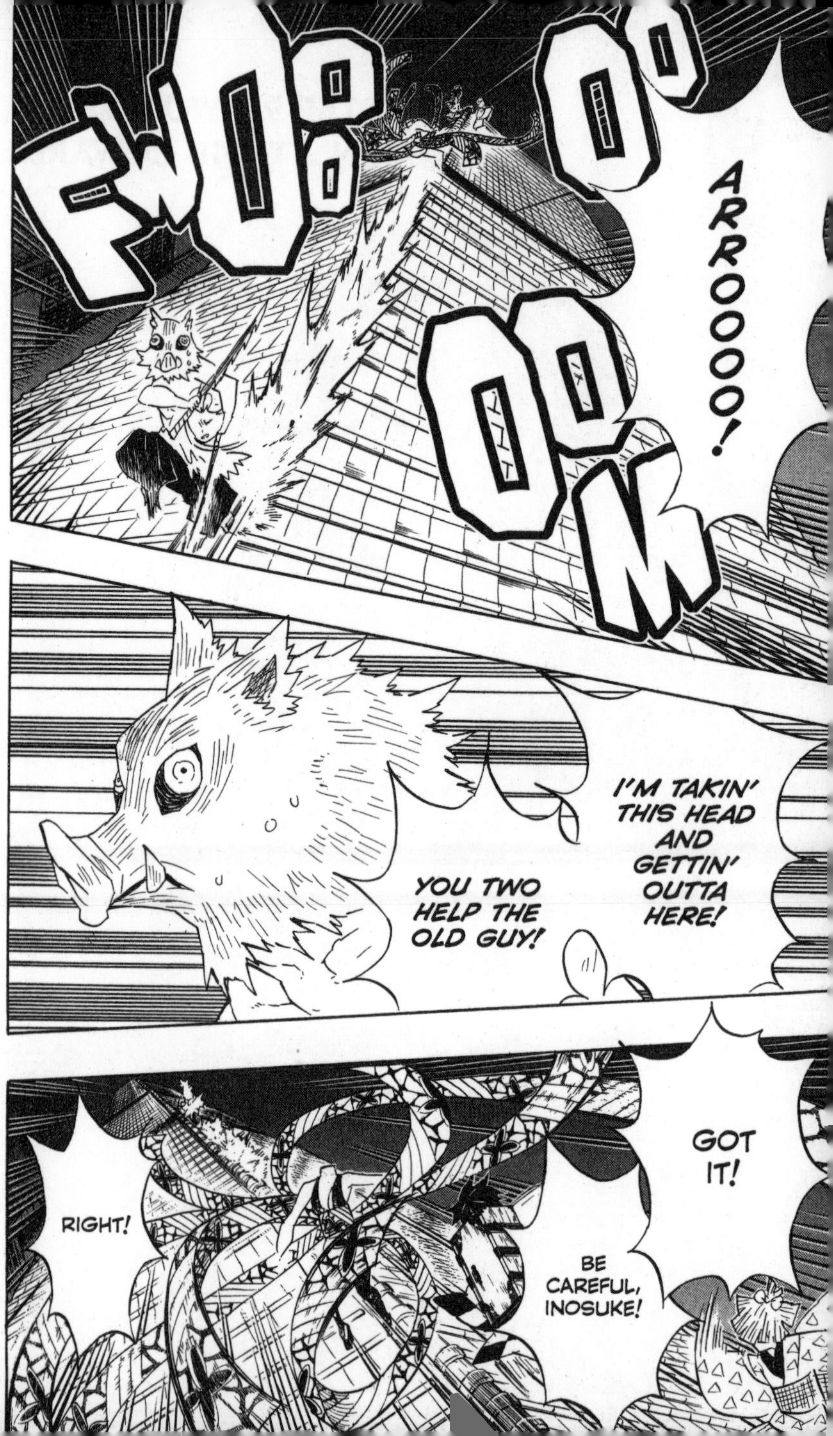
FWOOOOOOOM
ARROOOOO!
I'M TAKIN' THIS HEAD AND GETTIN' OUTTA HERE!
YOU TWO HELP THE OLD GUY!
GOT IT!
BE CAREFUL, INOSUKE!
RIGHT!

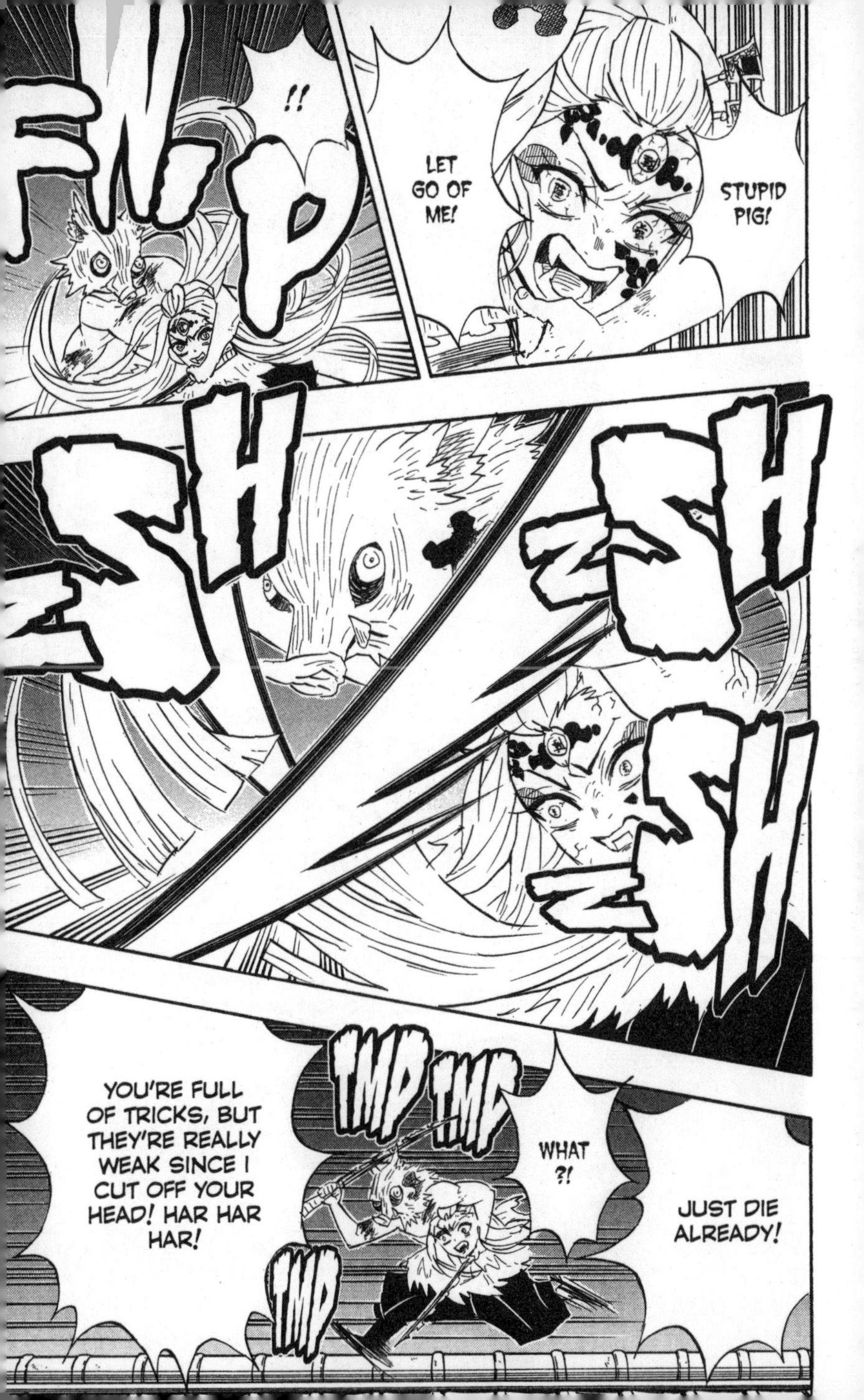
STUPID PIG!
LET GO OF ME!
!!
WHIP
SH
SH
SH
JUST DIE ALREADY!
WHAT ?!
TMP TMP
YOU'RE FULL OF TRICKS, BUT THEY'RE REALLY WEAK SINCE I CUT OFF YOUR HEAD! HAR HAR HAR!
TMP

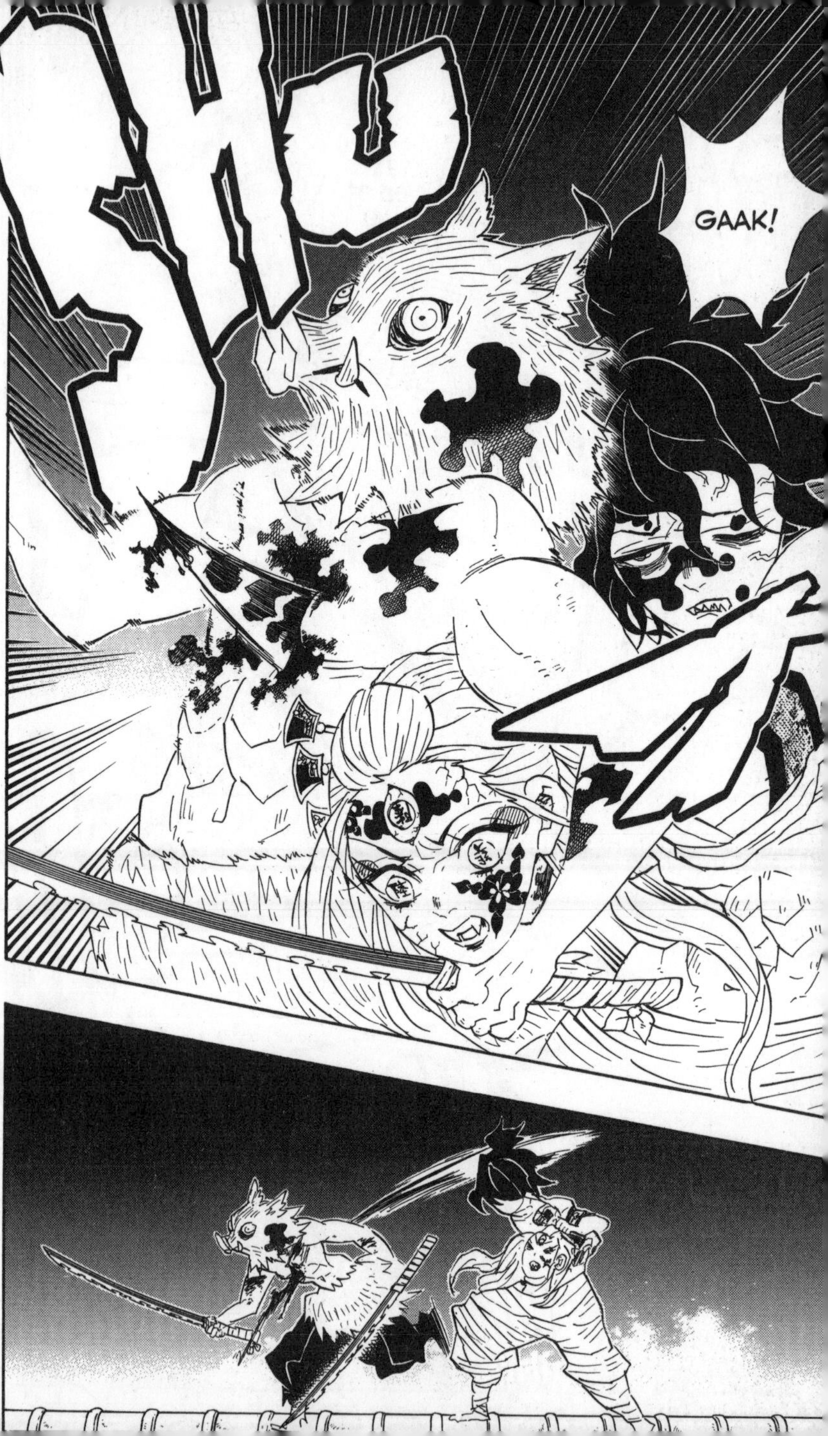
GAAK!

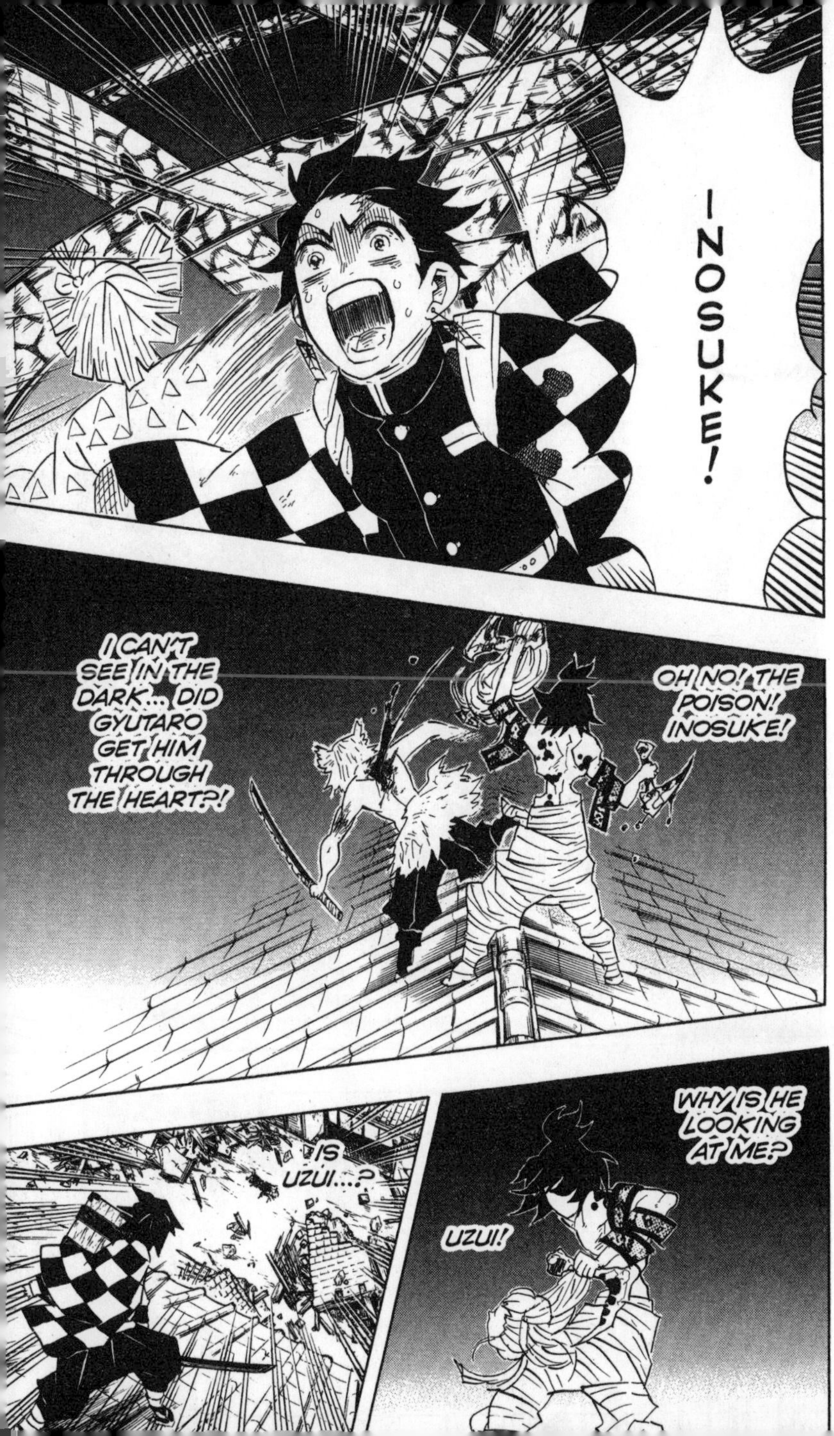
INOSUKE!
OH NO! THE POISON! INOSUKE!
I CAN'T SEE IN THE DARK... DID GYUTARO GET HIM THROUGH THE HEART?!
WHY IS HE LOOKING AT ME?
UZUI!
IS UZUI...?

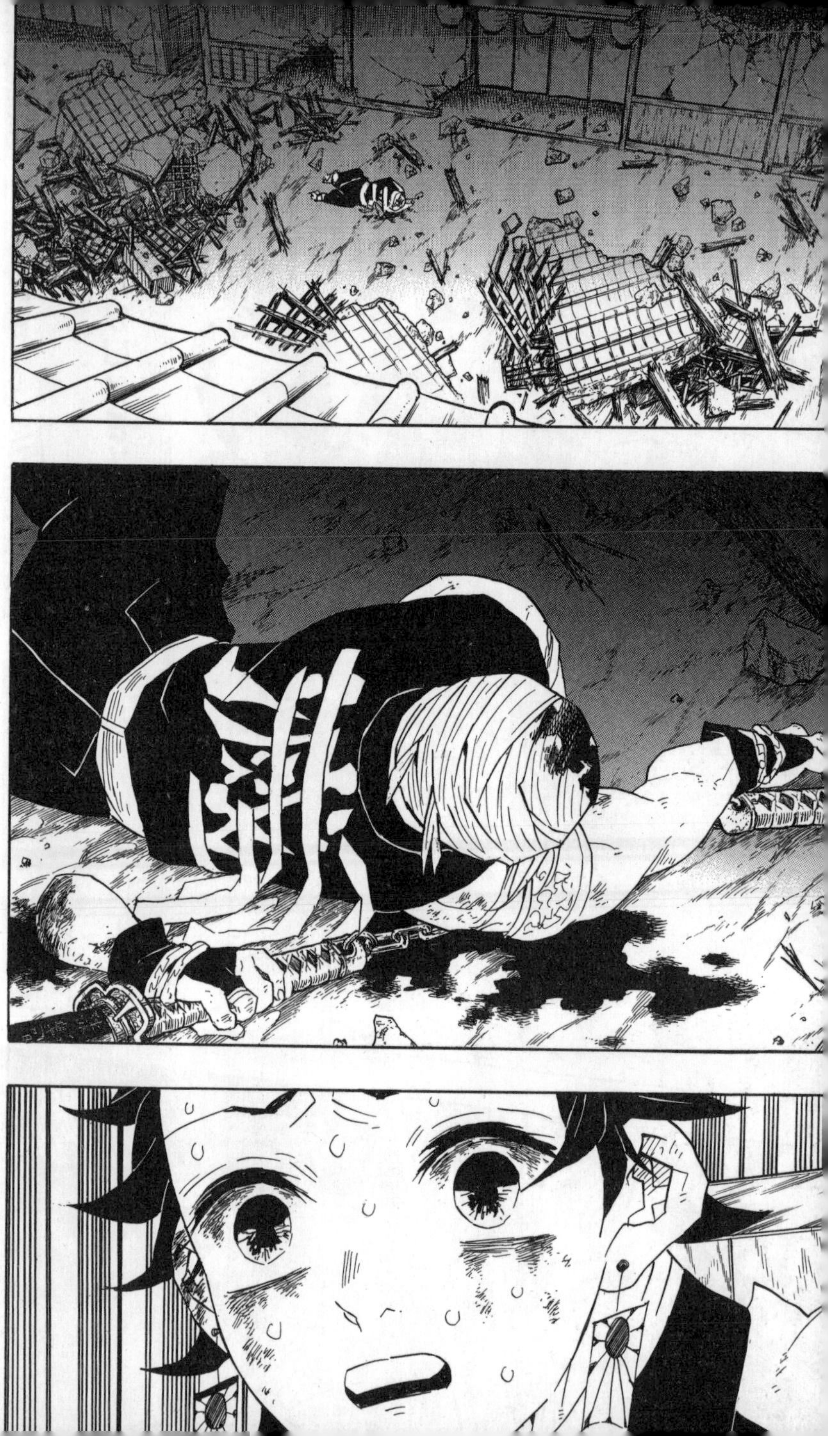

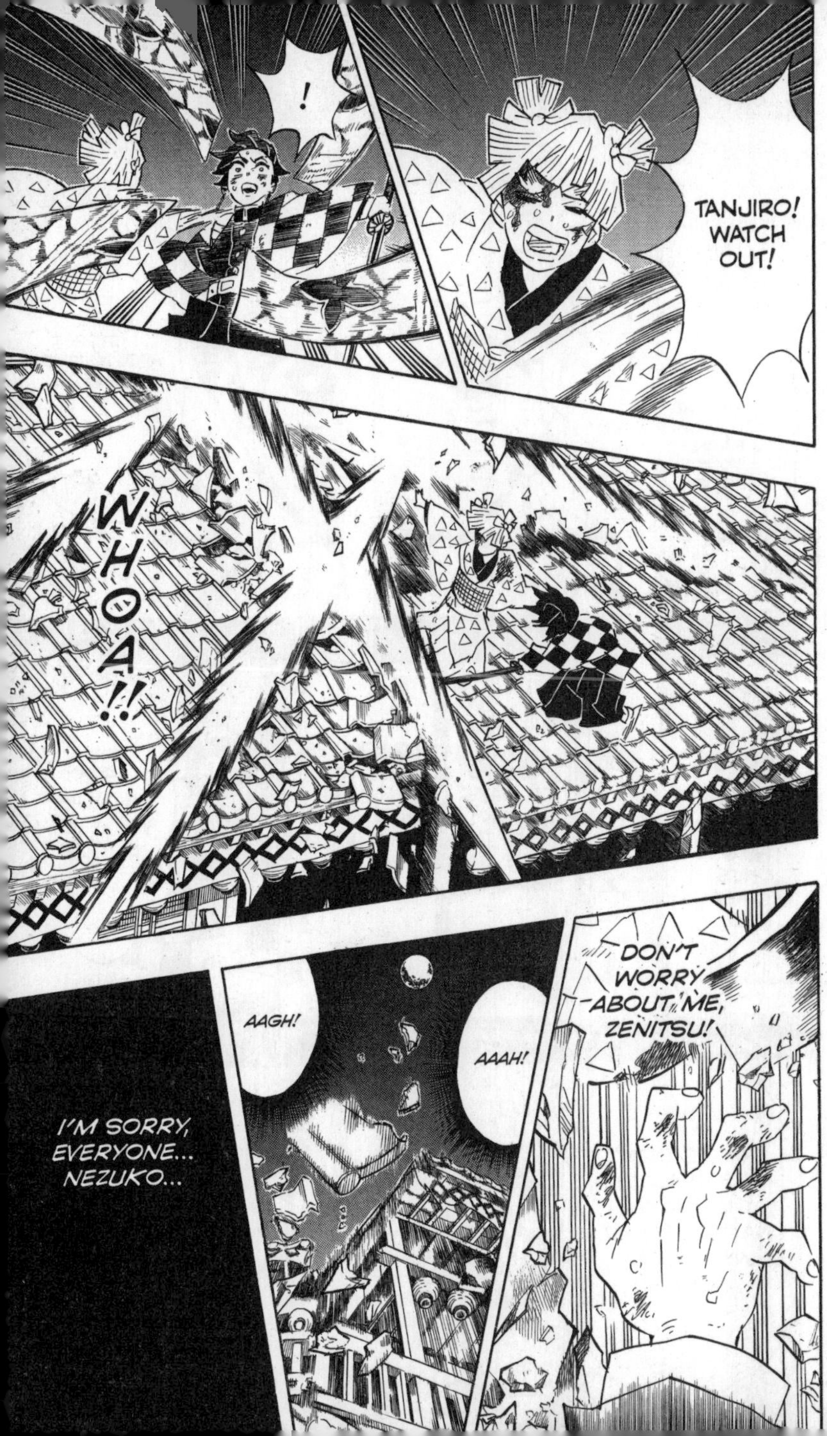
TANJIRO! WATCH OUT!
!
WHOA!!
DON'T WORRY ABOUT ME, ZENITSU!
AAAH!
AAGH!
I'M SORRY, EVERYONE... NEZUKO...

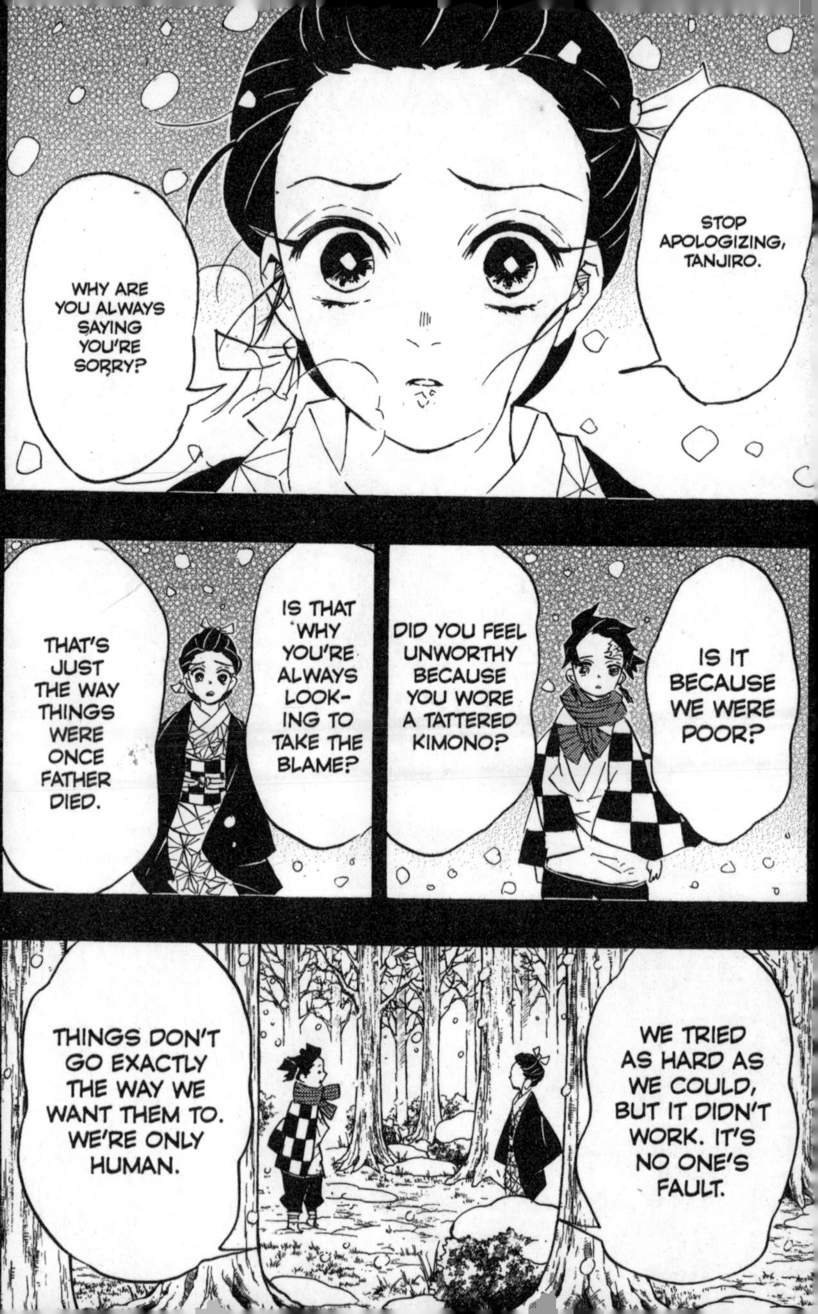
STOP APOLOGIZING, TANJIRO.
WHY ARE YOU ALWAYS SAYING YOU'RE SORRY?
IS IT BECAUSE WE WERE POOR?
DID YOU FEEL UNWORTHY BECAUSE YOU WORE A TATTERED KIMONO?
IS THAT WHY YOU'RE ALWAYS LOOKING TO TAKE THE BLAME?
THAT'S JUST THE WAY THINGS WERE ONCE FATHER DIED.
WE TRIED AS HARD AS WE COULD, BUT IT DIDN'T WORK. IT'S NO ONE'S FAULT.
THINGS DON'T GO EXACTLY THE WAY WE WANT THEM TO. WE'RE ONLY HUMAN.

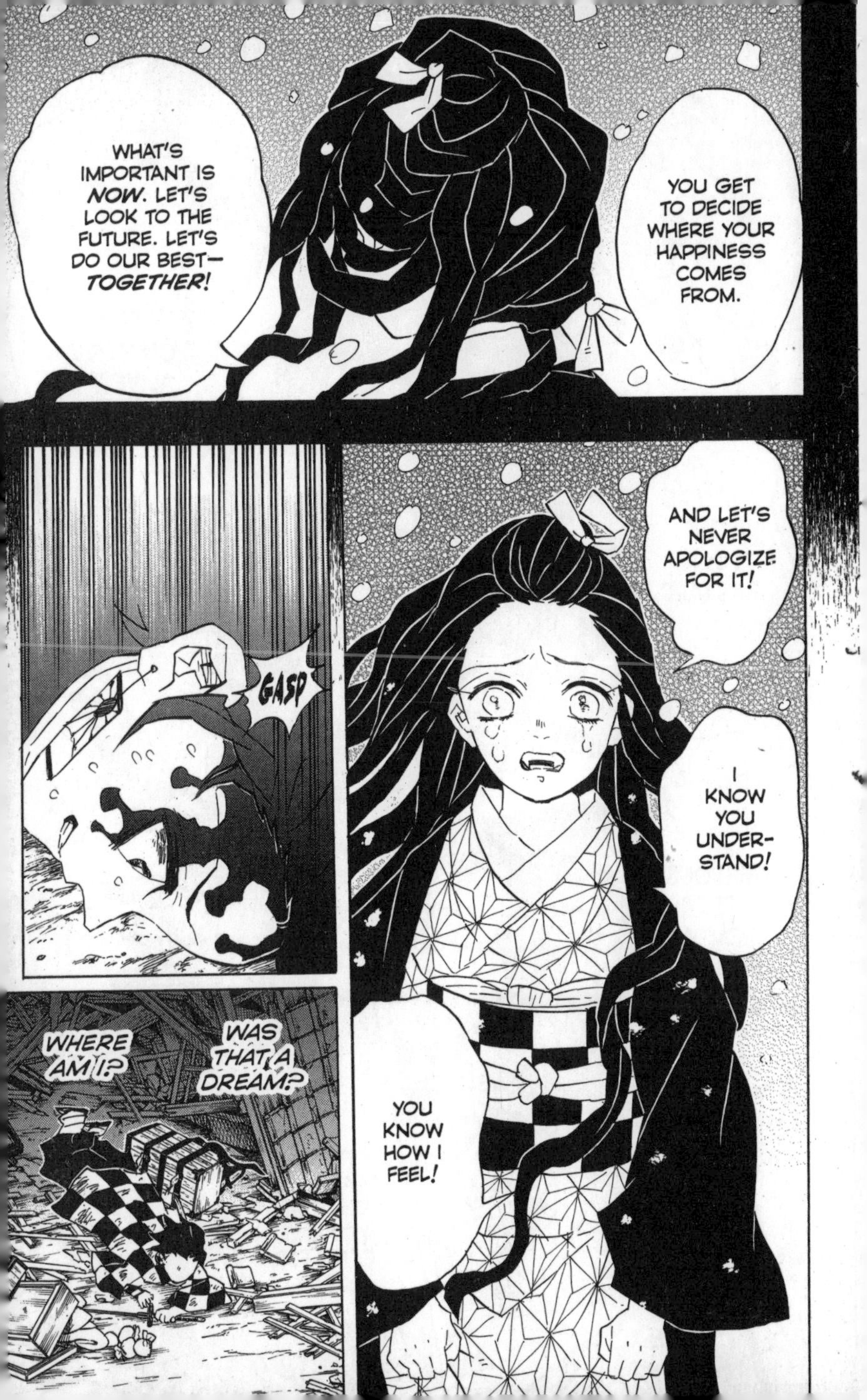
YOU GET TO DECIDE WHERE YOUR HAPPINESS COMES FROM.
WHAT'S IMPORTANT IS *NOW*. LET'S LOOK TO THE FUTURE. LET'S DO OUR BEST— *TOGETHER*!
AND LET'S NEVER APOLOGIZE FOR IT!
I KNOW YOU UNDER-STAND!
YOU KNOW HOW I FEEL!
GASP
WAS THAT A DREAM?
WHERE AM I?

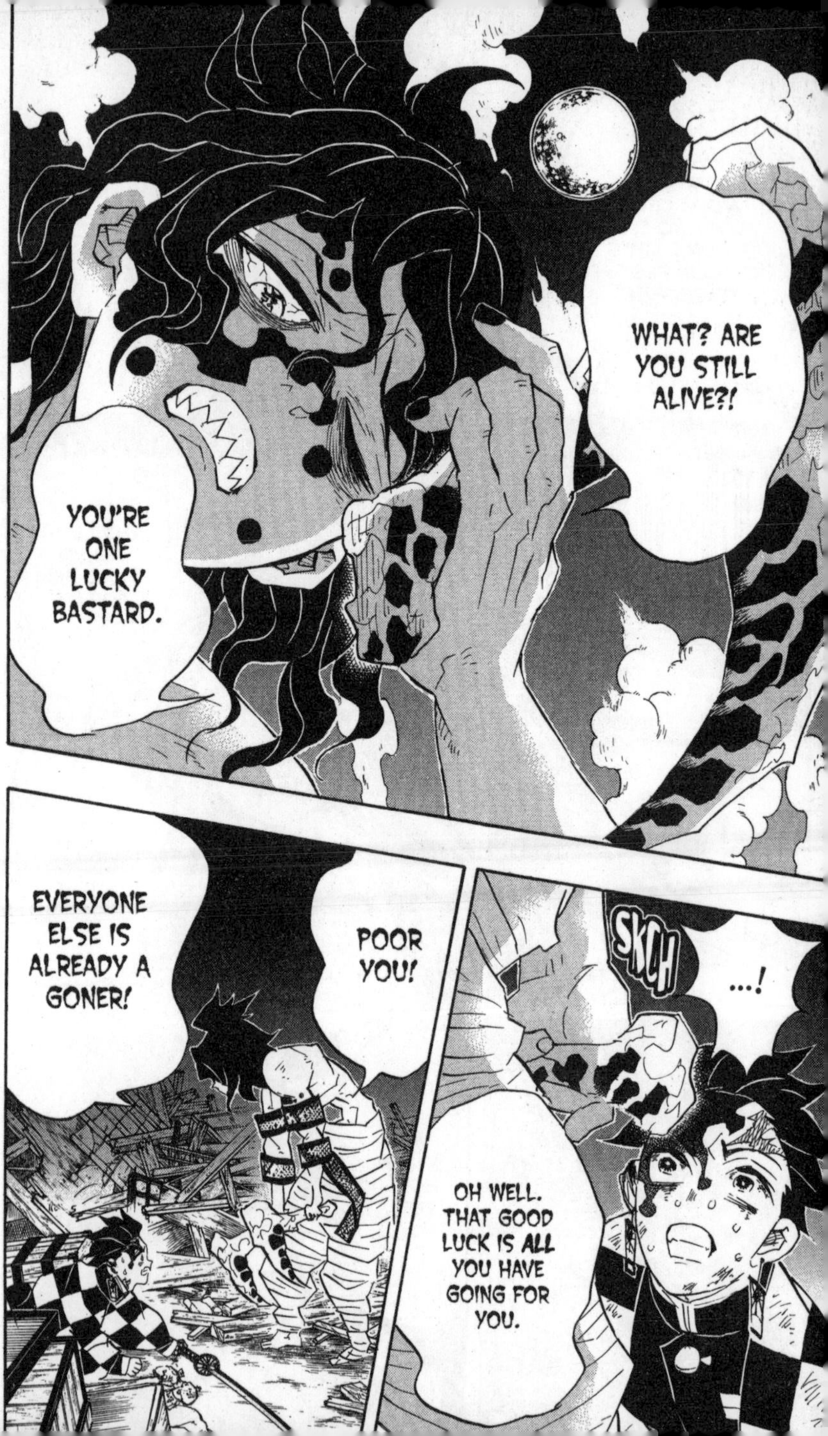
WHAT? ARE YOU STILL ALIVE?!
YOU'RE ONE LUCKY BASTARD.
SKCH
...!
OH WELL. THAT GOOD LUCK IS ALL YOU HAVE GOING FOR YOU.
POOR YOU!
EVERYONE ELSE IS ALREADY A GONER!

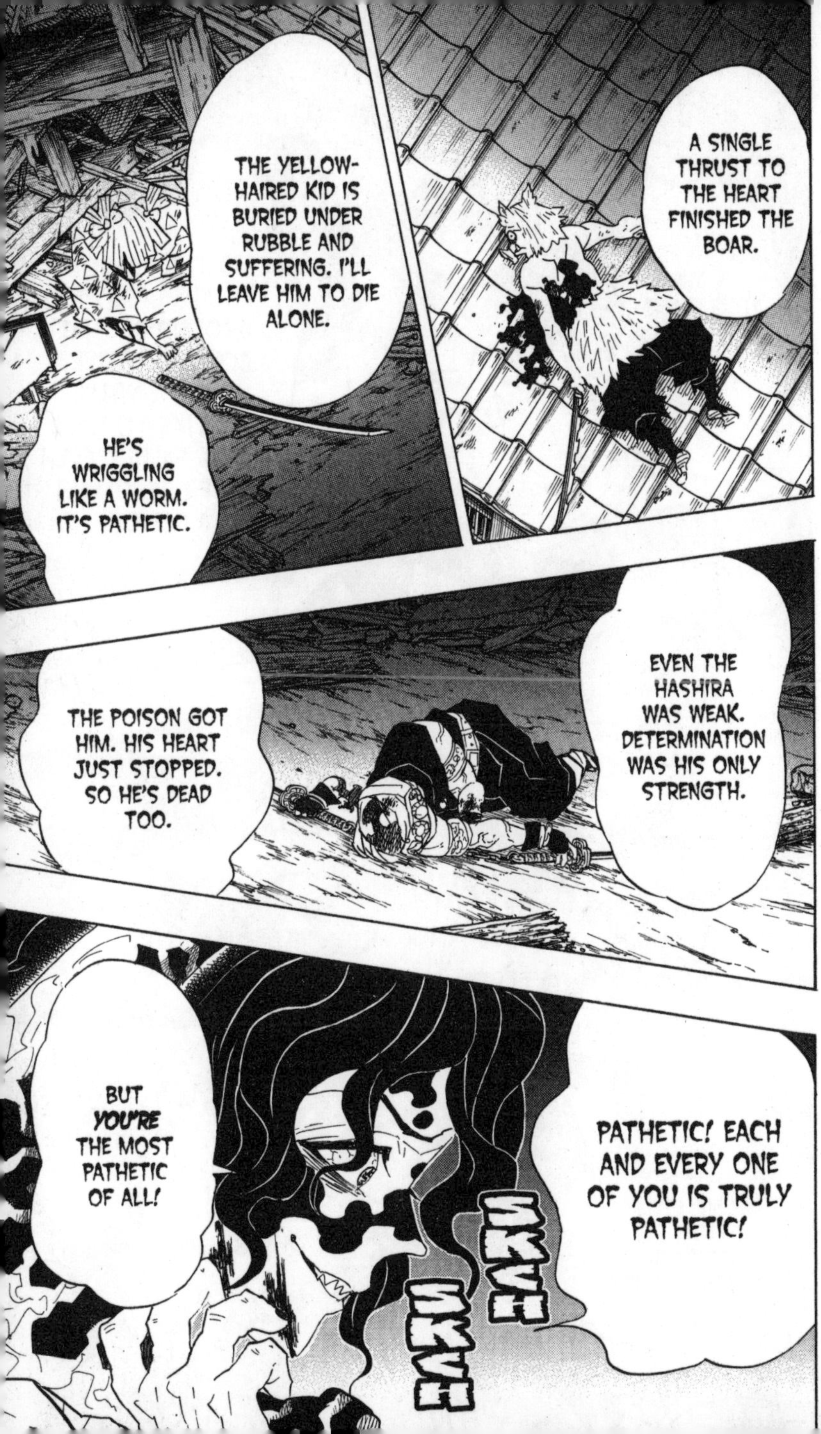
A SINGLE THRUST TO THE HEART FINISHED THE BOAR.
THE YELLOW-HAIRED KID IS BURIED UNDER RUBBLE AND SUFFERING. I'LL LEAVE HIM TO DIE ALONE.
HE'S WRIGGLING LIKE A WORM. IT'S PATHETIC.
EVEN THE HASHIRA WAS WEAK. DETERMINATION WAS HIS ONLY STRENGTH.
THE POISON GOT HIM. HIS HEART JUST STOPPED. SO HE'S DEAD TOO.
PATHETIC! EACH AND EVERY ONE OF YOU IS TRULY PATHETIC!
SKVH
SKVH
BUT *YOU'RE* THE MOST PATHETIC OF ALL!

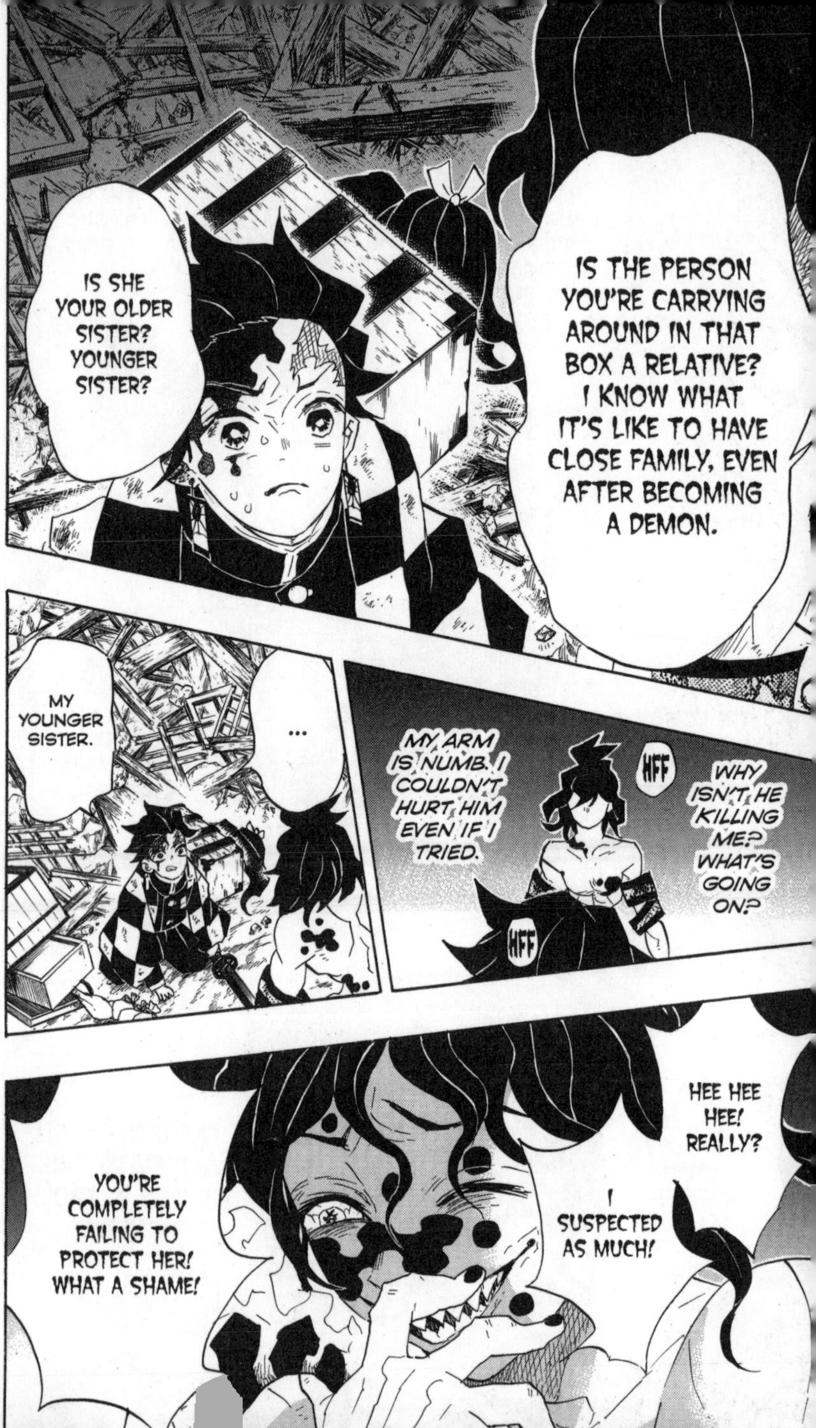
IS THE PERSON YOU'RE CARRYING AROUND IN THAT BOX A RELATIVE? I KNOW WHAT IT'S LIKE TO HAVE CLOSE FAMILY, EVEN AFTER BECOMING A DEMON.
IS SHE YOUR OLDER SISTER? YOUNGER SISTER?
WHY ISN'T HE KILLING ME? WHAT'S GOING ON?
HFF
MY ARM IS NUMB. I COULDN'T HURT HIM EVEN IF I TRIED.
HFF
...
MY YOUNGER SISTER.
HEE HEE HEE! REALLY?
I SUSPECTED AS MUCH!
YOU'RE COMPLETELY FAILING TO PROTECT HER! WHAT A SHAME!

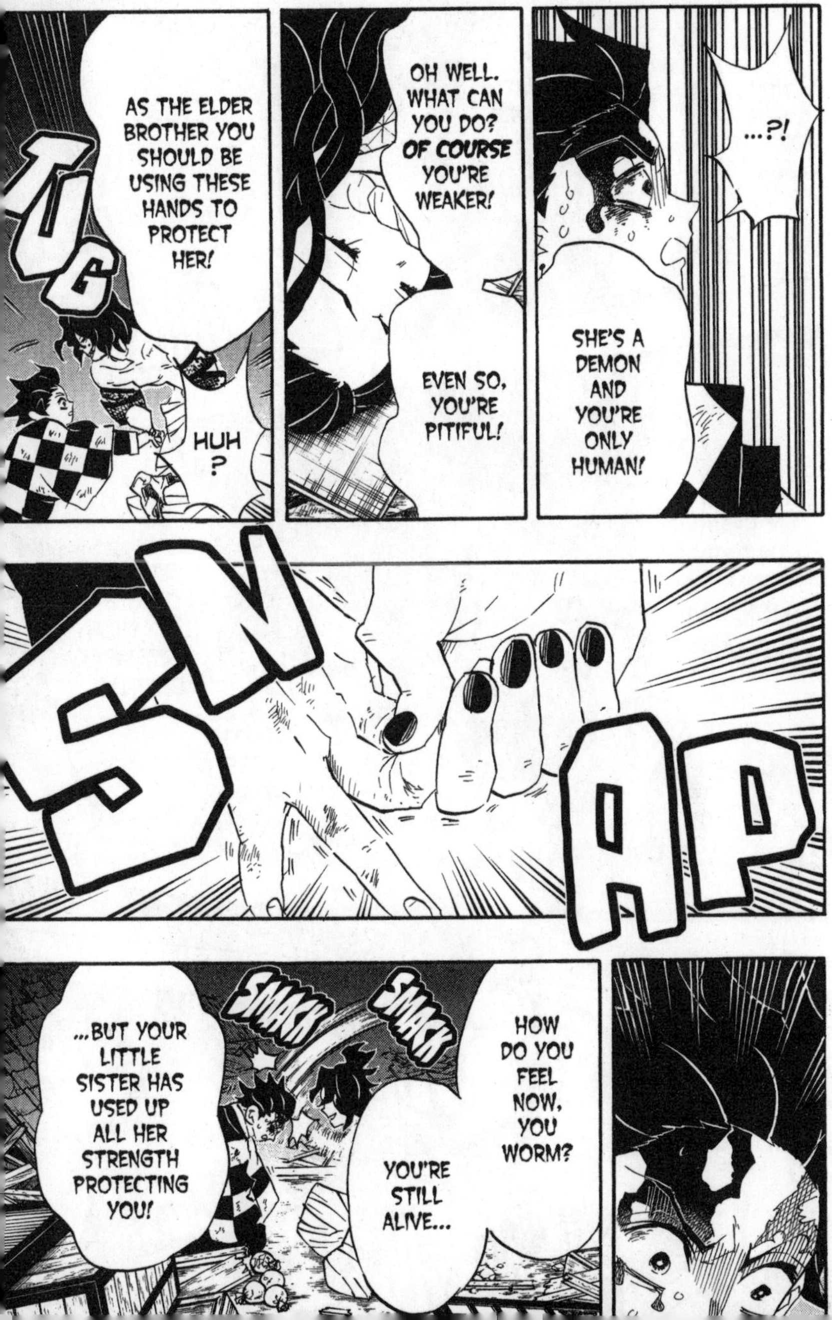
...?!
SHE'S A DEMON AND YOU'RE ONLY HUMAN!
OH WELL. WHAT CAN YOU DO? OF COURSE YOU'RE WEAKER!
EVEN SO, YOU'RE PITIFUL!
AS THE ELDER BROTHER YOU SHOULD BE USING THESE HANDS TO PROTECT HER!
TUG
HUH?
SNAP
HOW DO YOU FEEL NOW, YOU WORM?
SMACK
SMACK
YOU'RE STILL ALIVE...
...BUT YOUR LITTLE SISTER HAS USED UP ALL HER STRENGTH PROTECTING YOU!

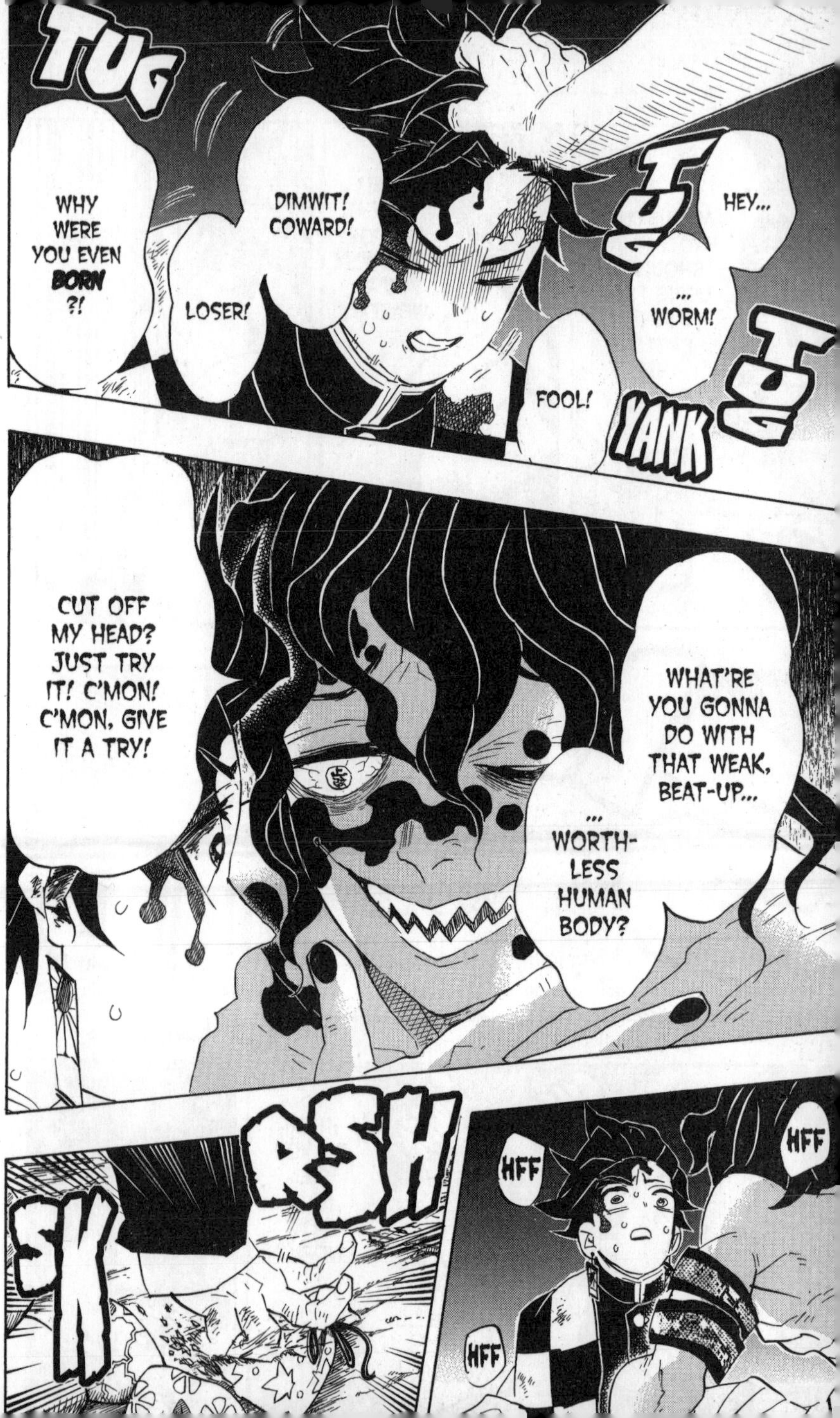
TUG
HEY...
...WORM!
TUG
YANK
FOOL!
DIMWIT! COWARD!
LOSER!
TUG
WHY WERE YOU EVEN BORN ?!
WHAT'RE YOU GONNA DO WITH THAT WEAK, BEAT-UP...
...WORTH-LESS HUMAN BODY?
CUT OFF MY HEAD? JUST TRY IT! C'MON! C'MON, GIVE IT A TRY!
HFF
HFF
HFF
RSH
SK

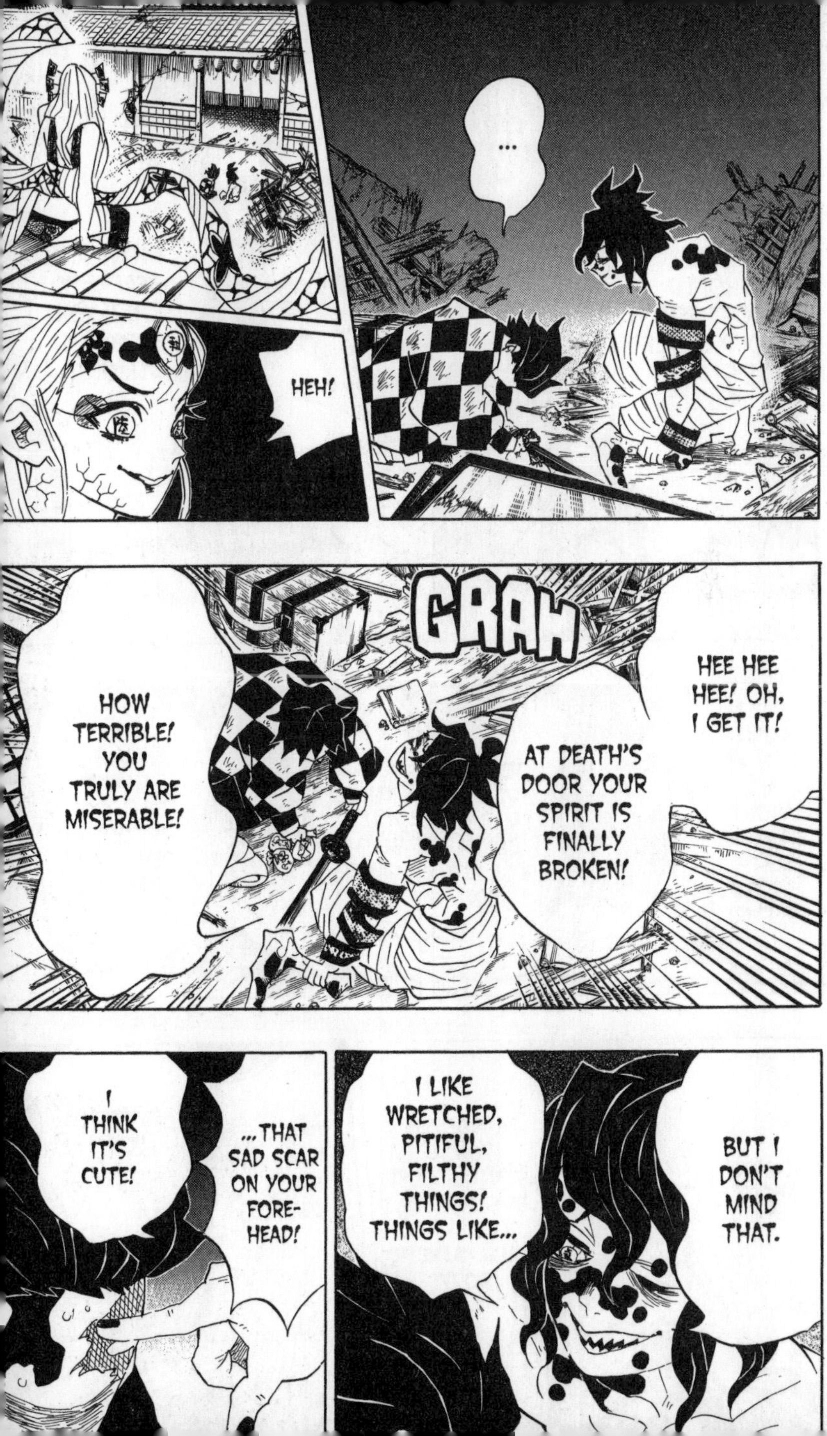
...
HEH!
HEE HEE HEE! OH, I GET IT!
GRAH
AT DEATH'S DOOR YOUR SPIRIT IS FINALLY BROKEN!
HOW TERRIBLE! YOU TRULY ARE MISERABLE!
BUT I DON'T MIND THAT.
I LIKE WRETCHED, PITIFUL, FILTHY THINGS! THINGS LIKE...
...THAT SAD SCAR ON YOUR FORE-HEAD!
I THINK IT'S CUTE!

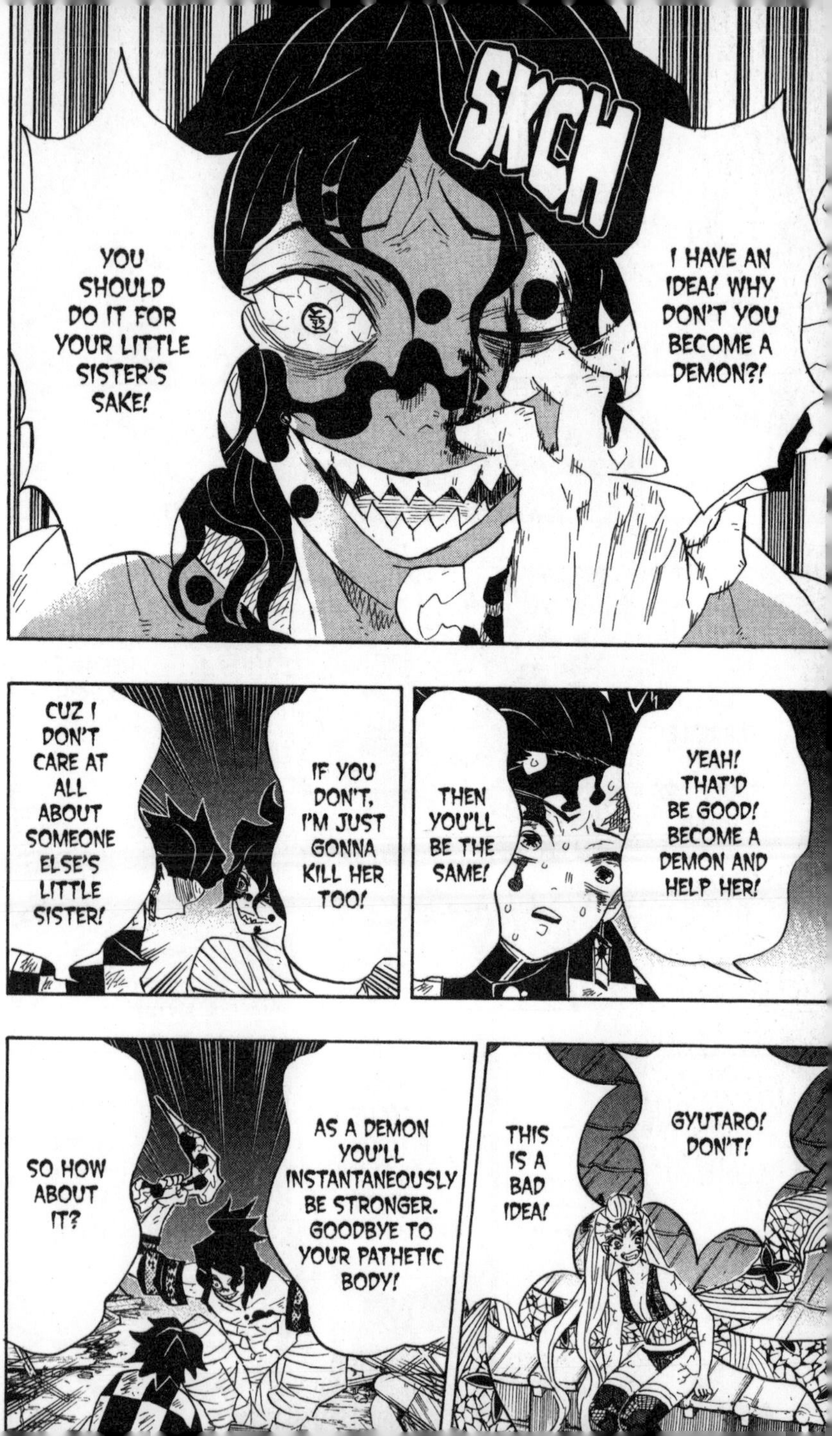
SKCH
I HAVE AN IDEA! WHY DON'T YOU BECOME A DEMON?!
YOU SHOULD DO IT FOR YOUR LITTLE SISTER'S SAKE!
YEAH! THAT'D BE GOOD! BECOME A DEMON AND HELP HER!
THEN YOU'LL BE THE SAME!
IF YOU DON'T, I'M JUST GONNA KILL HER TOO!
CUZ I DON'T CARE AT ALL ABOUT SOMEONE ELSE'S LITTLE SISTER!
GYUTARO! DON'T!
THIS IS A BAD IDEA!
AS A DEMON YOU'LL INSTANTANEOUSLY BE STRONGER. GOODBYE TO YOUR PATHETIC BODY!
SO HOW ABOUT IT?

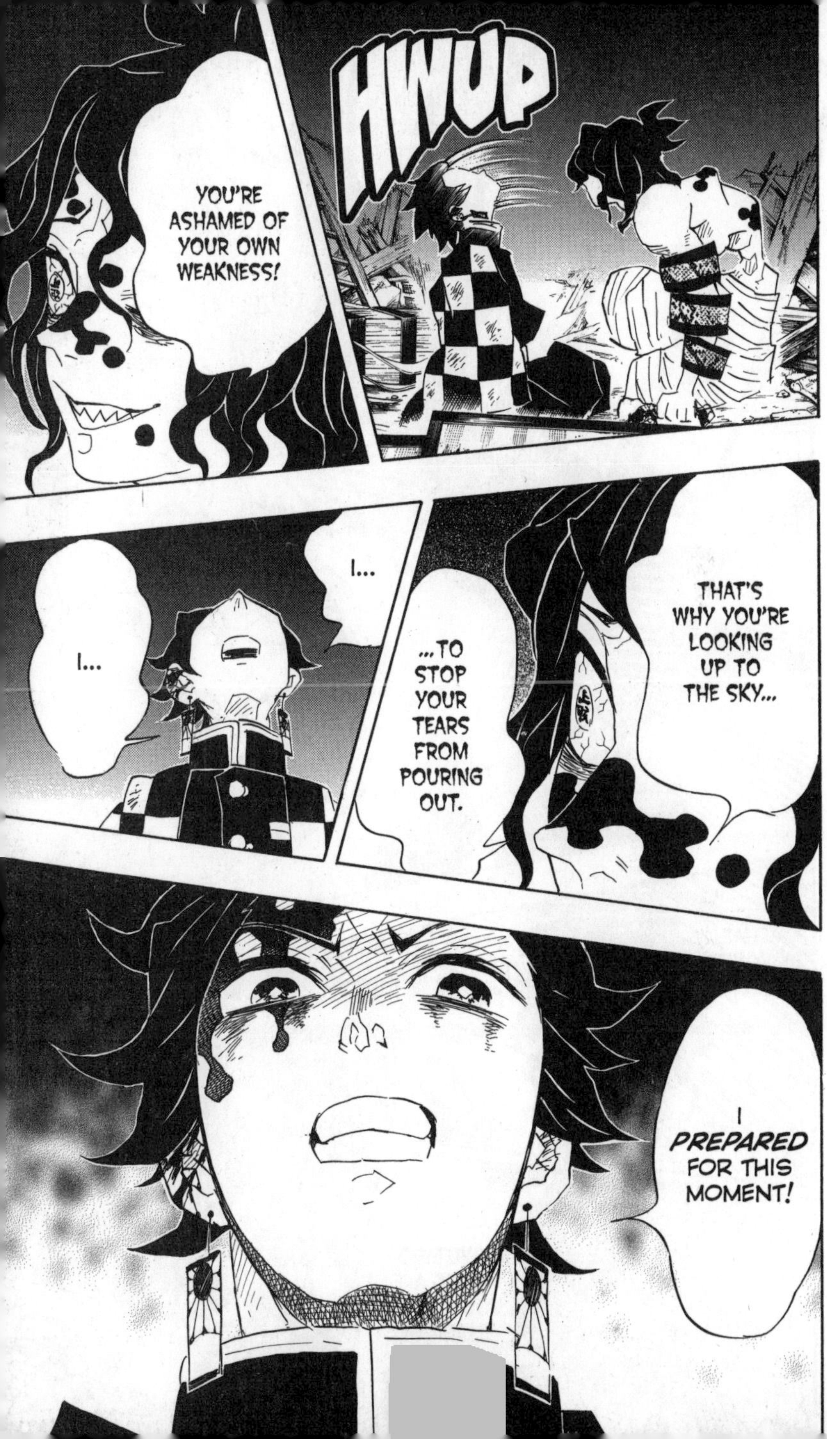
HWUP
YOU'RE ASHAMED OF YOUR OWN WEAKNESS!
THAT'S WHY YOU'RE LOOKING UP TO THE SKY...
...TO STOP YOUR TEARS FROM POURING OUT.
I...
I...
I *PREPARED* FOR THIS MOMENT!

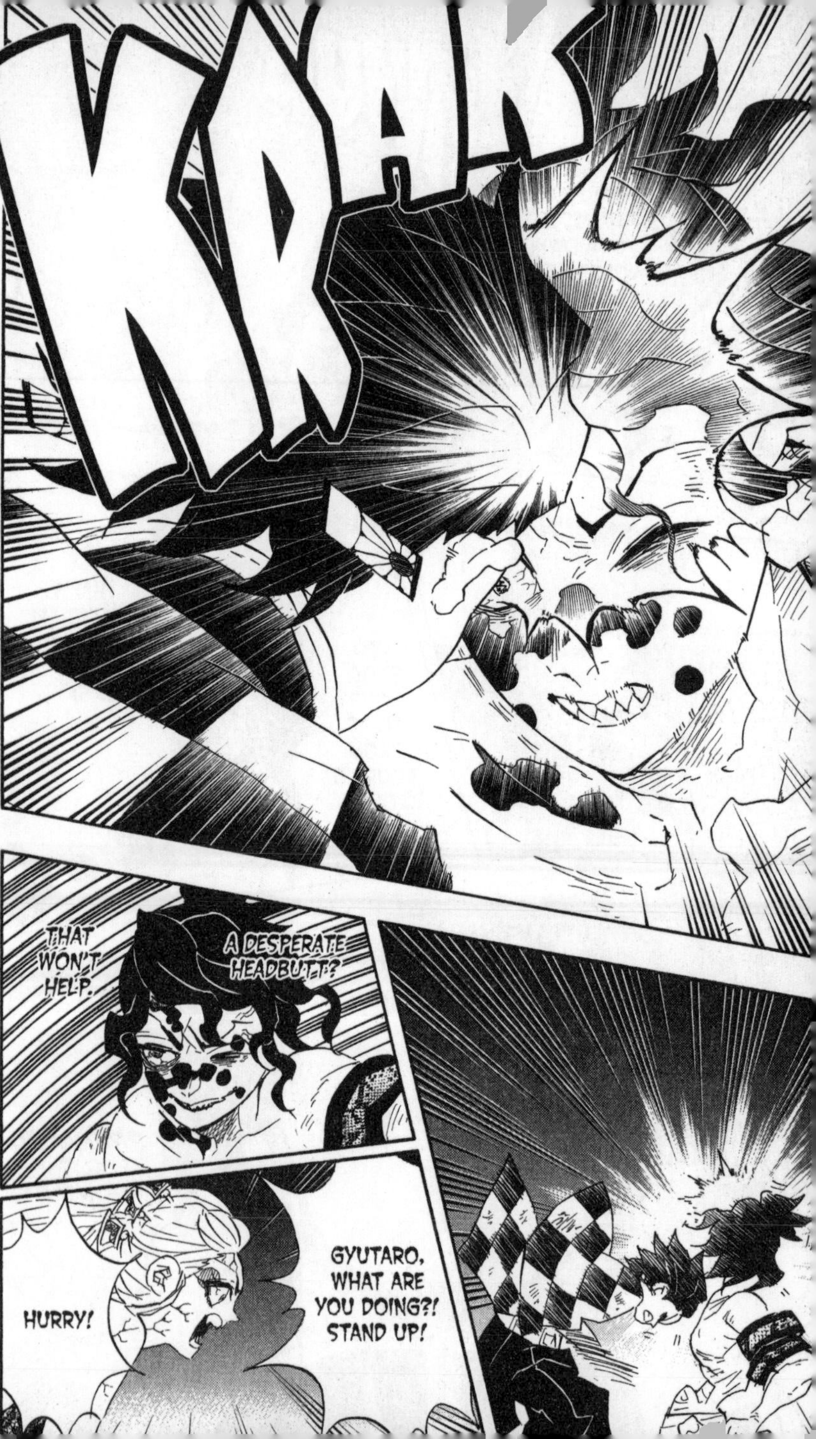
A DESPERATE HEADBUTT?
THAT WON'T HELP.
GYUTARO, WHAT ARE YOU DOING?! STAND UP!
HURRY!

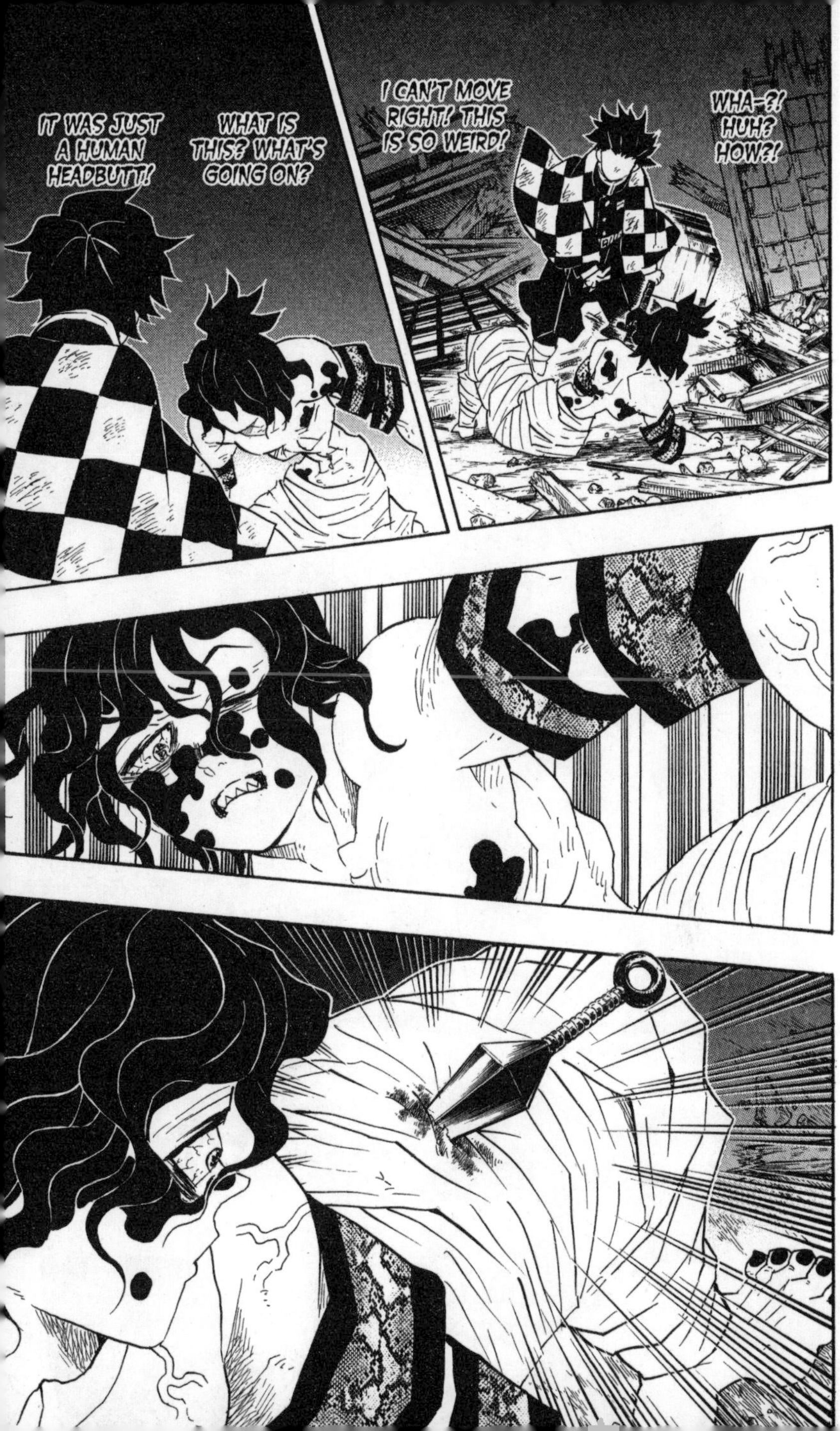
WHA-?! HUH? HOW?!
I CAN'T MOVE RIGHT! THIS IS SO WEIRD!
WHAT IS THIS? WHAT'S GOING ON?
IT WAS JUST A HUMAN HEADBUTT!

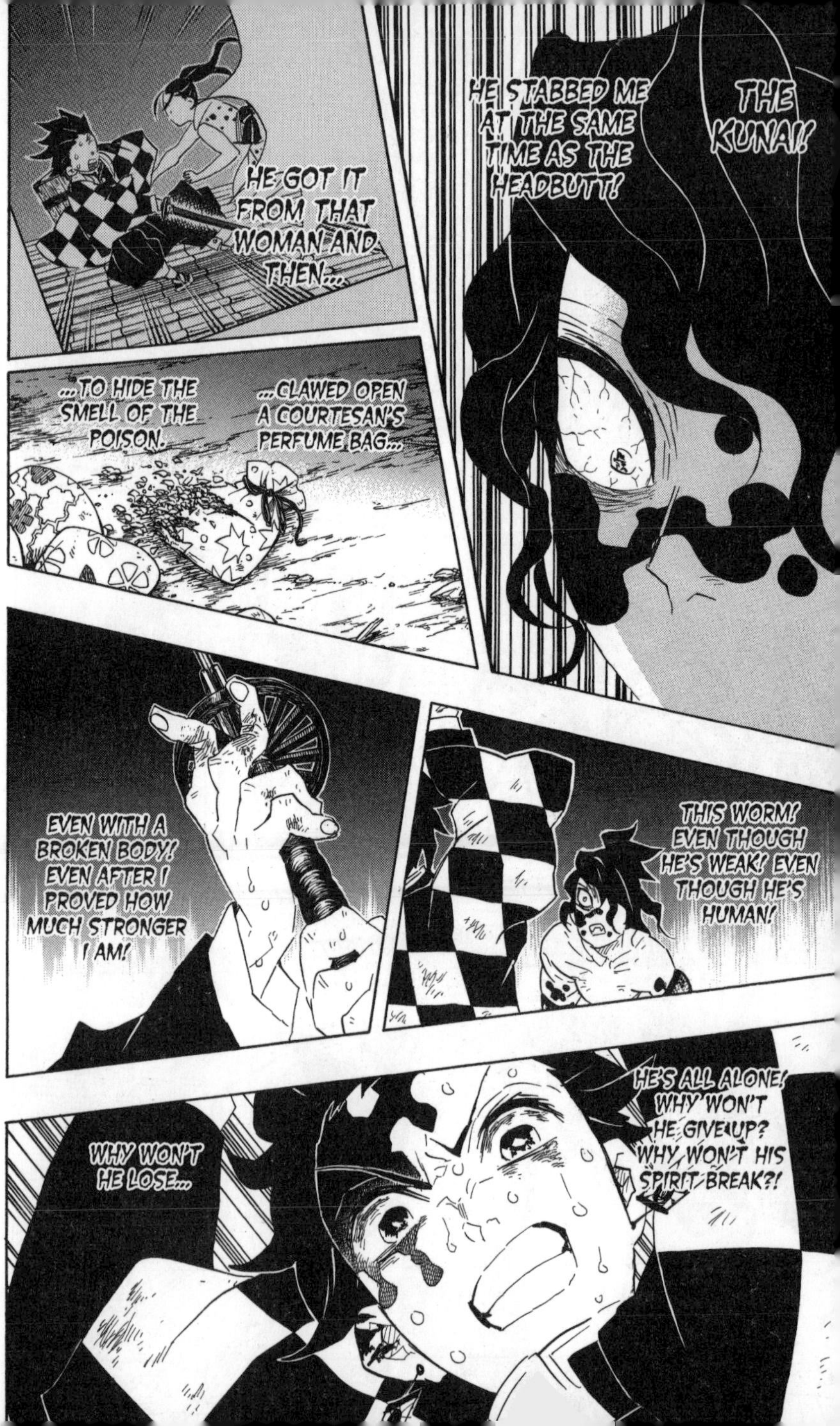
THE KUNAI!!
HE STABBED ME AT THE SAME TIME AS THE HEADBUTT!
HE GOT IT FROM THAT WOMAN AND THEN...
...CLAWED OPEN A COURTESAN'S PERFUME BAG...
...TO HIDE THE SMELL OF THE POISON.
THIS WORM! EVEN THOUGH HE'S WEAK! EVEN THOUGH HE'S HUMAN!
EVEN WITH A BROKEN BODY! EVEN AFTER I PROVED HOW MUCH STRONGER I AM!
HE'S ALL ALONE! WHY WON'T HE GIVE UP? WHY WON'T HIS SPIRIT BREAK?!
WHY WON'T HE LOSE...

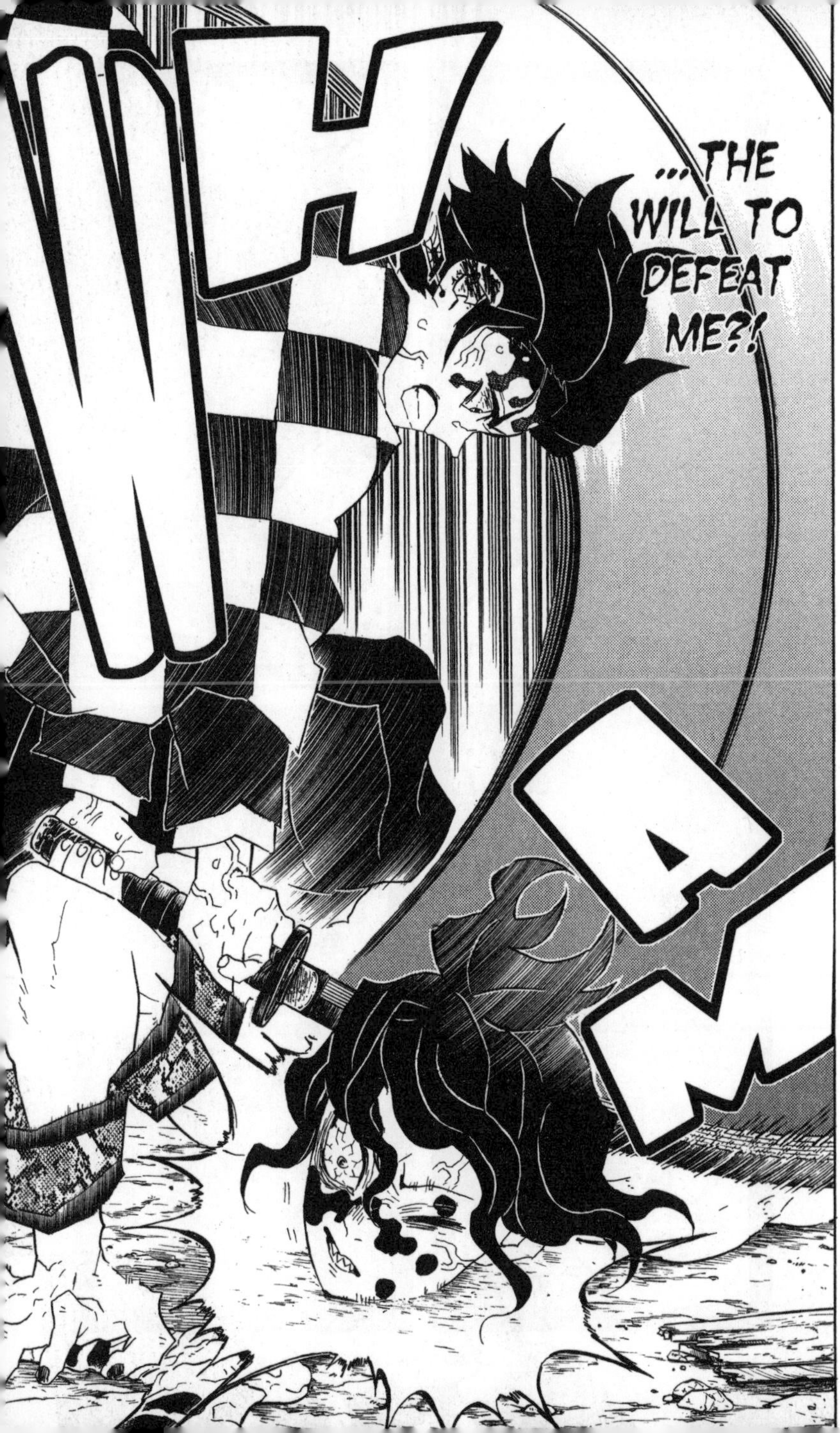
...THE WILL TO DEFEAT ME?!
WHAM

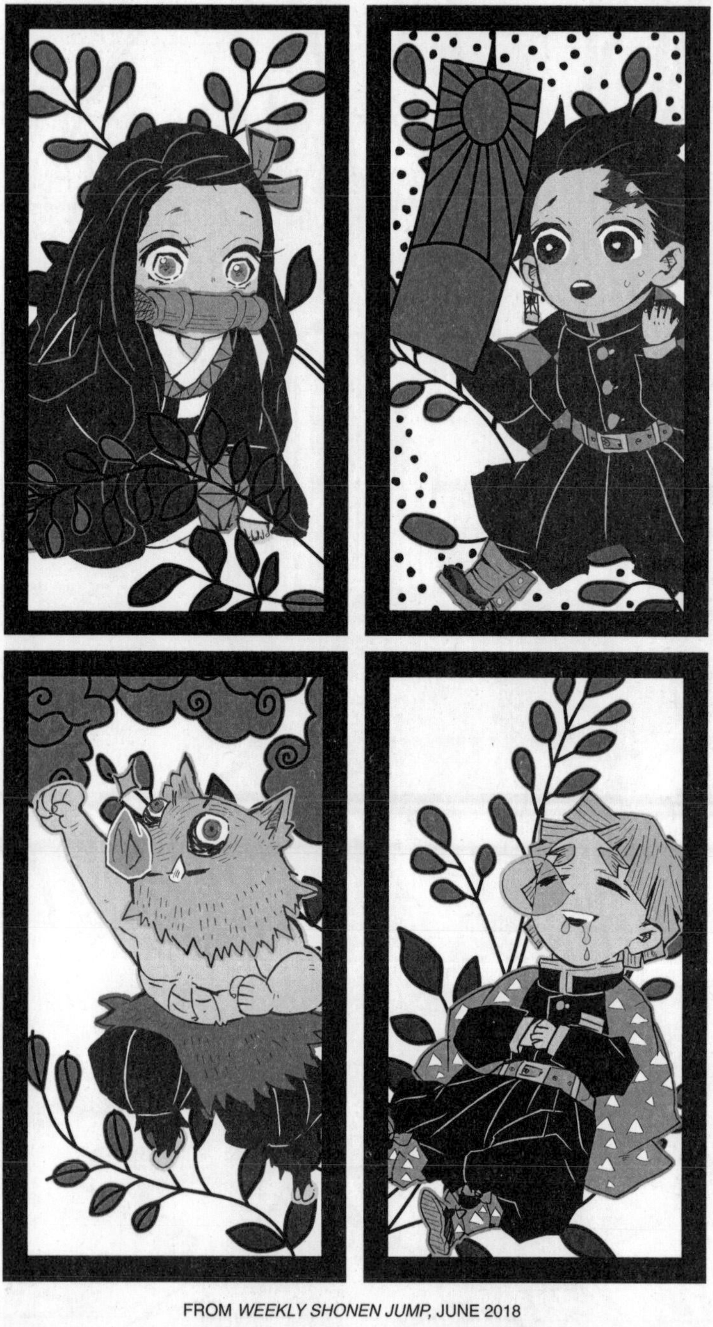

FROM *WEEKLY SHONEN JUMP,* JUNE 2018

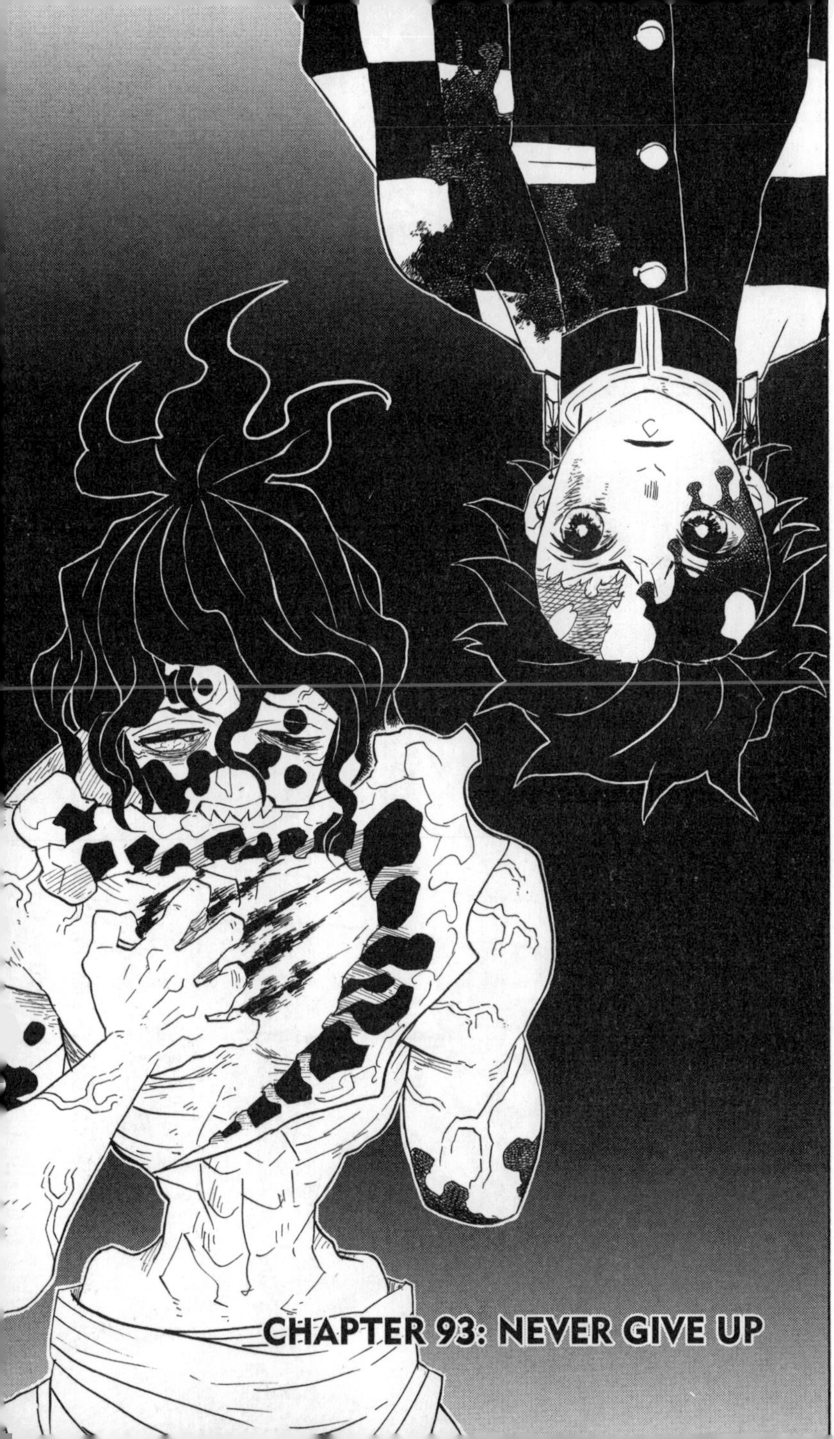

CHAPTER 93: NEVER GIVE UP

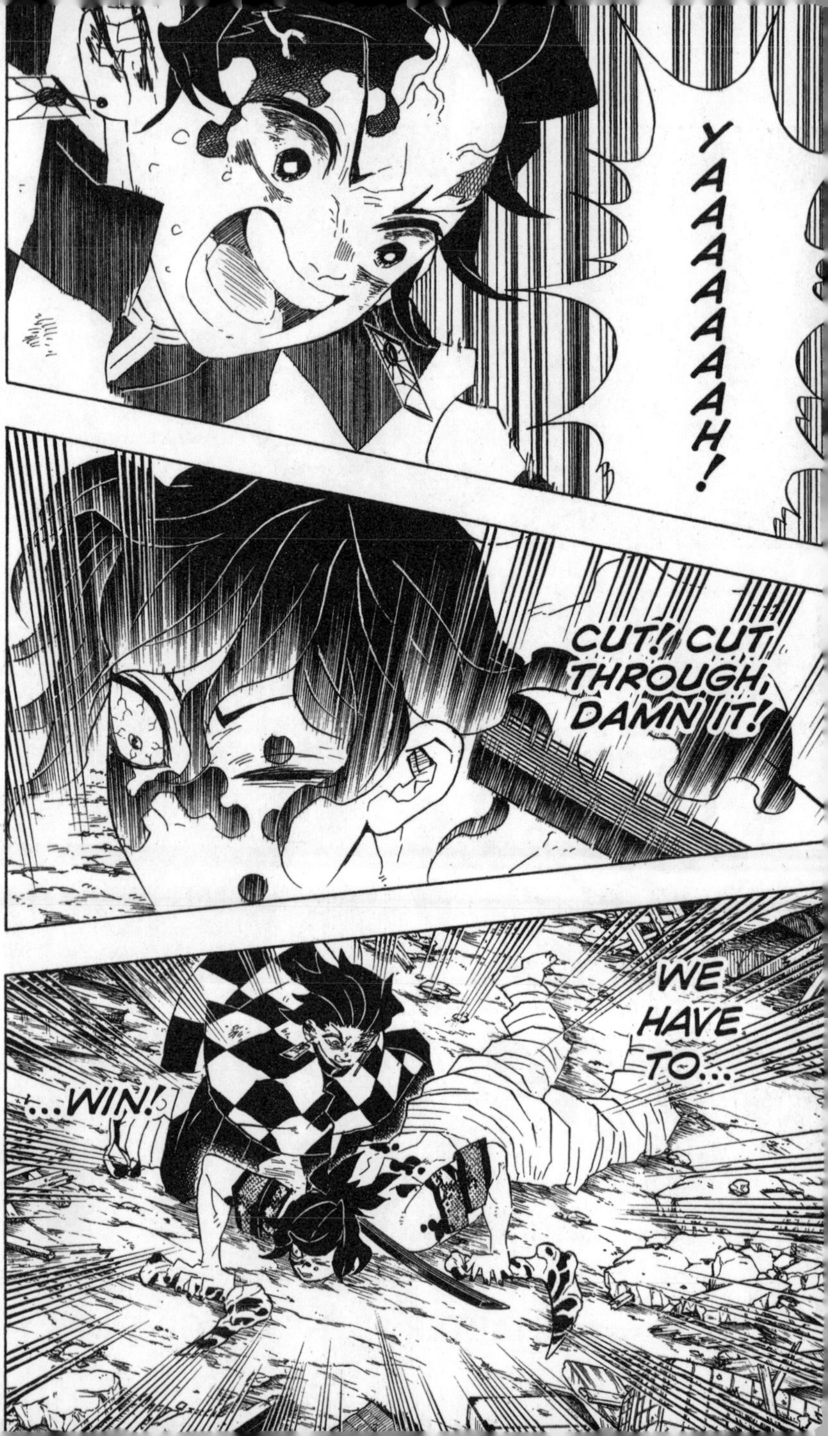
YAAAAAAAAH!
CUT! CUT THROUGH, DAMN IT!
WE HAVE TO...
...WIN!

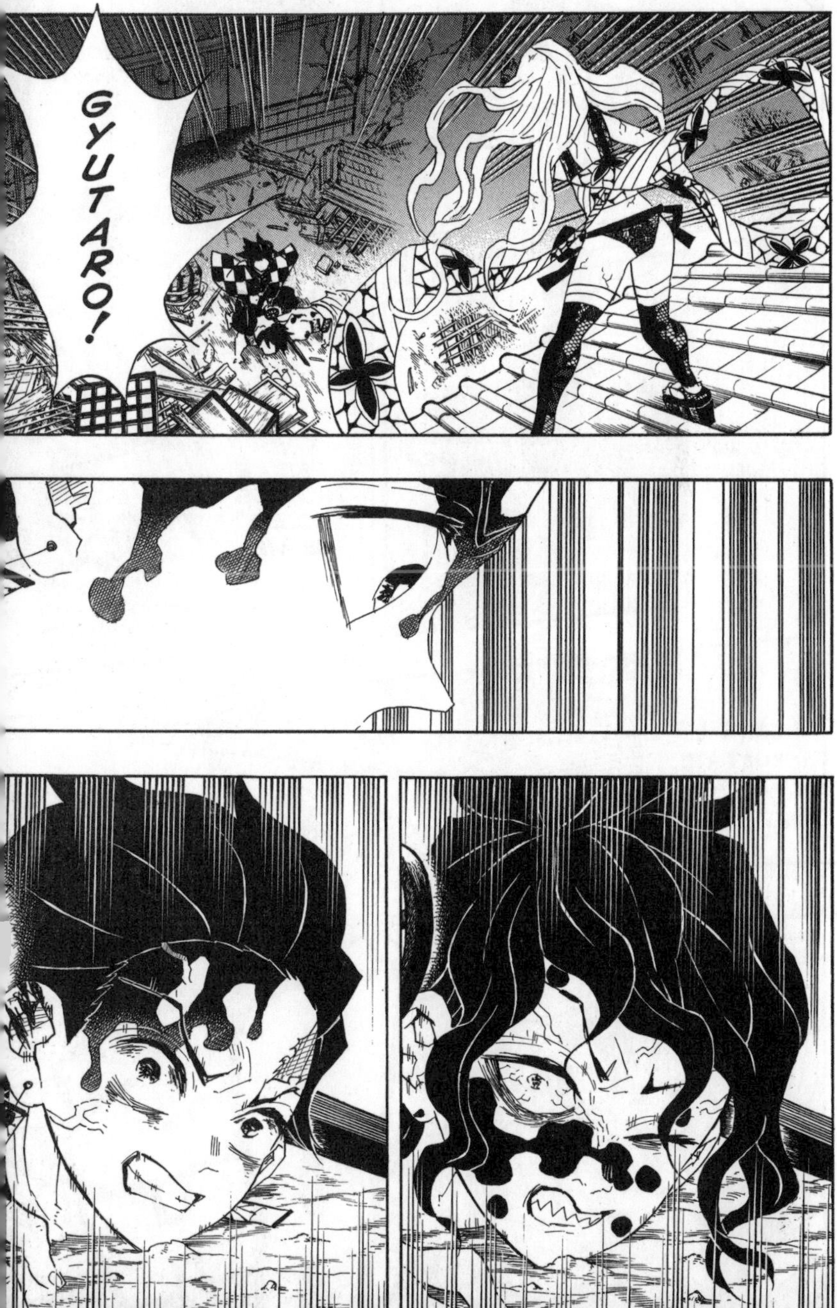
GYUTARO!

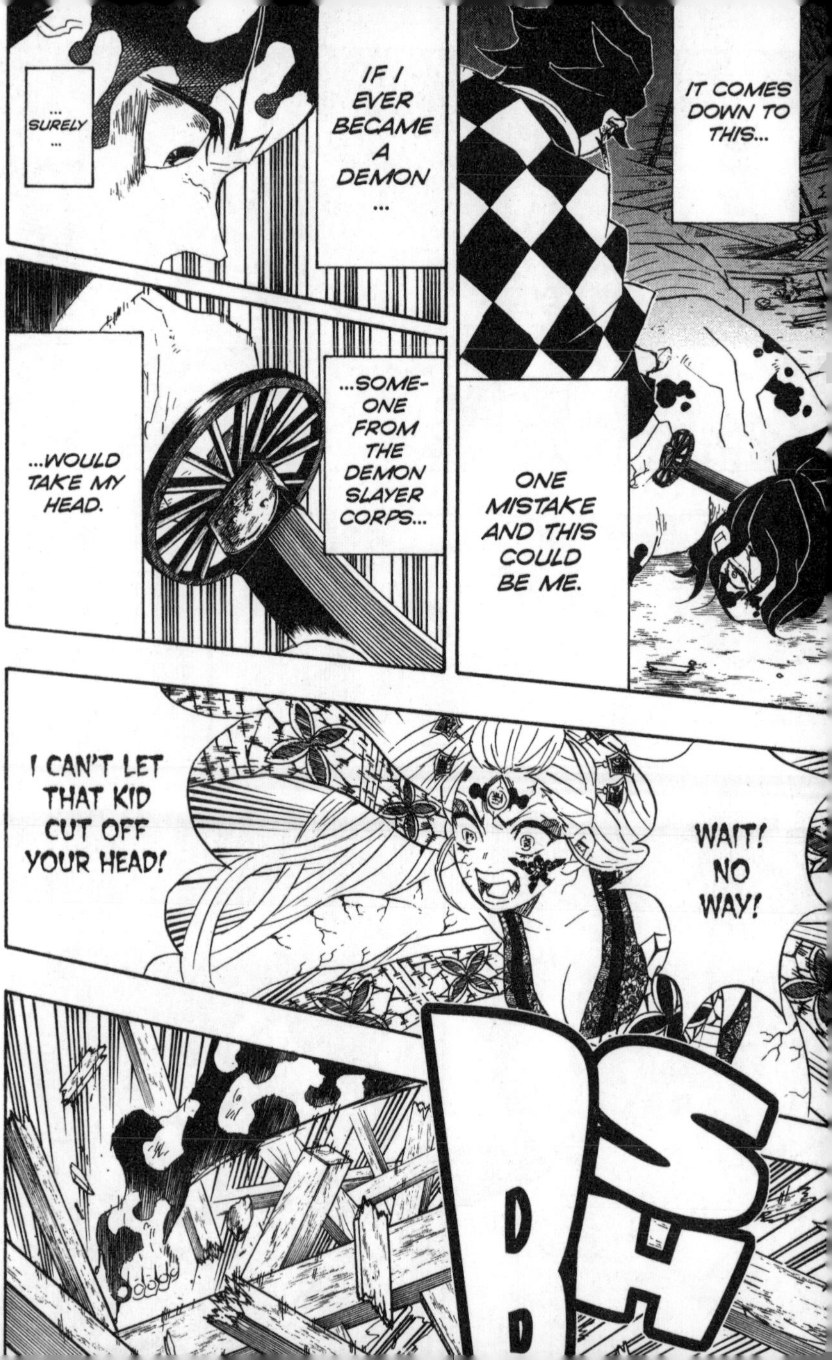
IT COMES DOWN TO THIS...
ONE MISTAKE AND THIS COULD BE ME.
IF I EVER BECAME A DEMON...
...SURELY...
...SOME-ONE FROM THE DEMON SLAYER CORPS...
...WOULD TAKE MY HEAD.
WAIT! NO WAY!
I CAN'T LET THAT KID CUT OFF YOUR HEAD!

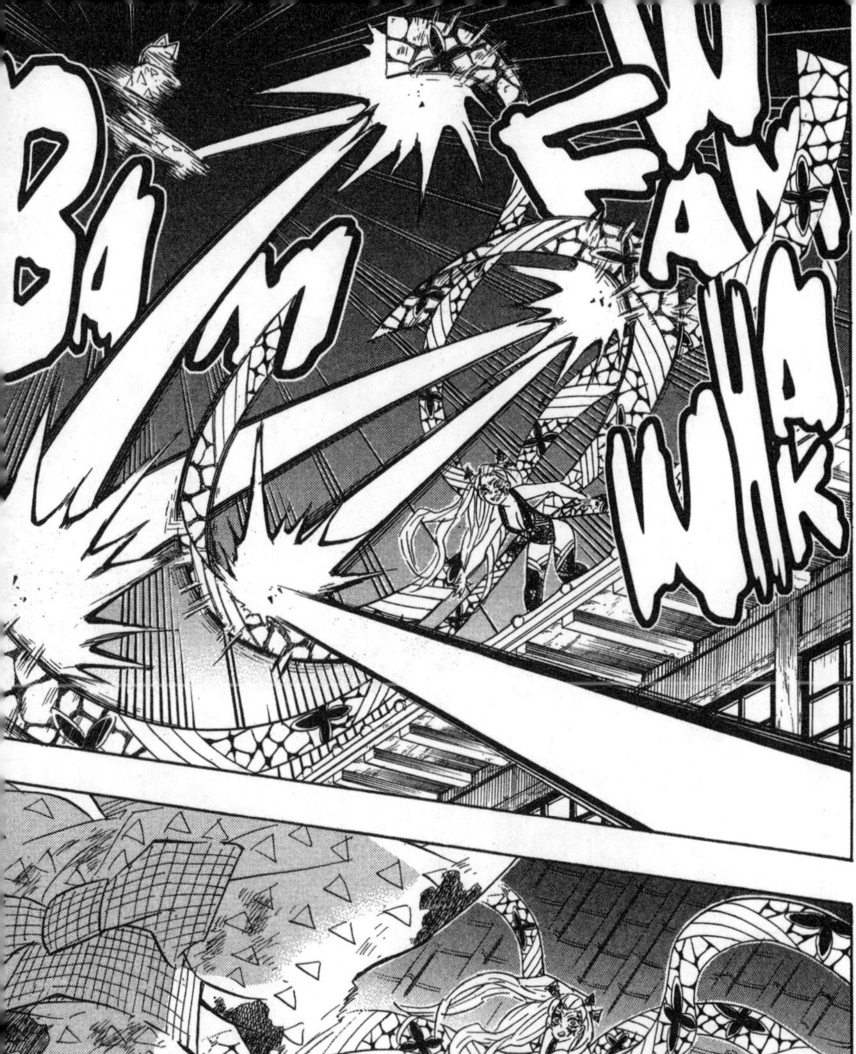
WHAM
WHAK
BAM
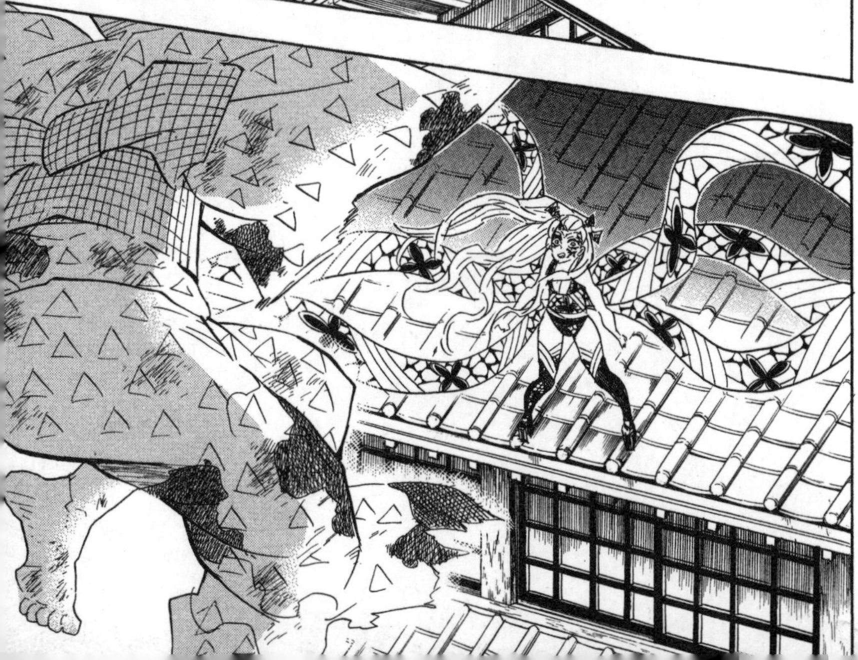

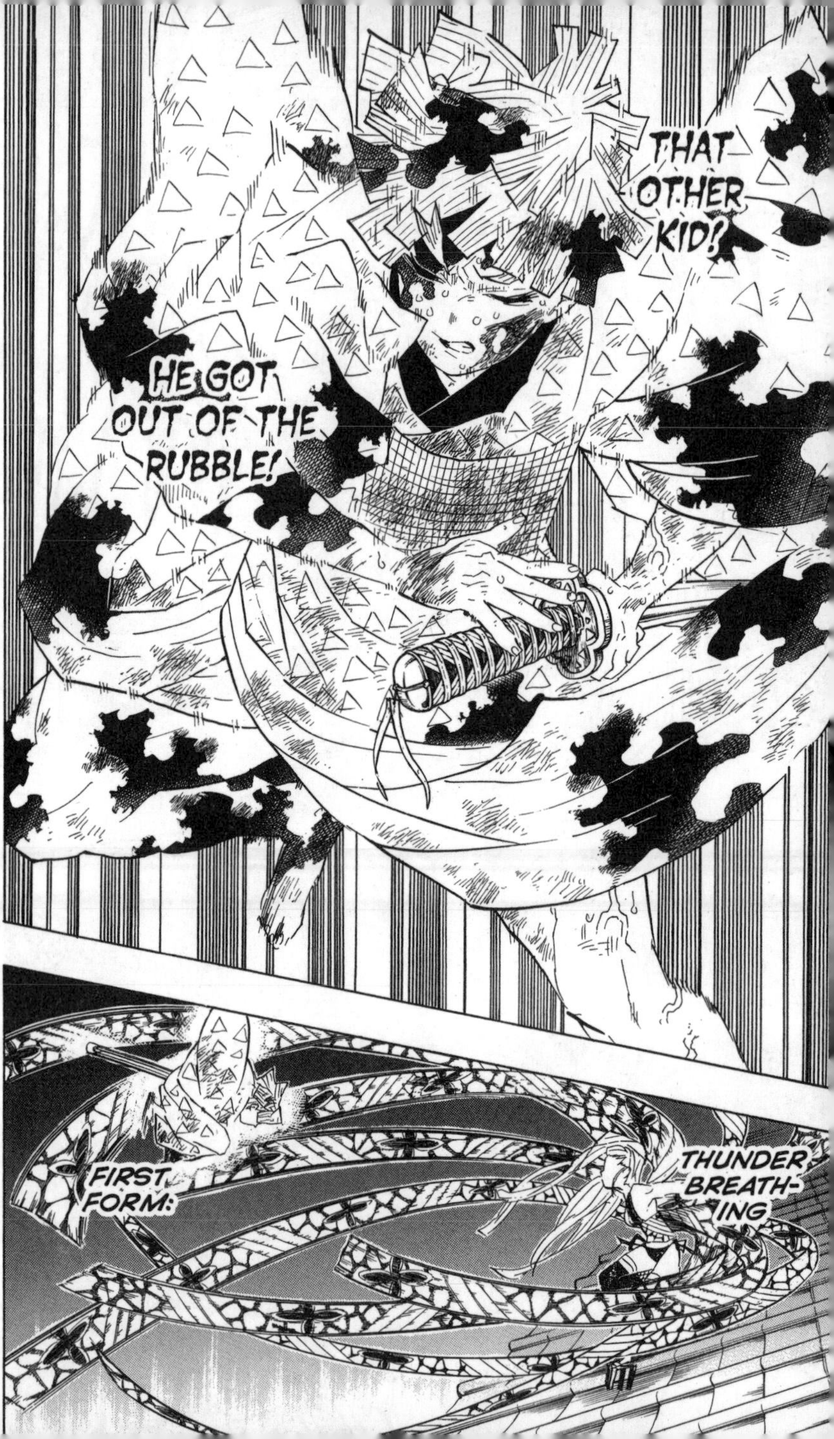
THAT OTHER KID!?
HE GOT OUT OF THE RUBBLE!
THUNDER-BREATH-ING
FIRST FORM:

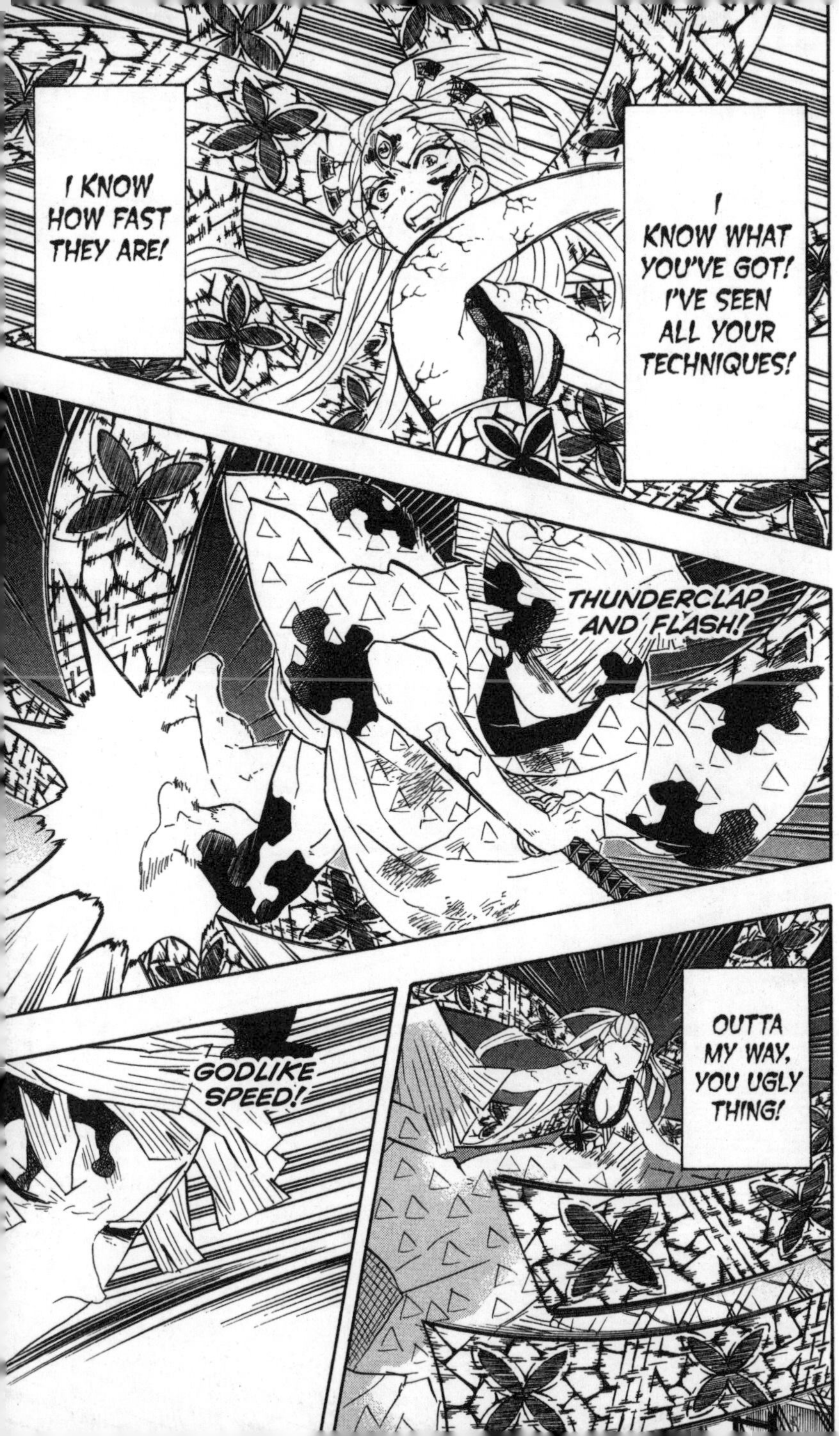
I KNOW WHAT YOU'VE GOT! I'VE SEEN ALL YOUR TECHNIQUES!
I KNOW HOW FAST THEY ARE!
THUNDERCLAP AND FLASH!
OUTTA MY WAY, YOU UGLY THING!
GODLIKE SPEED!

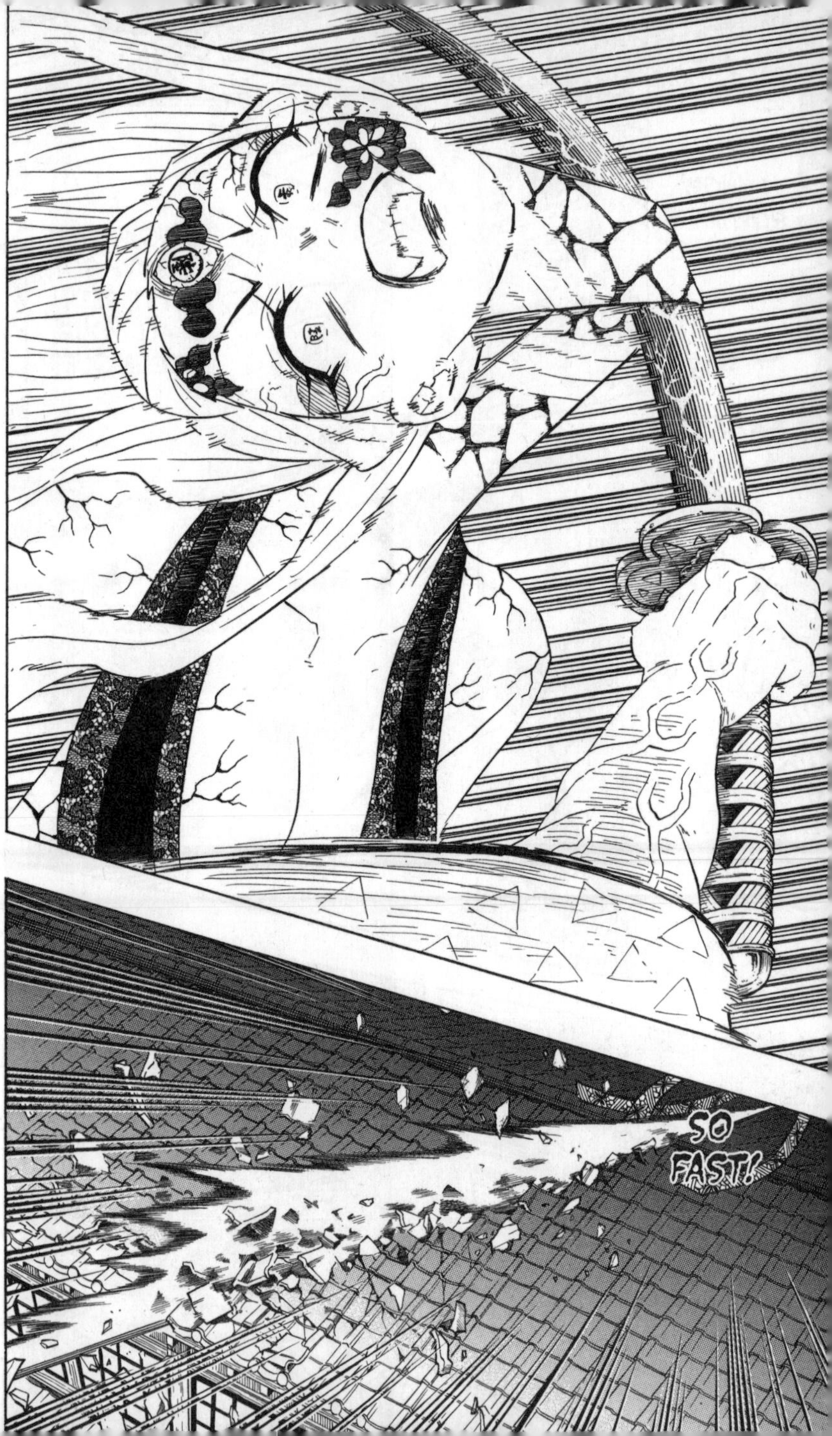
SO FAST!

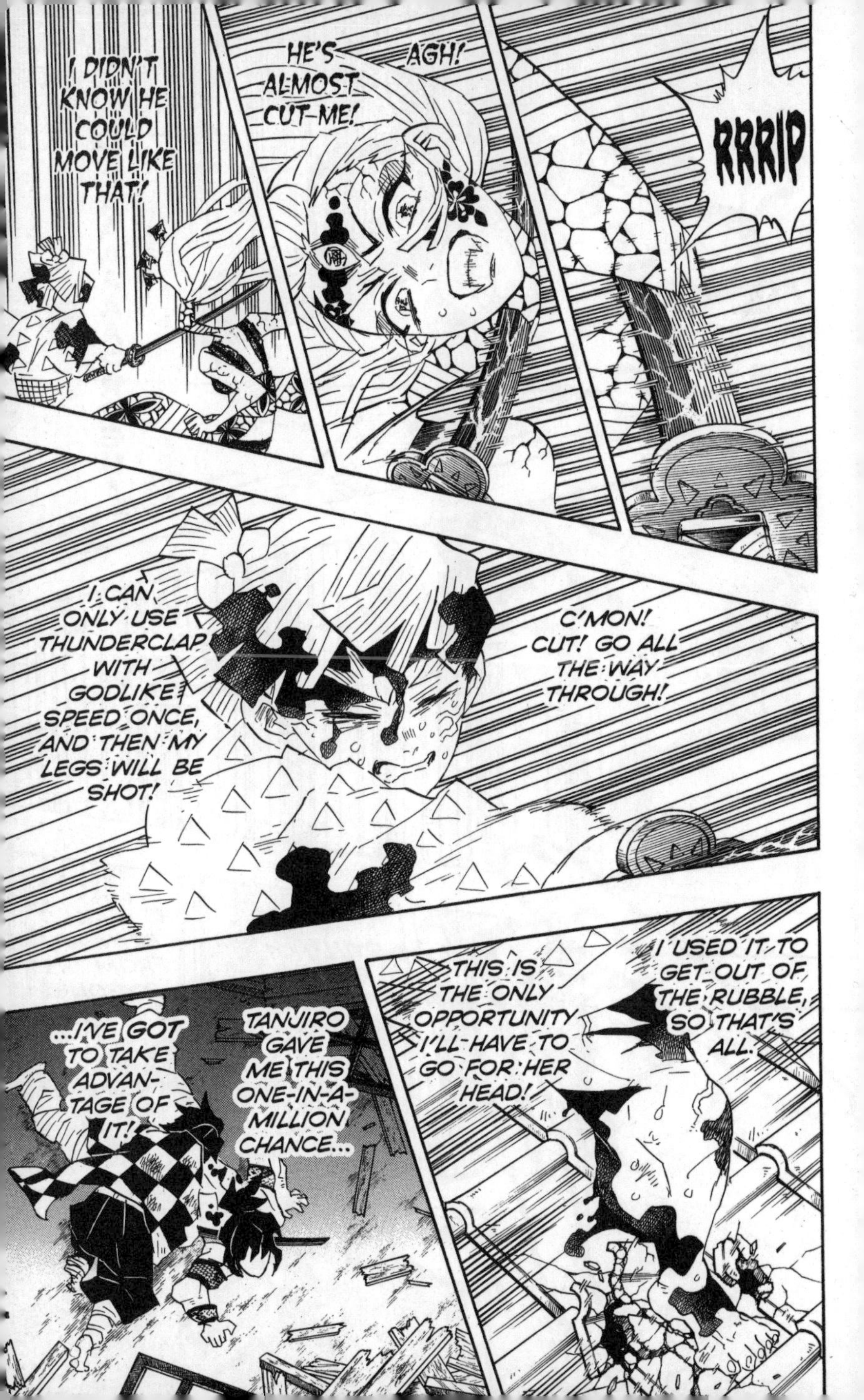
RRRIP
AGH!
HE'S ALMOST CUT ME!
I DIDN'T KNOW HE COULD MOVE LIKE THAT!
C'MON! CUT! GO ALL THE WAY THROUGH!
I CAN ONLY USE THUNDERCLAP WITH GODLIKE SPEED ONCE, AND THEN MY LEGS WILL BE SHOT!
I USED IT TO GET OUT OF THE RUBBLE, SO THAT'S ALL.
THIS IS THE ONLY OPPORTUNITY I'LL HAVE TO GO FOR HER HEAD!
TANJIRO GAVE ME THIS ONE-IN-A-MILLION CHANCE...
...I'VE GOT TO TAKE ADVAN-TAGE OF IT!

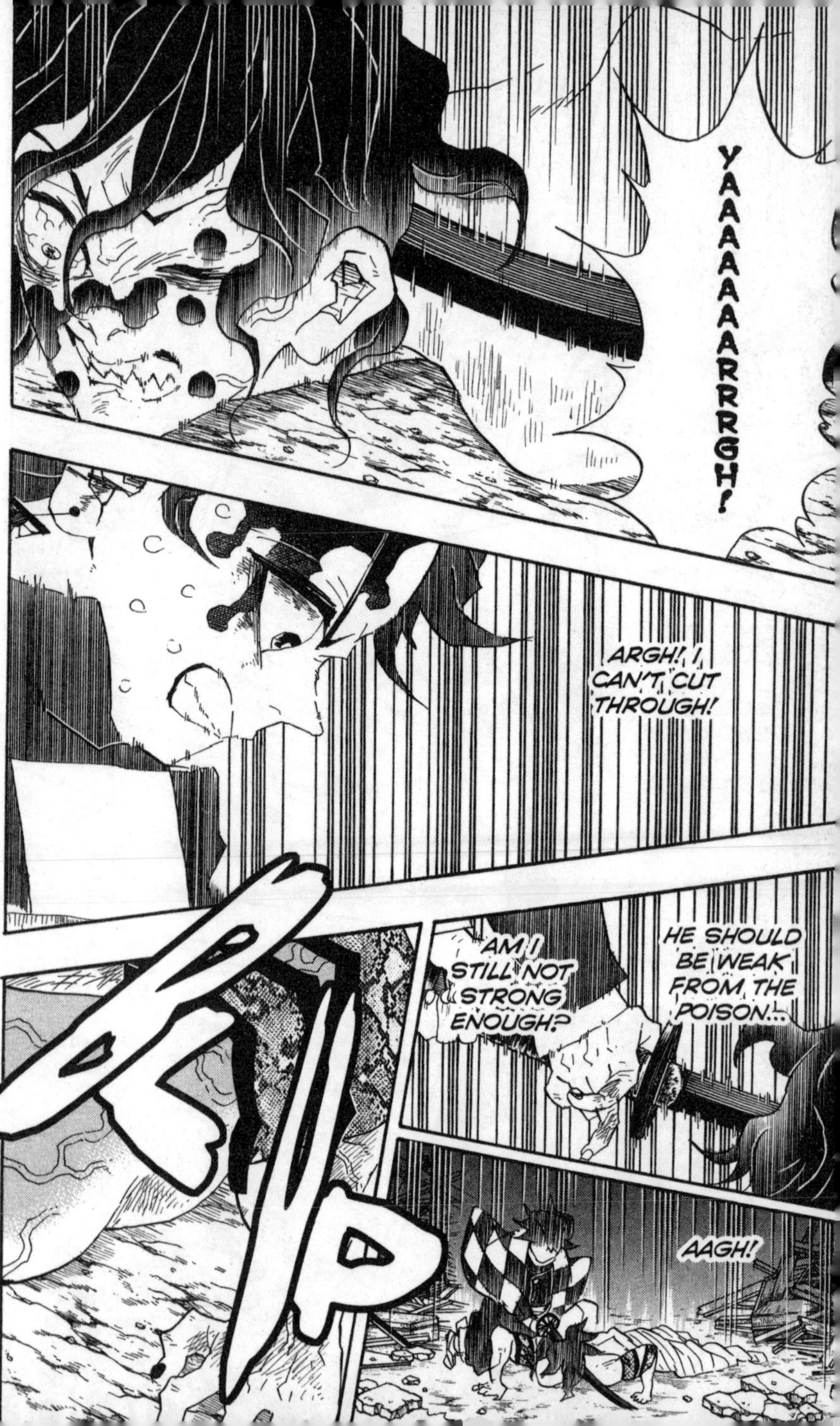
YAAAAAAARRRGH!
ARGH! I CAN'T CUT THROUGH!
HE SHOULD BE WEAK FROM THE POISON...
AM I STILL NOT STRONG ENOUGH?
AAGH!

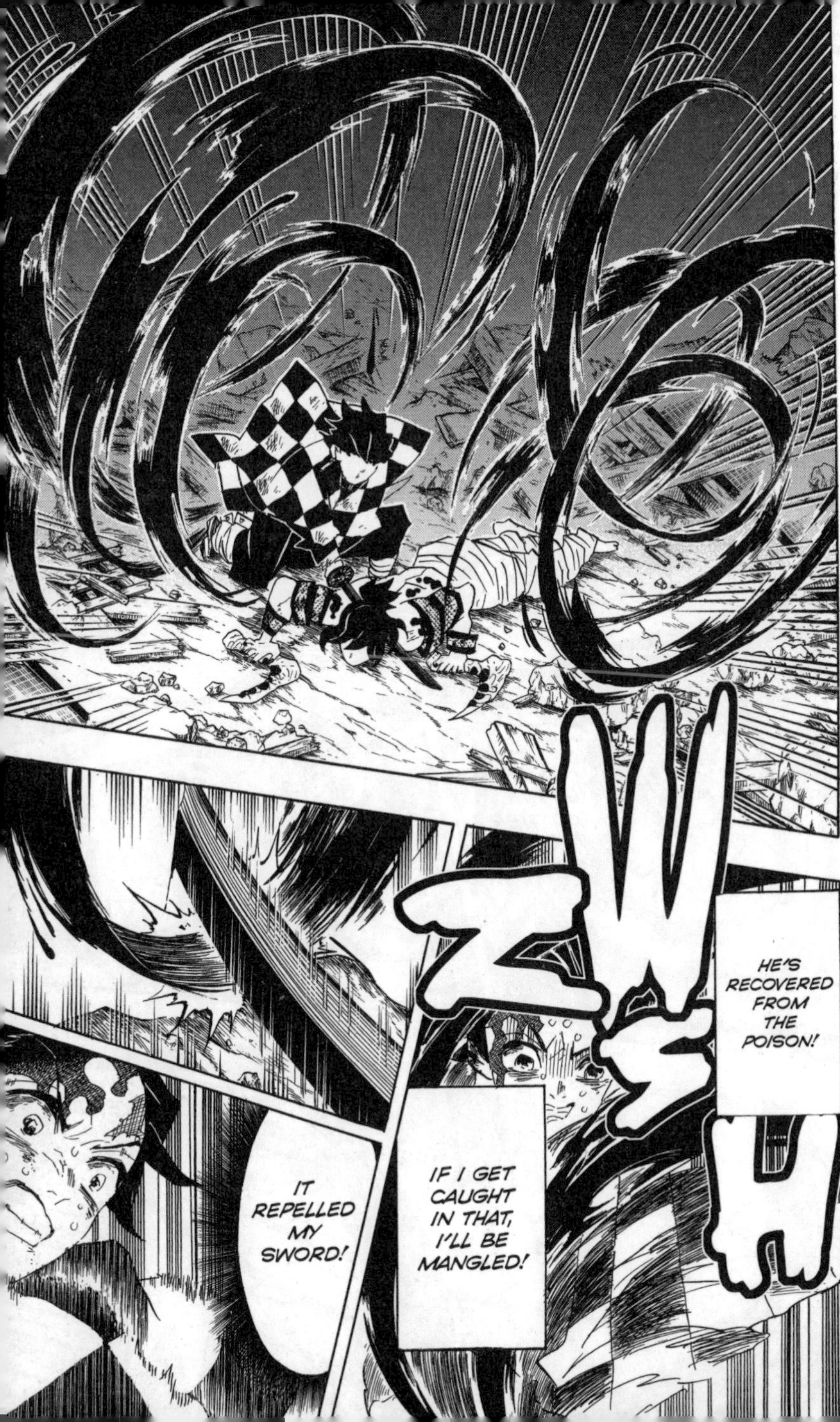
HE'S RECOVERED FROM THE POISON!
IF I GET CAUGHT IN THAT, I'LL BE MANGLED!
IT REPELLED MY SWORD!

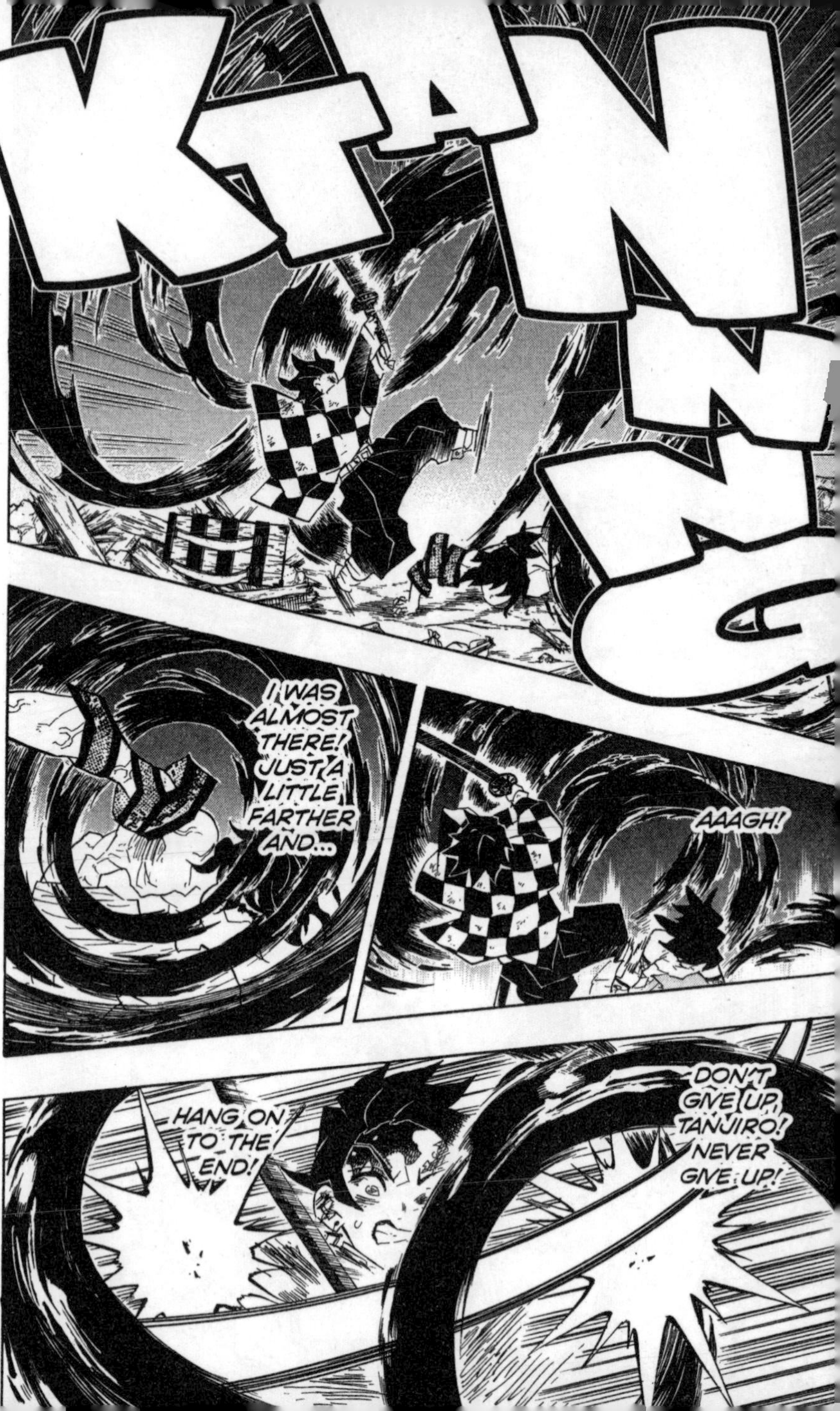
KANNNG
AAAGH!
I WAS ALMOST THERE! JUST A LITTLE FARTHER AND...
DON'T GIVE UP, TANJIRO! NEVER GIVE UP!
HANG ON TO THE END!

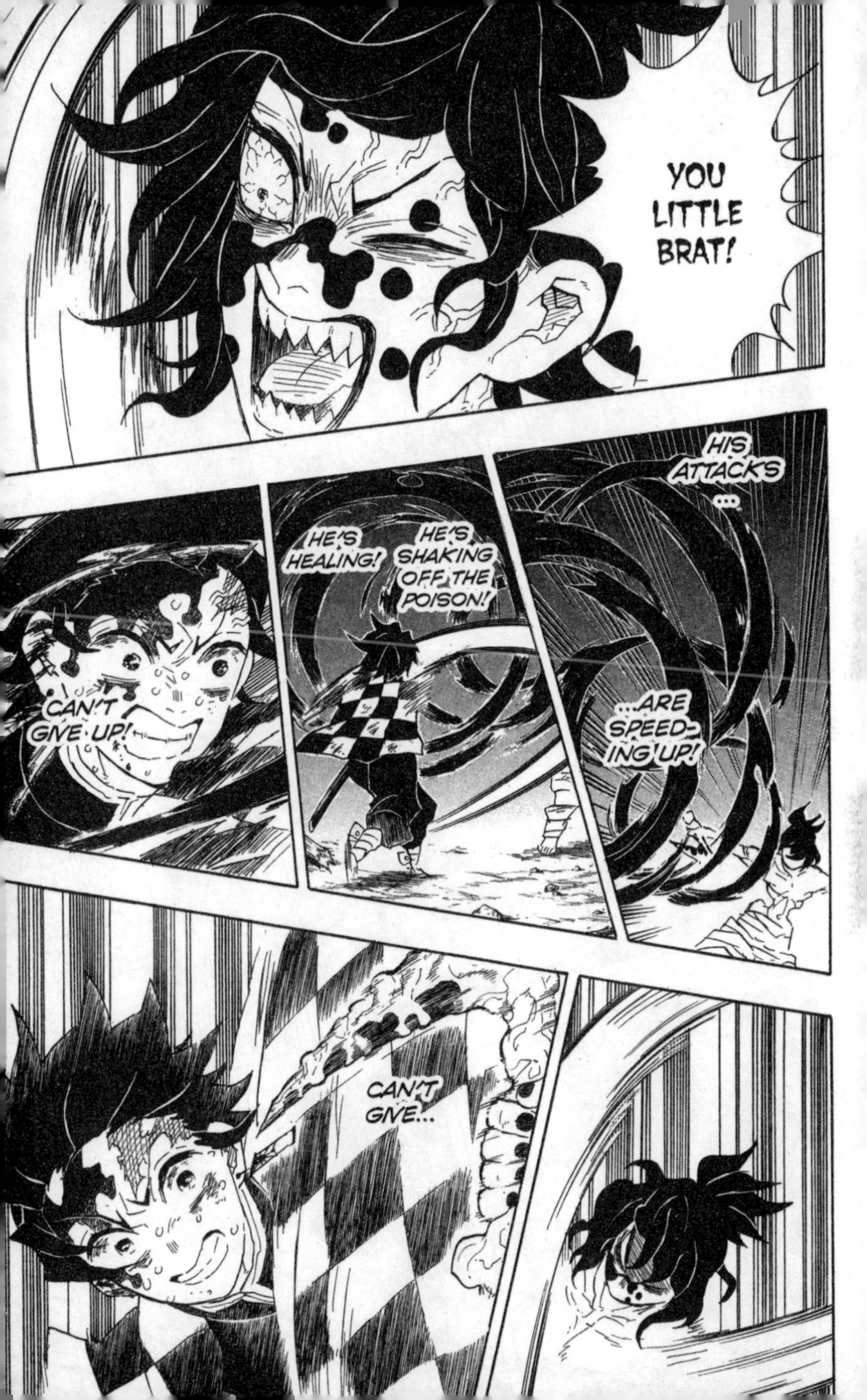
YOU LITTLE BRAT!
HIS ATTACKS...
...ARE SPEEDING UP!
HE'S SHAKING OFF THE POISON!
HE'S HEALING!
CAN'T GIVE UP!
CAN'T GIVE...

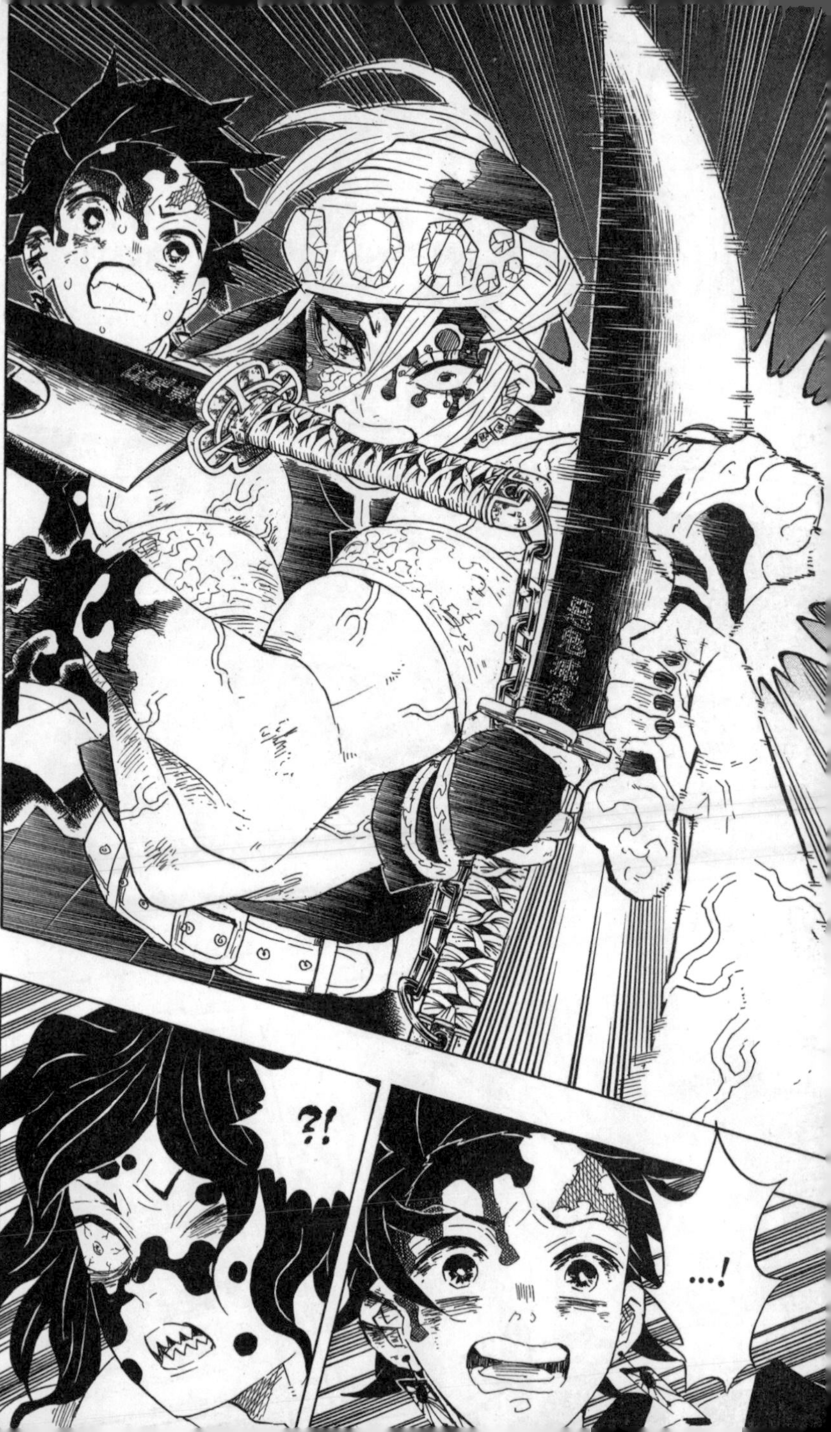
...!
?!

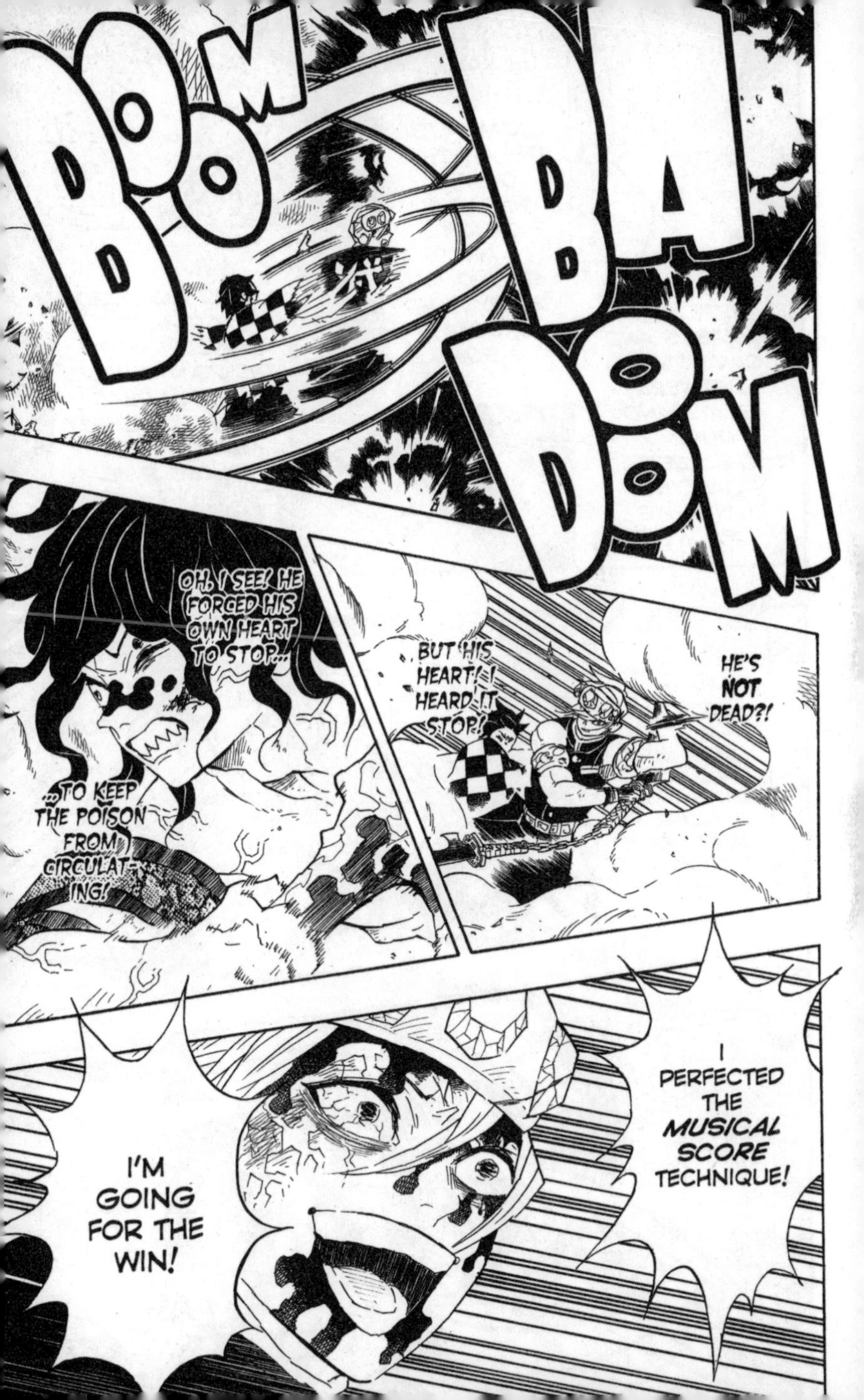

BA DOOM
DOOM
HE'S NOT DEAD?!
BUT HIS HEART! I HEARD IT STOP!
OH, I SEE! HE FORCED HIS OWN HEART TO STOP...
...TO KEEP THE POISON FROM CIRCULATING!
I PERFECTED THE *MUSICAL SCORE* TECHNIQUE!
I'M GOING FOR THE WIN!

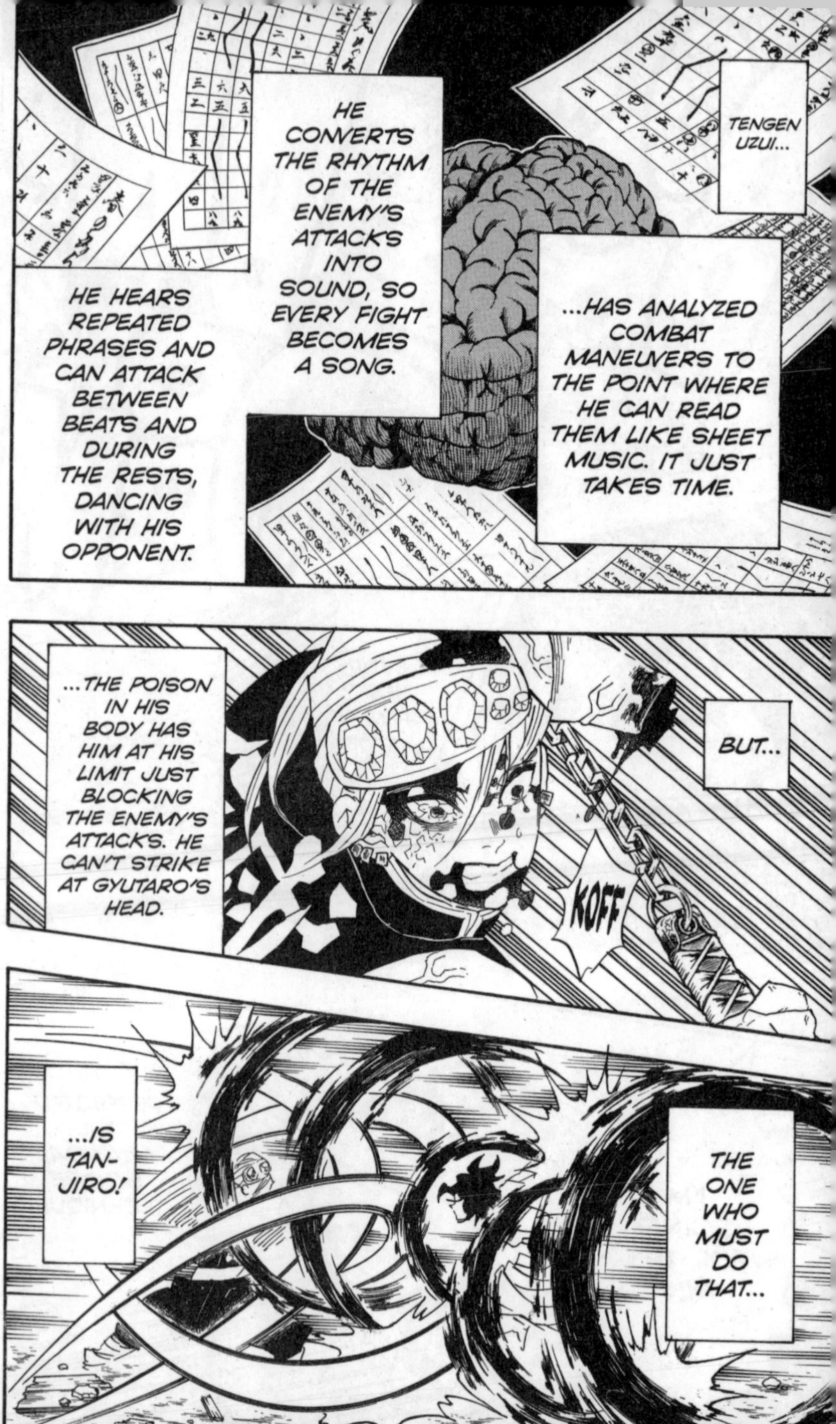
TENGEN UZUI...
...HAS ANALYZED COMBAT MANEUVERS TO THE POINT WHERE HE CAN READ THEM LIKE SHEET MUSIC. IT JUST TAKES TIME.
HE CONVERTS THE RHYTHM OF THE ENEMY'S ATTACKS INTO SOUND, SO EVERY FIGHT BECOMES A SONG.
HE HEARS REPEATED PHRASES AND CAN ATTACK BETWEEN BEATS AND DURING THE RESTS, DANCING WITH HIS OPPONENT.
BUT...
...THE POISON IN HIS BODY HAS HIM AT HIS LIMIT JUST BLOCKING THE ENEMY'S ATTACKS. HE CAN'T STRIKE AT GYUTARO'S HEAD.
KOFF
THE ONE WHO MUST DO THAT...
...IS TAN-JIRO!

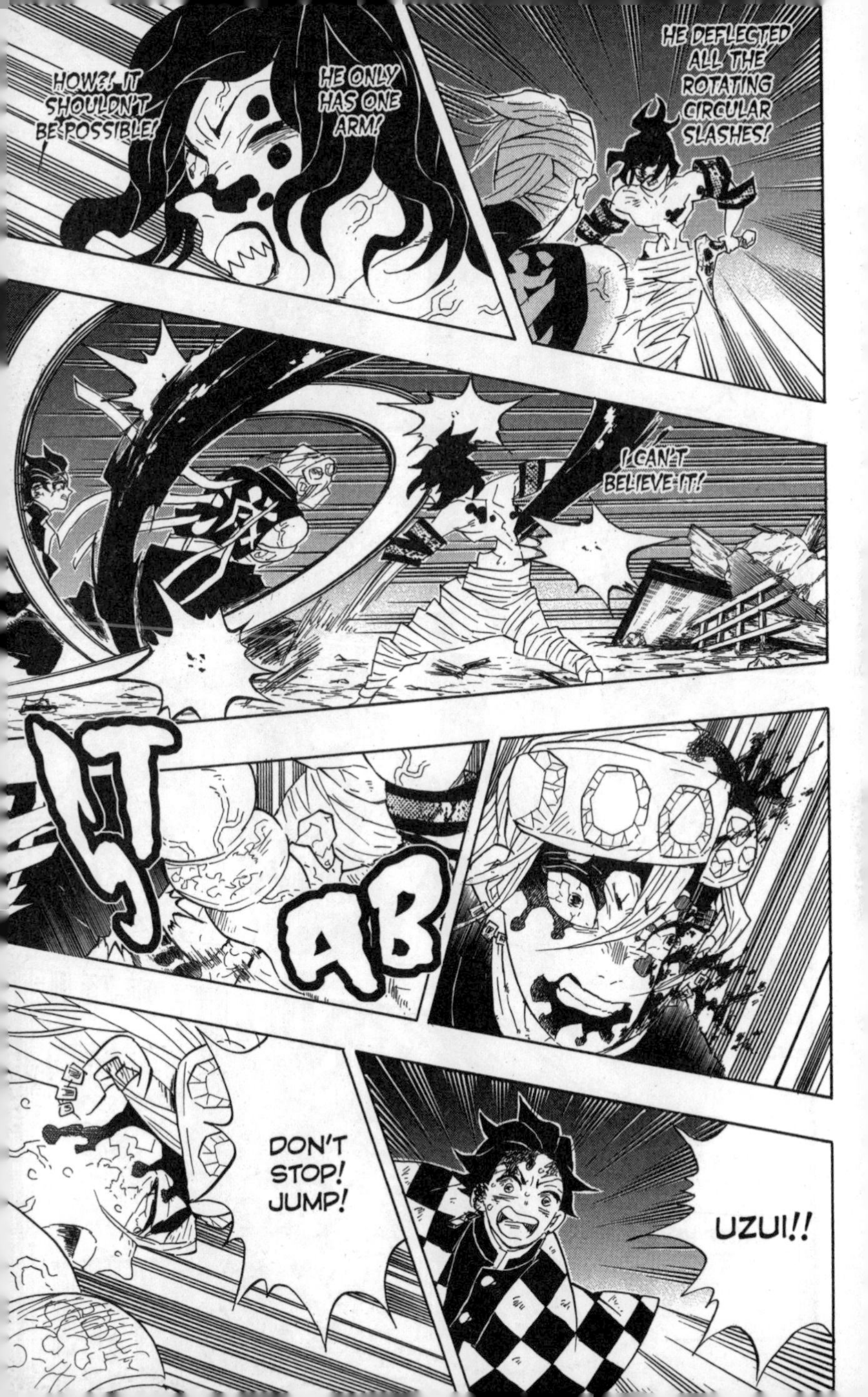
HE DEFLECTED ALL THE ROTATING CIRCULAR SLASHES!
HE ONLY HAS ONE ARM!
HOW?! IT SHOULDN'T BE POSSIBLE!
I CAN'T BELIEVE IT!
STAB
UZUI!!
DON'T STOP! JUMP!

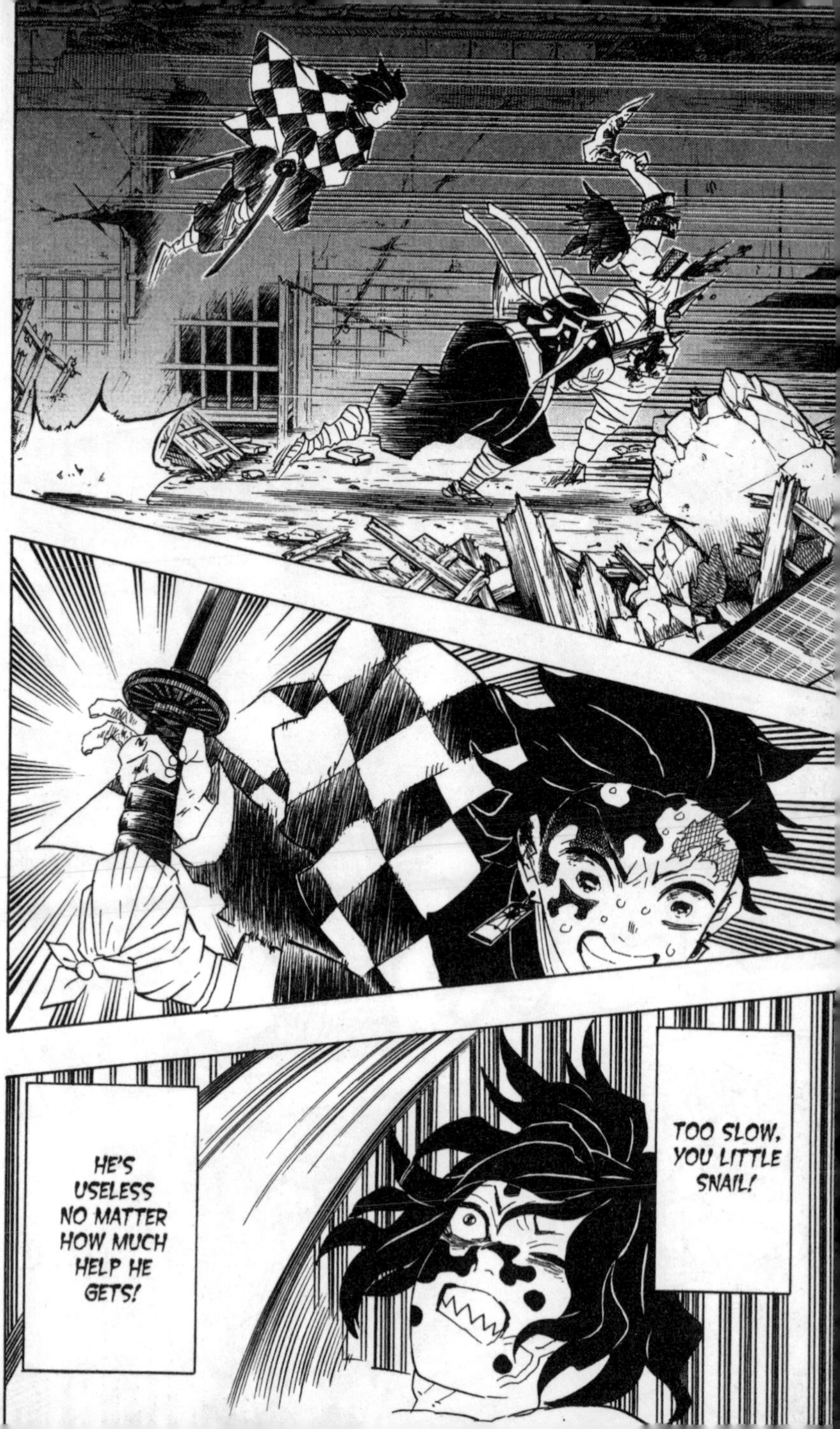
TOO SLOW, YOU LITTLE SNAIL!
HE'S USELESS NO MATTER HOW MUCH HELP HE GETS!

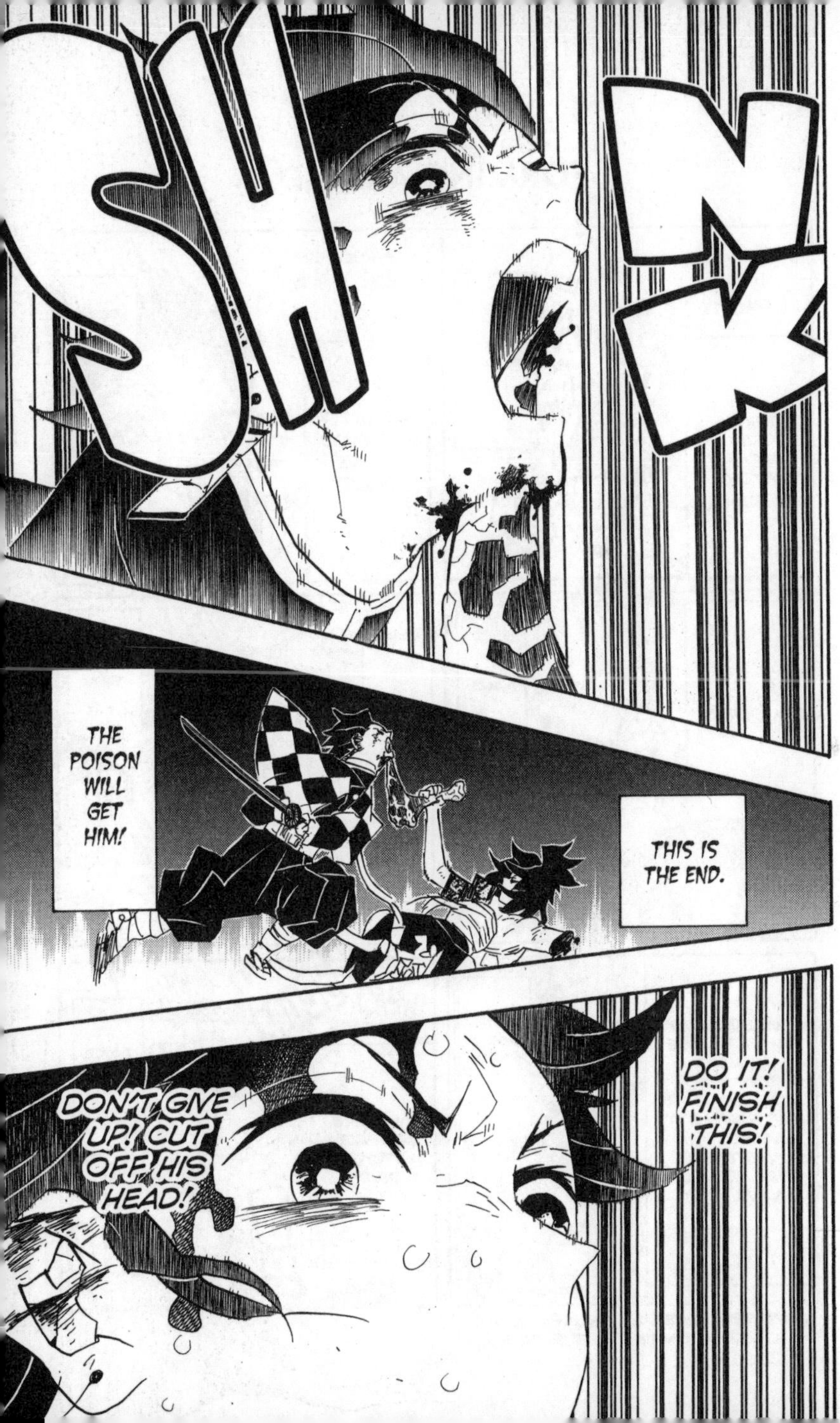
SHNK
THIS IS THE END.
THE POISON WILL GET HIM!
DO IT! FINISH THIS!
DON'T GIVE UP! CUT OFF HIS HEAD!

FORMING A BAND

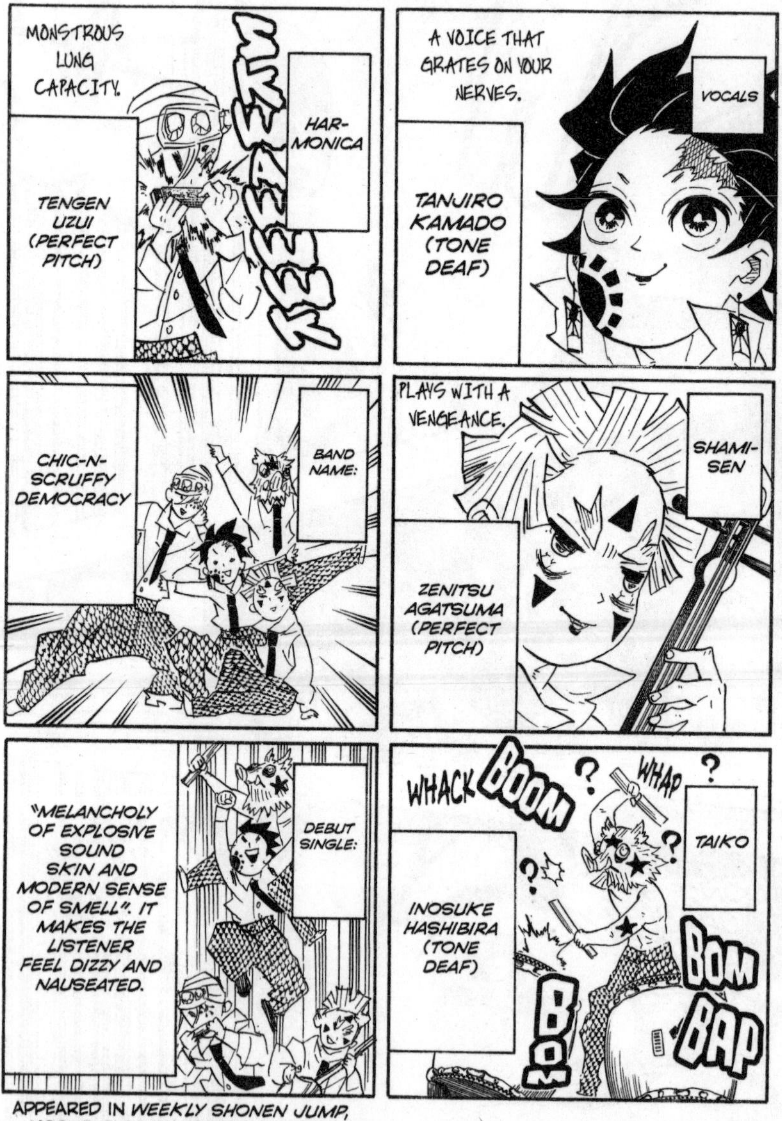
VOCALS
A VOICE THAT GRATES ON YOUR NERVES.
TANJIRO KAMADO (TONE DEAF)
HAR-MONICA
MONSTROUS LUNG CAPACITY.
TENGEN UZUI (PERFECT PITCH)
SHAMI-SEN
PLAYS WITH A VENGEANCE.
ZENITSU AGATSUMA (PERFECT PITCH)
BAND NAME:
CHIC-N-SCRUFFY DEMOCRACY
TAIKO
WHAP
BOOM
WHACK
INOSUKE HASHIBIRA (TONE DEAF)
BOM
BAP
BOM
DEBUT SINGLE:
"MELANCHOLY OF EXPLOSIVE SOUND SKIN AND MODERN SENSE OF SMELL". IT MAKES THE LISTENER FEEL DIZZY AND NAUSEATED.

APPEARED IN *WEEKLY SHONEN JUMP*, NOS. 2-3 COMBINED ISSUE, 2018.

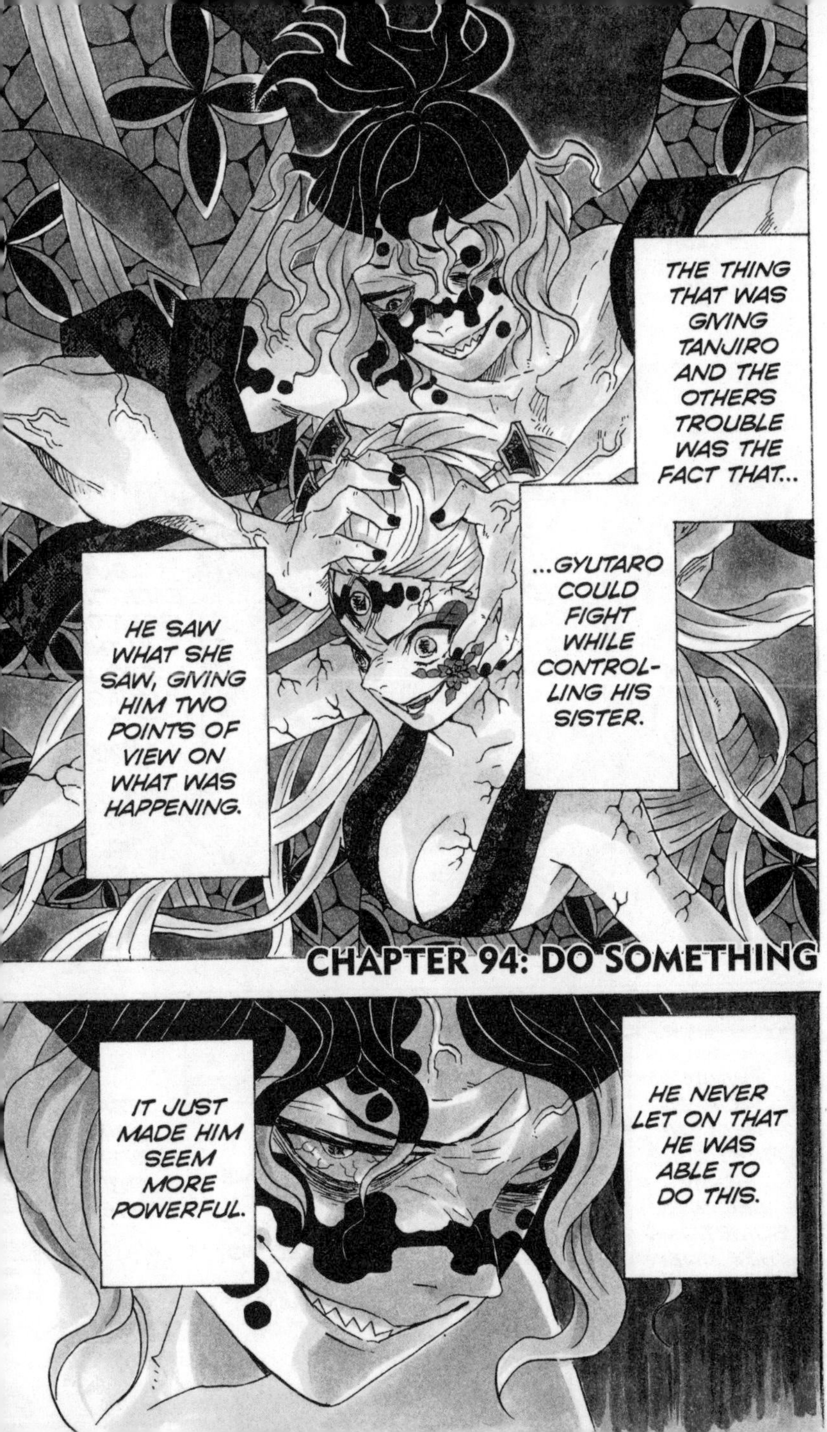
THE THING THAT WAS GIVING TANJIRO AND THE OTHERS TROUBLE WAS THE FACT THAT...
...GYUTARO COULD FIGHT WHILE CONTROL-LING HIS SISTER.
HE SAW WHAT SHE SAW, GIVING HIM TWO POINTS OF VIEW ON WHAT WAS HAPPENING.
CHAPTER 94: DO SOMETHING
HE NEVER LET ON THAT HE WAS ABLE TO DO THIS.
IT JUST MADE HIM SEEM MORE POWERFUL.

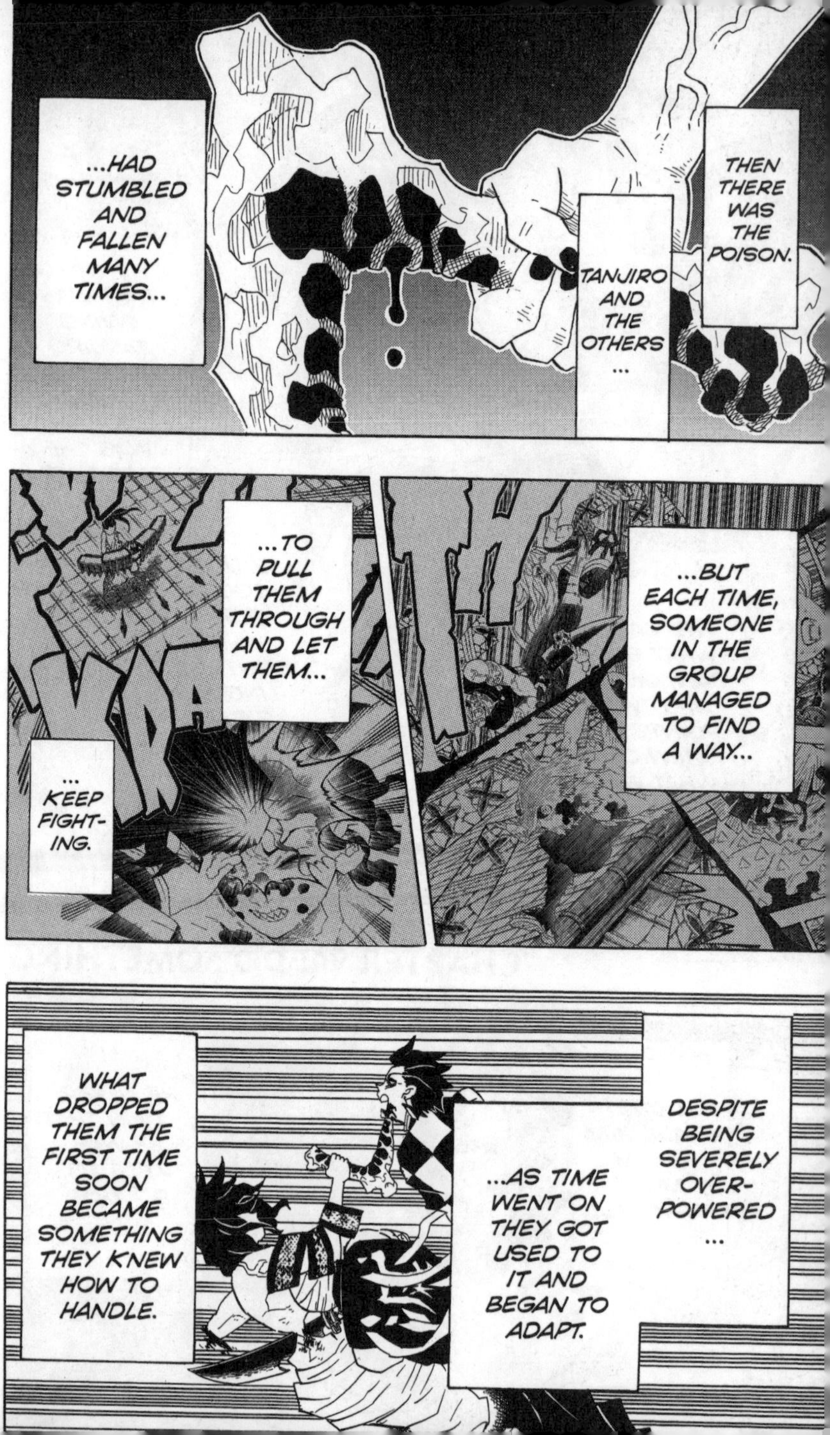
THEN THERE WAS THE POISON.
TANJIRO AND THE OTHERS ...
...HAD STUMBLED AND FALLEN MANY TIMES...
...BUT EACH TIME, SOMEONE IN THE GROUP MANAGED TO FIND A WAY...
...TO PULL THEM THROUGH AND LET THEM...
... KEEP FIGHT-ING.
DESPITE BEING SEVERELY OVER-POWERED ...
...AS TIME WENT ON THEY GOT USED TO IT AND BEGAN TO ADAPT.
WHAT DROPPED THEM THE FIRST TIME SOON BECAME SOMETHING THEY KNEW HOW TO HANDLE.

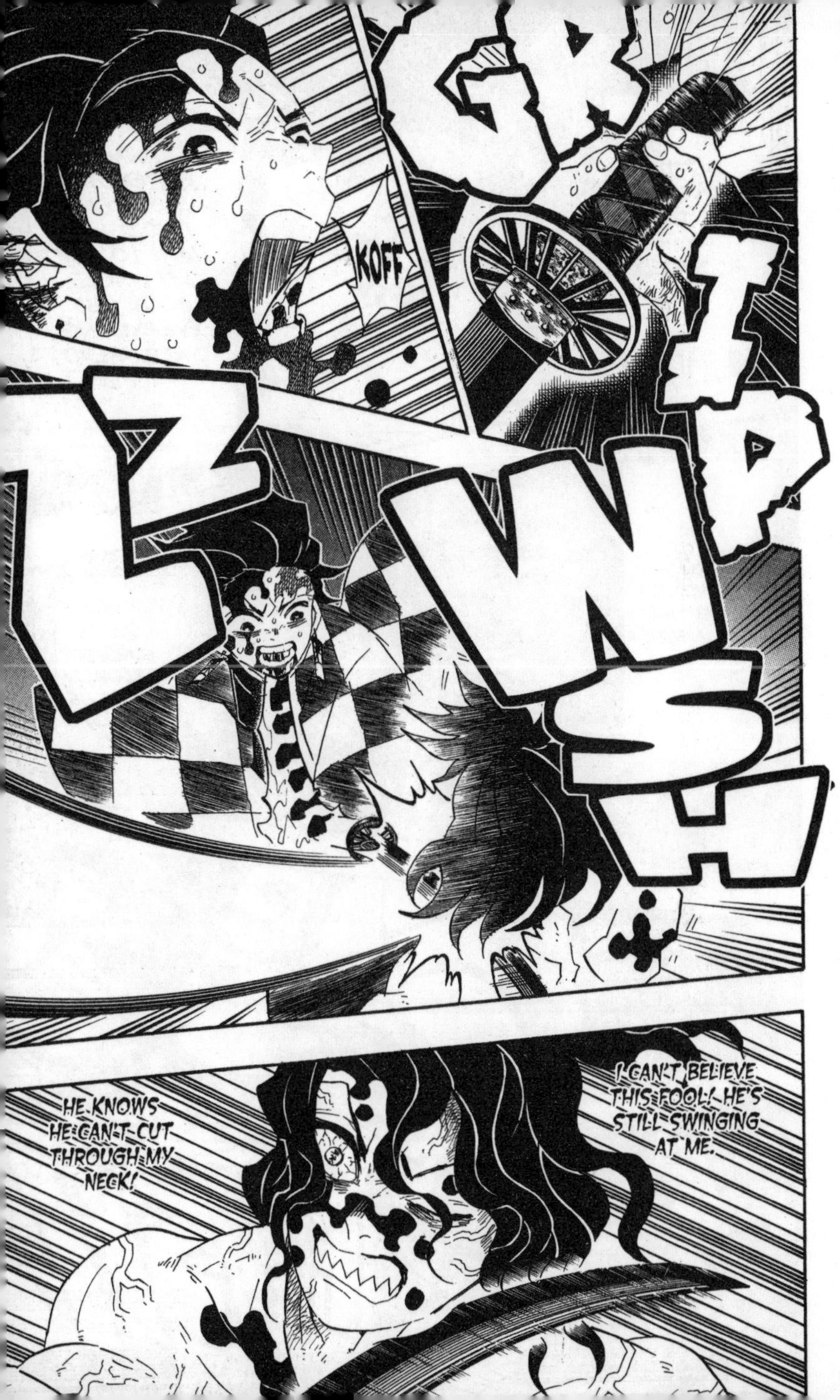
GRIP
KOFF
ZWISH
I CAN'T BELIEVE THIS FOOL! HE'S STILL SWINGING AT ME.
HE KNOWS HE CAN'T CUT THROUGH MY NECK!

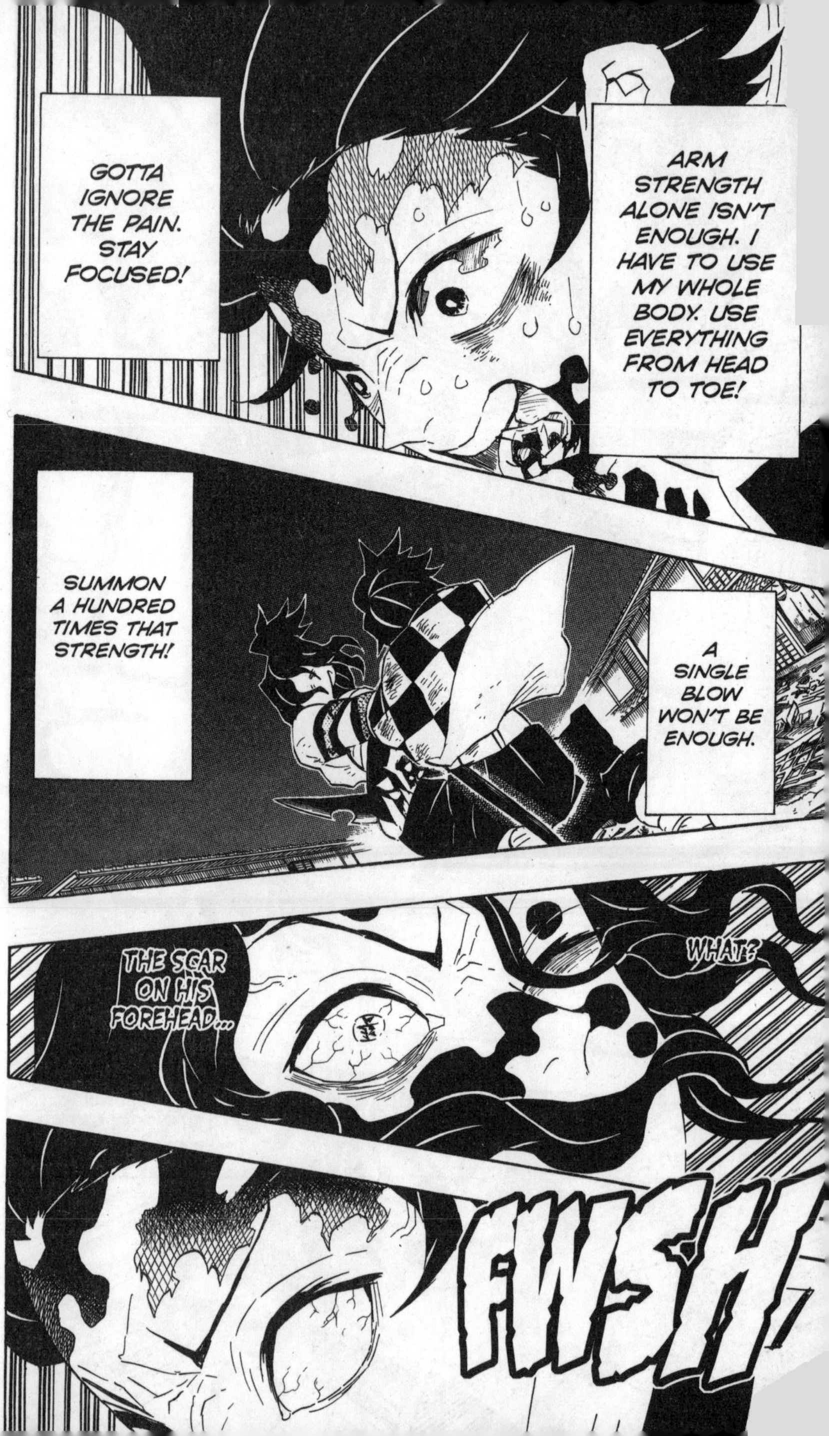
ARM STRENGTH ALONE ISN'T ENOUGH. I HAVE TO USE MY WHOLE BODY. USE EVERYTHING FROM HEAD TO TOE!
GOTTA IGNORE THE PAIN. STAY FOCUSED!
A SINGLE BLOW WON'T BE ENOUGH.
SUMMON A HUNDRED TIMES THAT STRENGTH!
WHAT?
THE SCAR ON HIS FOREHEAD...
FWSH

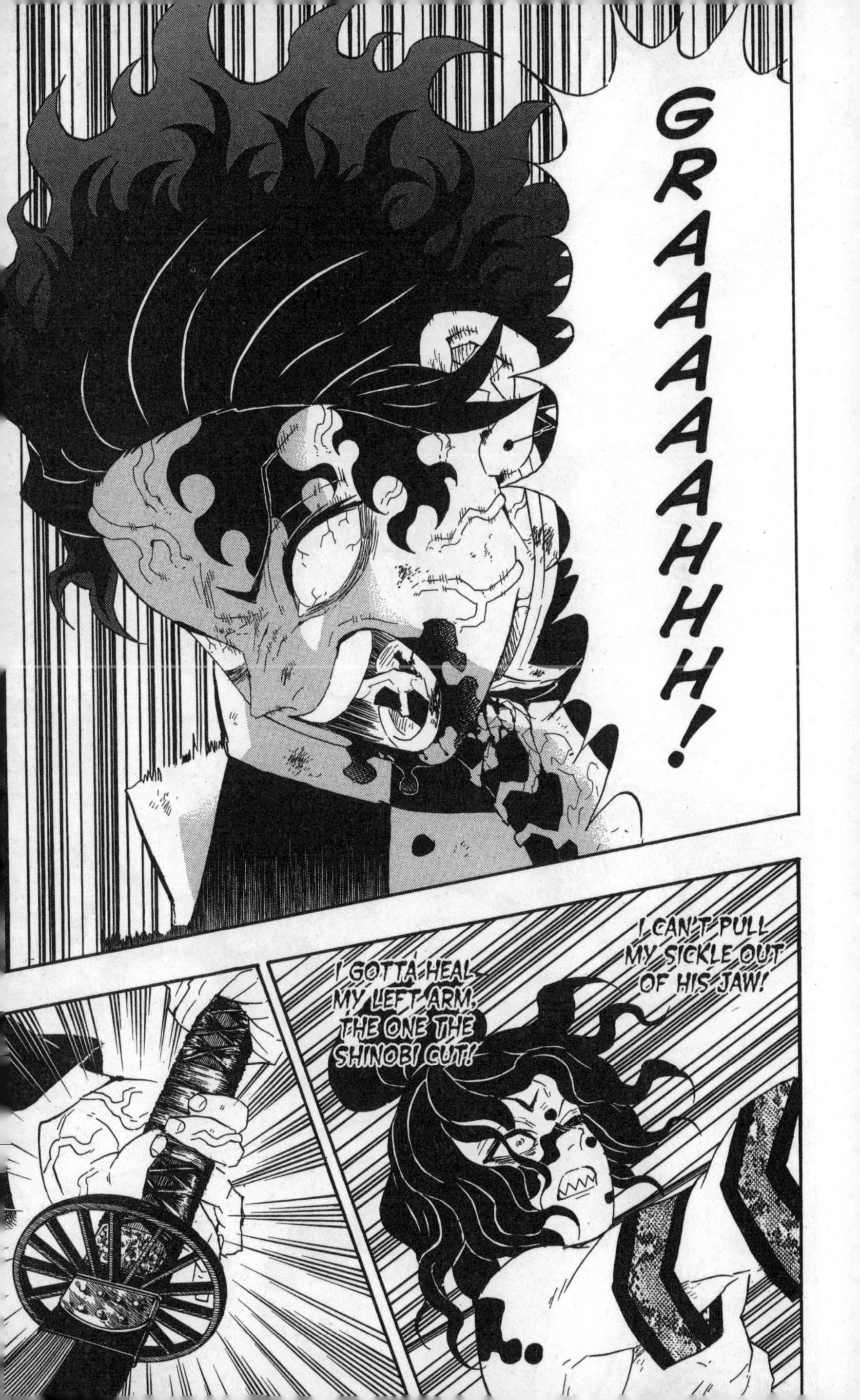
GRAAAAAHHH!
I CAN'T PULL MY SICKLE OUT OF HIS JAW!
I GOTTA HEAL MY LEFT ARM, THE ONE THE SHINOBI CUT!

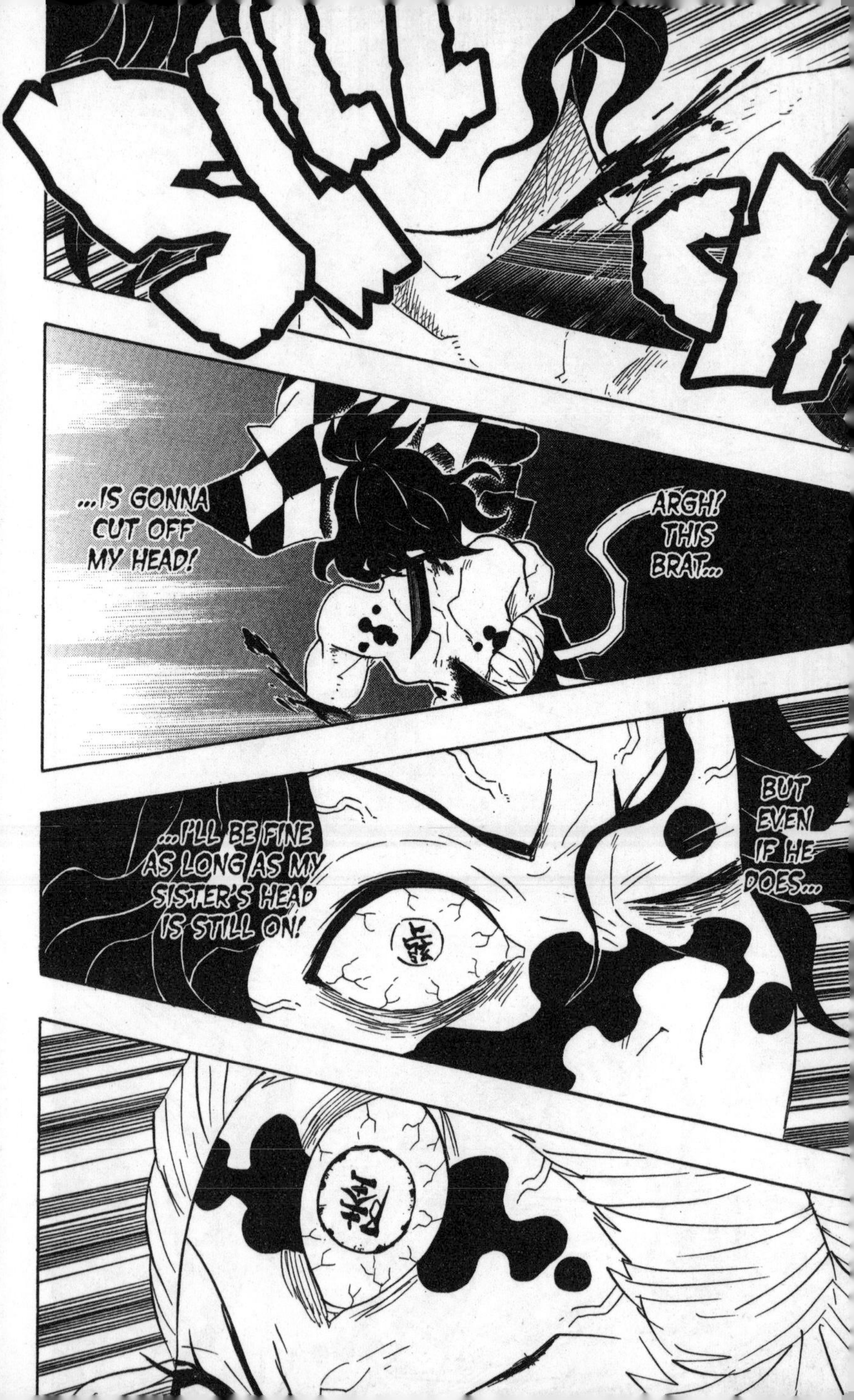
ARGH! THIS BRAT...
...IS GONNA CUT OFF MY HEAD!
BUT EVEN IF HE DOES...
...I'LL BE FINE AS LONG AS MY SISTER'S HEAD IS STILL ON!

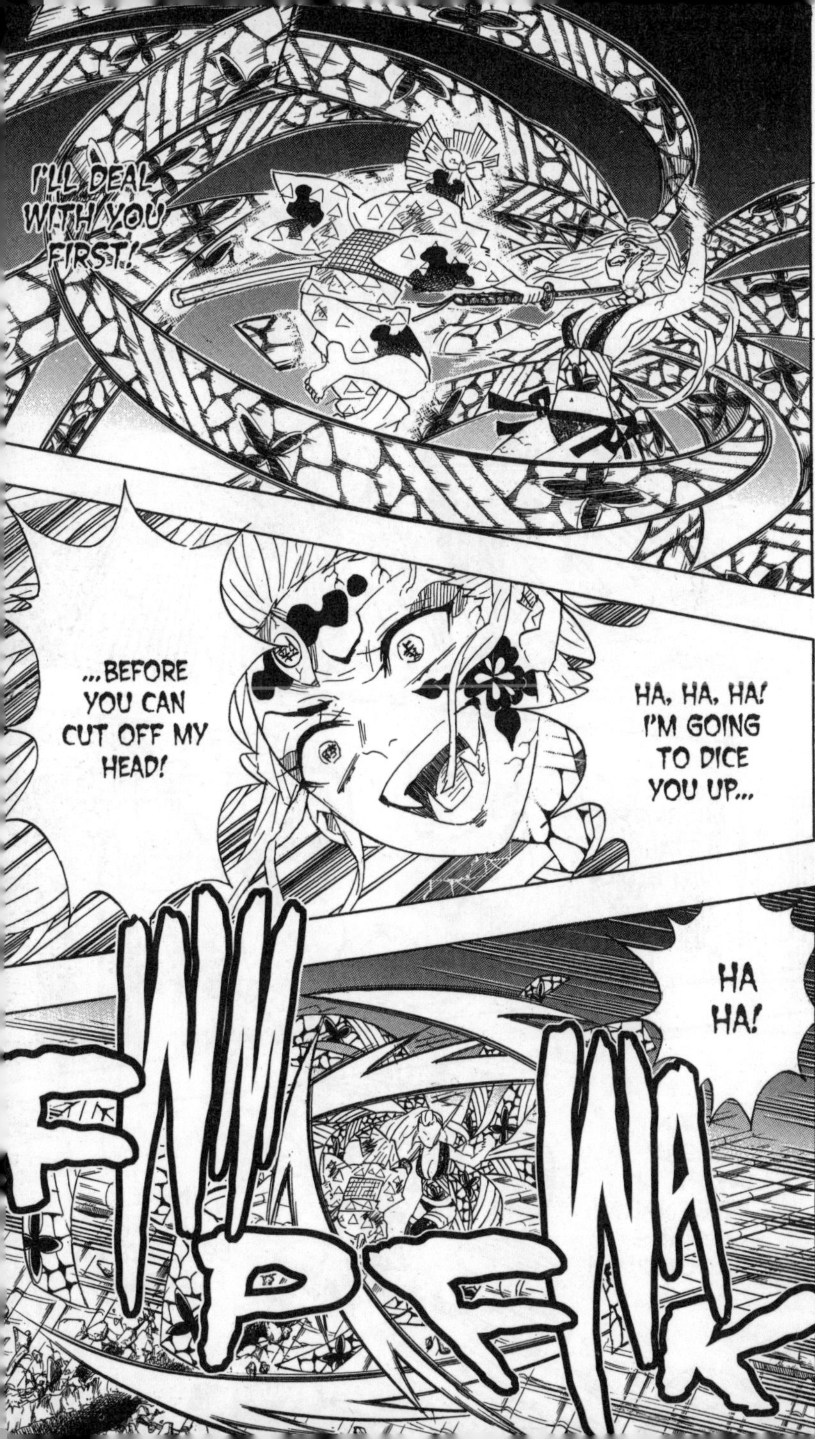
I'LL DEAL WITH YOU FIRST!
HA, HA, HA! I'M GOING TO DICE YOU UP...
...BEFORE YOU CAN CUT OFF MY HEAD!
HA HA!

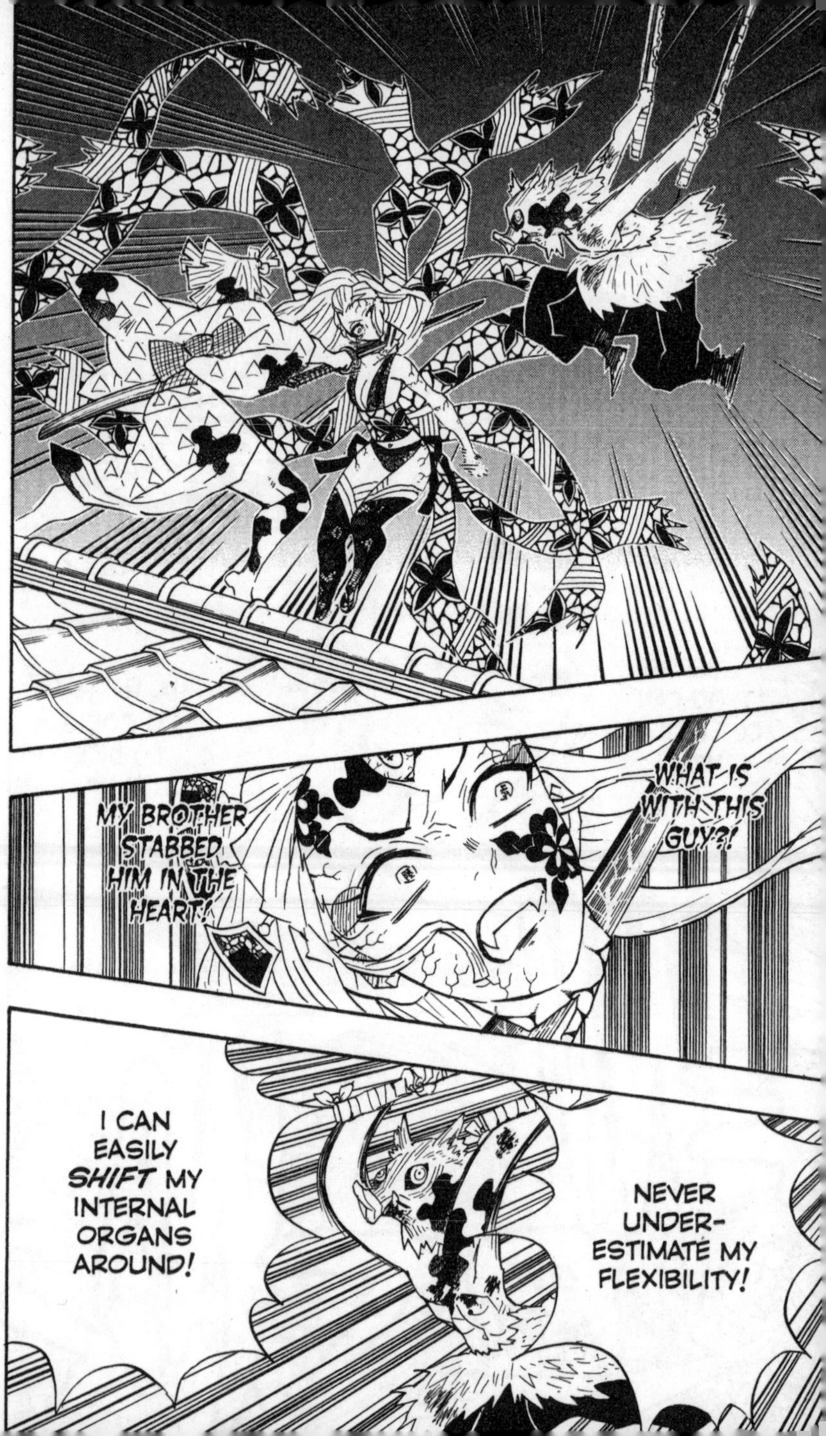
WHAT IS WITH THIS GUY?!
MY BROTHER STABBED HIM IN THE HEART!
NEVER UNDER-ESTIMATE MY FLEXIBILITY!
I CAN EASILY SHIFT MY INTERNAL ORGANS AROUND!

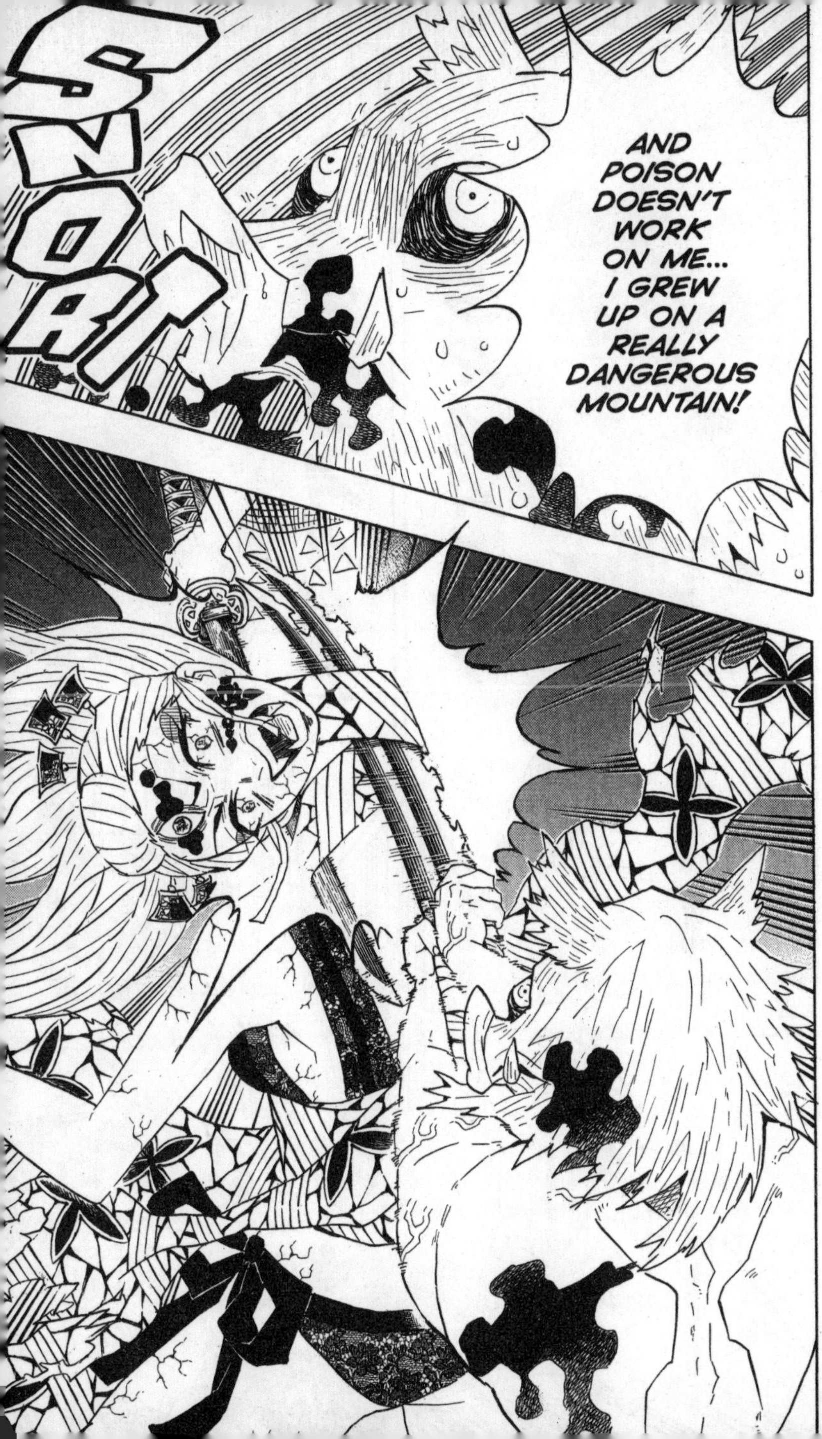
AND POISON DOESN'T WORK ON ME... I GREW UP ON A REALLY DANGEROUS MOUNTAIN!
SNORT!

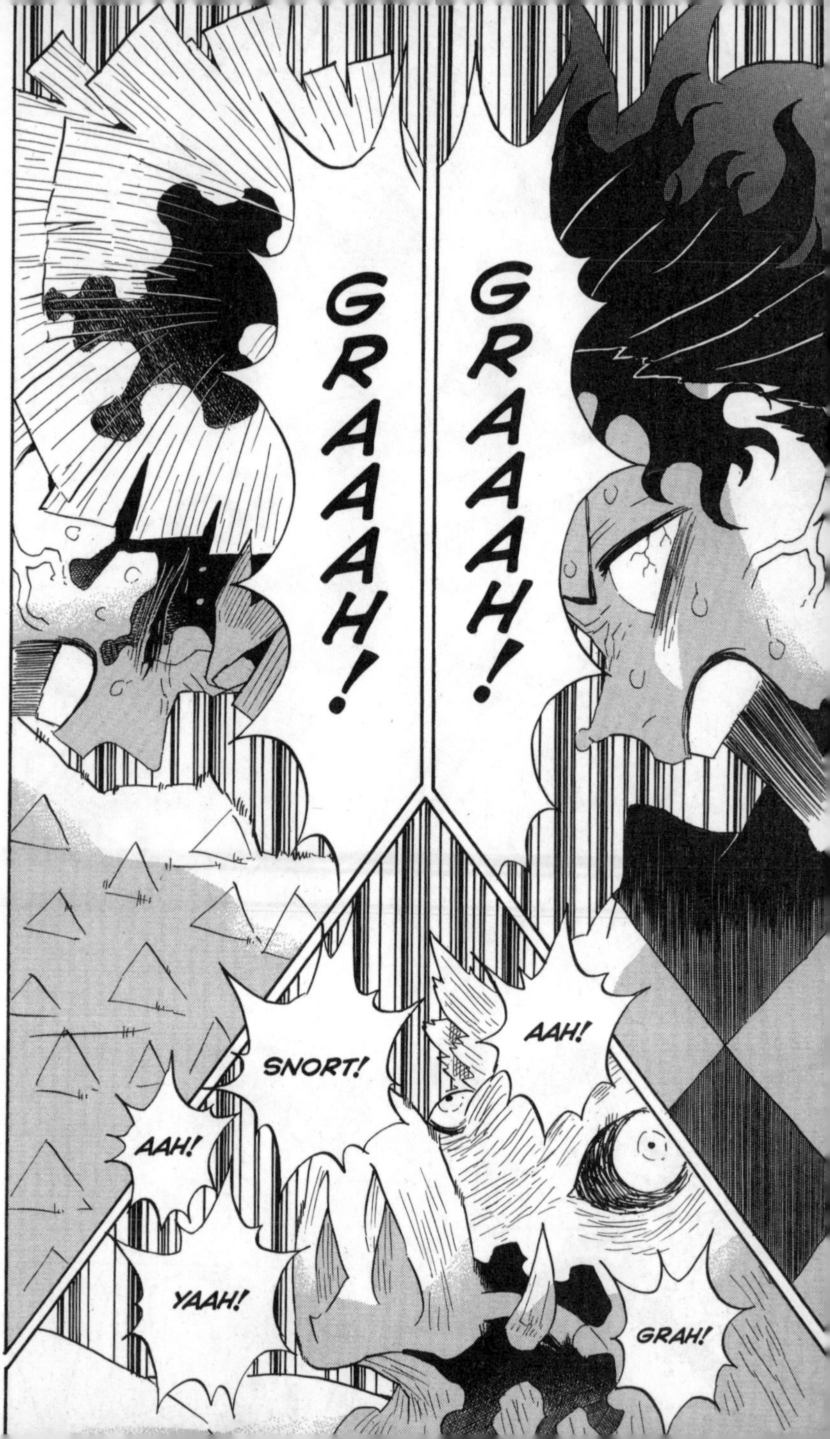
GRAAAAH!
GRAAAAH!
AAH!
SNORT!
AAH!
YAAH!
GRAH!

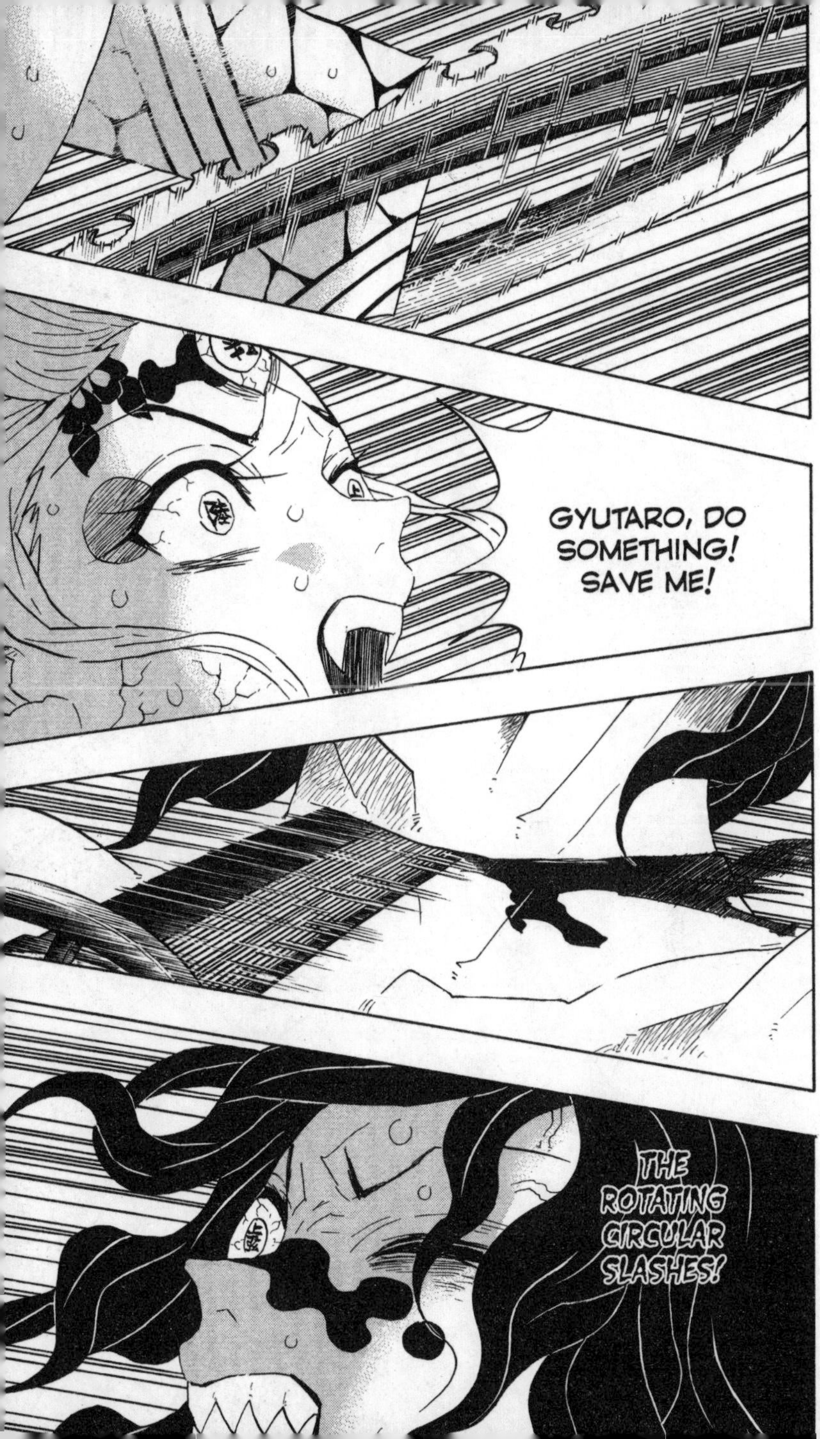
GYUTARO, DO SOMETHING! SAVE ME!
THE ROTATING CIRCULAR SLASHES!

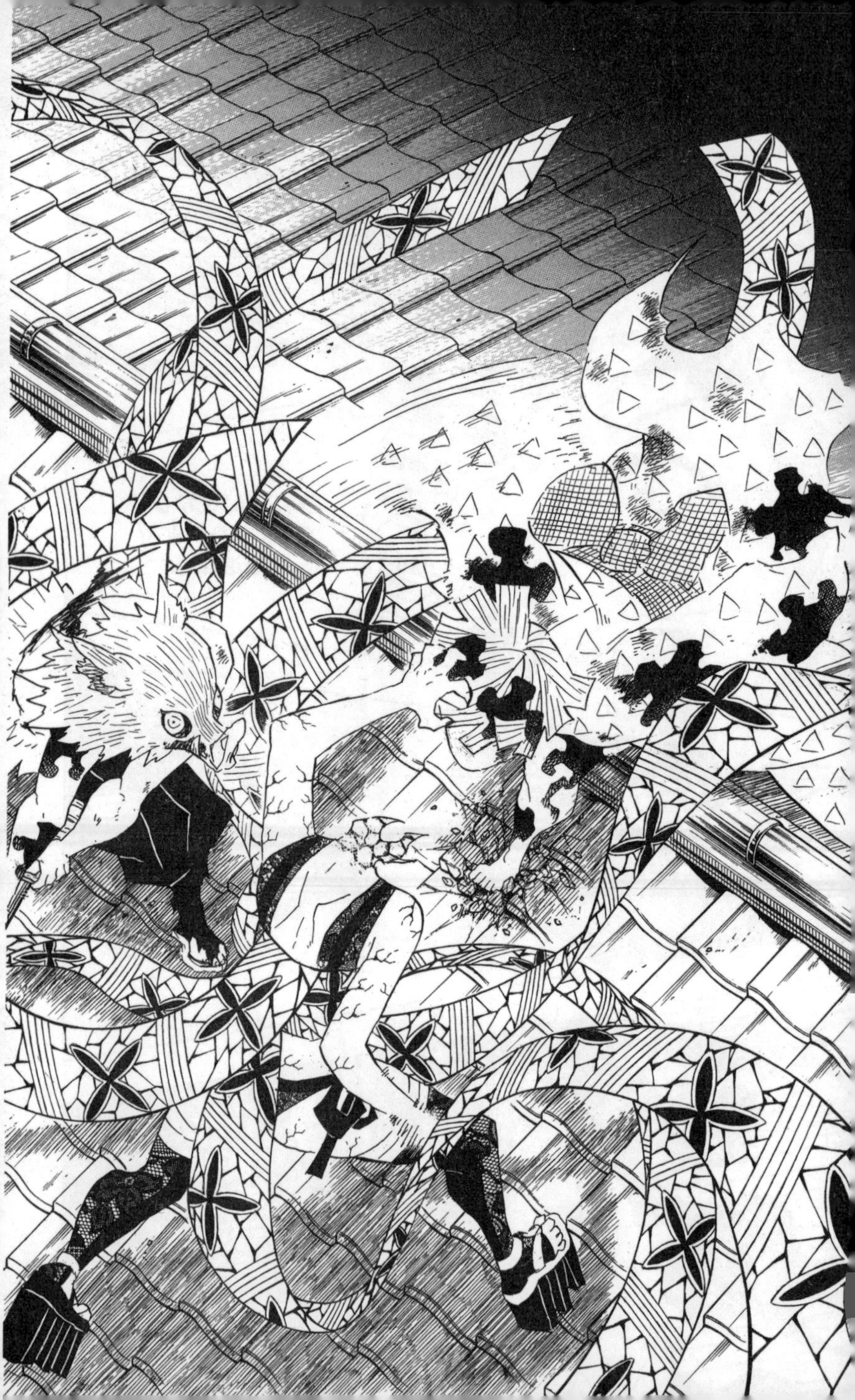

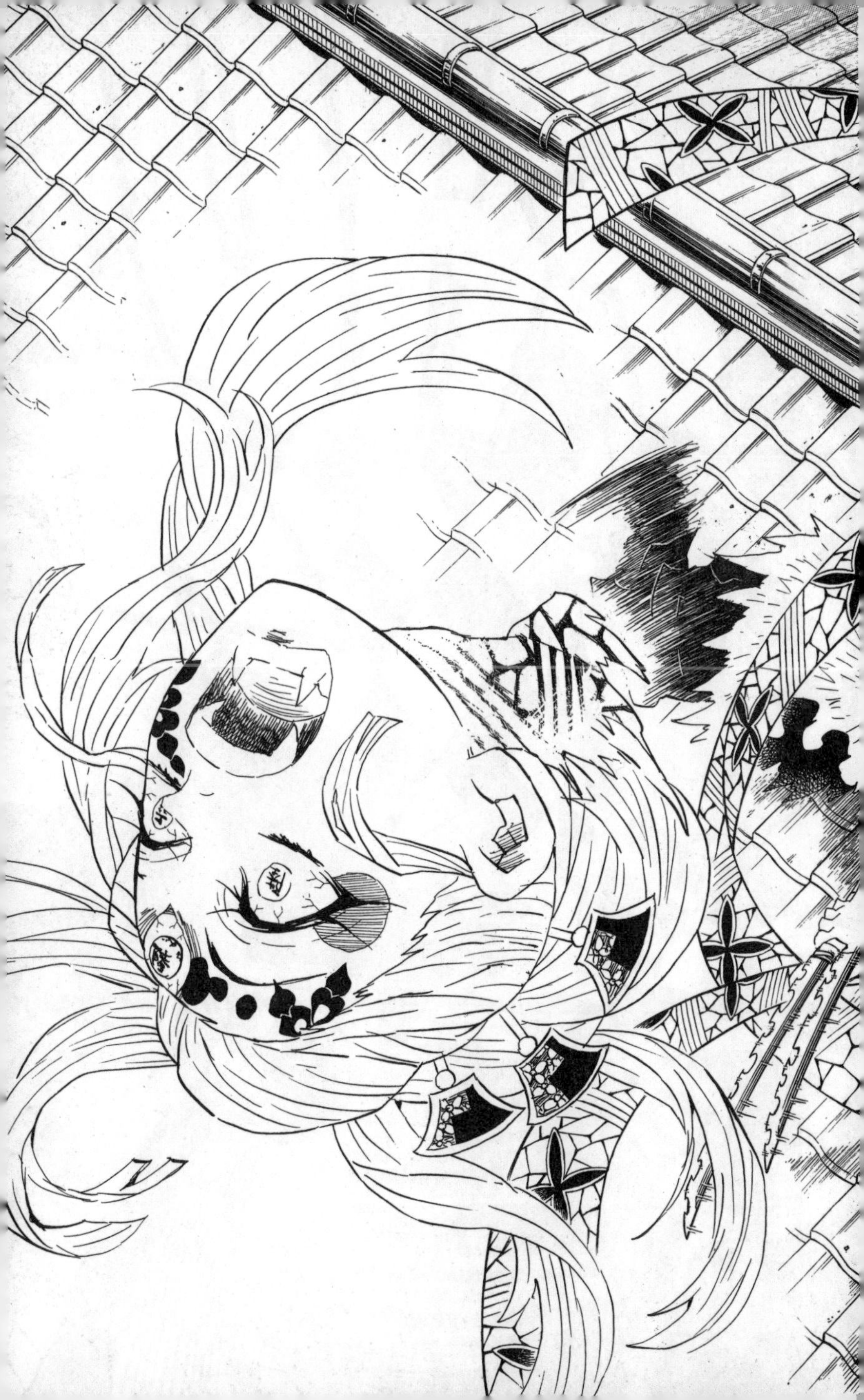

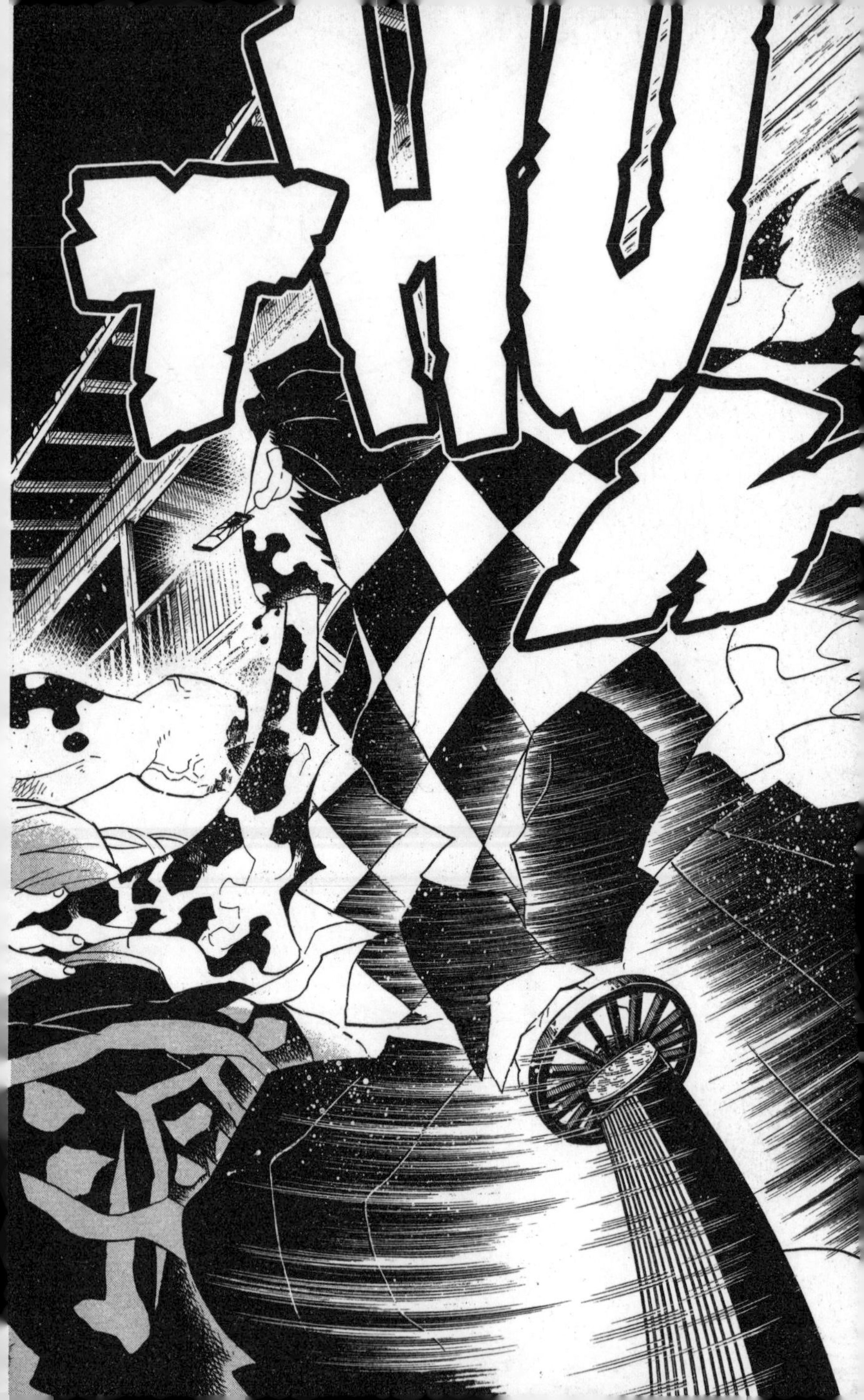
THU

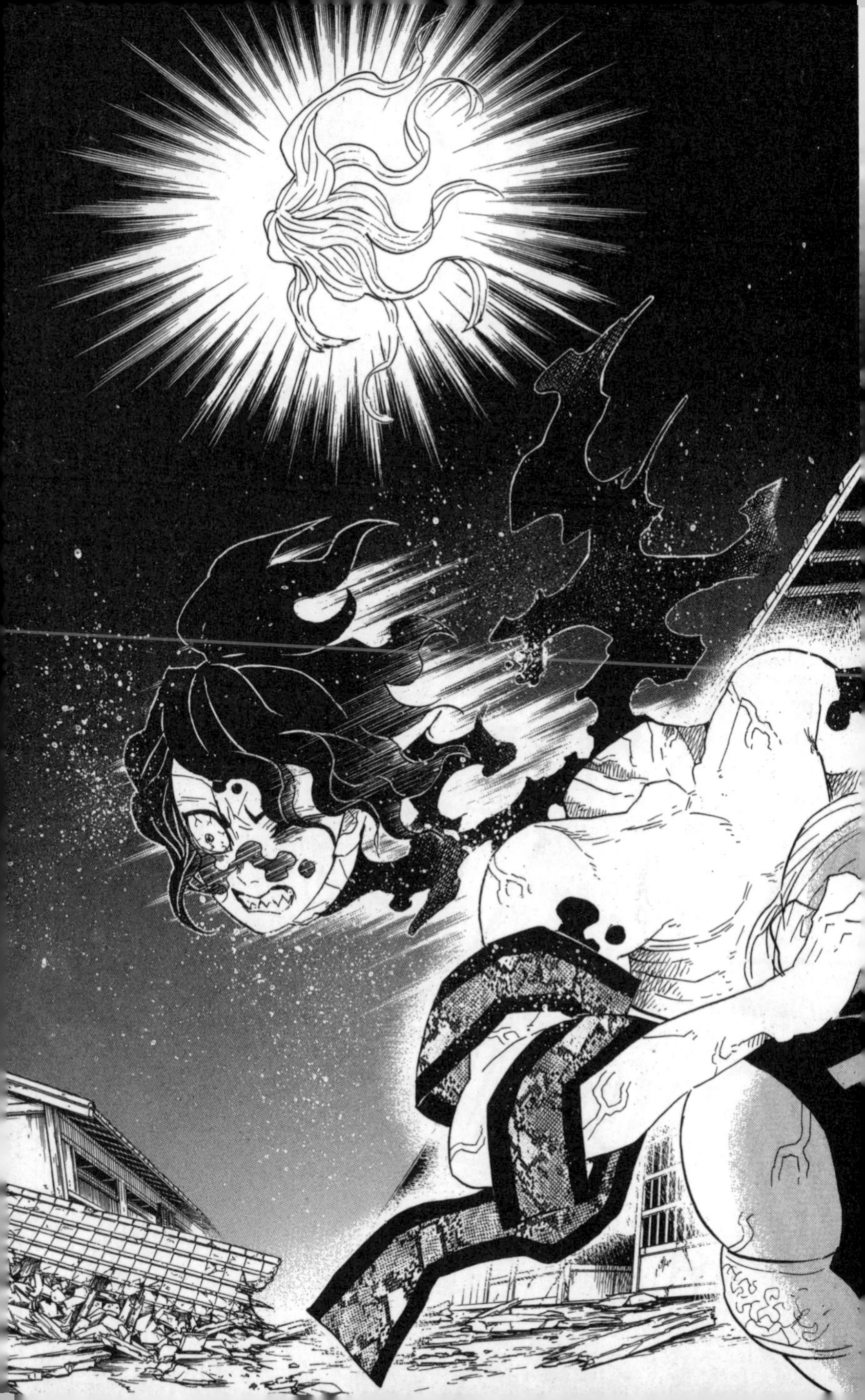

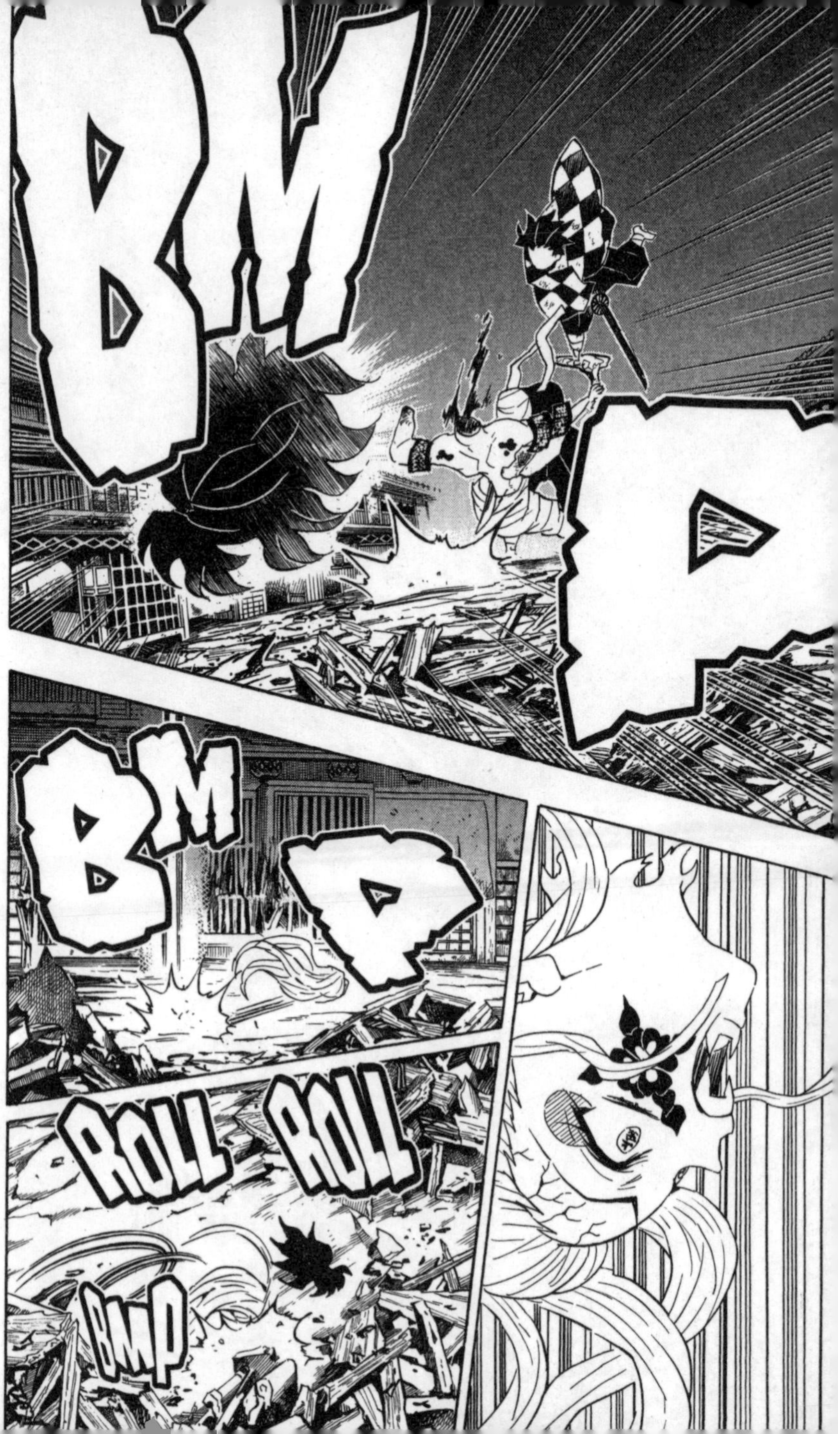
BMP
BMP
ROLL ROLL
BMP

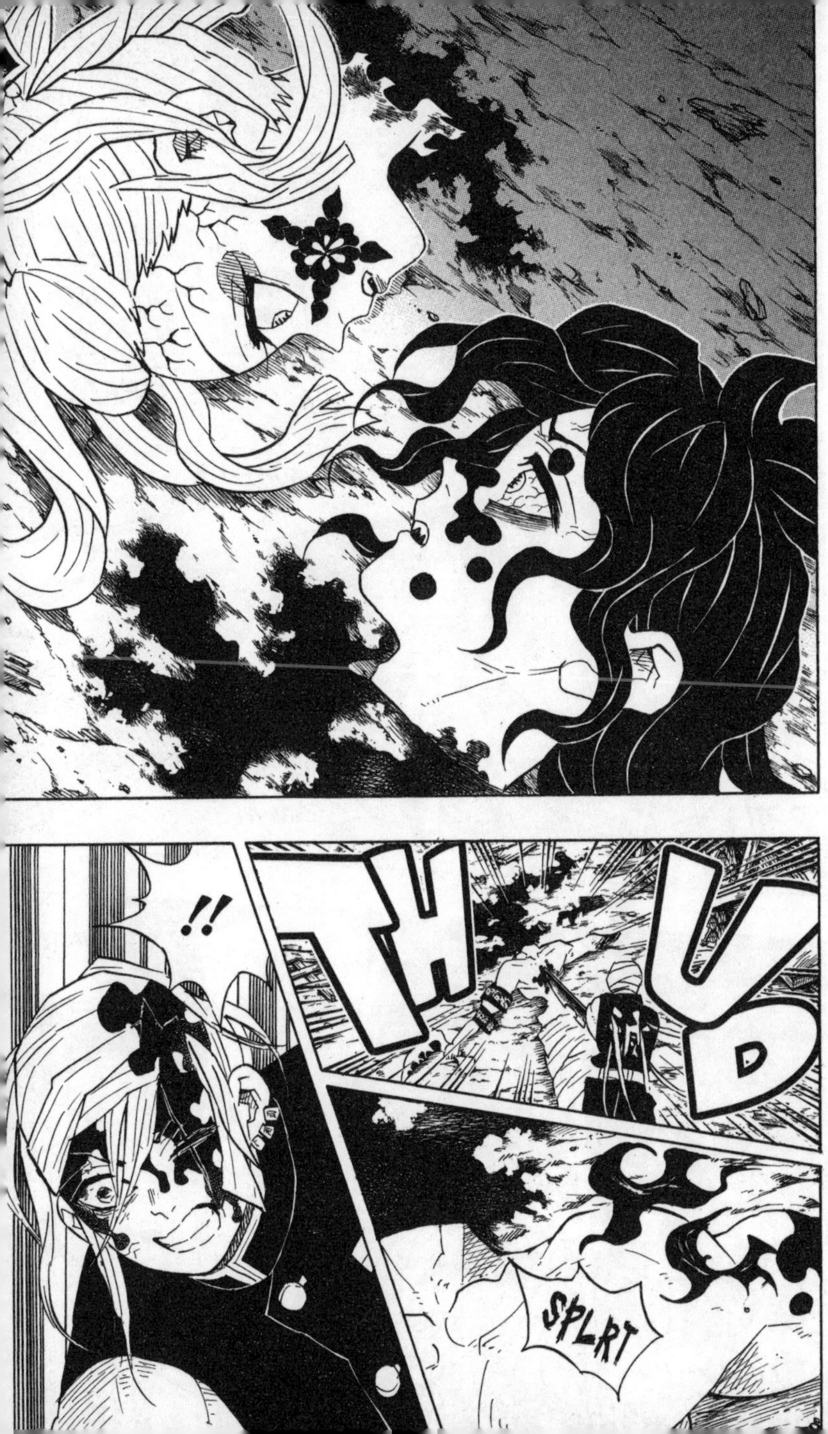
THUD
SPLRT
!!

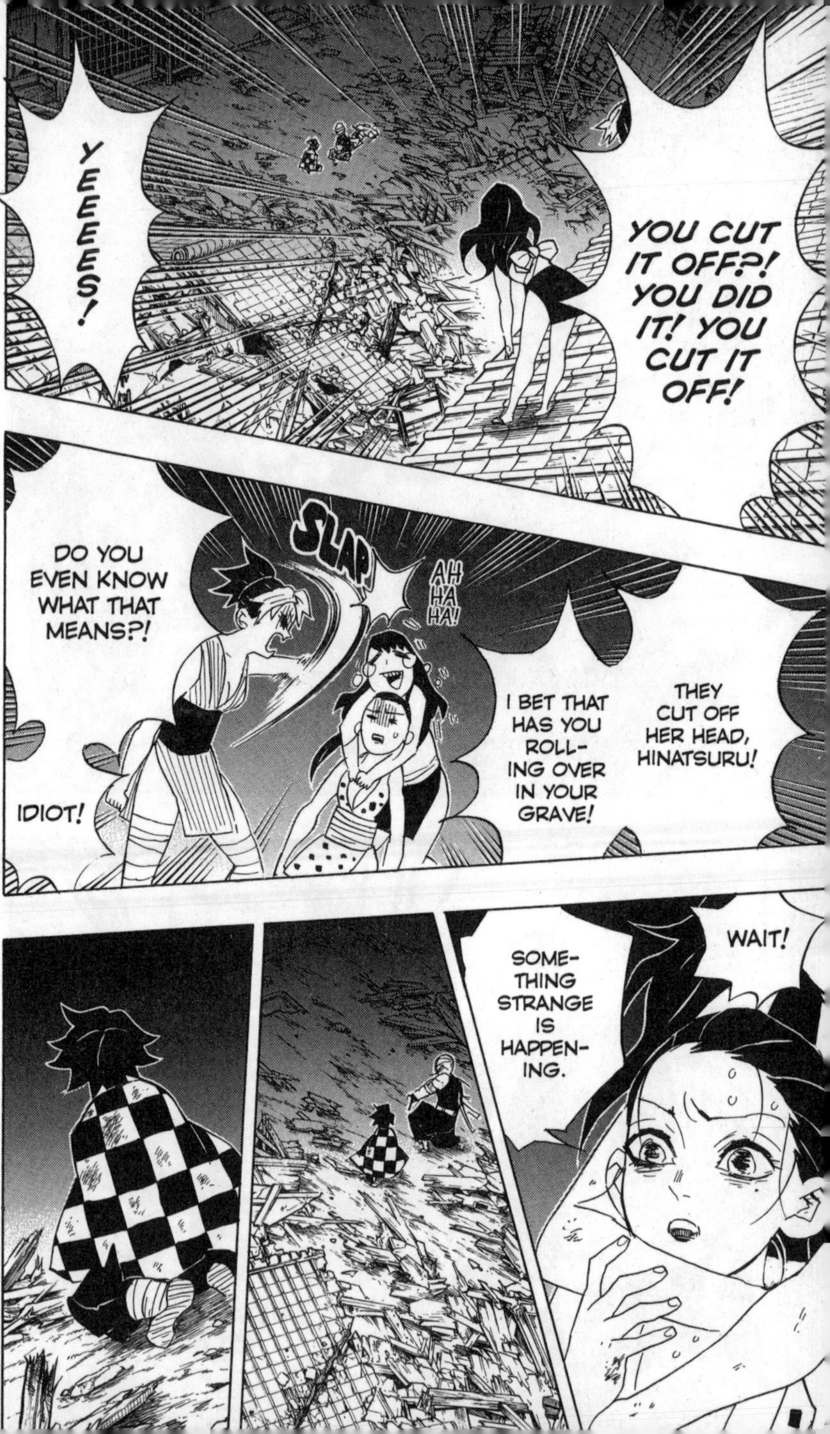
YOU CUT IT OFF?! YOU DID IT! YOU CUT IT OFF!
YEEEEES!
THEY CUT OFF HER HEAD, HINATSURU!
I BET THAT HAS YOU ROLLING OVER IN YOUR GRAVE!
AH HA HA!
SLAP
DO YOU EVEN KNOW WHAT THAT MEANS?!
IDIOT!
WAIT!
SOMETHING STRANGE IS HAPPENING.

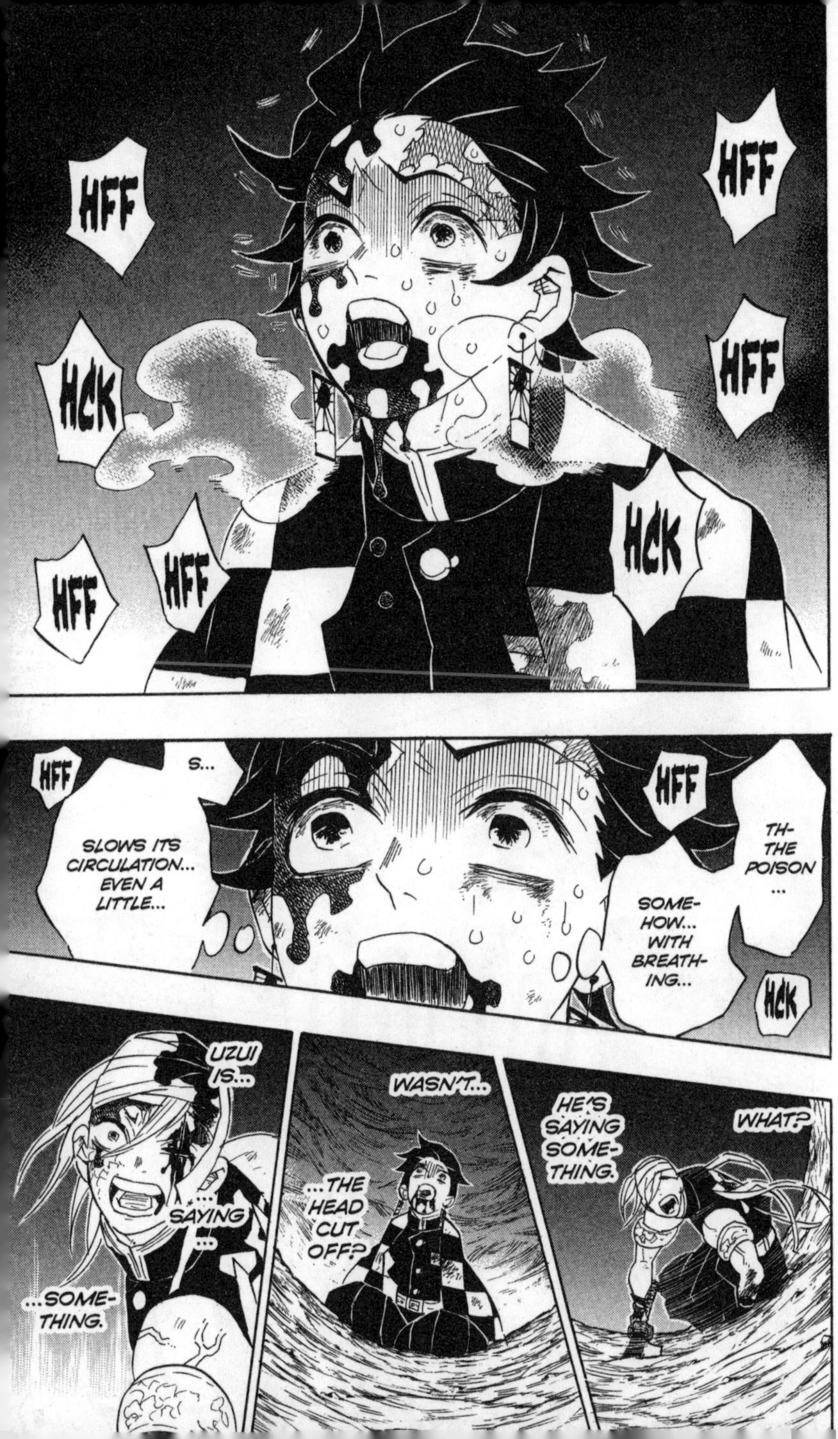
HFF
HFF
HCK
HFF
HCK
HFF
HFF
HFF
TH- THE POISON ...
SOME-HOW... WITH BREATH-ING...
HCK
HFF
S...
SLOWS ITS CIRCULATION... EVEN A LITTLE...
WHAT?
HE'S SAYING SOME-THING.
WASN'T...
...THE HEAD CUT OFF?
UZUI IS...
...SAYING...
...SOME-THING.

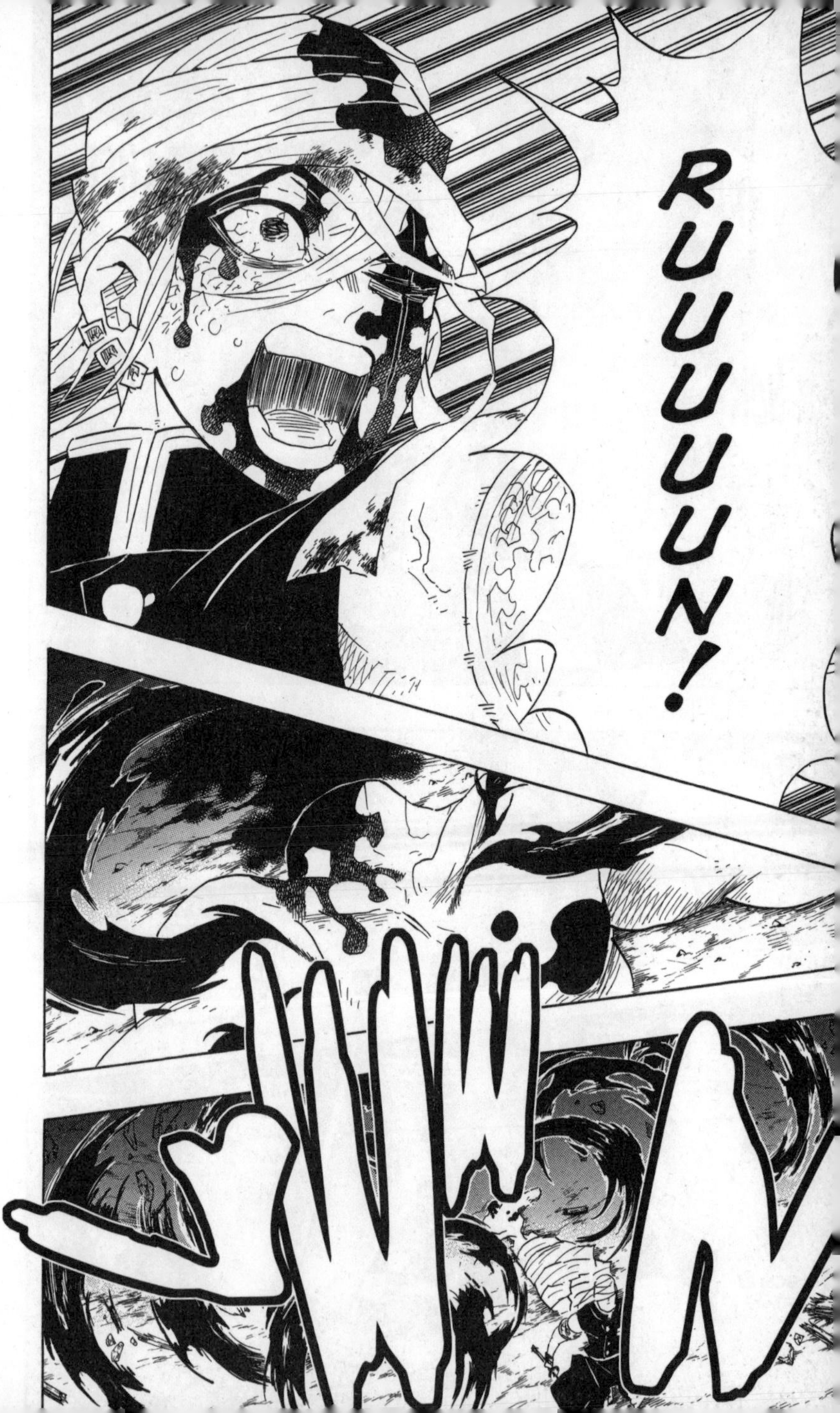
RUUUUUN!

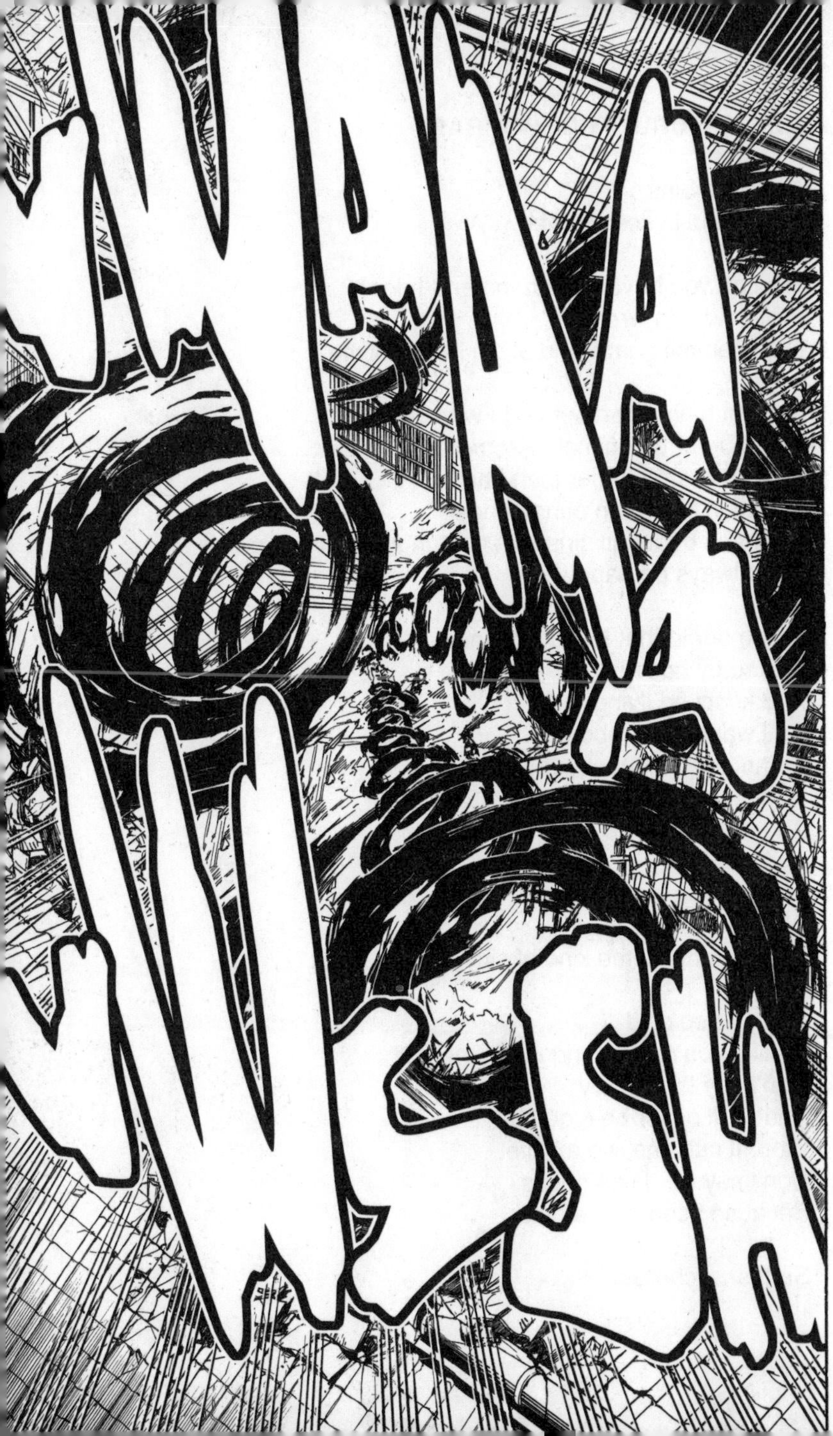

CHIC-N-SCRUFFY DEMOCRACY

Past Life Sins
Music and Lyrics: zenithu ☆ A

Why do you have a girlfriend and I don't?
What did I do wrong?
Did I commit some kind of sin in a past life?

It might have been better if I was born
As a bug or an animal or something.
If I was even dumber than I am
And didn't have an ounce pride
I'd chase beautiful girls with my tongue hanging out
And always be happy.

I'm so dumb that I'm totally fine.
Kicked by hooves
And knocked flying.
So I want to be reborn.
An animal is fine, or even a bug.
I want to touch a girl
And really be able to smell her.

Why do you have a girlfriend and I don't?
What did I do wrong?
Did I commit some kind of sin in a past life?

Don't be so cold.
It's like you're shooting me in the gut.
Don't say I'm creepy
And we'll never be together.
Stop. It cuts me like a knife.
Don't say it… I can guess.
Because I can take a hint.

Siiiiins… (chorus)

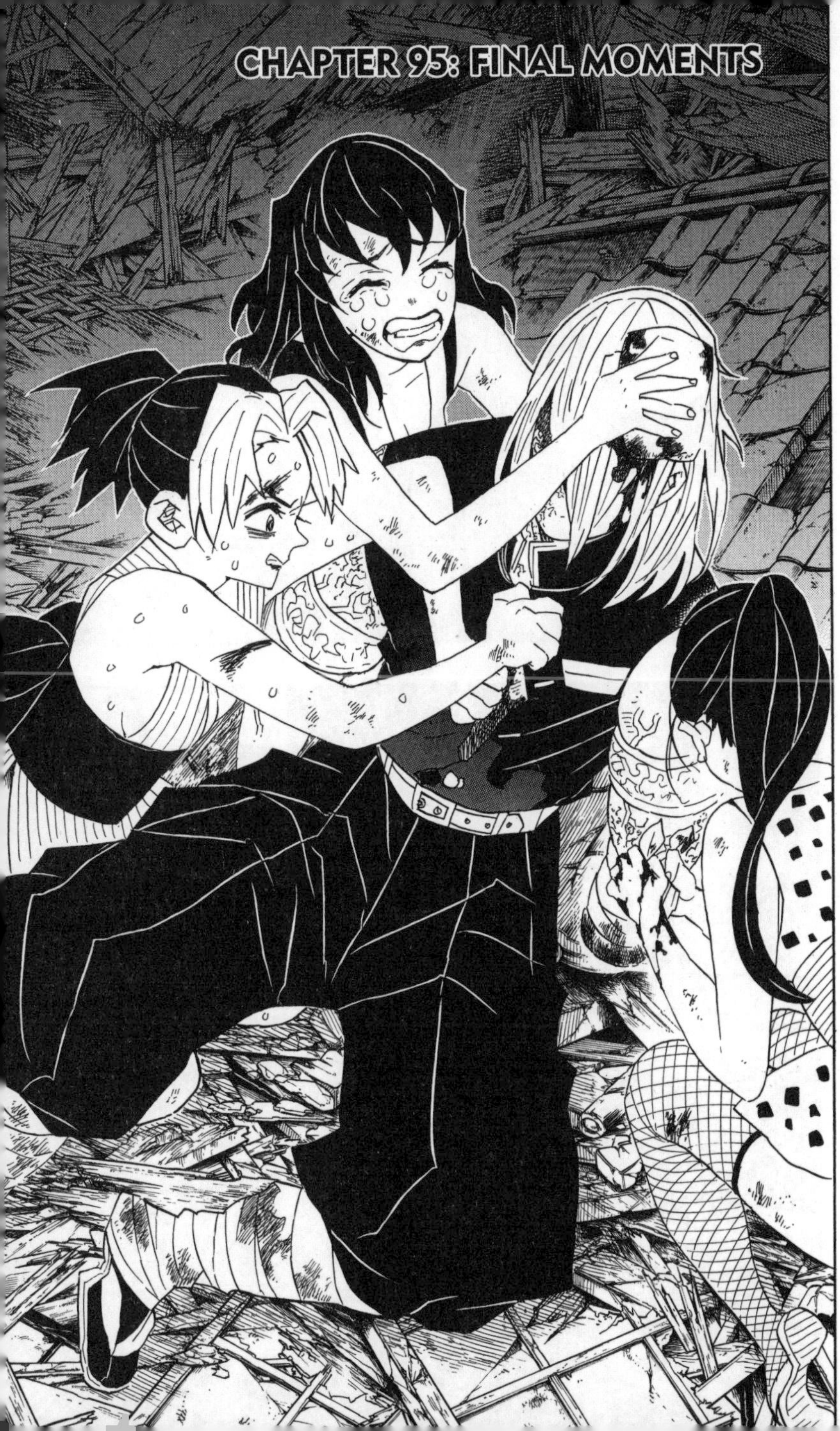
CHAPTER 95: FINAL MOMENTS

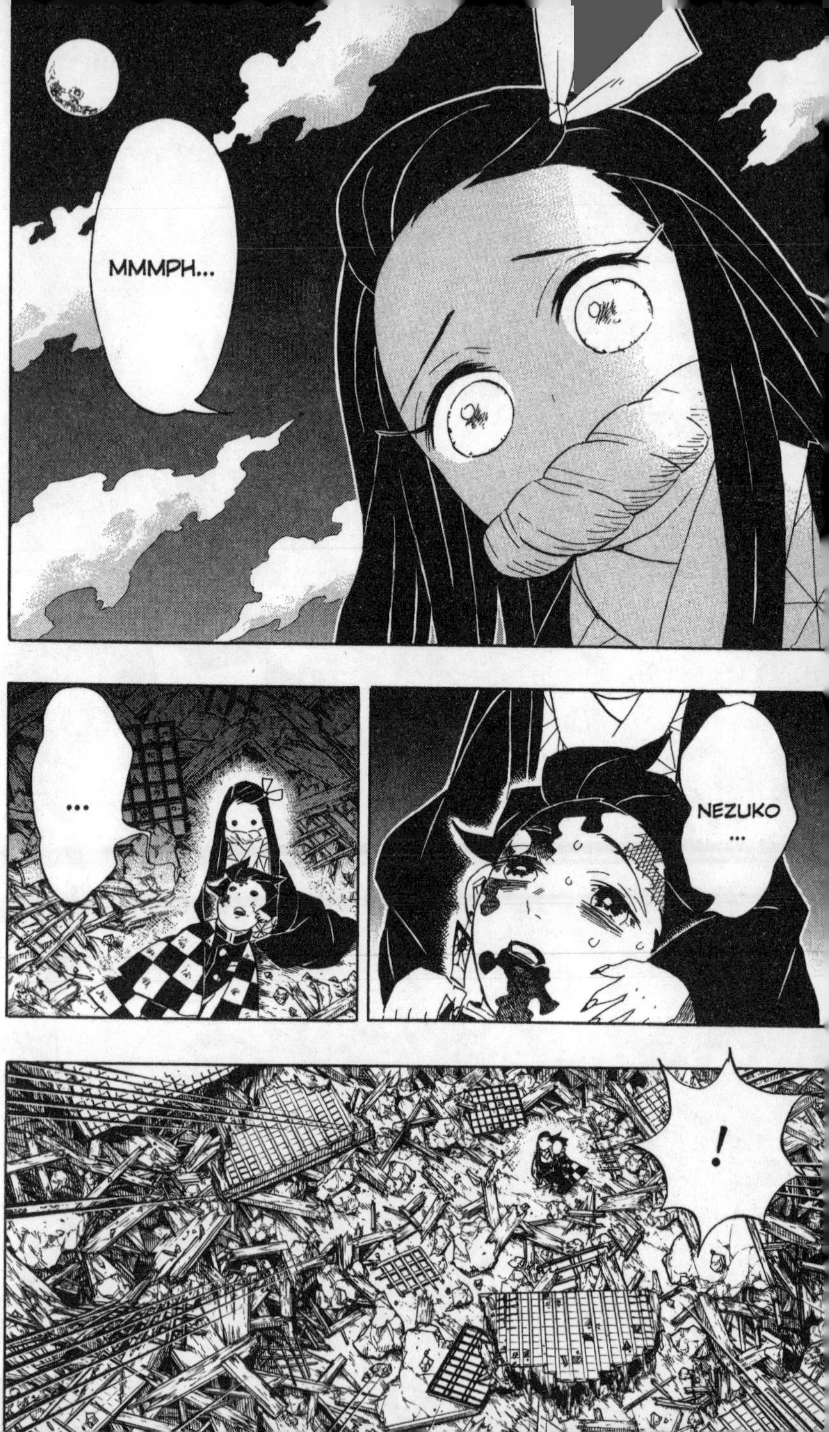
MMMPH...
NEZUKO ...
...
!

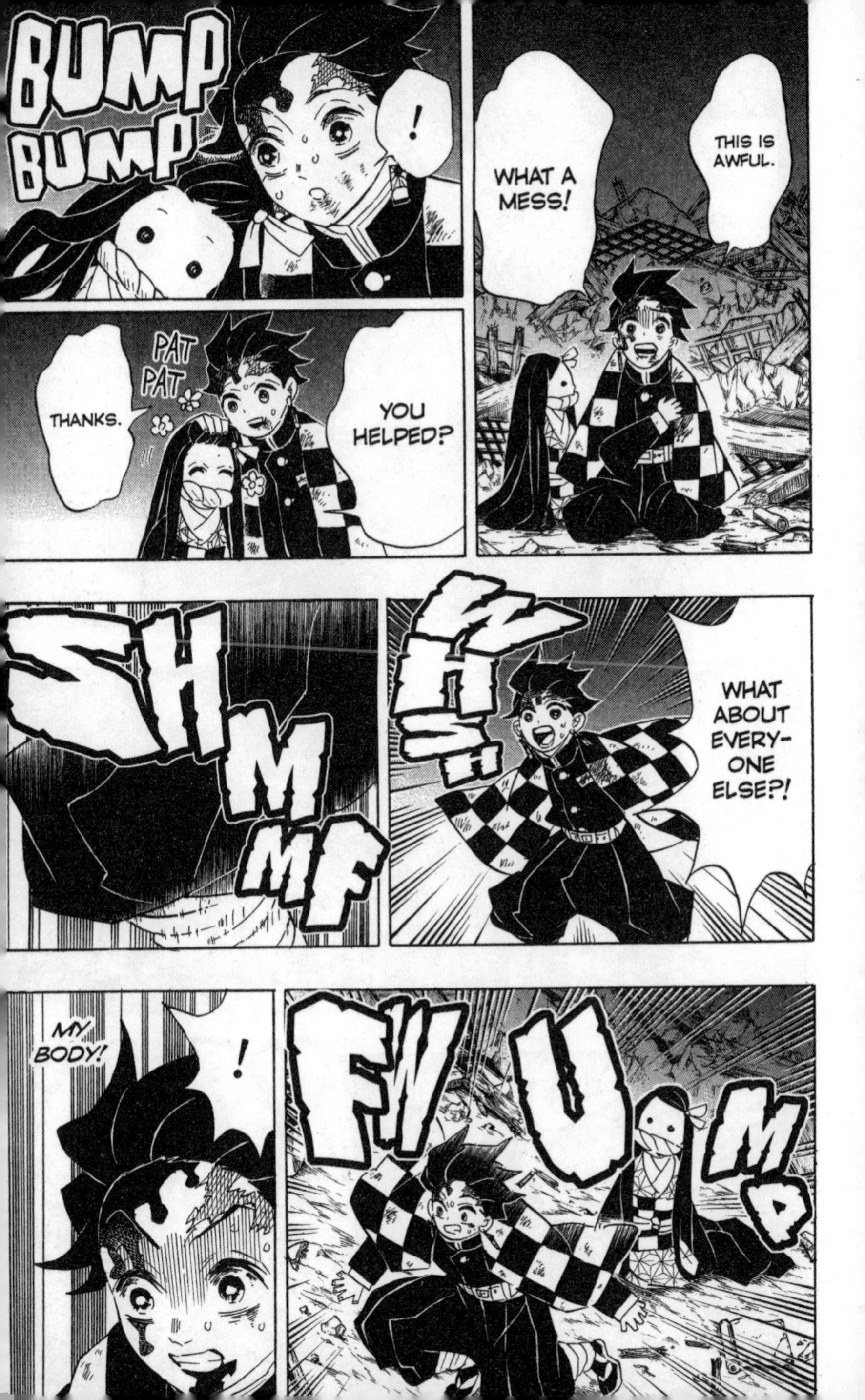
THIS IS AWFUL.
WHAT A MESS!
BUMP BUMP
!
YOU HELPED?
PAT PAT
THANKS.
WHAT ABOUT EVERY-ONE ELSE?!
SHMMF
FWUMP
!
MY BODY!

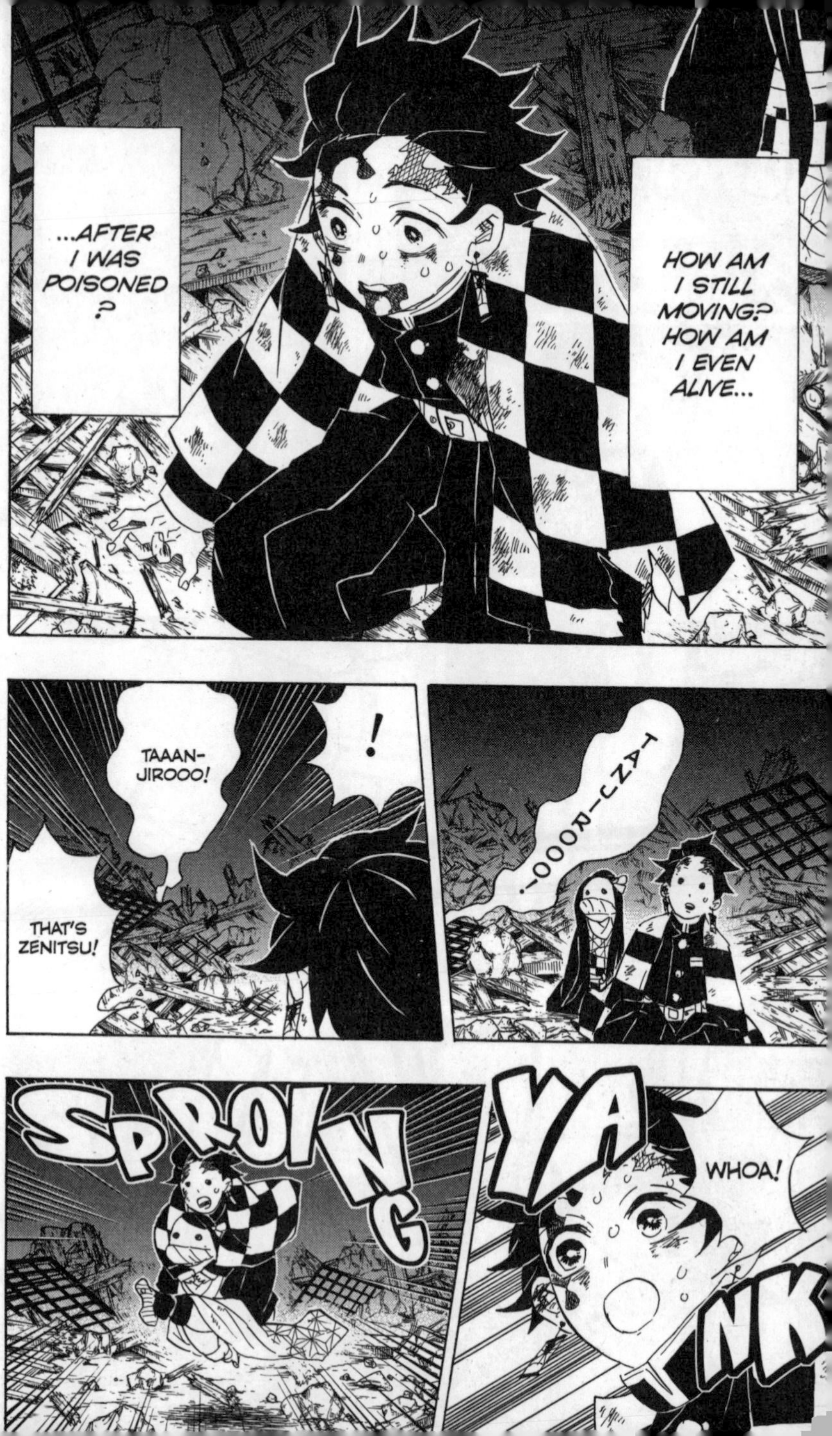
HOW AM I STILL MOVING? HOW AM I EVEN ALIVE...
...AFTER I WAS POISONED?
TANJI-ROOO...
!
TAAAN-JIROOO!
THAT'S ZENITSU!
YANK
WHOA!
SPROING

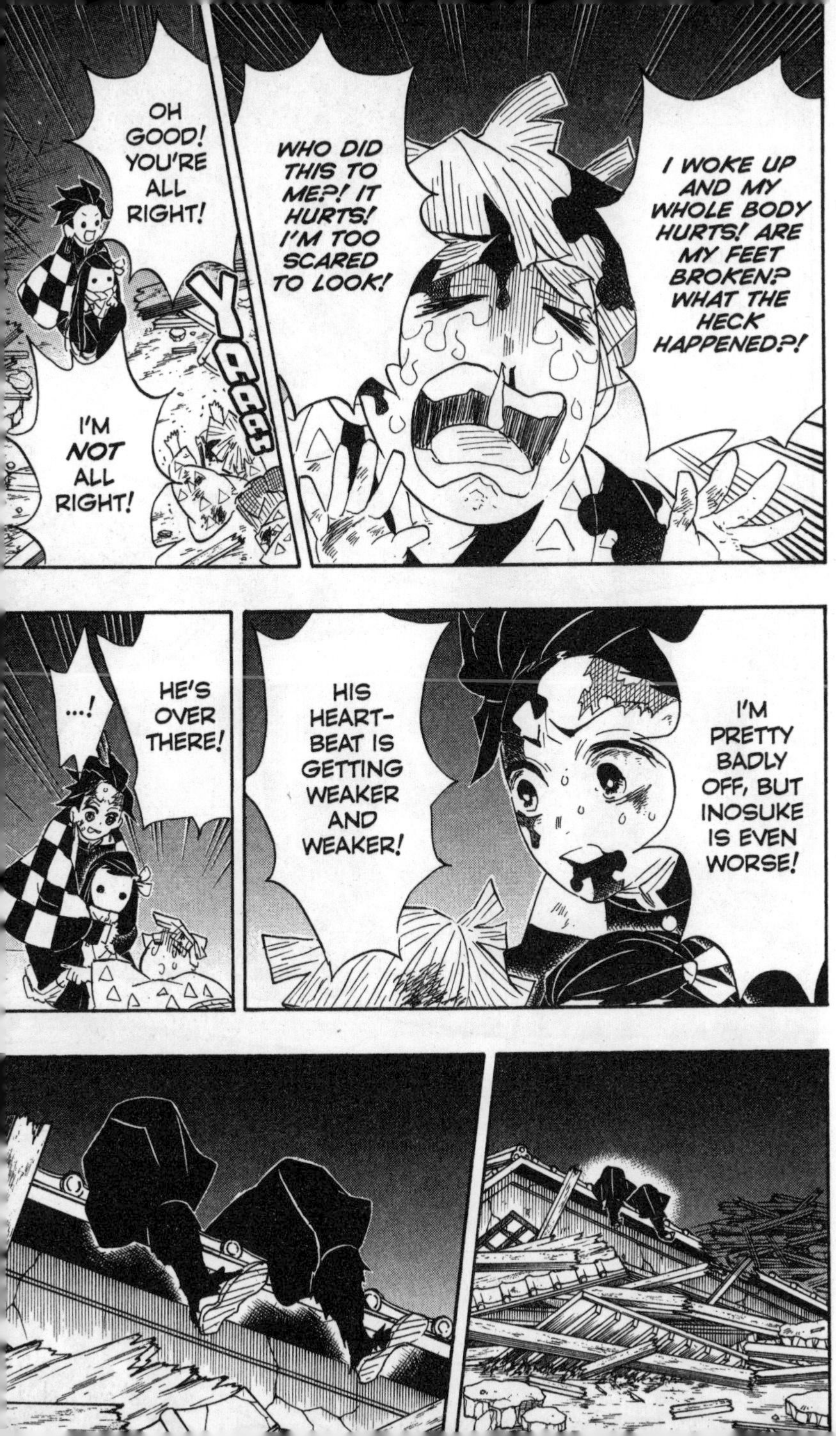
I WOKE UP AND MY WHOLE BODY HURTS! ARE MY FEET BROKEN? WHAT THE HECK HAPPENED?!
WHO DID THIS TO ME?! IT HURTS! I'M TOO SCARED TO LOOK!
OH GOOD! YOU'RE ALL RIGHT!
I'M *NOT* ALL RIGHT!
I'M PRETTY BADLY OFF, BUT INOSUKE IS EVEN WORSE!
HIS HEART-BEAT IS GETTING WEAKER AND WEAKER!
HE'S OVER THERE!
...!

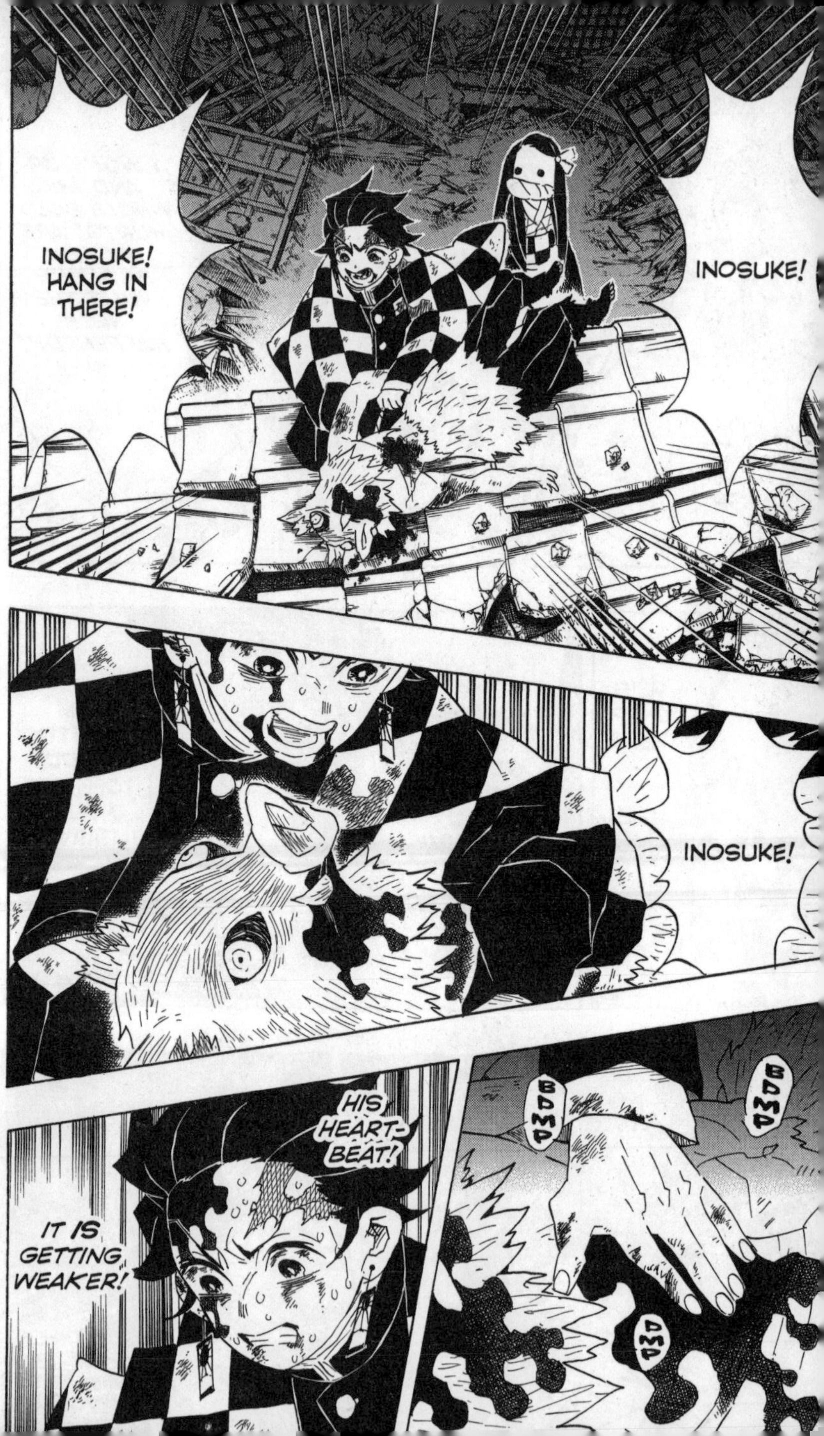
INOSUKE!
INOSUKE! HANG IN THERE!
INOSUKE!
BDMP
BDMP
DMP
HIS HEART-BEAT!
IT IS GETTING WEAKER!

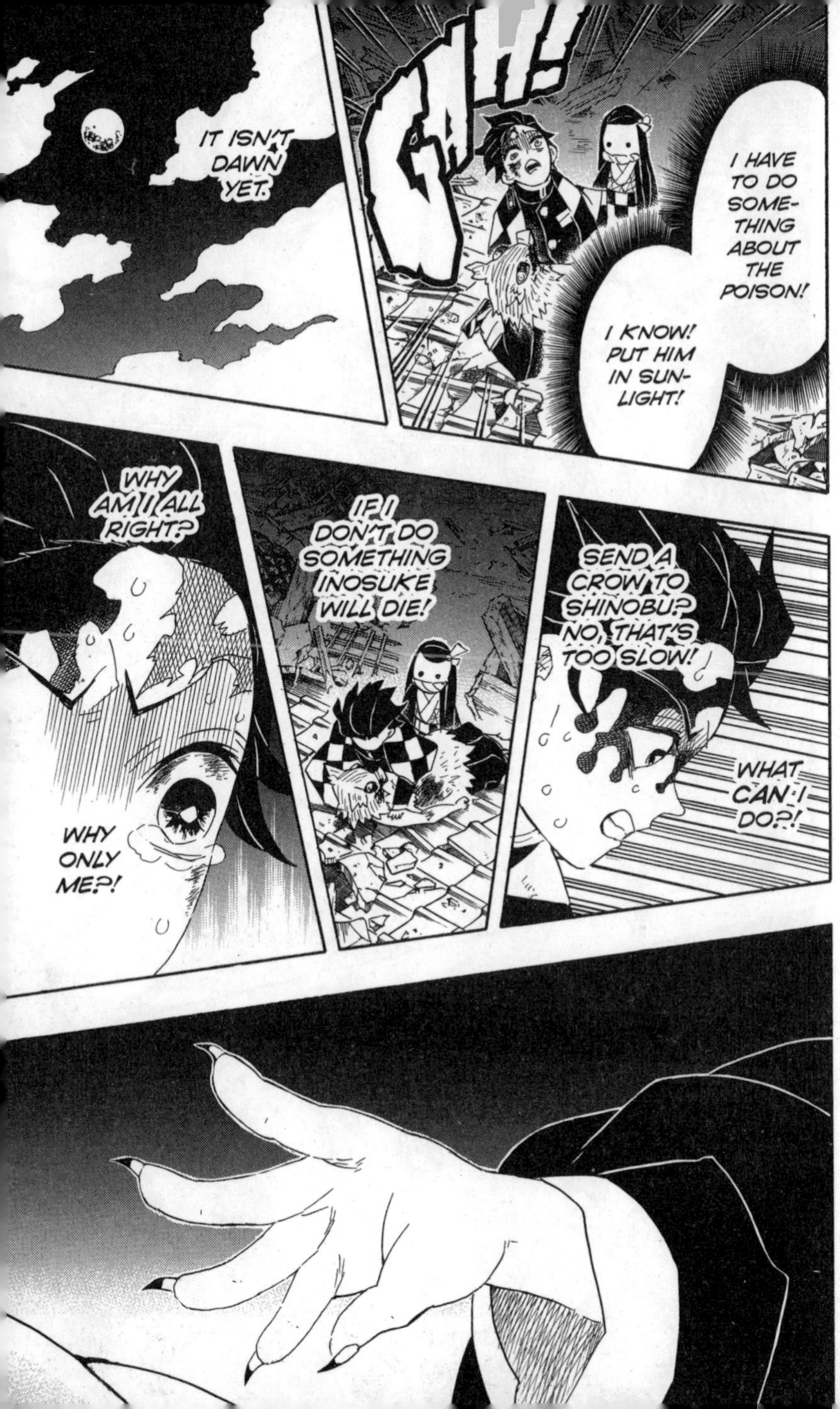
GAH!
I HAVE TO DO SOMETHING ABOUT THE POISON!
I KNOW! PUT HIM IN SUNLIGHT!
IT ISN'T DAWN YET.
SEND A CROW TO SHINOBU? NO, THAT'S TOO SLOW!
WHAT CAN I DO?!
IF I DON'T DO SOMETHING INOSUKE WILL DIE!
WHY AM I ALL RIGHT?
WHY ONLY ME?!

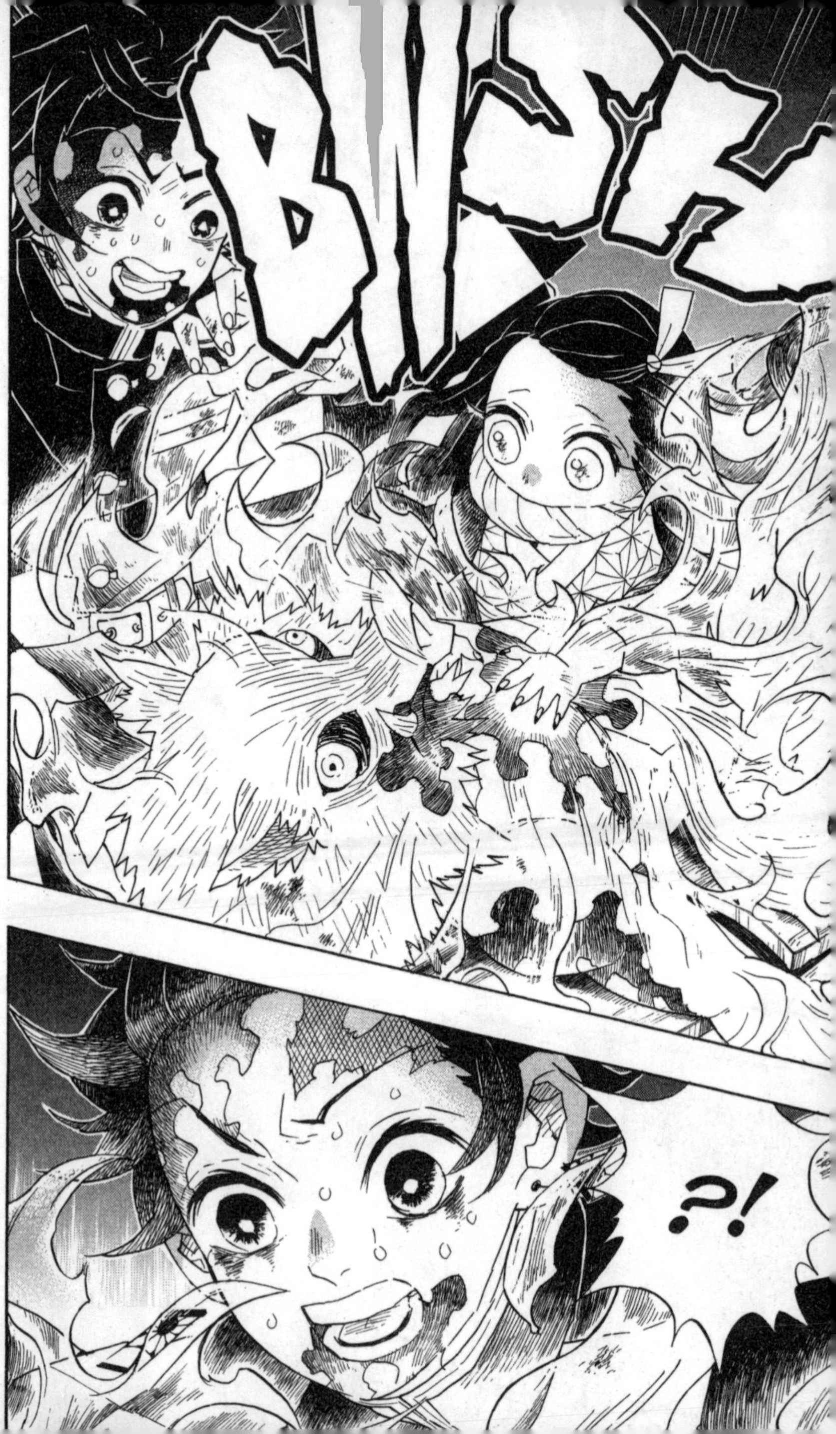
?!

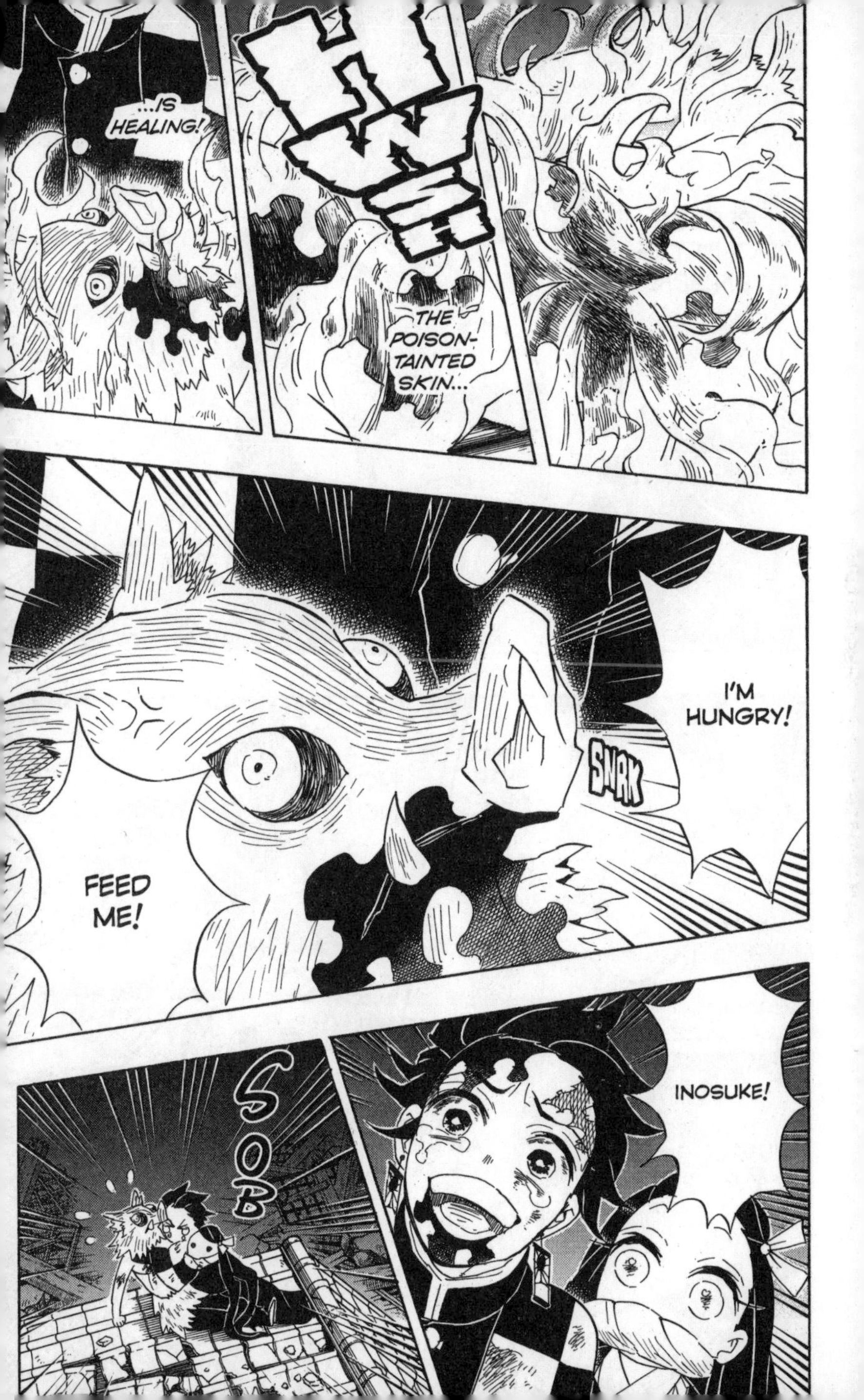
THE POISON-TAINTED SKIN...
...IS HEALING!
I'M HUNGRY!
SNAK
FEED ME!
INOSUKE!
SOB

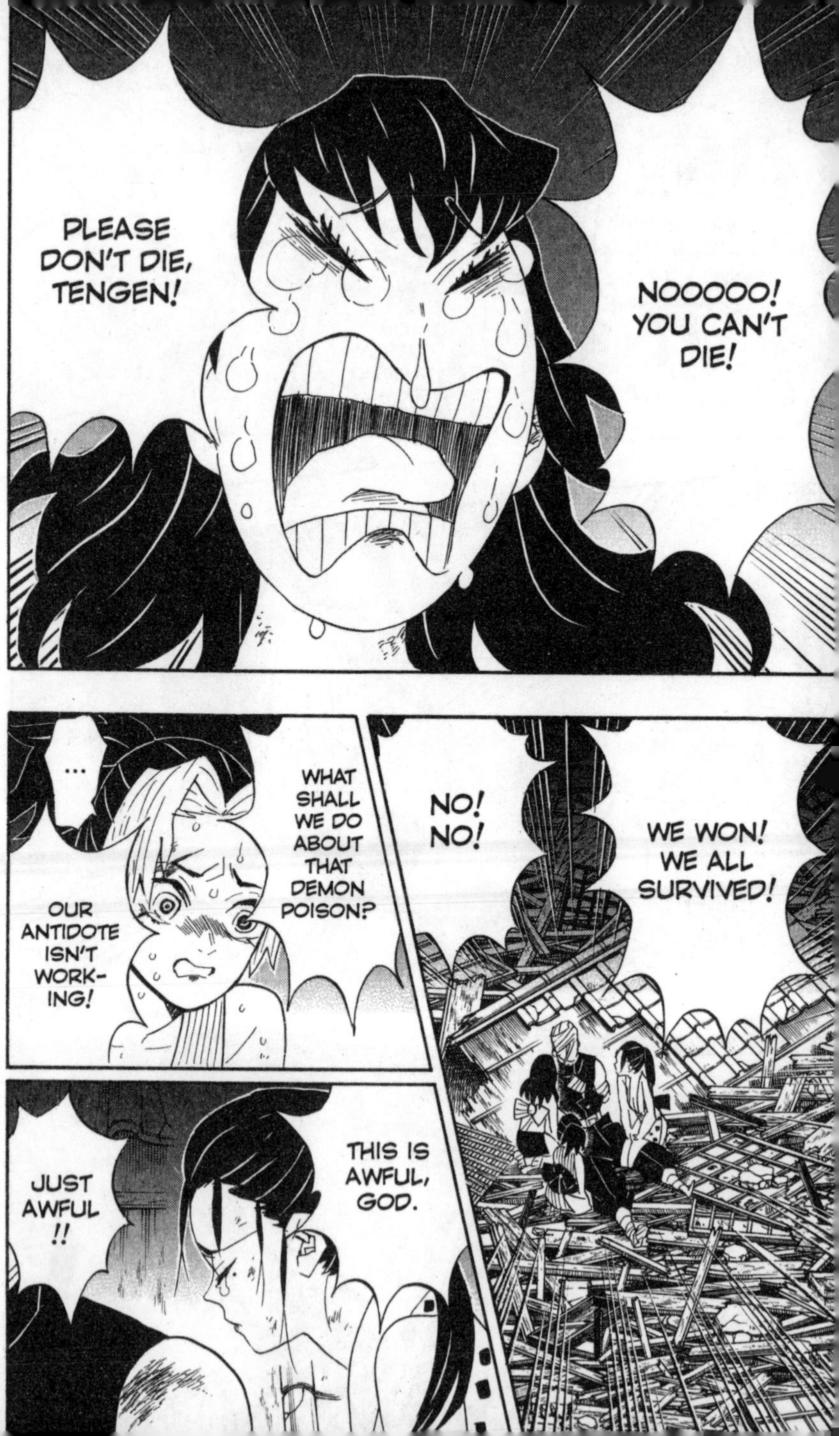
NOOOOO! YOU CAN'T DIE!
PLEASE DON'T DIE, TENGEN!
WE WON! WE ALL SURVIVED!
NO! NO!
WHAT SHALL WE DO ABOUT THAT DEMON POISON?
...
OUR ANTIDOTE ISN'T WORK-ING!
THIS IS AWFUL, GOD.
JUST AWFUL!!

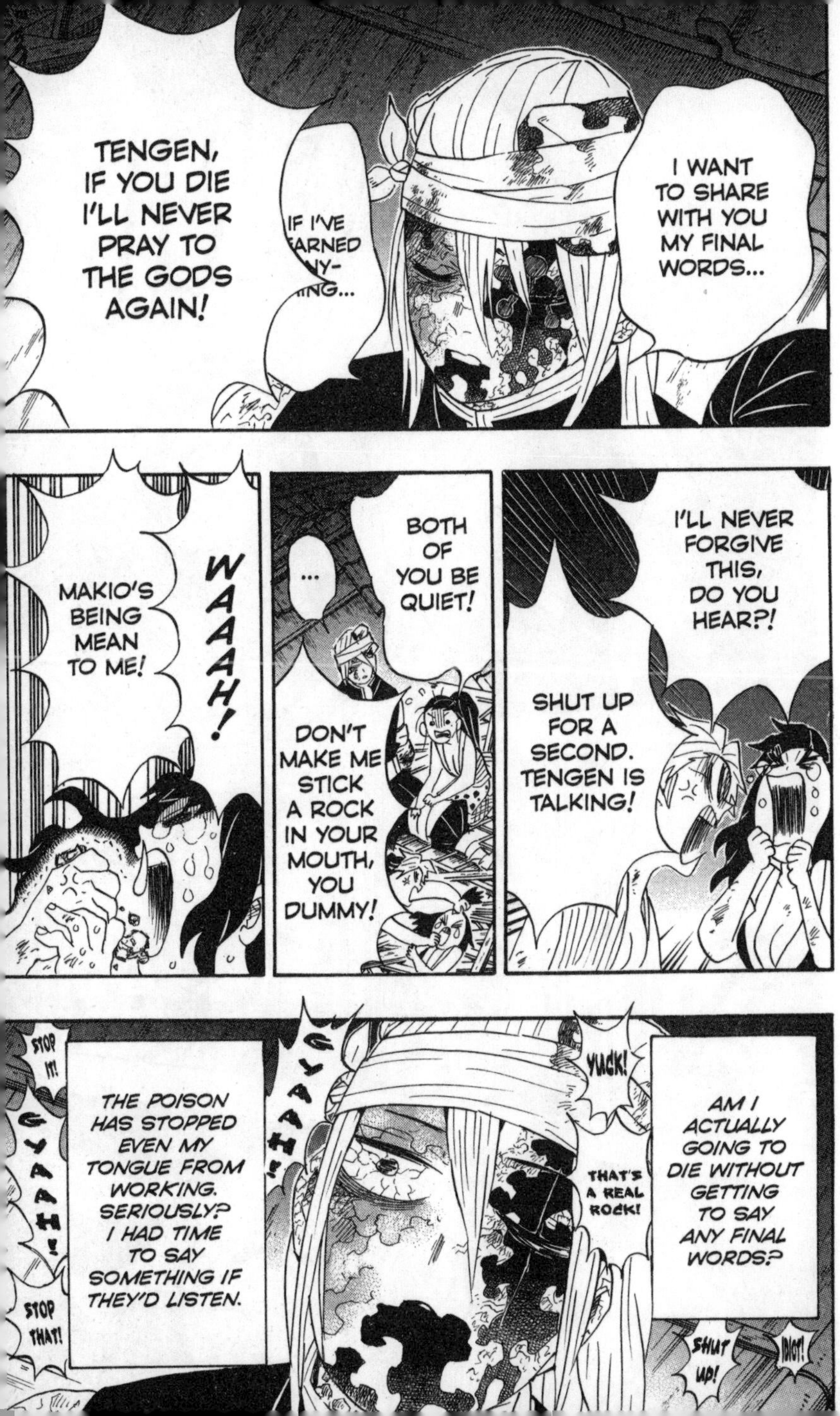
I WANT TO SHARE WITH YOU MY FINAL WORDS...
IF I'VE ARNED NY- ING...
TENGEN, IF YOU DIE I'LL NEVER PRAY TO THE GODS AGAIN!
I'LL NEVER FORGIVE THIS, DO YOU HEAR?!
SHUT UP FOR A SECOND. TENGEN IS TALKING!
BOTH OF YOU BE QUIET!
...
DON'T MAKE ME STICK A ROCK IN YOUR MOUTH, YOU DUMMY!
WAAAAH!
MAKIO'S BEING MEAN TO ME!
AM I ACTUALLY GOING TO DIE WITHOUT GETTING TO SAY ANY FINAL WORDS?
YUCK!
THAT'S A REAL ROCK!
IDIOT!
SHUT UP!
GYAAAH!
THE POISON HAS STOPPED EVEN MY TONGUE FROM WORKING. SERIOUSLY? I HAD TIME TO SAY SOMETHING IF THEY'D LISTEN.
STOP IT!
GYAAAH!
STOP THAT!

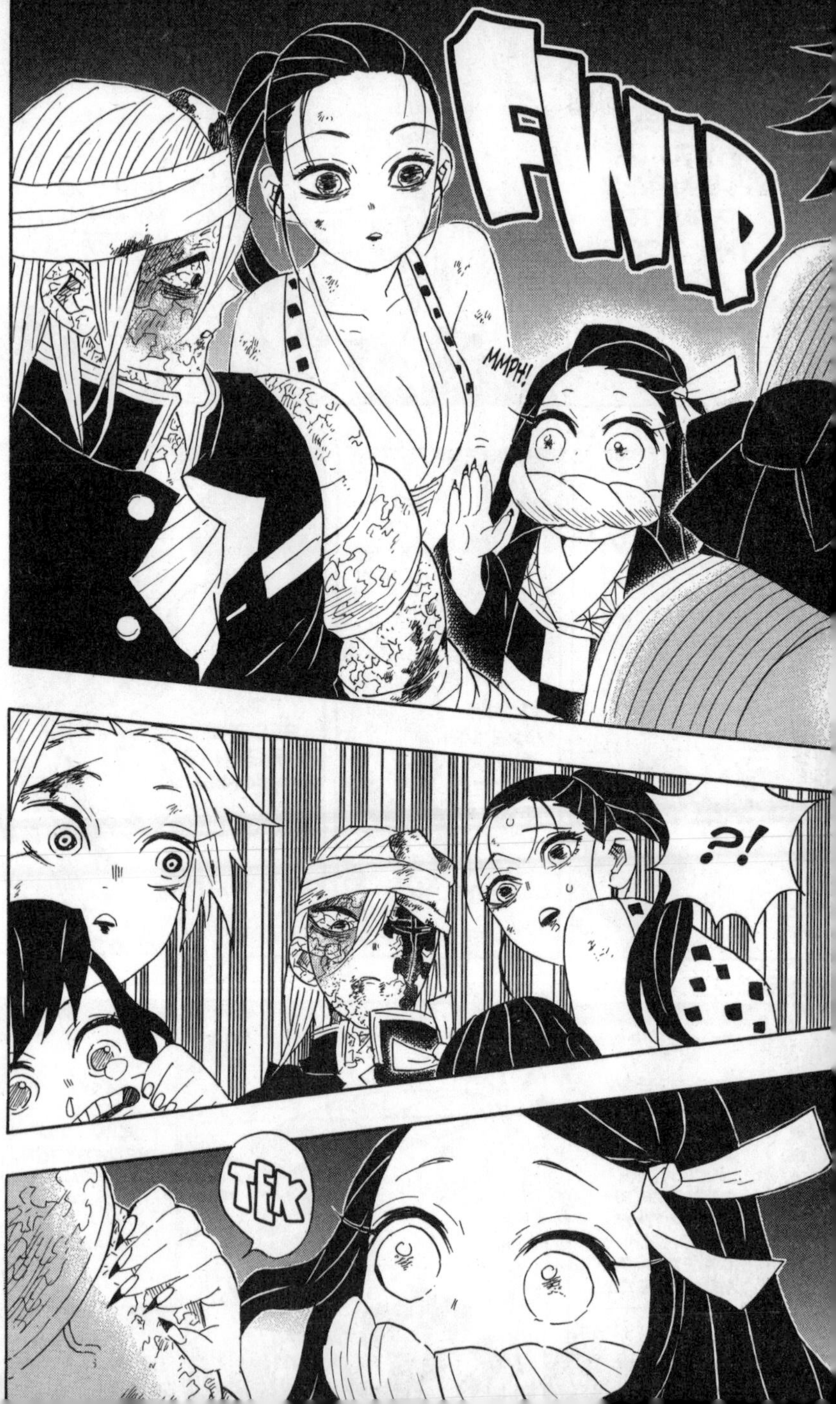
F-WIP
MMPH!
?!
TEK

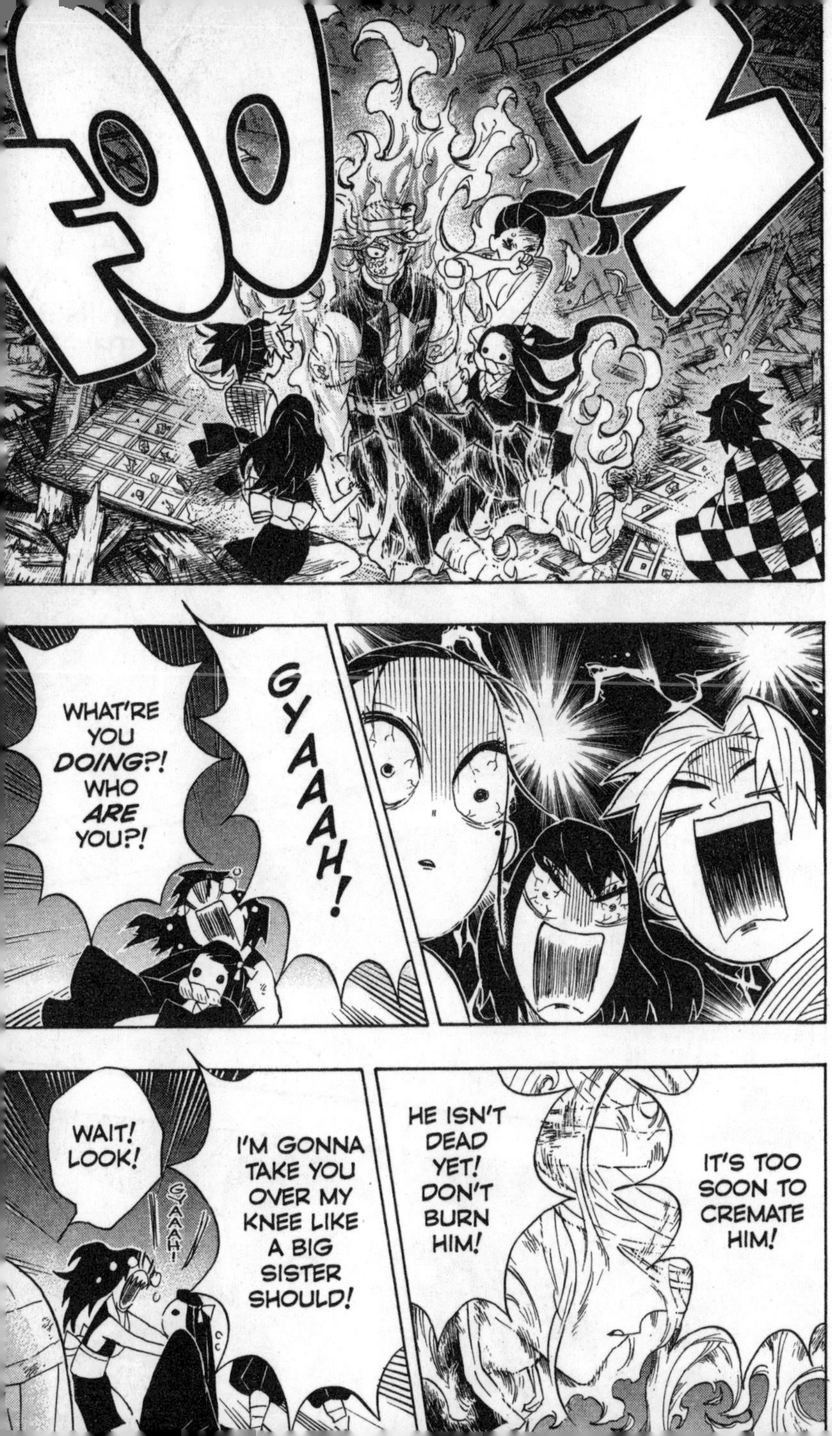
FOOM
GYAAAH!
WHAT'RE YOU *DOING*?! WHO *ARE* YOU?!
IT'S TOO SOON TO CREMATE HIM!
HE ISN'T DEAD YET! DON'T BURN HIM!
I'M GONNA TAKE YOU OVER MY KNEE LIKE A BIG SISTER SHOULD!
WAIT! LOOK!
GYAAAH!

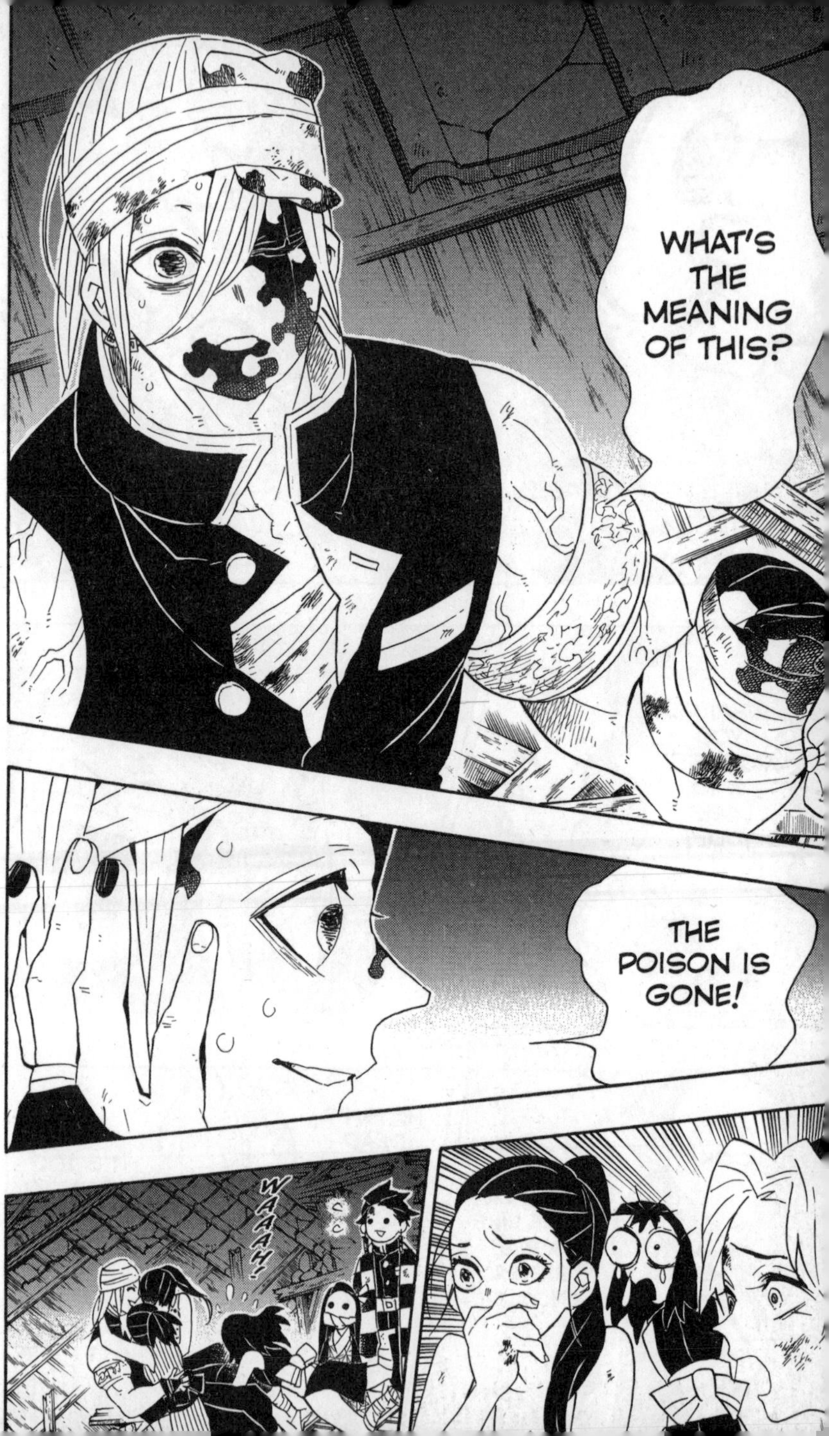
WHAT'S THE MEANING OF THIS?
THE POISON IS GONE!
WAAAAH!

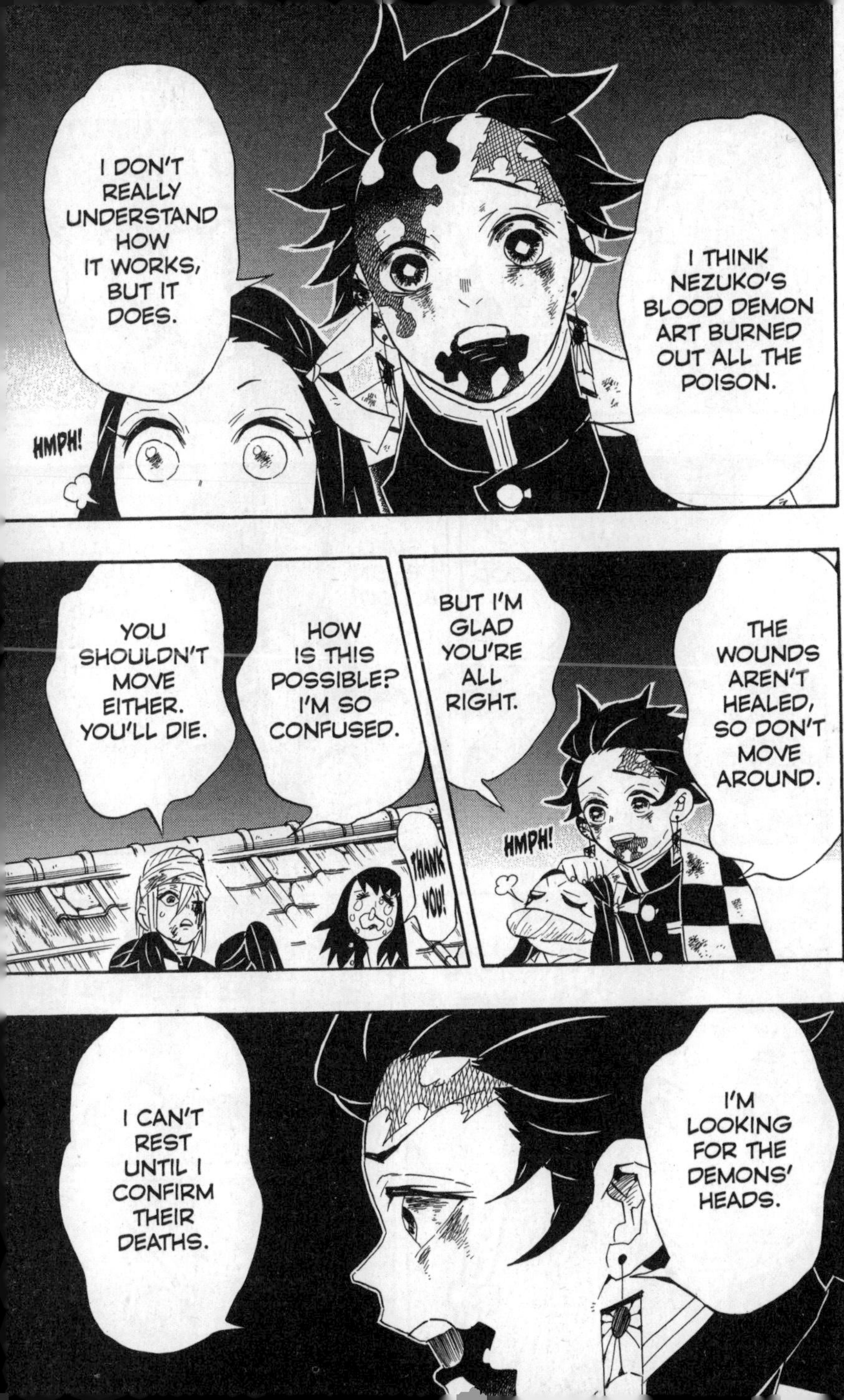
I THINK NEZUKO'S BLOOD DEMON ART BURNED OUT ALL THE POISON.
I DON'T REALLY UNDERSTAND HOW IT WORKS, BUT IT DOES.
HMPH!
THE WOUNDS AREN'T HEALED, SO DON'T MOVE AROUND.
BUT I'M GLAD YOU'RE ALL RIGHT.
HMPH!
HOW IS THIS POSSIBLE? I'M SO CONFUSED.
YOU SHOULDN'T MOVE EITHER. YOU'LL DIE.
THANK YOU!
I'M LOOKING FOR THE DEMONS' HEADS.
I CAN'T REST UNTIL I CONFIRM THEIR DEATHS.

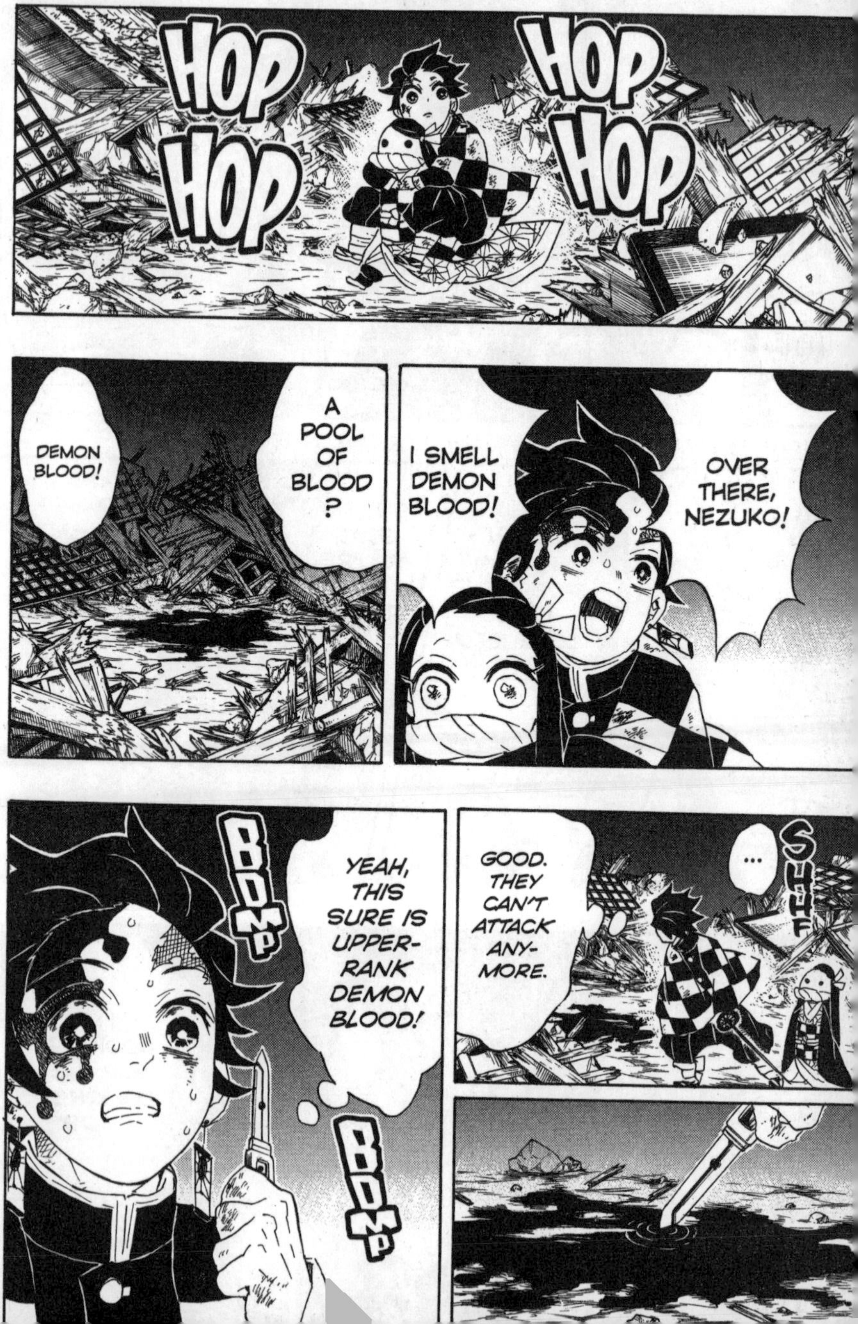
HOP HOP
HOP HOP
OVER THERE, NEZUKO!
I SMELL DEMON BLOOD!
A POOL OF BLOOD?
DEMON BLOOD!
SHHF
...
GOOD. THEY CAN'T ATTACK ANYMORE.
YEAH, THIS SURE IS UPPER-RANK DEMON BLOOD!
BDMP
BDMP

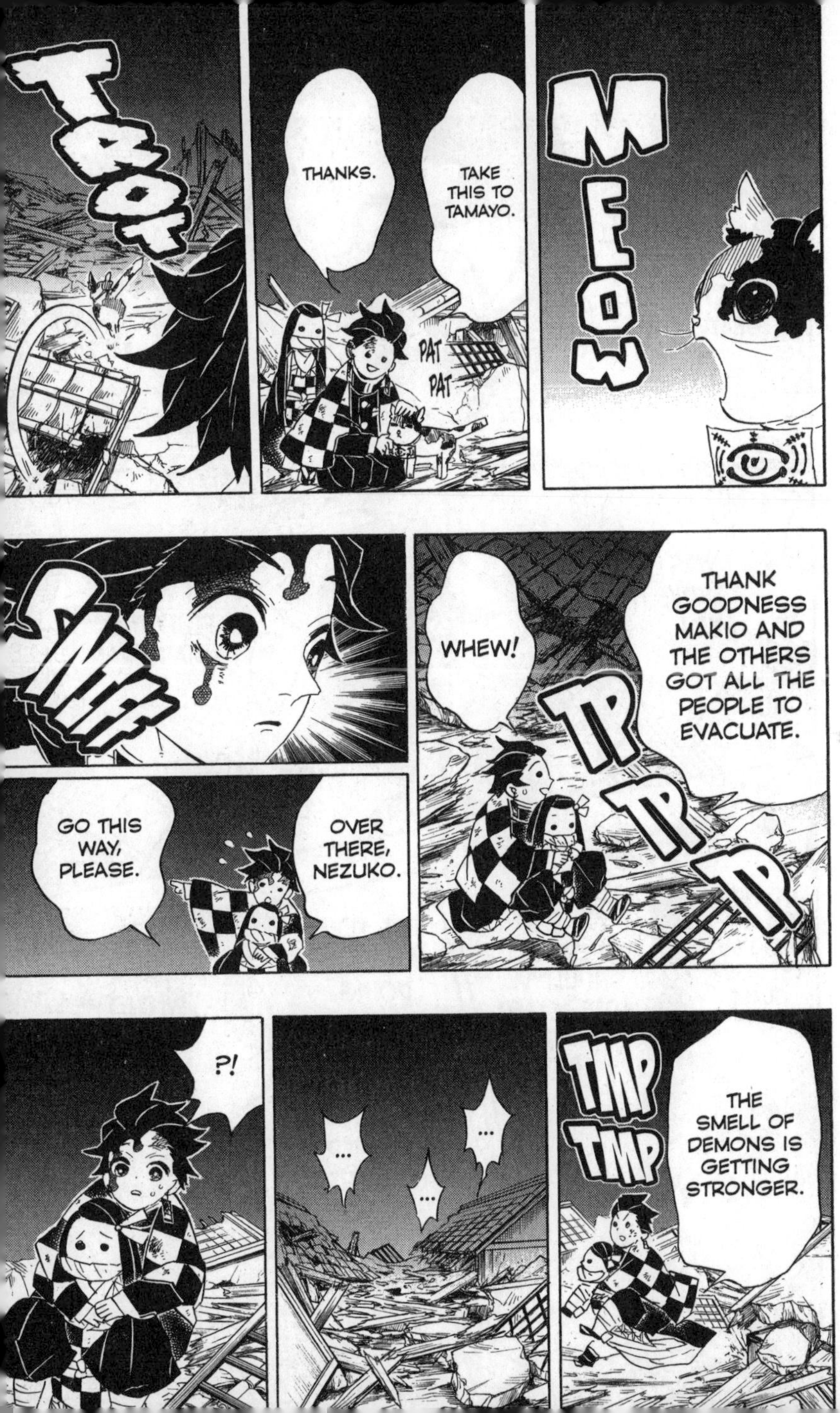
MEOW
TAKE THIS TO TAMAYO.
THANKS.
PAT PAT
TROT
THANK GOODNESS MAKIO AND THE OTHERS GOT ALL THE PEOPLE TO EVACUATE.
WHEW!
TP TP TP
SNIFF
OVER THERE, NEZUKO.
GO THIS WAY, PLEASE.
TMP TMP
THE SMELL OF DEMONS IS GETTING STRONGER.
...
...
...
?!

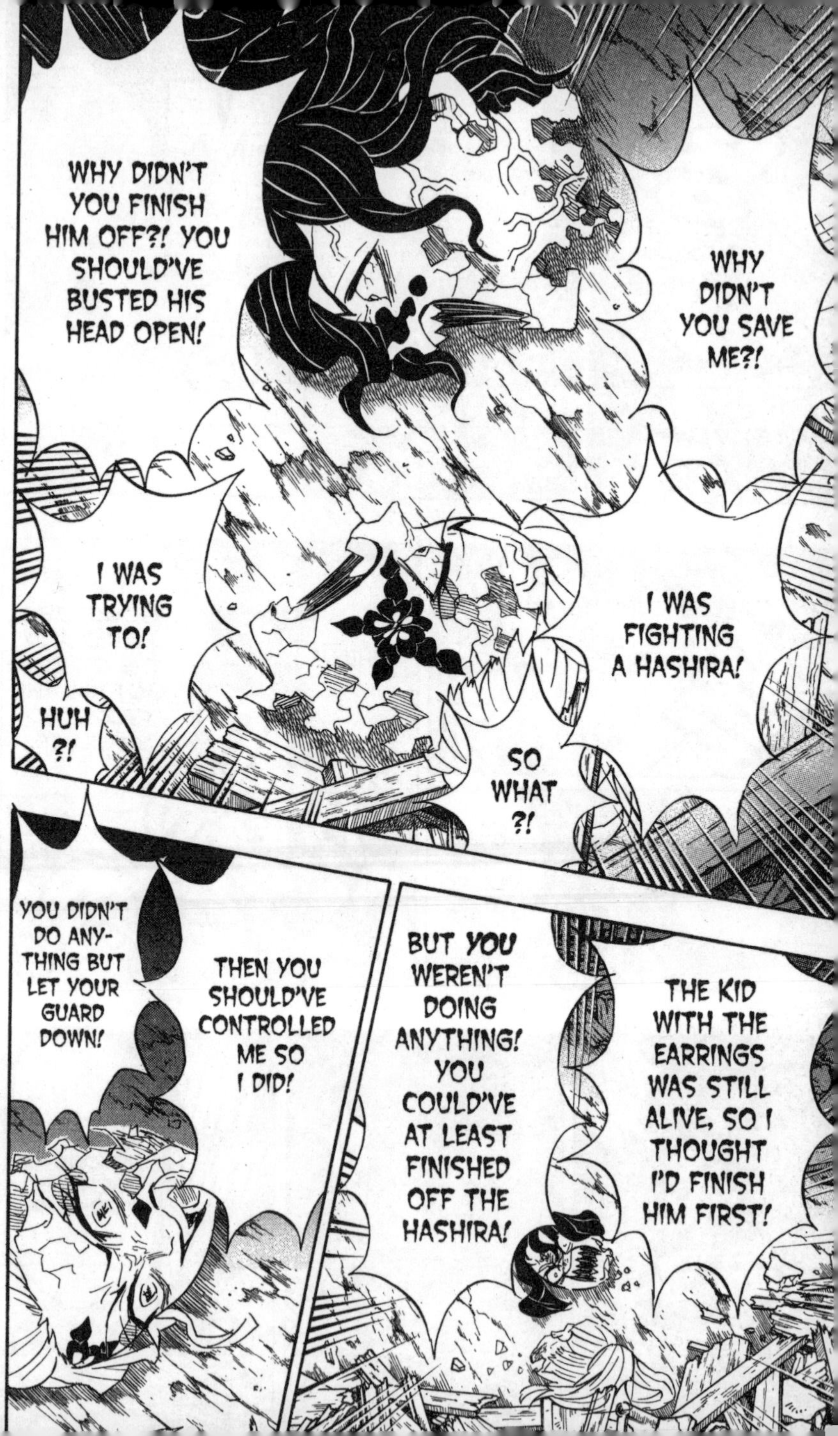

WHY DIDN'T YOU SAVE ME?!
WHY DIDN'T YOU FINISH HIM OFF?! YOU SHOULD'VE BUSTED HIS HEAD OPEN!
I WAS FIGHTING A HASHIRA!
I WAS TRYING TO!
SO WHAT?!
HUH?!
THE KID WITH THE EARRINGS WAS STILL ALIVE, SO I THOUGHT I'D FINISH HIM FIRST!
BUT *YOU* WEREN'T DOING ANYTHING! YOU COULD'VE AT LEAST FINISHED OFF THE HASHIRA!
THEN YOU SHOULD'VE CONTROLLED ME SO I DID!
YOU DIDN'T DO ANY-THING BUT LET YOUR GUARD DOWN!

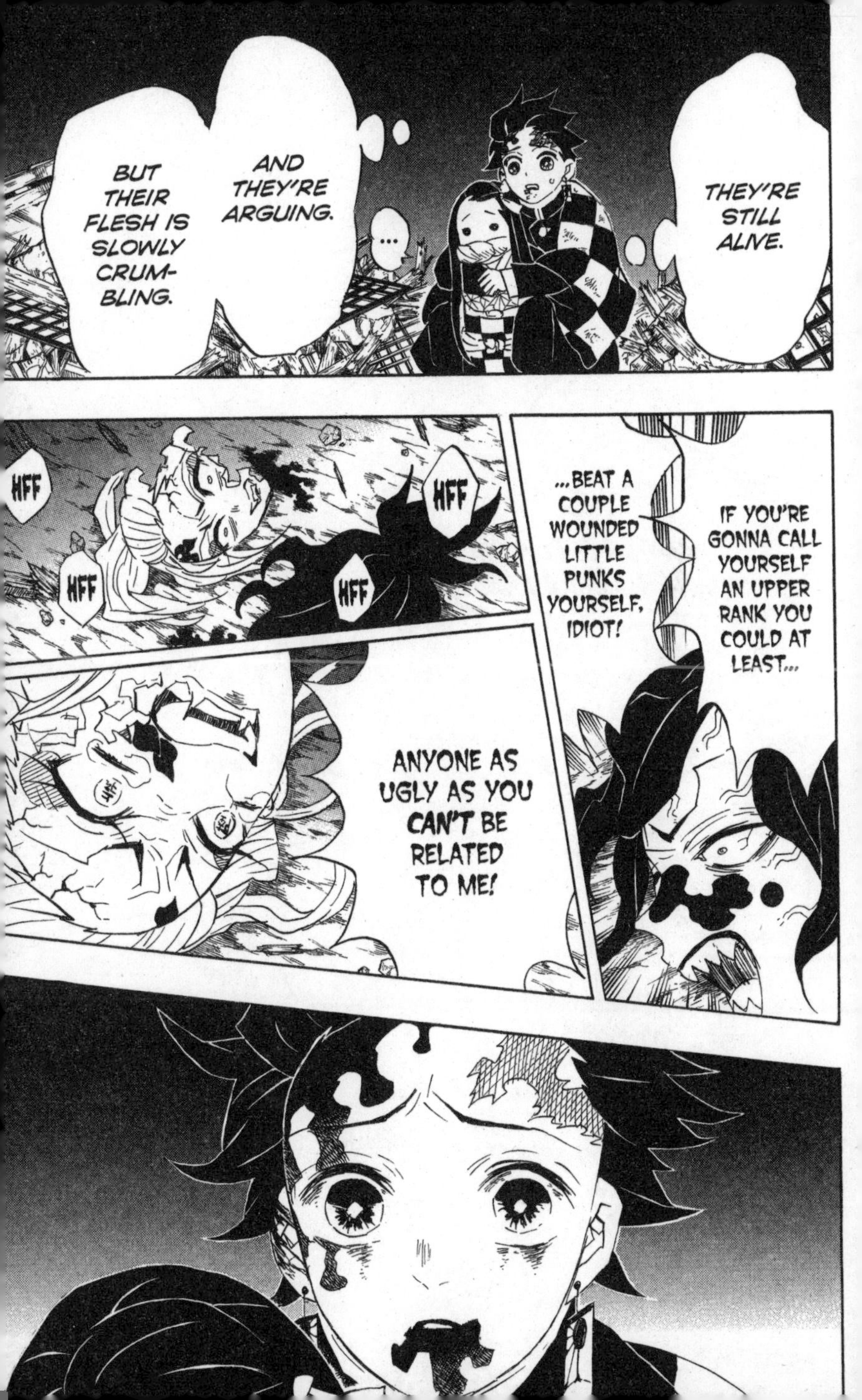
THEY'RE STILL ALIVE.
...
AND THEY'RE ARGUING.
BUT THEIR FLESH IS SLOWLY CRUMBLING.
IF YOU'RE GONNA CALL YOURSELF AN UPPER RANK YOU COULD AT LEAST...
...BEAT A COUPLE WOUNDED LITTLE PUNKS YOURSELF, IDIOT!
HFF
HFF
HFF
HFF
ANYONE AS UGLY AS YOU CAN'T BE RELATED TO ME!

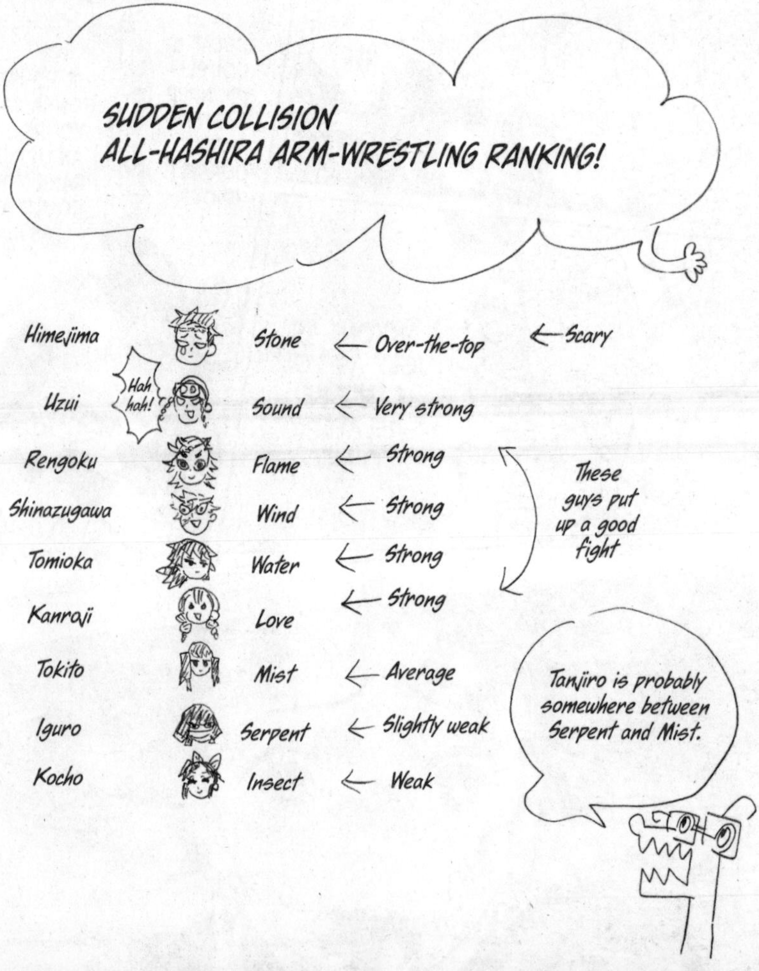
SUDDEN COLLISION
ALL-HASHIRA ARM-WRESTLING RANKING!
Himejima Stone ← Over-the-top ← Scary
Hah hah!
Uzui Sound ← Very strong
Rengoku Flame ← Strong
Shinazugawa Wind ← Strong
Tomioka Water ← Strong
Kanroji Love ← Strong
These guys put up a good fight
Tokito Mist ← Average
Iguro Serpent ← Slightly weak
Kocho Insect ← Weak
Tanjiro is probably somewhere between Serpent and Mist.

CHAPTER 96: NO MATTER HOW MANY LIVES, PART 1

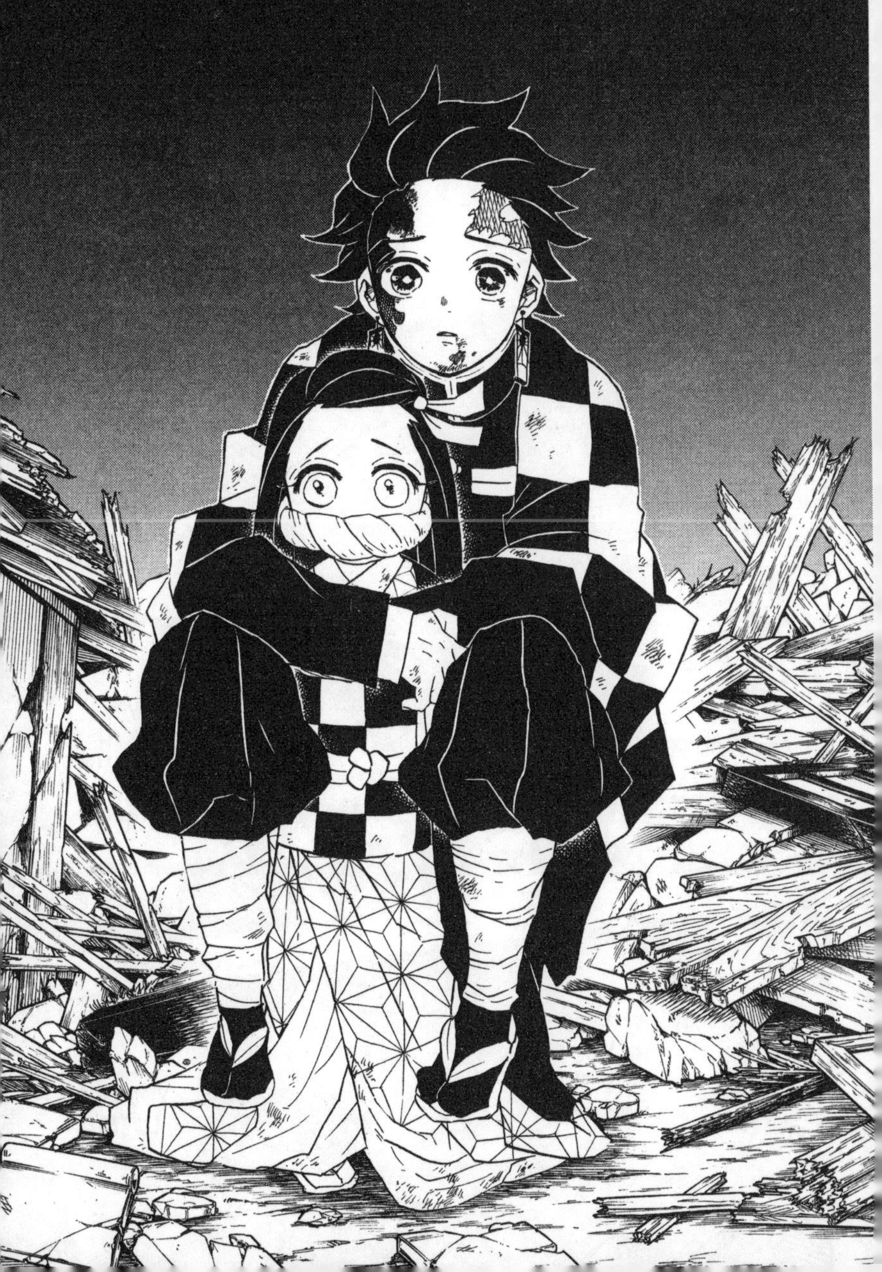

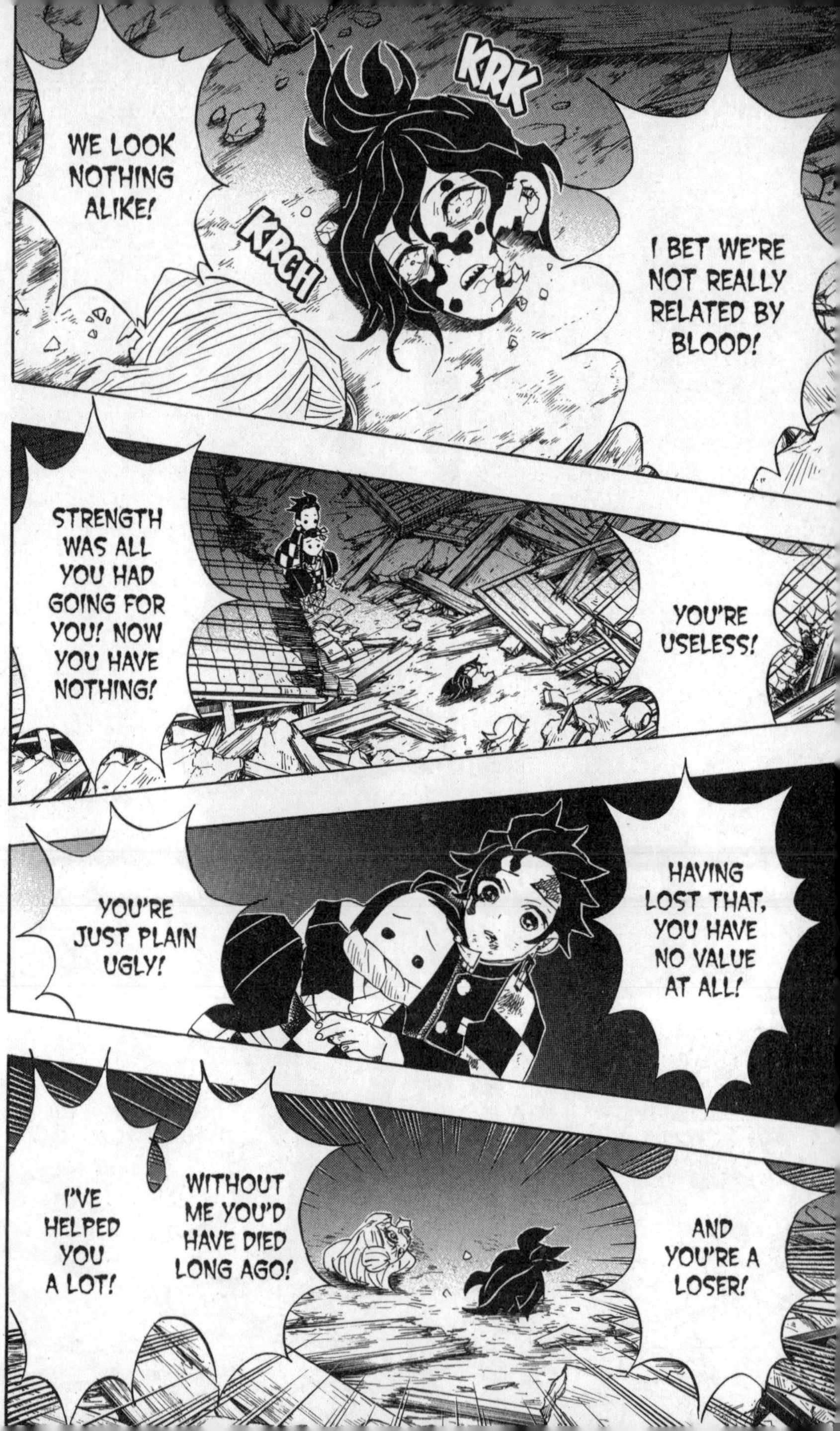
I BET WE'RE NOT REALLY RELATED BY BLOOD!
KRK
KRCH
WE LOOK NOTHING ALIKE!
YOU'RE USELESS!
STRENGTH WAS ALL YOU HAD GOING FOR YOU! NOW YOU HAVE NOTHING!
HAVING LOST THAT, YOU HAVE NO VALUE AT ALL!
YOU'RE JUST PLAIN UGLY!
AND YOU'RE A LOSER!
WITHOUT ME YOU'D HAVE DIED LONG AGO!
I'VE HELPED YOU A LOT!

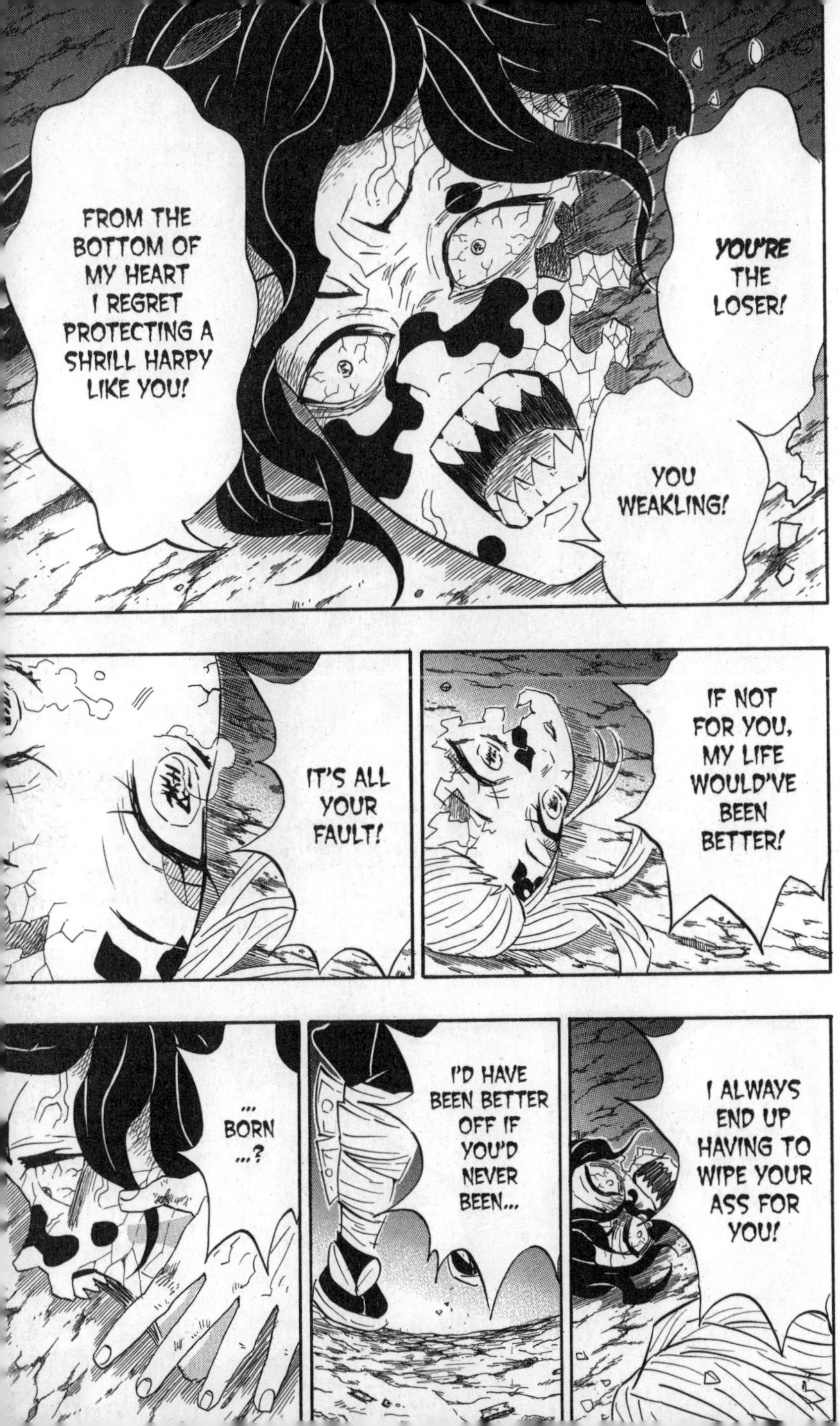
YOU'RE THE LOSER!
YOU WEAKLING!
FROM THE BOTTOM OF MY HEART I REGRET PROTECTING A SHRILL HARPY LIKE YOU!
IF NOT FOR YOU, MY LIFE WOULD'VE BEEN BETTER!
IT'S ALL YOUR FAULT!
I ALWAYS END UP HAVING TO WIPE YOUR ASS FOR YOU!
I'D HAVE BEEN BETTER OFF IF YOU'D NEVER BEEN...
... BORN ...?

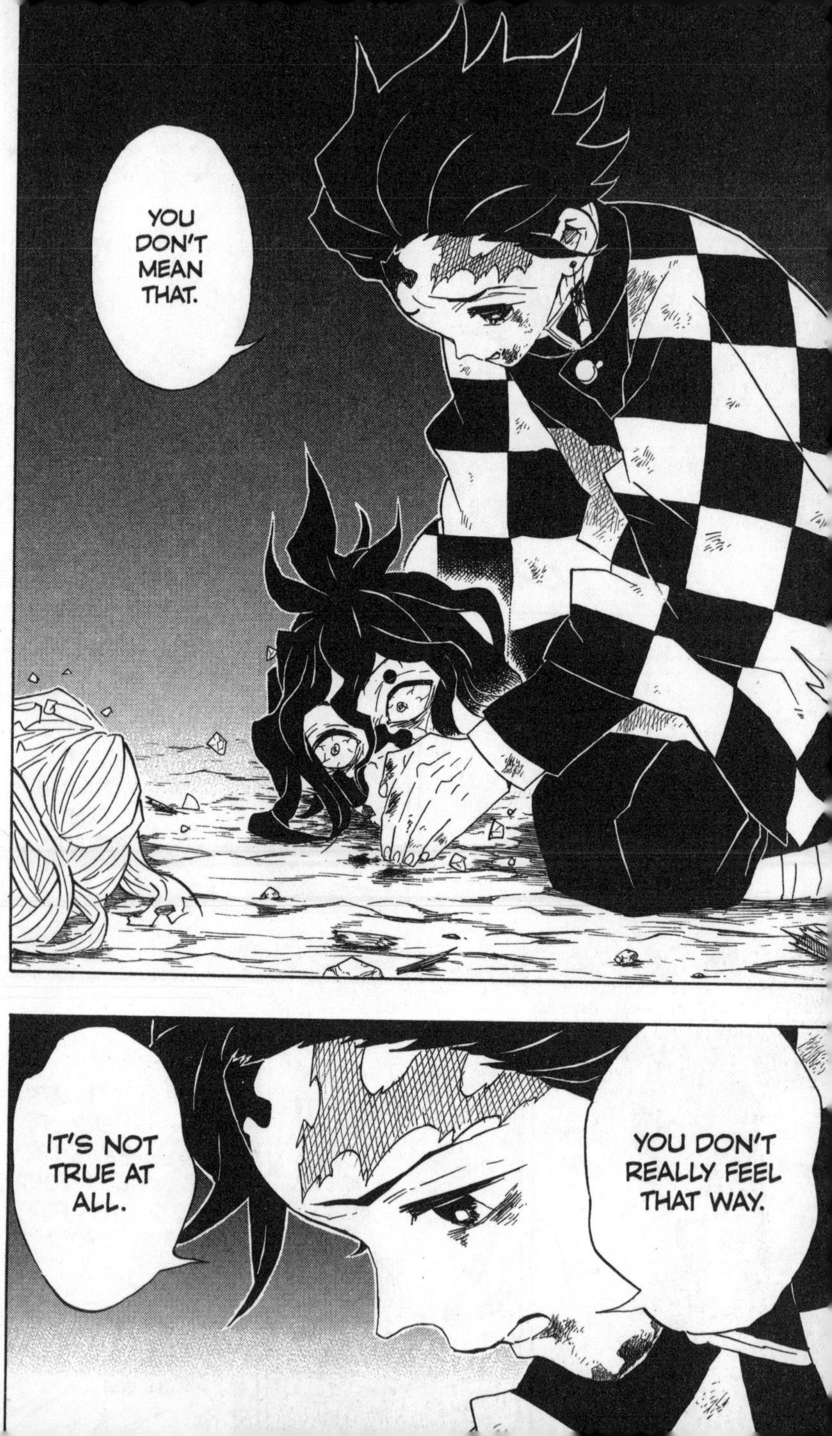
YOU DON'T MEAN THAT.
YOU DON'T REALLY FEEL THAT WAY.
IT'S NOT TRUE AT ALL.

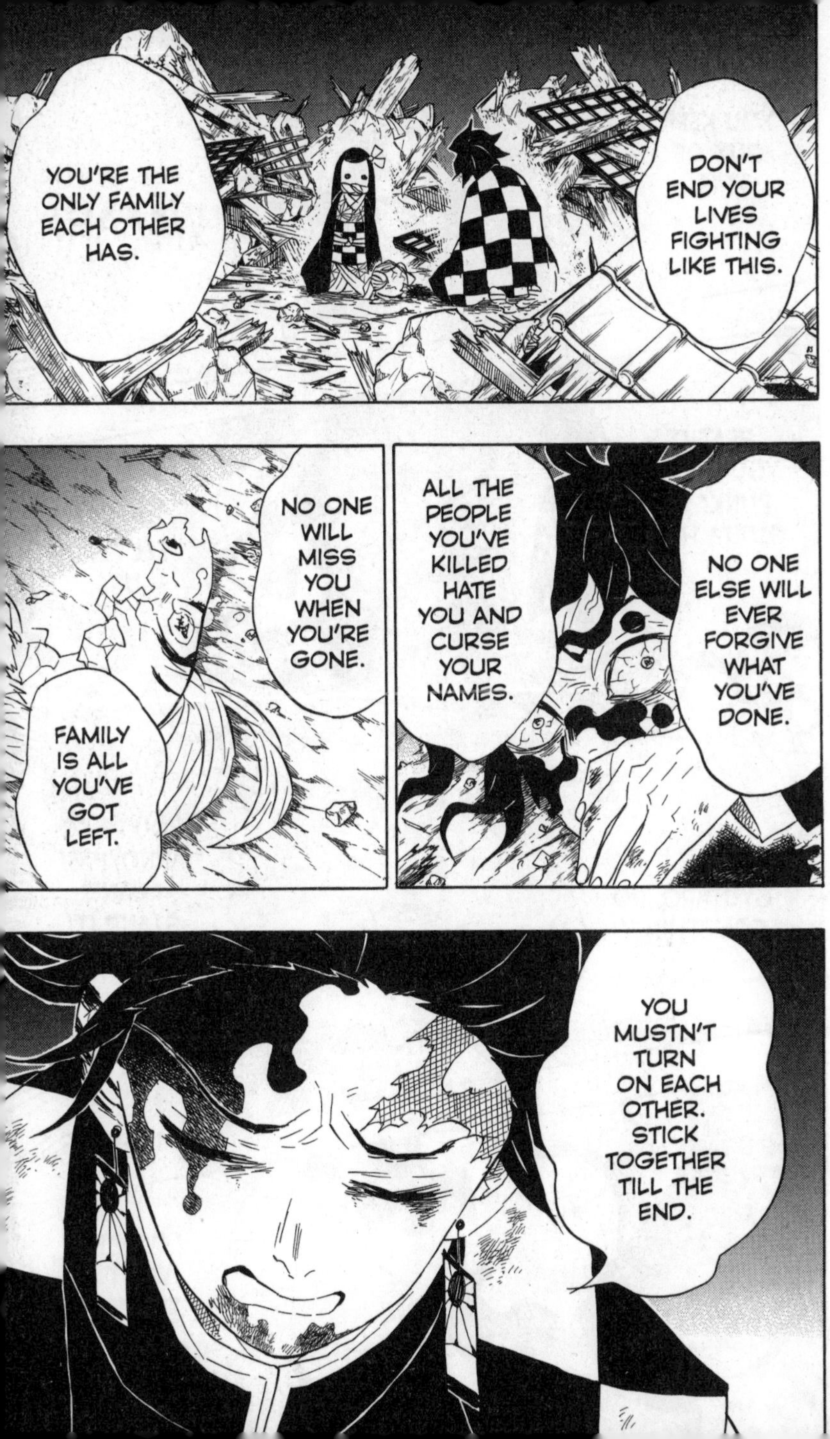
DON'T END YOUR LIVES FIGHTING LIKE THIS.
YOU'RE THE ONLY FAMILY EACH OTHER HAS.
NO ONE ELSE WILL EVER FORGIVE WHAT YOU'VE DONE.
ALL THE PEOPLE YOU'VE KILLED HATE YOU AND CURSE YOUR NAMES.
NO ONE WILL MISS YOU WHEN YOU'RE GONE.
FAMILY IS ALL YOU'VE GOT LEFT.
YOU MUSTN'T TURN ON EACH OTHER. STICK TOGETHER TILL THE END.

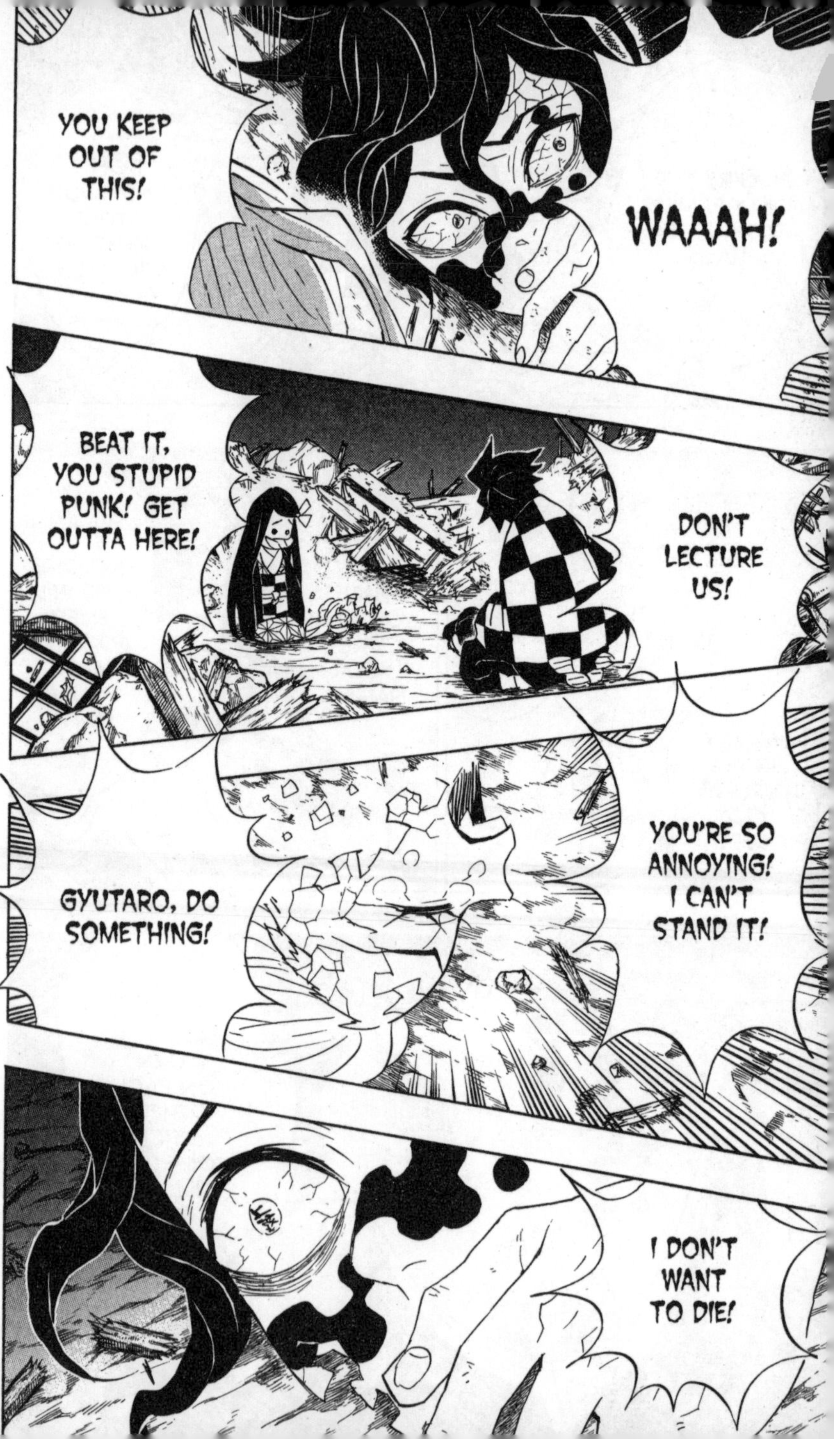
WAAAH!
YOU KEEP OUT OF THIS!
DON'T LECTURE US!
BEAT IT, YOU STUPID PUNK! GET OUTTA HERE!
YOU'RE SO ANNOYING! I CAN'T STAND IT!
GYUTARO, DO SOMETHING!
I DON'T WANT TO DIE!

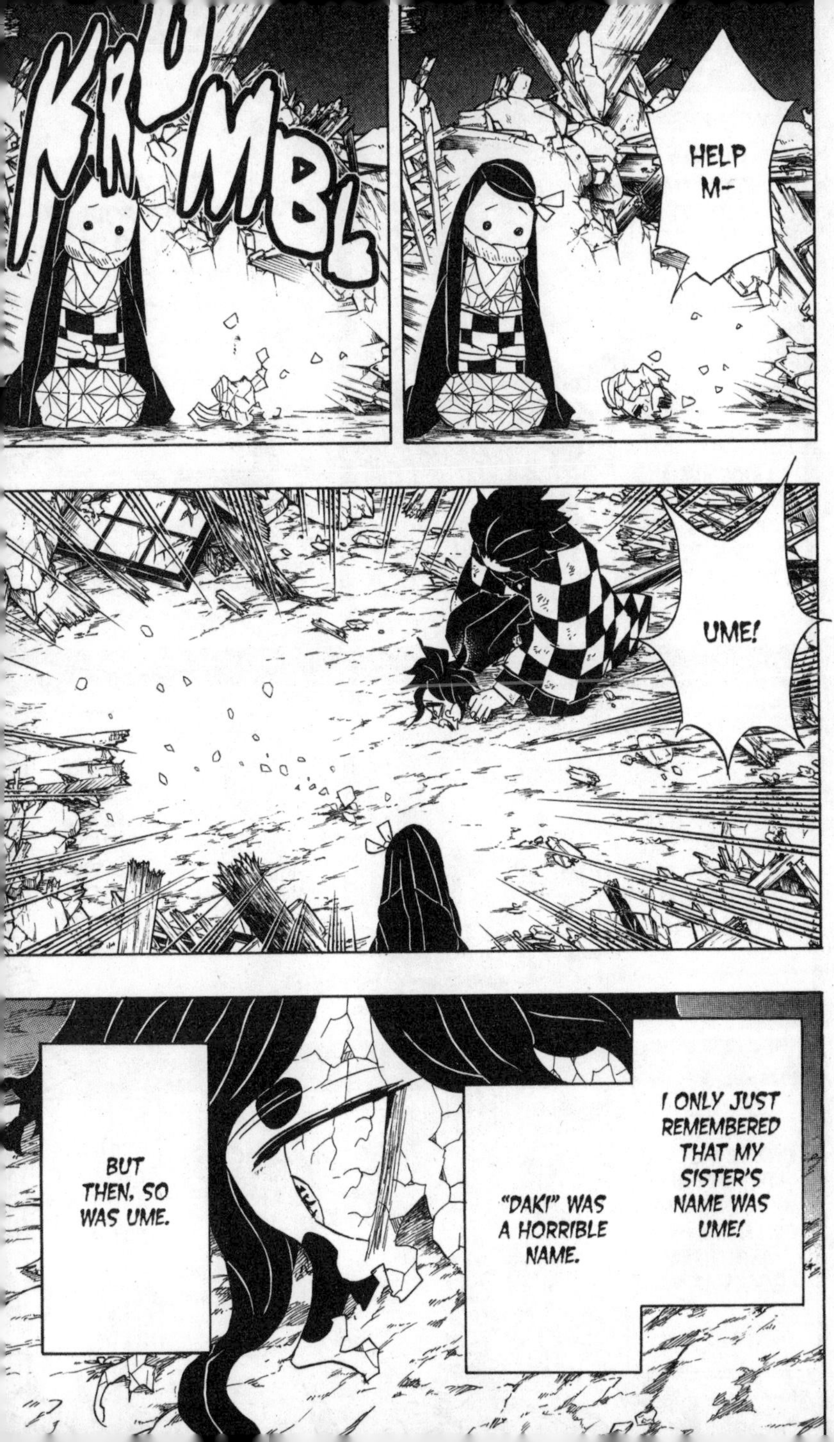
HELP M-
KRUMBL
UME!
I ONLY JUST REMEMBERED THAT MY SISTER'S NAME WAS UME!
"DAKI" WAS A HORRIBLE NAME.
BUT THEN, SO WAS UME.

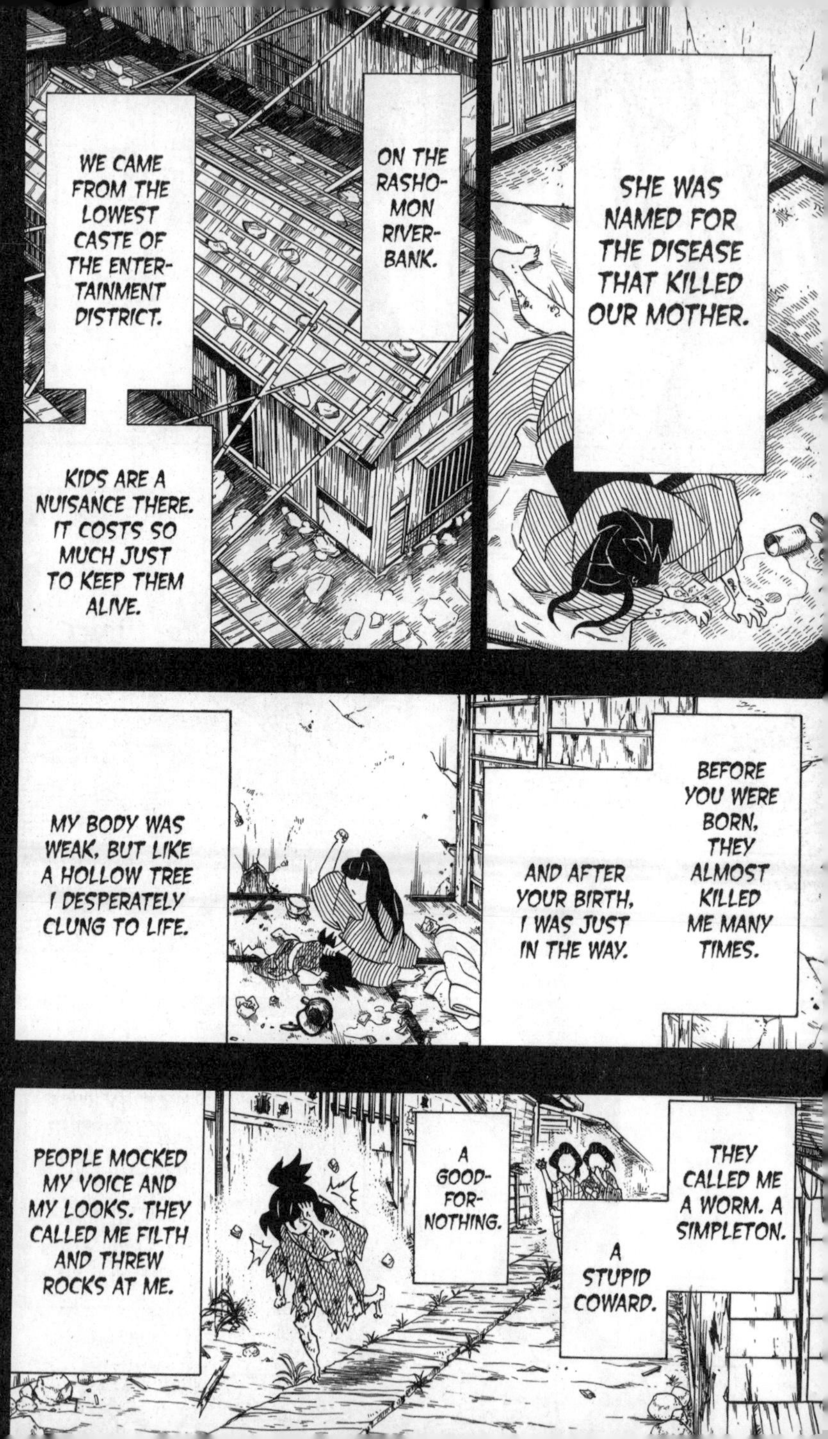
SHE WAS NAMED FOR THE DISEASE THAT KILLED OUR MOTHER.
ON THE RASHOMON RIVERBANK.
WE CAME FROM THE LOWEST CASTE OF THE ENTERTAINMENT DISTRICT.
KIDS ARE A NUISANCE THERE. IT COSTS SO MUCH JUST TO KEEP THEM ALIVE.
BEFORE YOU WERE BORN, THEY ALMOST KILLED ME MANY TIMES.
AND AFTER YOUR BIRTH, I WAS JUST IN THE WAY.
MY BODY WAS WEAK, BUT LIKE A HOLLOW TREE I DESPERATELY CLUNG TO LIFE.
THEY CALLED ME A WORM. A SIMPLETON.
A STUPID COWARD.
A GOOD-FOR-NOTHING.
PEOPLE MOCKED MY VOICE AND MY LOOKS. THEY CALLED ME FILTH AND THREW ROCKS AT ME.

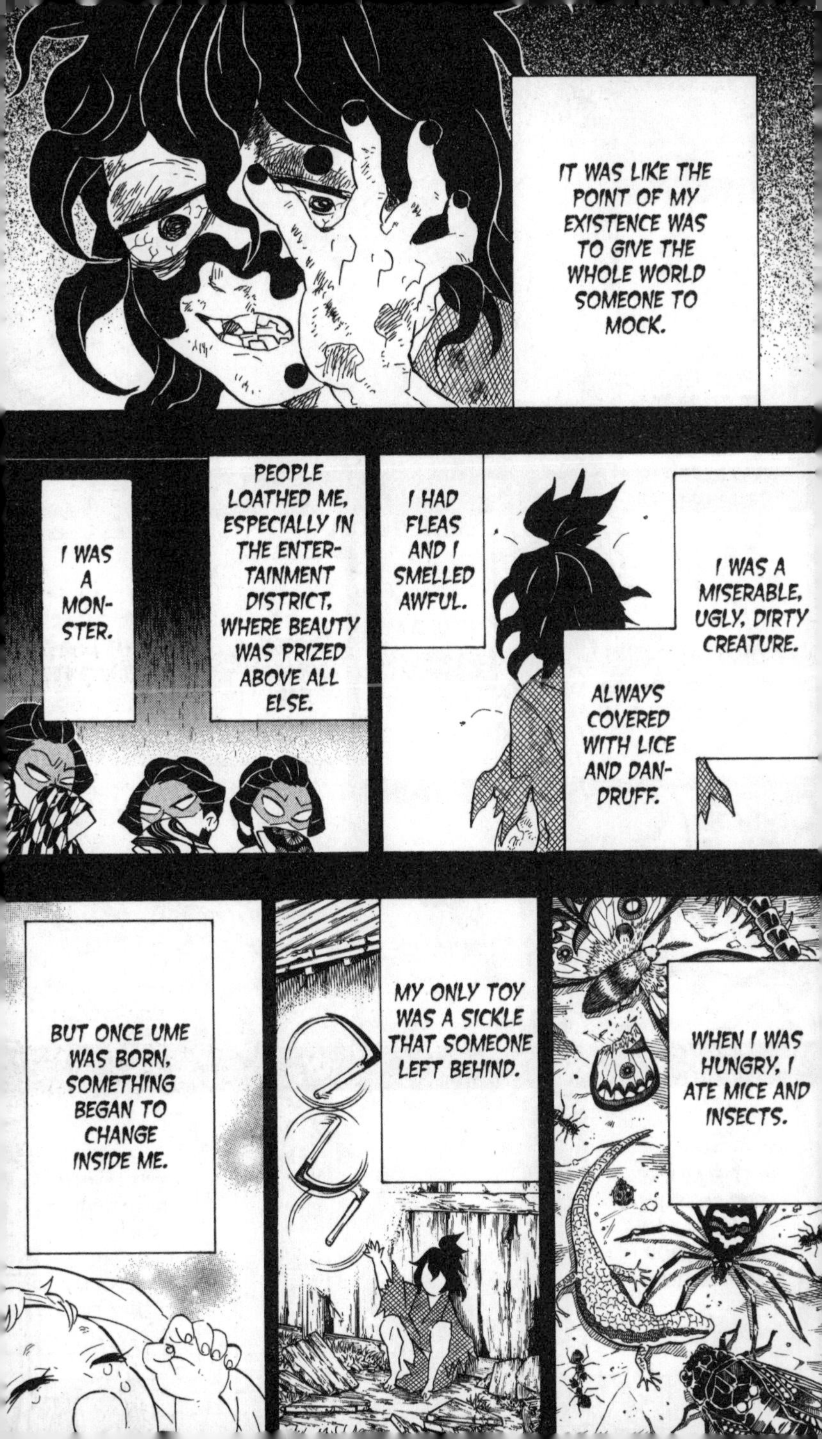
IT WAS LIKE THE POINT OF MY EXISTENCE WAS TO GIVE THE WHOLE WORLD SOMEONE TO MOCK.
I WAS A MISERABLE, UGLY, DIRTY CREATURE.
ALWAYS COVERED WITH LICE AND DAN-DRUFF.
I HAD FLEAS AND I SMELLED AWFUL.
PEOPLE LOATHED ME, ESPECIALLY IN THE ENTER-TAINMENT DISTRICT, WHERE BEAUTY WAS PRIZED ABOVE ALL ELSE.
I WAS A MON-STER.
WHEN I WAS HUNGRY, I ATE MICE AND INSECTS.
MY ONLY TOY WAS A SICKLE THAT SOMEONE LEFT BEHIND.
BUT ONCE UME WAS BORN, SOMETHING BEGAN TO CHANGE INSIDE ME.

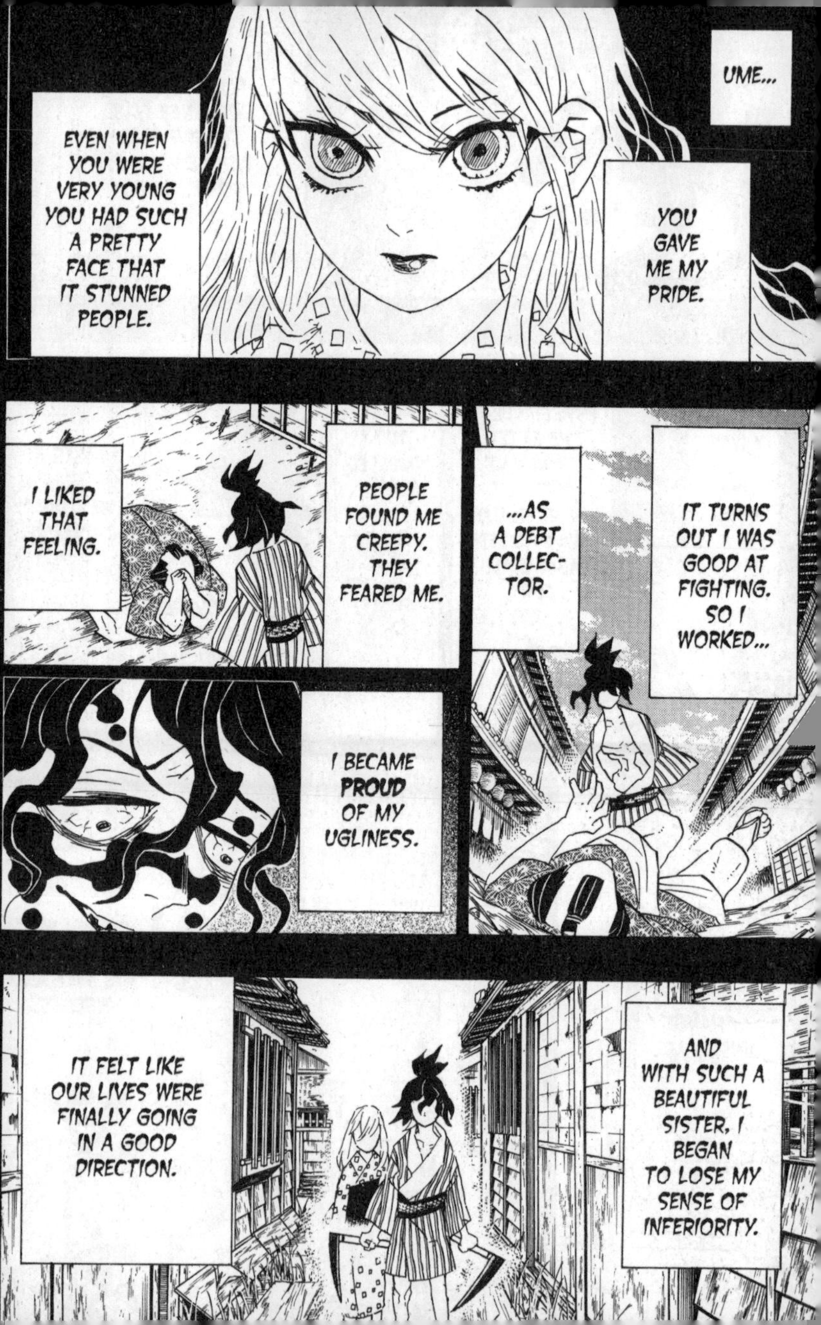
UME...
YOU GAVE ME MY PRIDE.
EVEN WHEN YOU WERE VERY YOUNG YOU HAD SUCH A PRETTY FACE THAT IT STUNNED PEOPLE.
IT TURNS OUT I WAS GOOD AT FIGHTING. SO I WORKED...
...AS A DEBT COLLEC-TOR.
PEOPLE FOUND ME CREEPY. THEY FEARED ME.
I LIKED THAT FEELING.
I BECAME **PROUD** OF MY UGLINESS.
AND WITH SUCH A BEAUTIFUL SISTER, I BEGAN TO LOSE MY SENSE OF INFERIORITY.
IT FELT LIKE OUR LIVES WERE FINALLY GOING IN A GOOD DIRECTION.

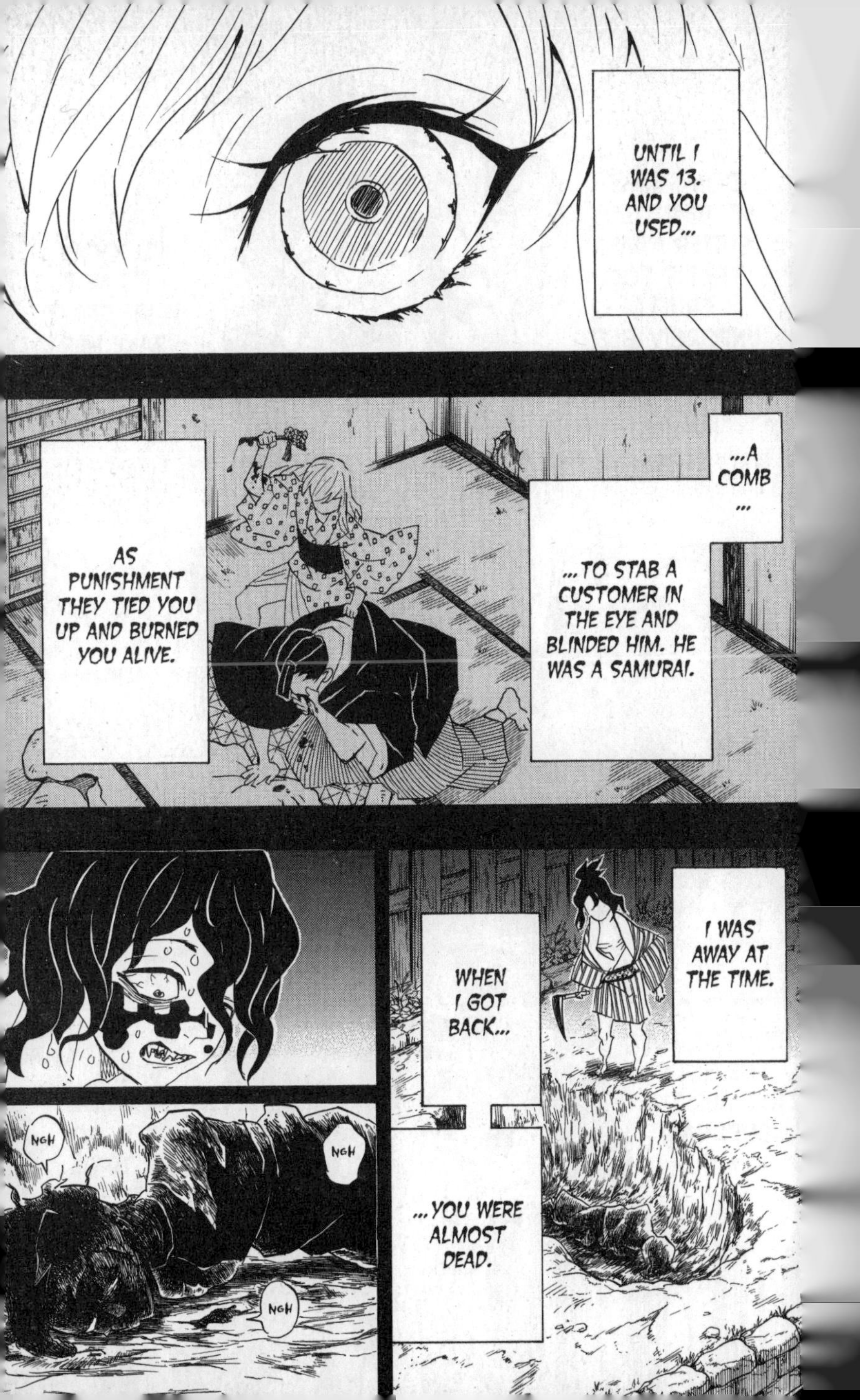
UNTIL I WAS 13. AND YOU USED...
...A COMB ...
...TO STAB A CUSTOMER IN THE EYE AND BLINDED HIM. HE WAS A SAMURAI.
AS PUNISHMENT THEY TIED YOU UP AND BURNED YOU ALIVE.
I WAS AWAY AT THE TIME.
WHEN I GOT BACK...
...YOU WERE ALMOST DEAD.
NGH
NGH
NGH

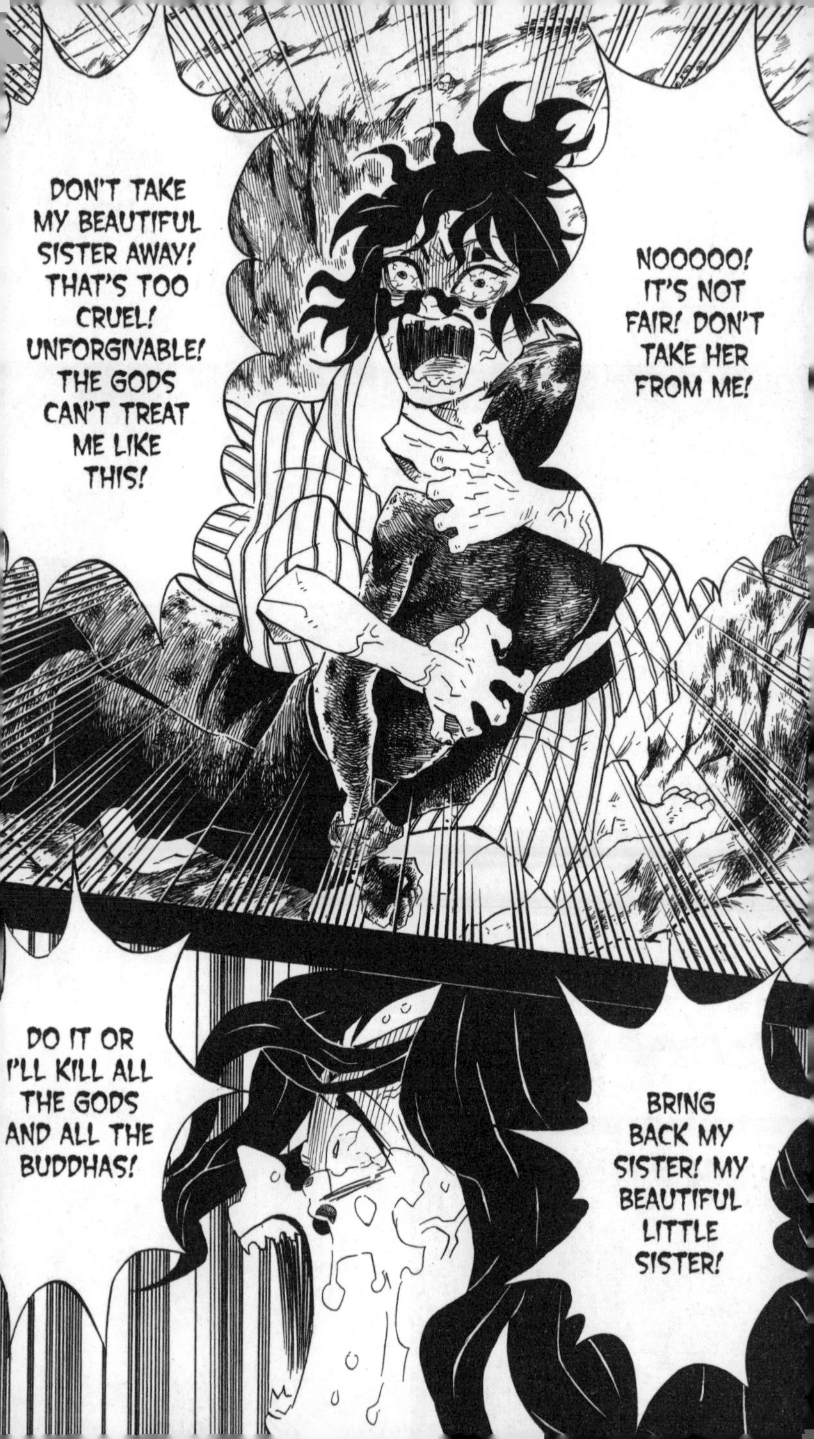
NOOOOO! IT'S NOT FAIR! DON'T TAKE HER FROM ME!
DON'T TAKE MY BEAUTIFUL SISTER AWAY! THAT'S TOO CRUEL! UNFORGIVABLE! THE GODS CAN'T TREAT ME LIKE THIS!
BRING BACK MY SISTER! MY BEAUTIFUL LITTLE SISTER!
DO IT OR I'LL KILL ALL THE GODS AND ALL THE BUDDHAS!

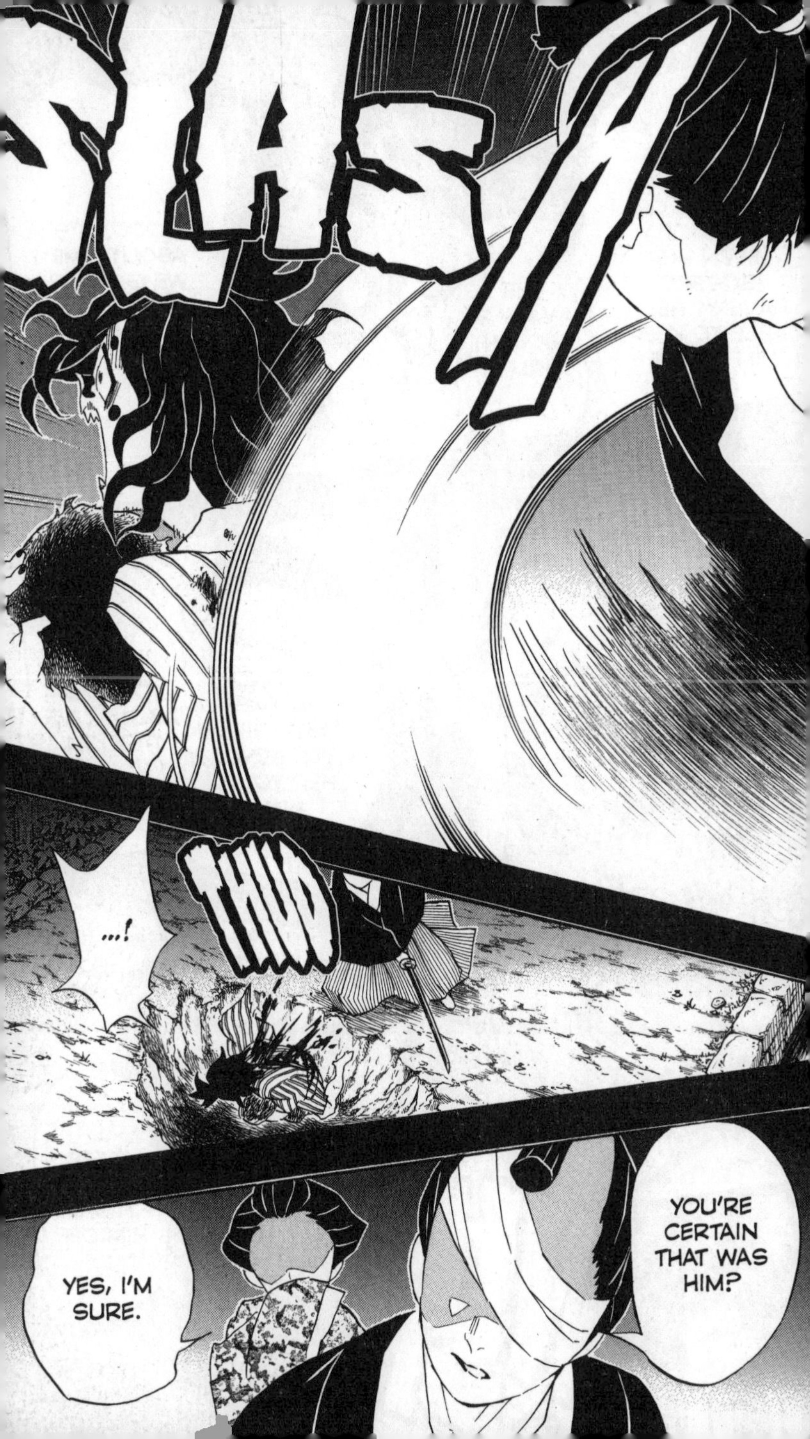
LAS
THUD
...!
YOU'RE CERTAIN THAT WAS HIM?
YES, I'M SURE.

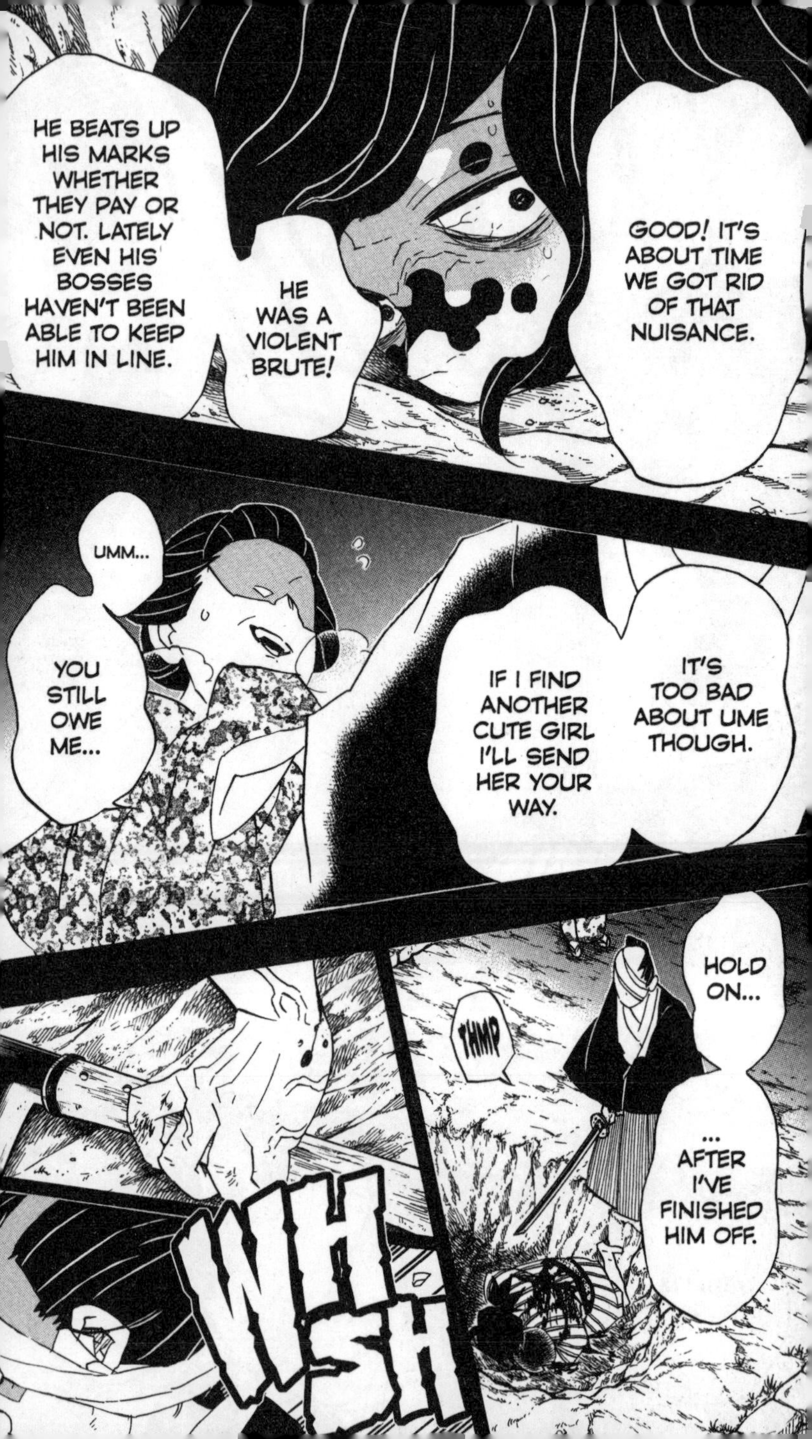
GOOD! IT'S ABOUT TIME WE GOT RID OF THAT NUISANCE.
HE WAS A VIOLENT BRUTE!
HE BEATS UP HIS MARKS WHETHER THEY PAY OR NOT. LATELY EVEN HIS BOSSES HAVEN'T BEEN ABLE TO KEEP HIM IN LINE.
IT'S TOO BAD ABOUT UME THOUGH.
IF I FIND ANOTHER CUTE GIRL I'LL SEND HER YOUR WAY.
UMM...
YOU STILL OWE ME...
HOLD ON...
... AFTER I'VE FINISHED HIM OFF.
THMP
WHSH

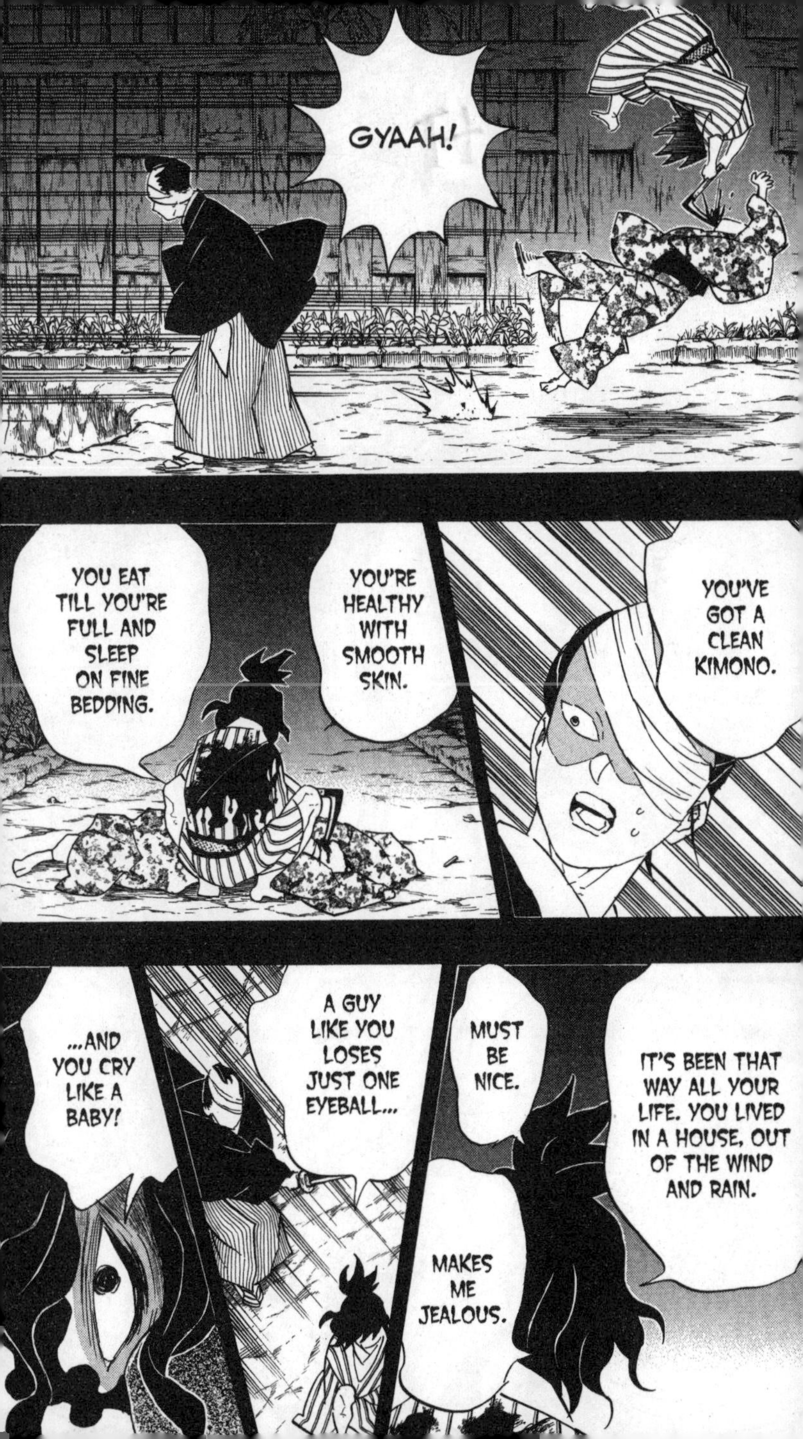
GYAAH!
YOU'VE GOT A CLEAN KIMONO.
YOU'RE HEALTHY WITH SMOOTH SKIN.
YOU EAT TILL YOU'RE FULL AND SLEEP ON FINE BEDDING.
IT'S BEEN THAT WAY ALL YOUR LIFE. YOU LIVED IN A HOUSE, OUT OF THE WIND AND RAIN.
MUST BE NICE.
MAKES ME JEALOUS.
A GUY LIKE YOU LOSES JUST ONE EYEBALL...
...AND YOU CRY LIKE A BABY!

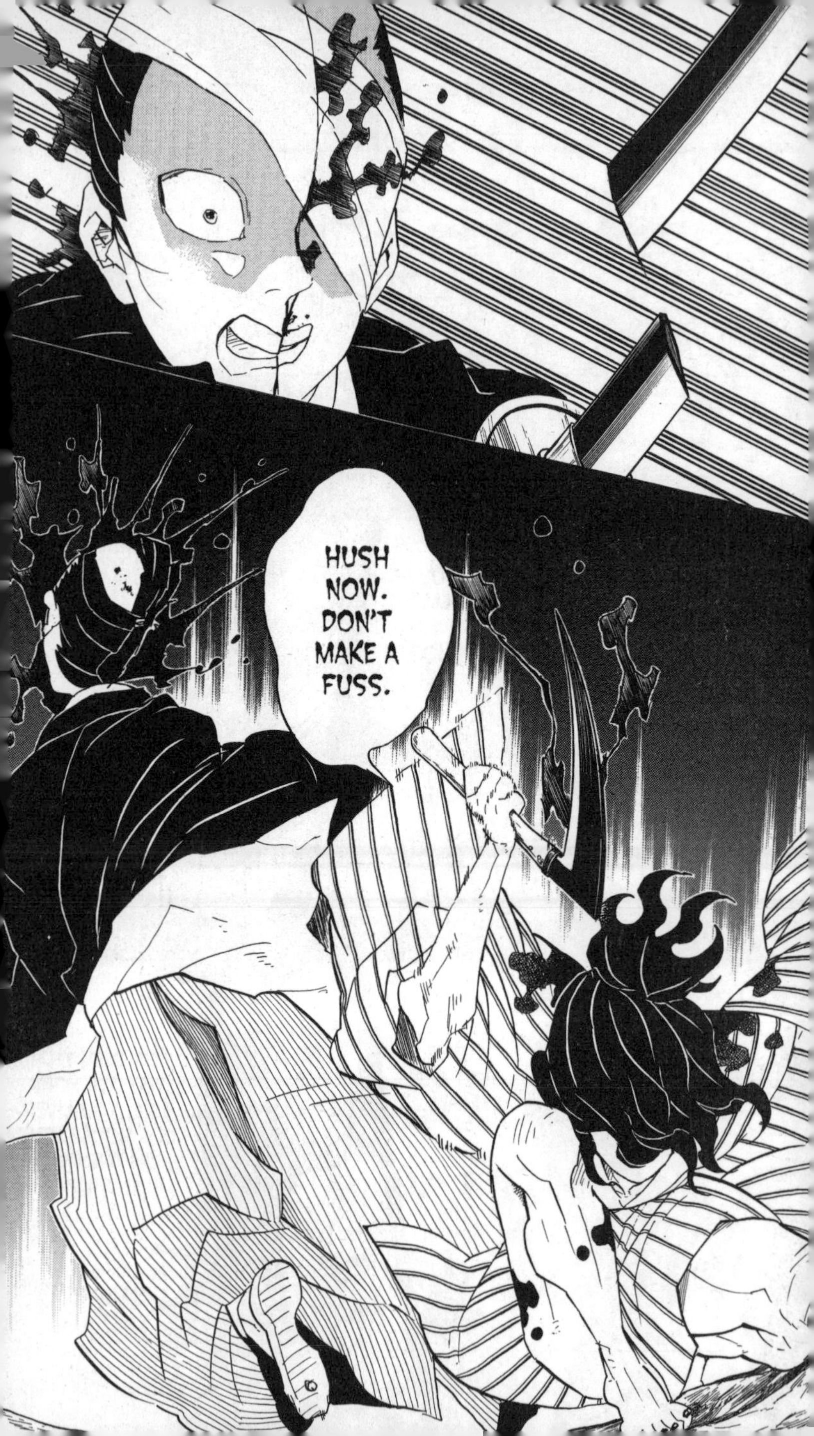
HUSH NOW. DON'T MAKE A FUSS.

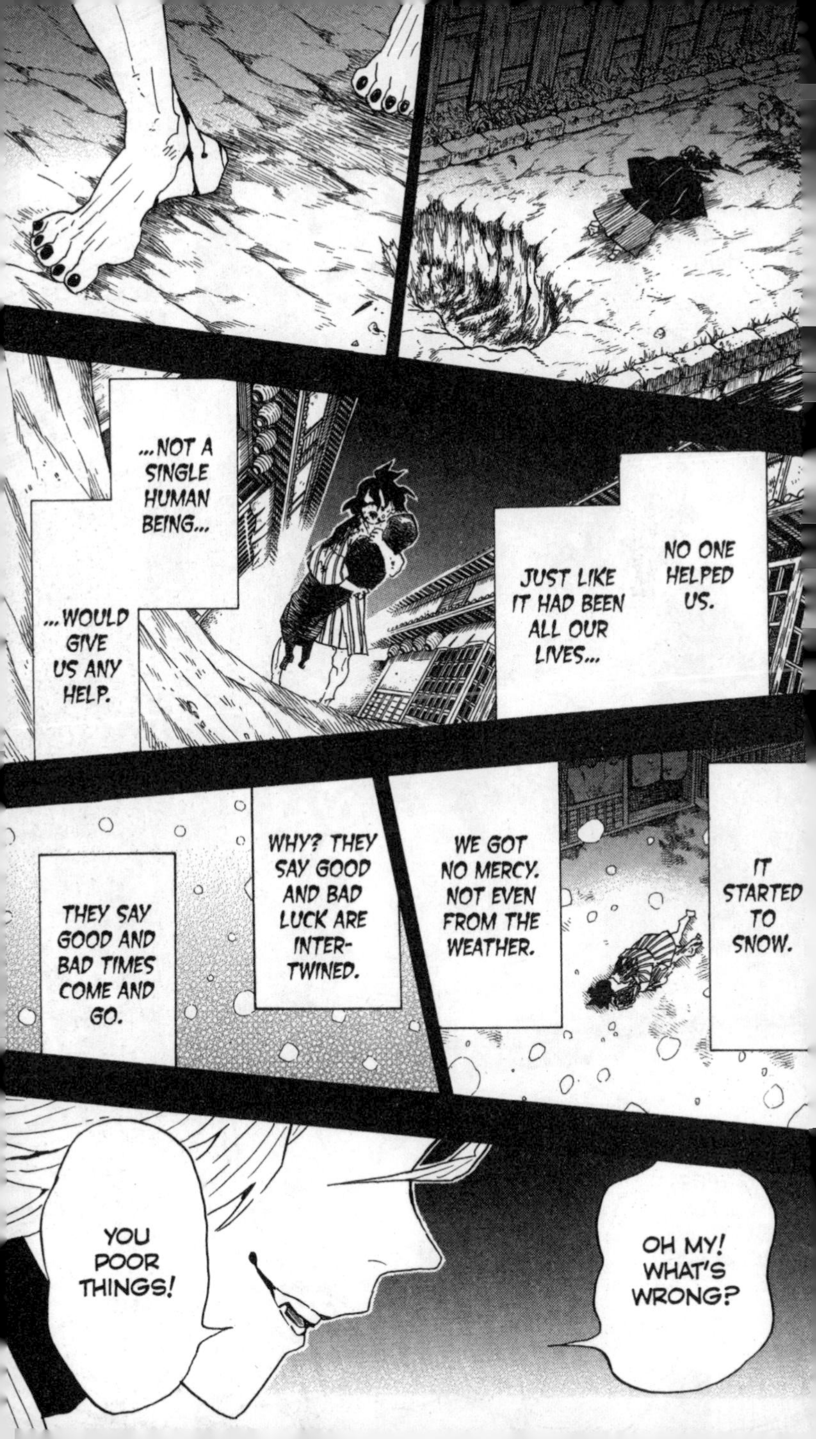
NO ONE HELPED US.
JUST LIKE IT HAD BEEN ALL OUR LIVES...
...NOT A SINGLE HUMAN BEING...
...WOULD GIVE US ANY HELP.
IT STARTED TO SNOW.
WE GOT NO MERCY. NOT EVEN FROM THE WEATHER.
WHY? THEY SAY GOOD AND BAD LUCK ARE INTER-TWINED.
THEY SAY GOOD AND BAD TIMES COME AND GO.
OH MY! WHAT'S WRONG?
YOU POOR THINGS!

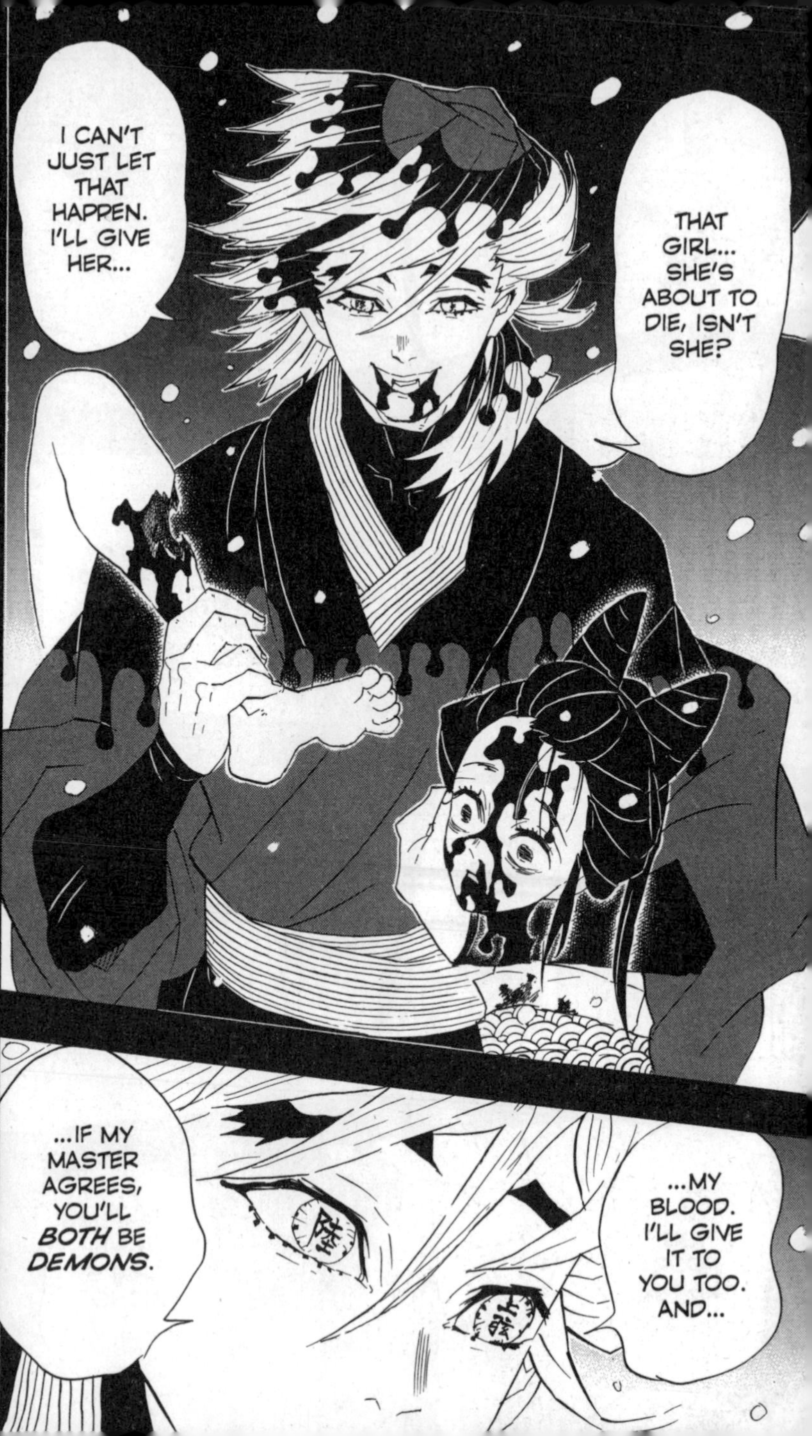
THAT GIRL... SHE'S ABOUT TO DIE, ISN'T SHE?
I CAN'T JUST LET THAT HAPPEN. I'LL GIVE HER...
...MY BLOOD. I'LL GIVE IT TO YOU TOO. AND...
...IF MY MASTER AGREES, YOU'LL *BOTH* BE *DEMONS*.

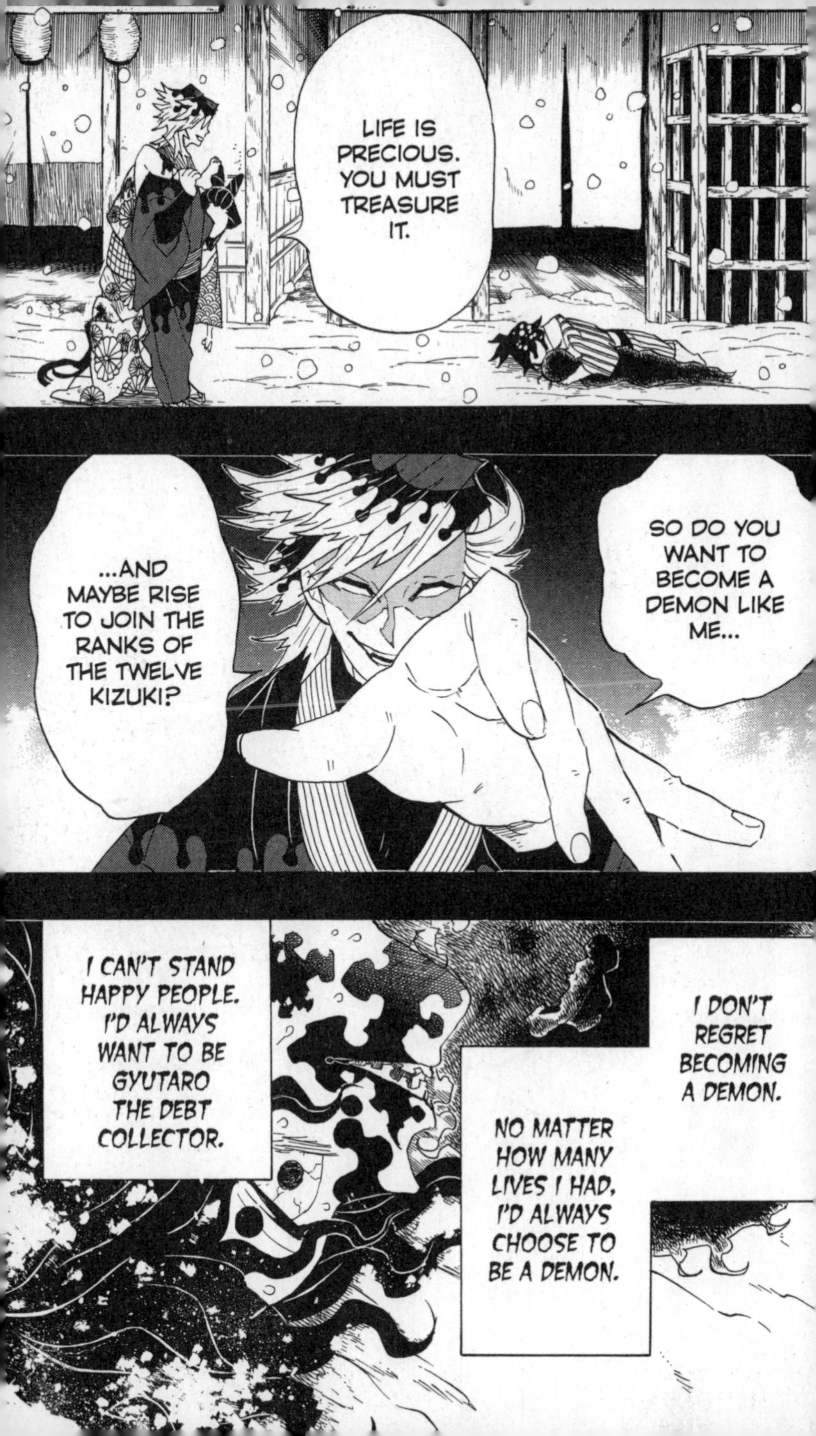
LIFE IS PRECIOUS. YOU MUST TREASURE IT.
SO DO YOU WANT TO BECOME A DEMON LIKE ME...
...AND MAYBE RISE TO JOIN THE RANKS OF THE TWELVE KIZUKI?
I DON'T REGRET BECOMING A DEMON.
NO MATTER HOW MANY LIVES I HAD, I'D ALWAYS CHOOSE TO BE A DEMON.
I CAN'T STAND HAPPY PEOPLE. I'D ALWAYS WANT TO BE GYUTARO THE DEBT COLLECTOR.

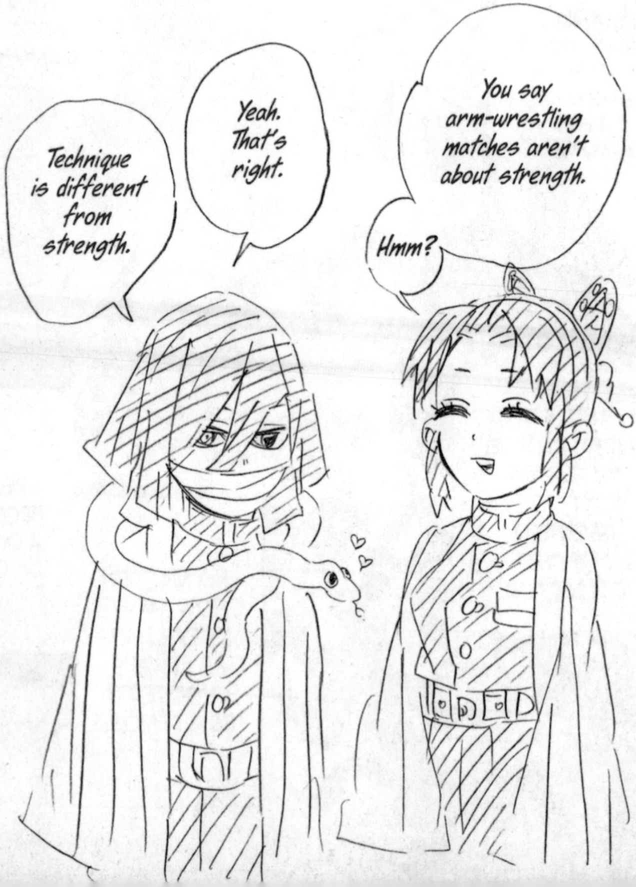
Hmm?
You say arm-wrestling matches aren't about strength.
Yeah. That's right.
Technique is different from strength.

CHAPTER 97: NO MATTER HOW MANY LIVES, PART 2

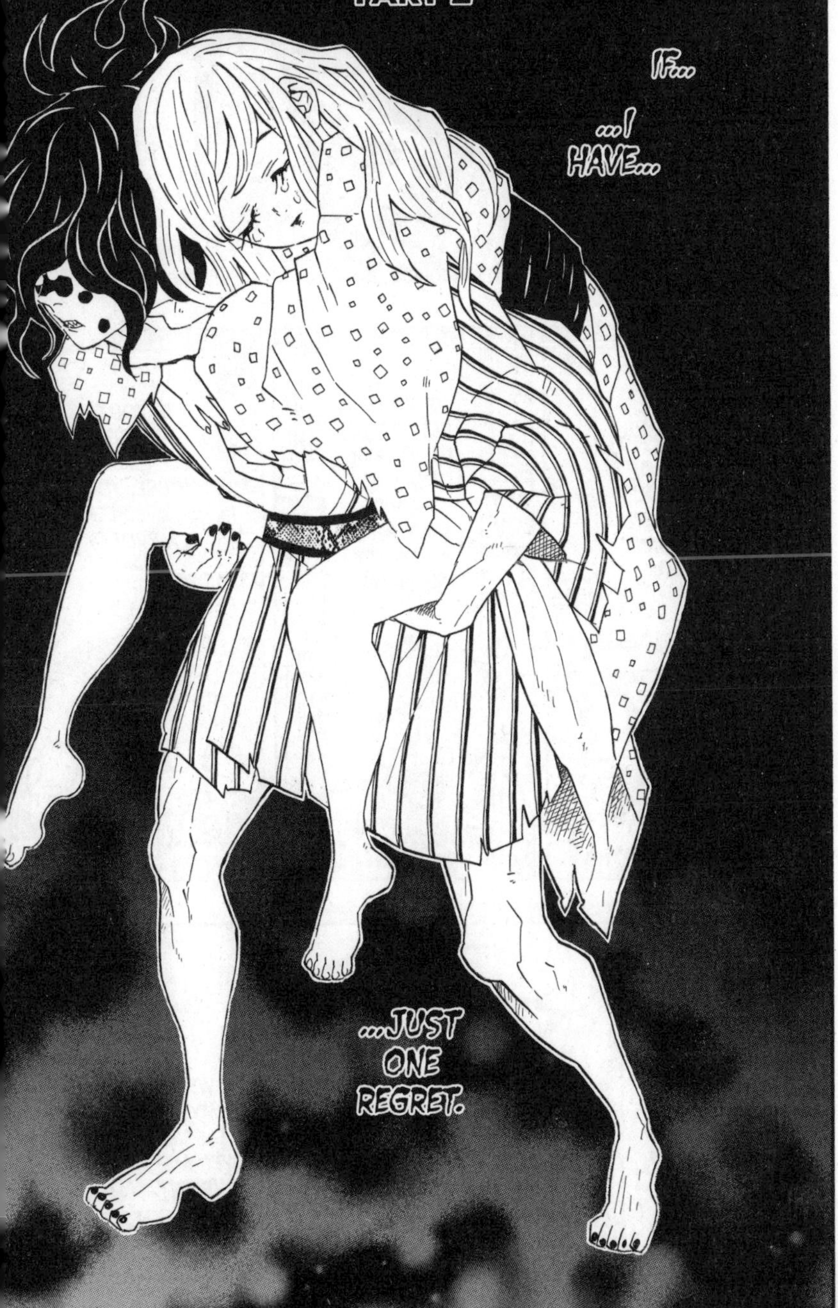
IF...
...I HAVE...
...JUST ONE REGRET.

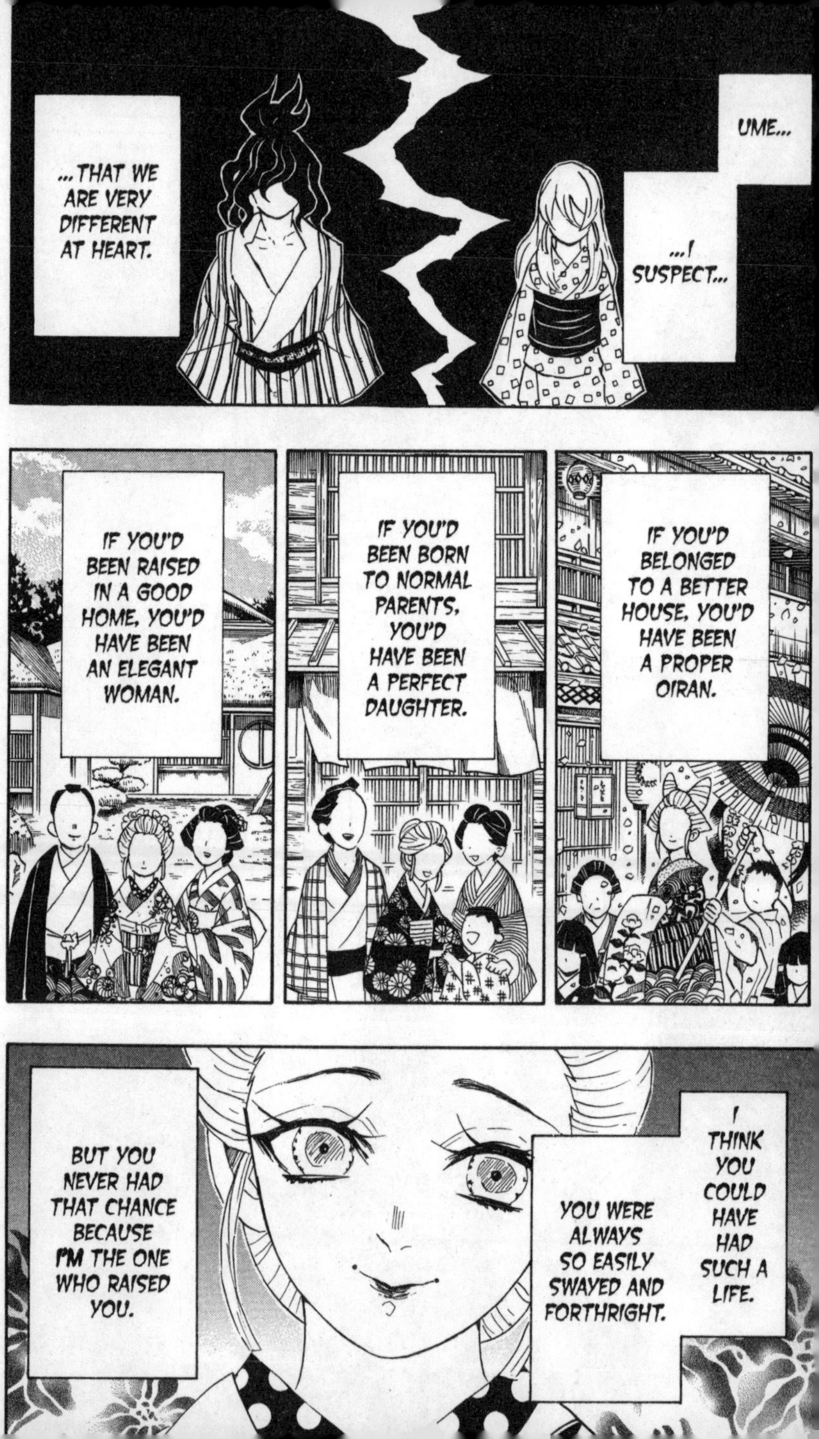
UME...
...I SUSPECT...
...THAT WE ARE VERY DIFFERENT AT HEART.
IF YOU'D BELONGED TO A BETTER HOUSE, YOU'D HAVE BEEN A PROPER OIRAN.
IF YOU'D BEEN BORN TO NORMAL PARENTS, YOU'D HAVE BEEN A PERFECT DAUGHTER.
IF YOU'D BEEN RAISED IN A GOOD HOME, YOU'D HAVE BEEN AN ELEGANT WOMAN.
I THINK YOU COULD HAVE HAD SUCH A LIFE.
YOU WERE ALWAYS SO EASILY SWAYED AND FORTHRIGHT.
BUT YOU NEVER HAD THAT CHANCE BECAUSE I'M THE ONE WHO RAISED YOU.

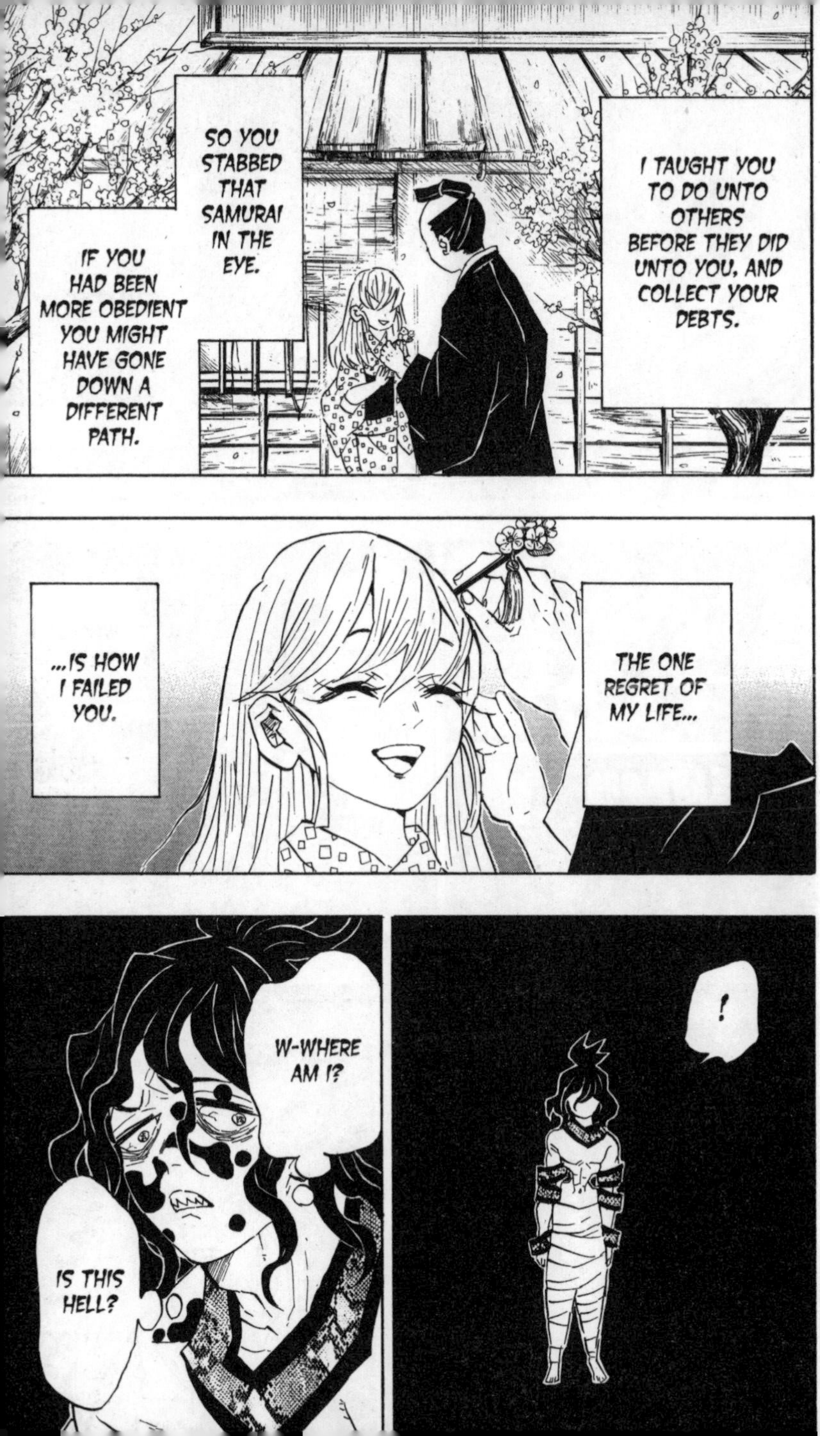
I TAUGHT YOU TO DO UNTO OTHERS BEFORE THEY DID UNTO YOU, AND COLLECT YOUR DEBTS.
SO YOU STABBED THAT SAMURAI IN THE EYE.
IF YOU HAD BEEN MORE OBEDIENT YOU MIGHT HAVE GONE DOWN A DIFFERENT PATH.
THE ONE REGRET OF MY LIFE...
...IS HOW I FAILED YOU.
!
W-WHERE AM I?
IS THIS HELL?

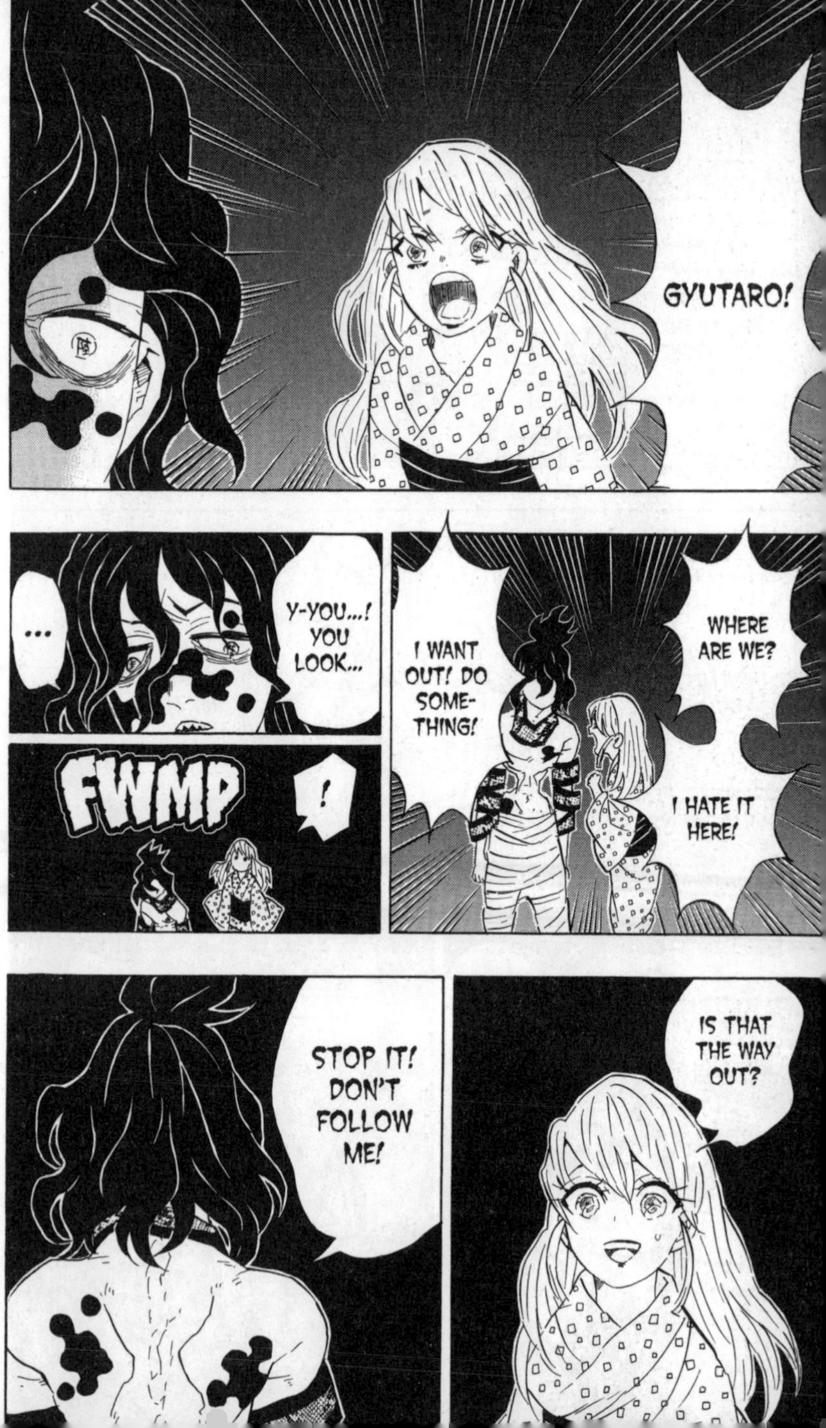
GYUTARO!
WHERE ARE WE?
I HATE IT HERE!
I WANT OUT! DO SOME-THING!
Y-YOU...! YOU LOOK...
...
FWMP
!
IS THAT THE WAY OUT?
STOP IT! DON'T FOLLOW ME!

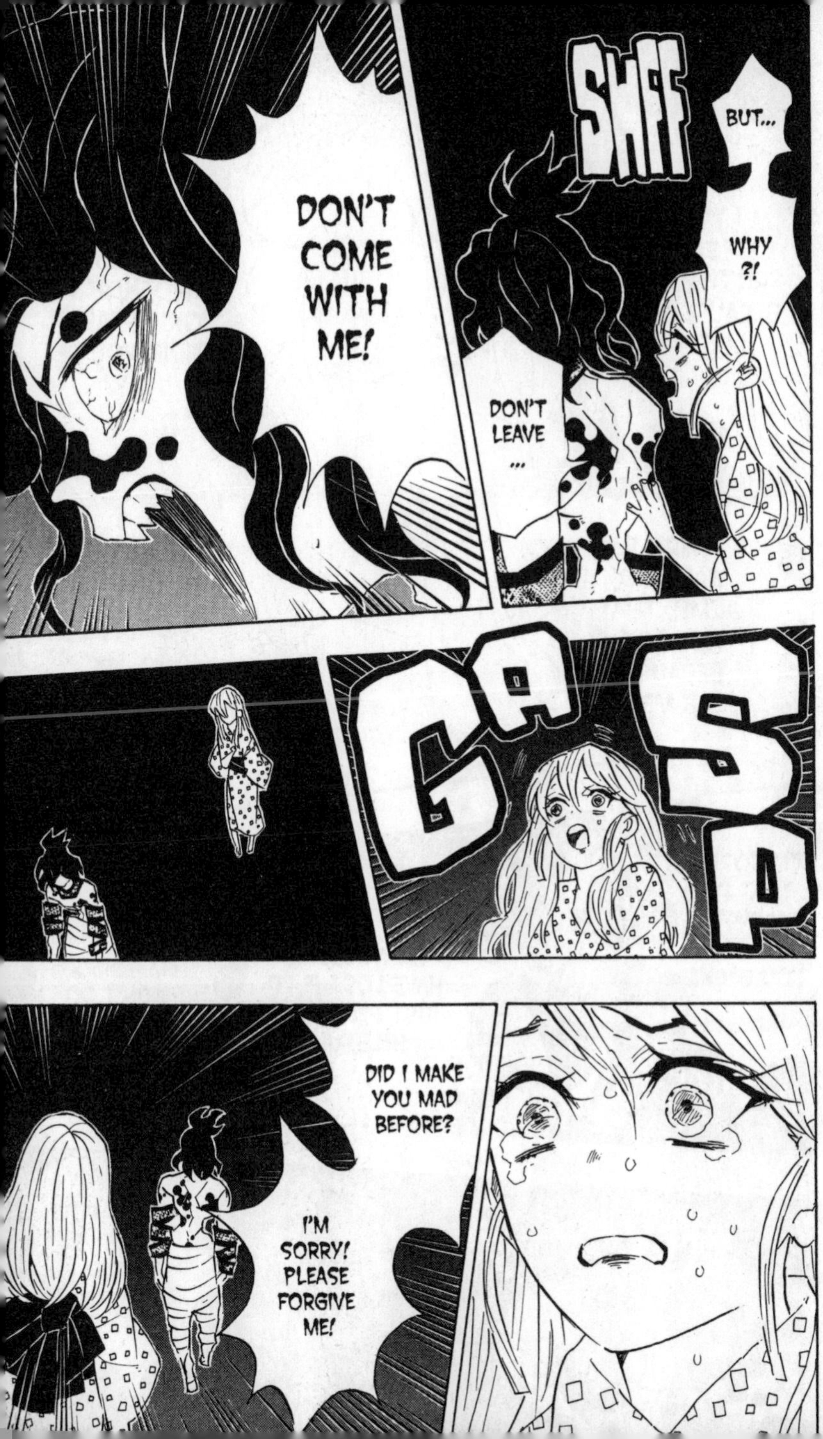
BUT...
SHFF
WHY?!
DON'T LEAVE...
DON'T COME WITH ME!
GASP
DID I MAKE YOU MAD BEFORE?
I'M SORRY! PLEASE FORGIVE ME!

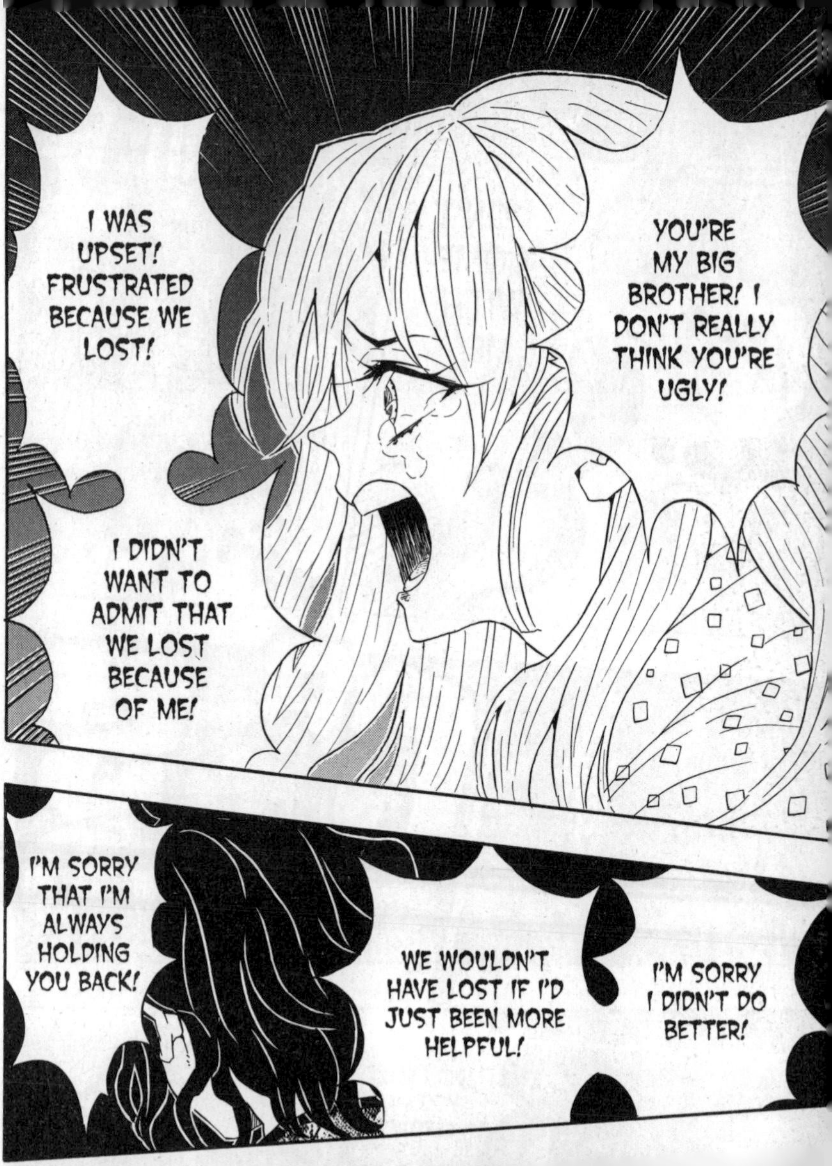
YOU'RE MY BIG BROTHER! I DON'T REALLY THINK YOU'RE UGLY!
I WAS UPSET! FRUSTRATED BECAUSE WE LOST!
I DIDN'T WANT TO ADMIT THAT WE LOST BECAUSE OF ME!
I'M SORRY I DIDN'T DO BETTER!
WE WOULDN'T HAVE LOST IF I'D JUST BEEN MORE HELPFUL!
I'M SORRY THAT I'M ALWAYS HOLDING YOU BACK!

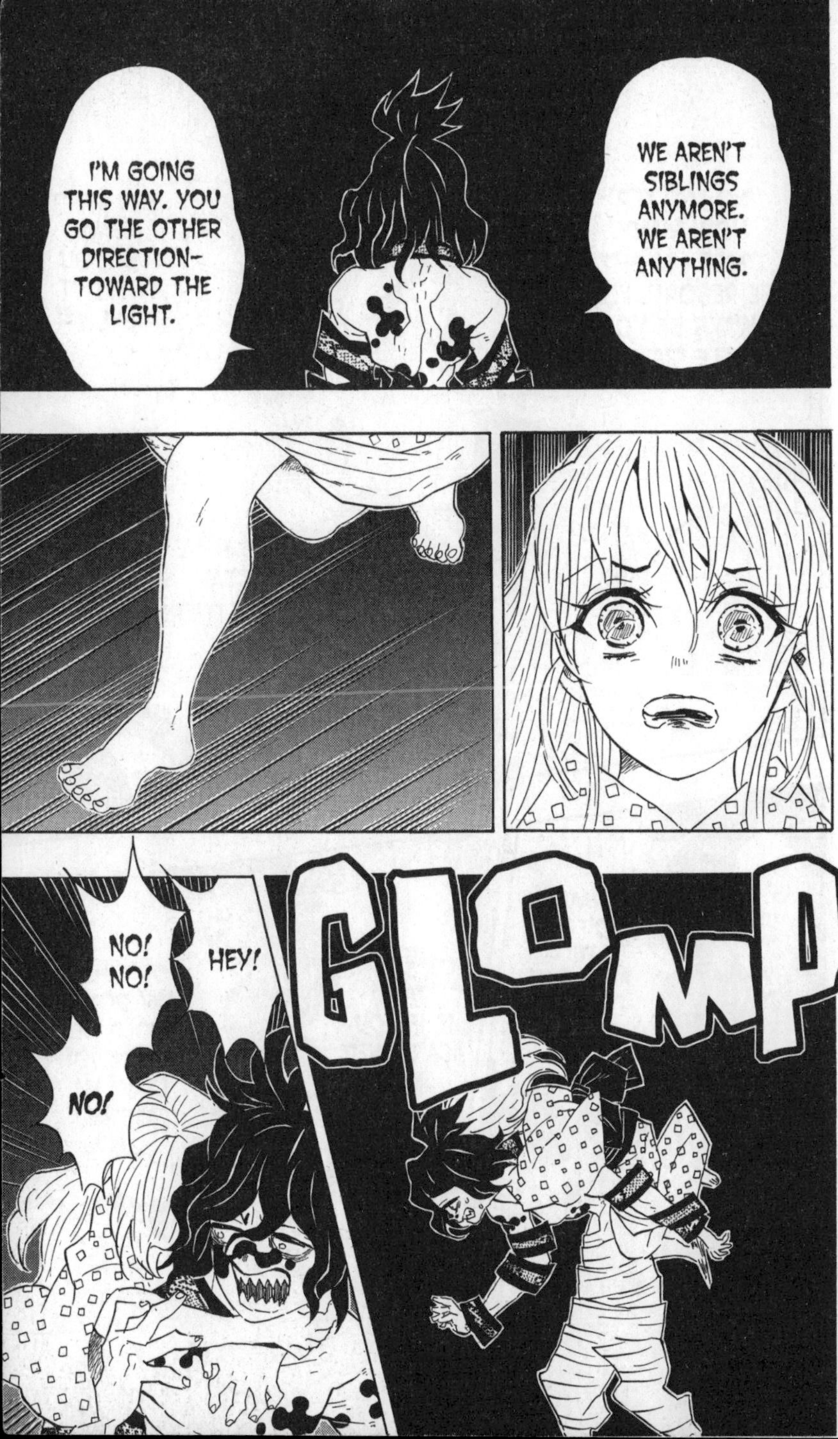
WE AREN'T SIBLINGS ANYMORE. WE AREN'T ANYTHING.
I'M GOING THIS WAY. YOU GO THE OTHER DIRECTION—TOWARD THE LIGHT.
GLOMP
HEY!
NO! NO!
NO!

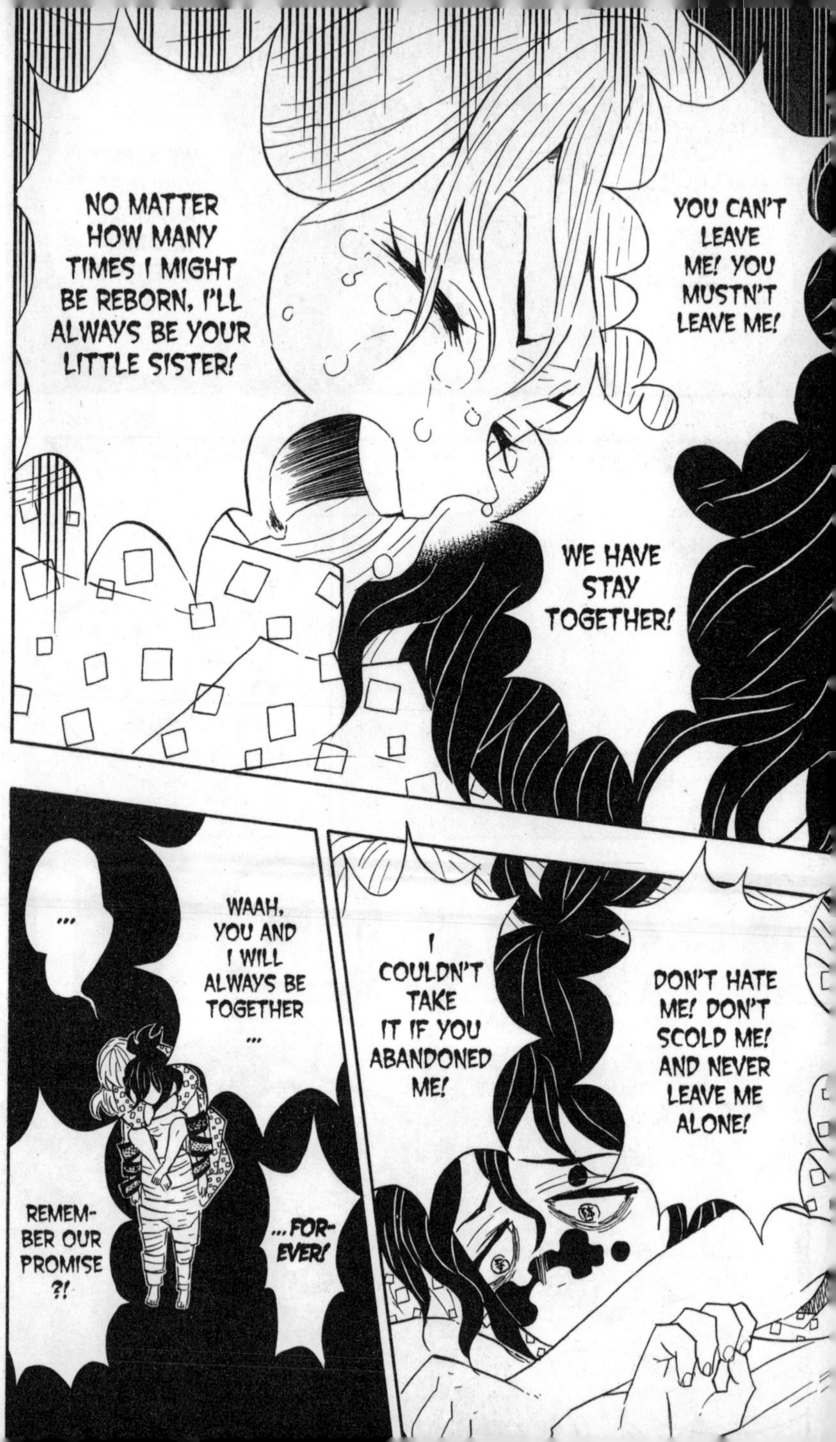
YOU CAN'T LEAVE ME! YOU MUSTN'T LEAVE ME!
NO MATTER HOW MANY TIMES I MIGHT BE REBORN, I'LL ALWAYS BE YOUR LITTLE SISTER!
WE HAVE STAY TOGETHER!
DON'T HATE ME! DON'T SCOLD ME! AND NEVER LEAVE ME ALONE!
I COULDN'T TAKE IT IF YOU ABANDONED ME!
WAAH, YOU AND I WILL ALWAYS BE TOGETHER ...
...
...FOR-EVER!
REMEM-BER OUR PROMISE ?!

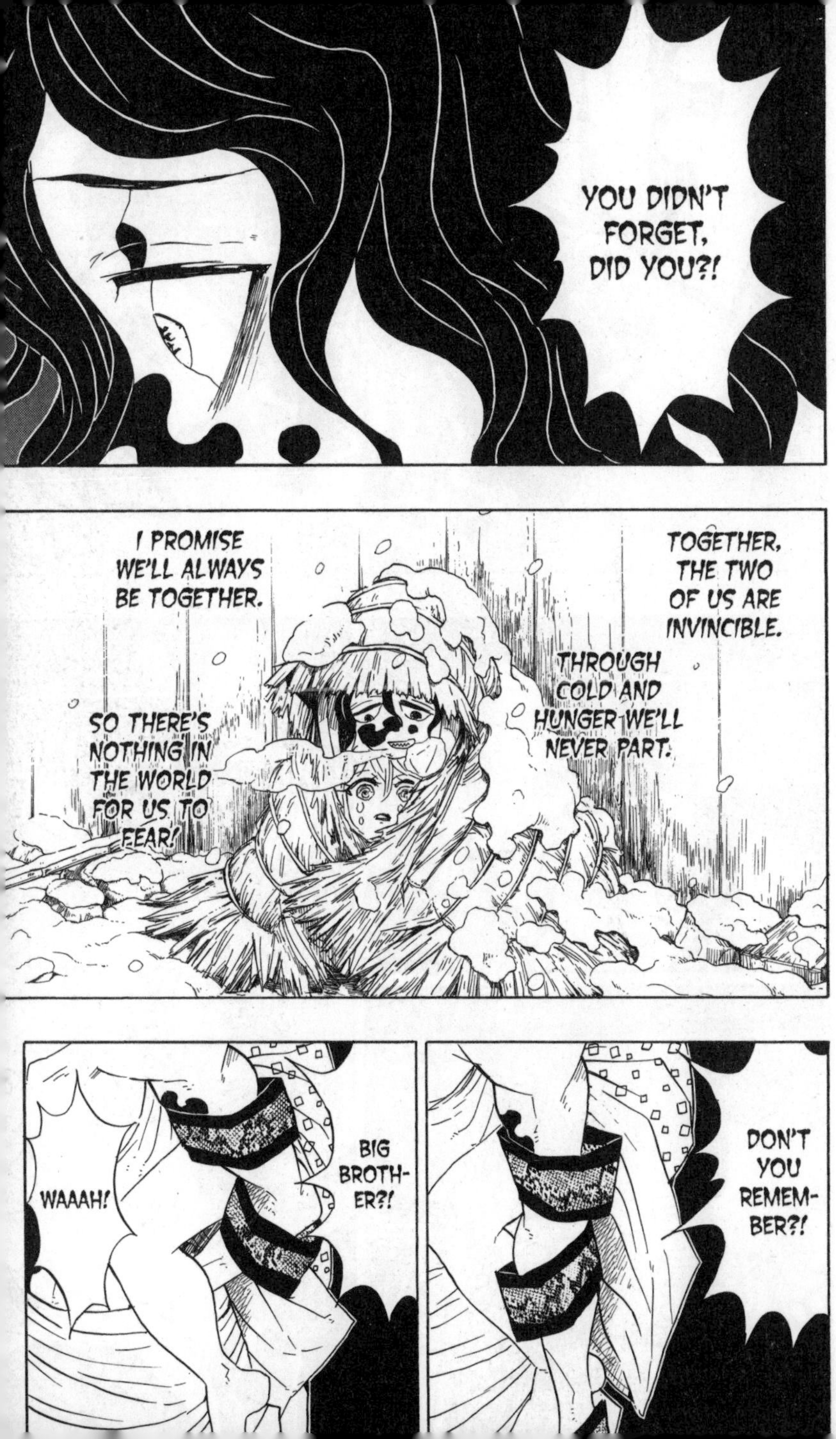
YOU DIDN'T FORGET, DID YOU?!
TOGETHER, THE TWO OF US ARE INVINCIBLE.
THROUGH COLD AND HUNGER WE'LL NEVER PART.
I PROMISE WE'LL ALWAYS BE TOGETHER.
SO THERE'S NOTHING IN THE WORLD FOR US TO FEAR!
DON'T YOU REMEMBER?!
BIG BROTHER?!
WAAAH!

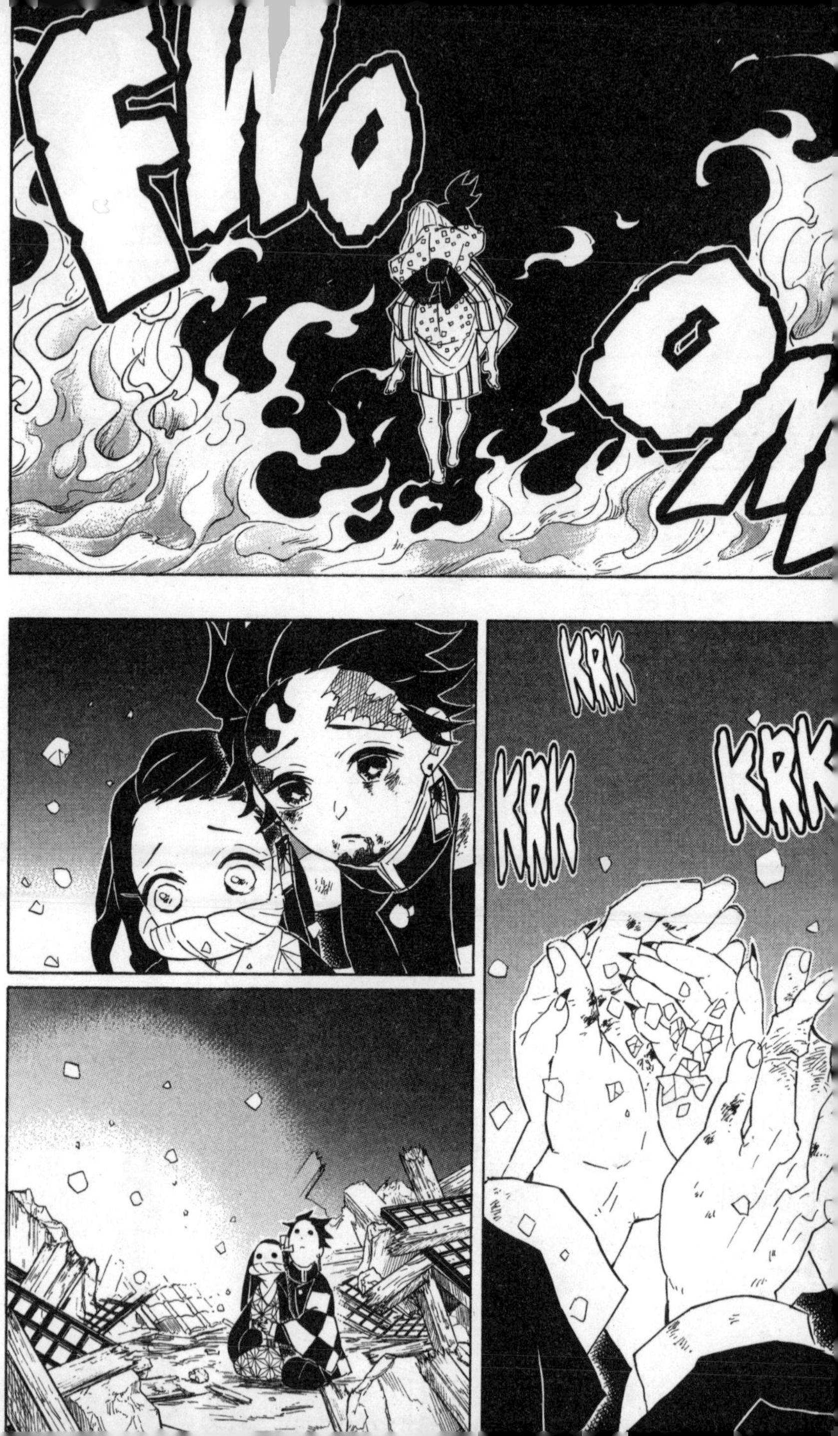
FWOOM
KRK
KRK
KRK

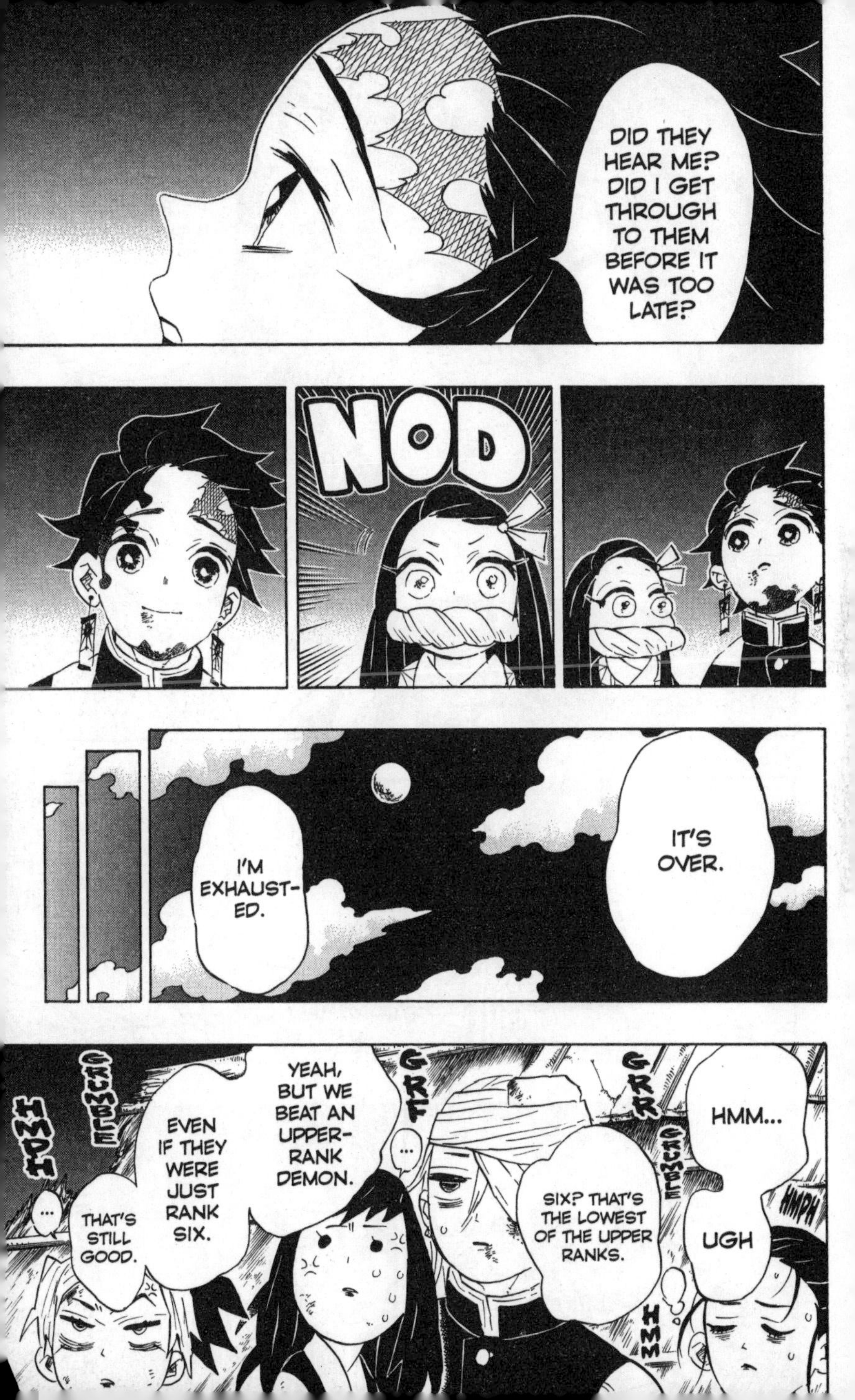
DID THEY HEAR ME? DID I GET THROUGH TO THEM BEFORE IT WAS TOO LATE?
NOD
IT'S OVER.
I'M EXHAUST-ED.
HMM...
GRR
GRUMBLE
SIX? THAT'S THE LOWEST OF THE UPPER RANKS.
HMPH
UGH
HMM
YEAH, BUT WE BEAT AN UPPER-RANK DEMON.
GRF
...
EVEN IF THEY WERE JUST RANK SIX.
GRUMBLE
HMPH
...
THAT'S STILL GOOD.

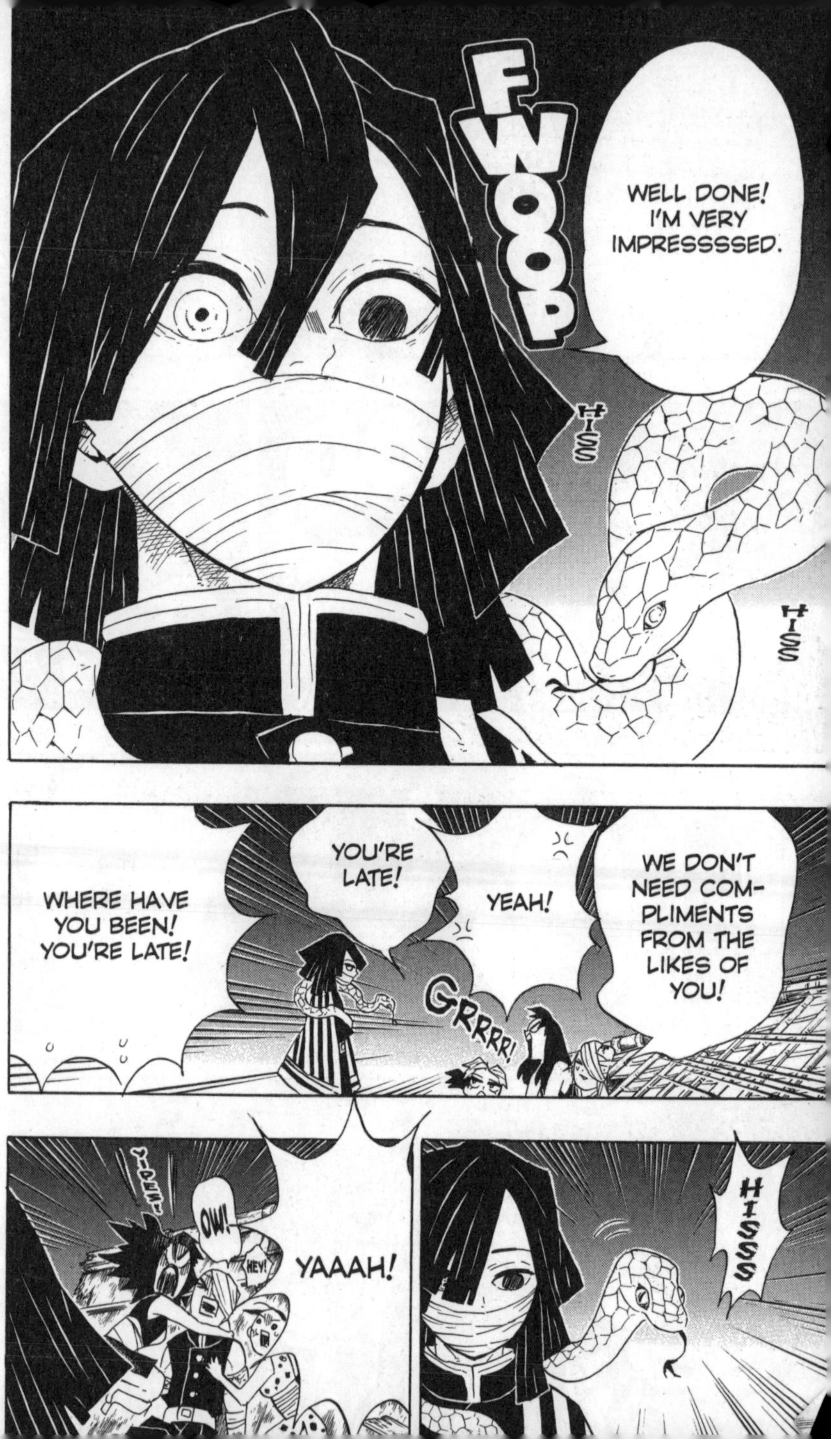
FWOOP
WELL DONE! I'M VERY IMPRESSSSED.
HISS
HISS
WE DON'T NEED COMPLIMENTS FROM THE LIKES OF YOU!
YEAH!
YOU'RE LATE!
GRRRRR!
WHERE HAVE YOU BEEN! YOU'RE LATE!
HISSS
YAAAH!
HEY!
OW!
YIPES!

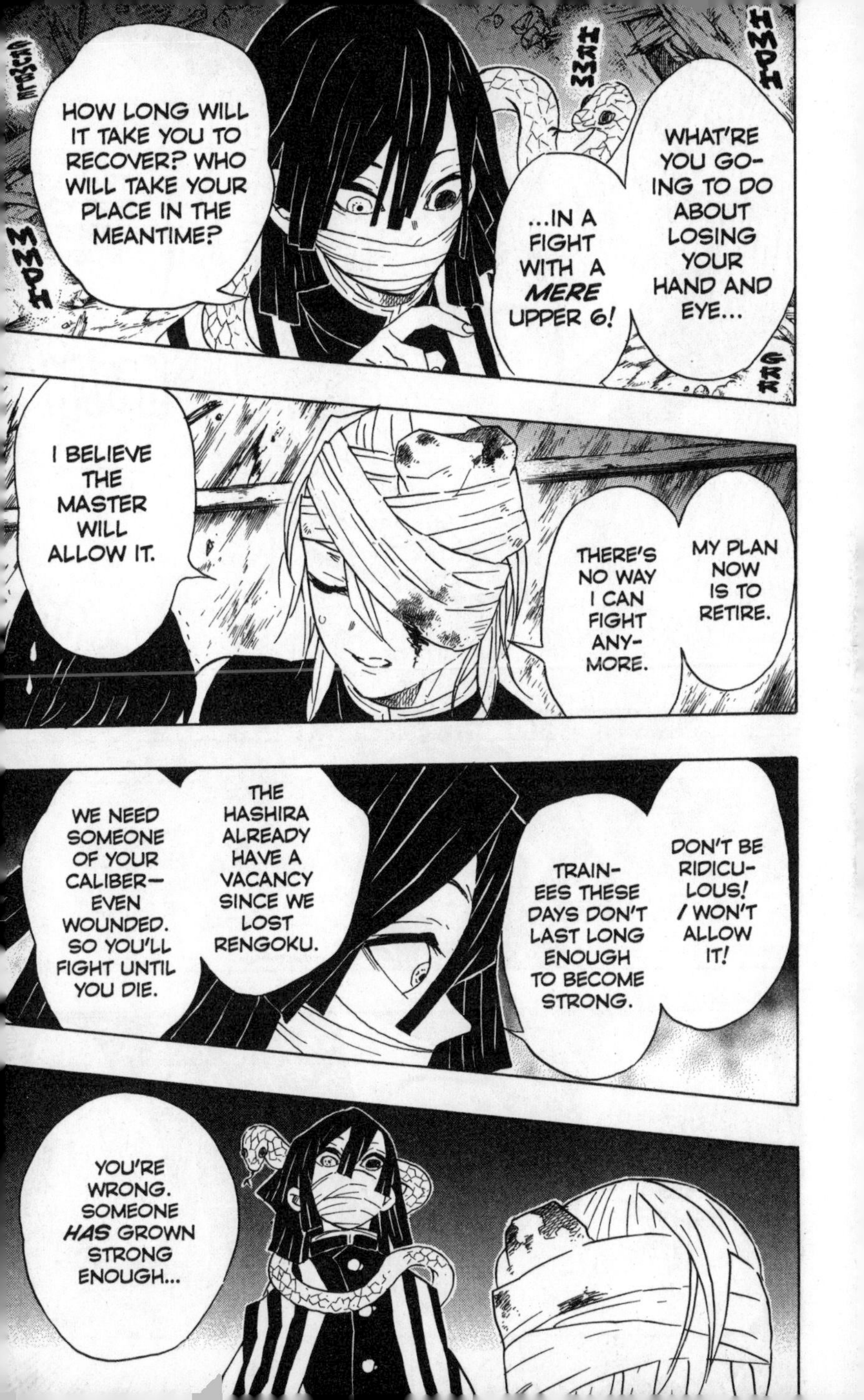
HMPH
WHAT'RE YOU GOING TO DO ABOUT LOSING YOUR HAND AND EYE...
GRR
HRMM
...IN A FIGHT WITH A *MERE* UPPER 6!
CRUMBLE
HOW LONG WILL IT TAKE YOU TO RECOVER? WHO WILL TAKE YOUR PLACE IN THE MEANTIME?
MMPH
MY PLAN NOW IS TO RETIRE.
THERE'S NO WAY I CAN FIGHT ANYMORE.
I BELIEVE THE MASTER WILL ALLOW IT.
DON'T BE RIDICULOUS! *I* WON'T ALLOW IT!
TRAINEES THESE DAYS DON'T LAST LONG ENOUGH TO BECOME STRONG.
THE HASHIRA ALREADY HAVE A VACANCY SINCE WE LOST RENGOKU.
WE NEED SOMEONE OF YOUR CALIBER—EVEN WOUNDED. SO YOU'LL FIGHT UNTIL YOU DIE.
YOU'RE WRONG. SOMEONE *HAS* GROWN STRONG ENOUGH...

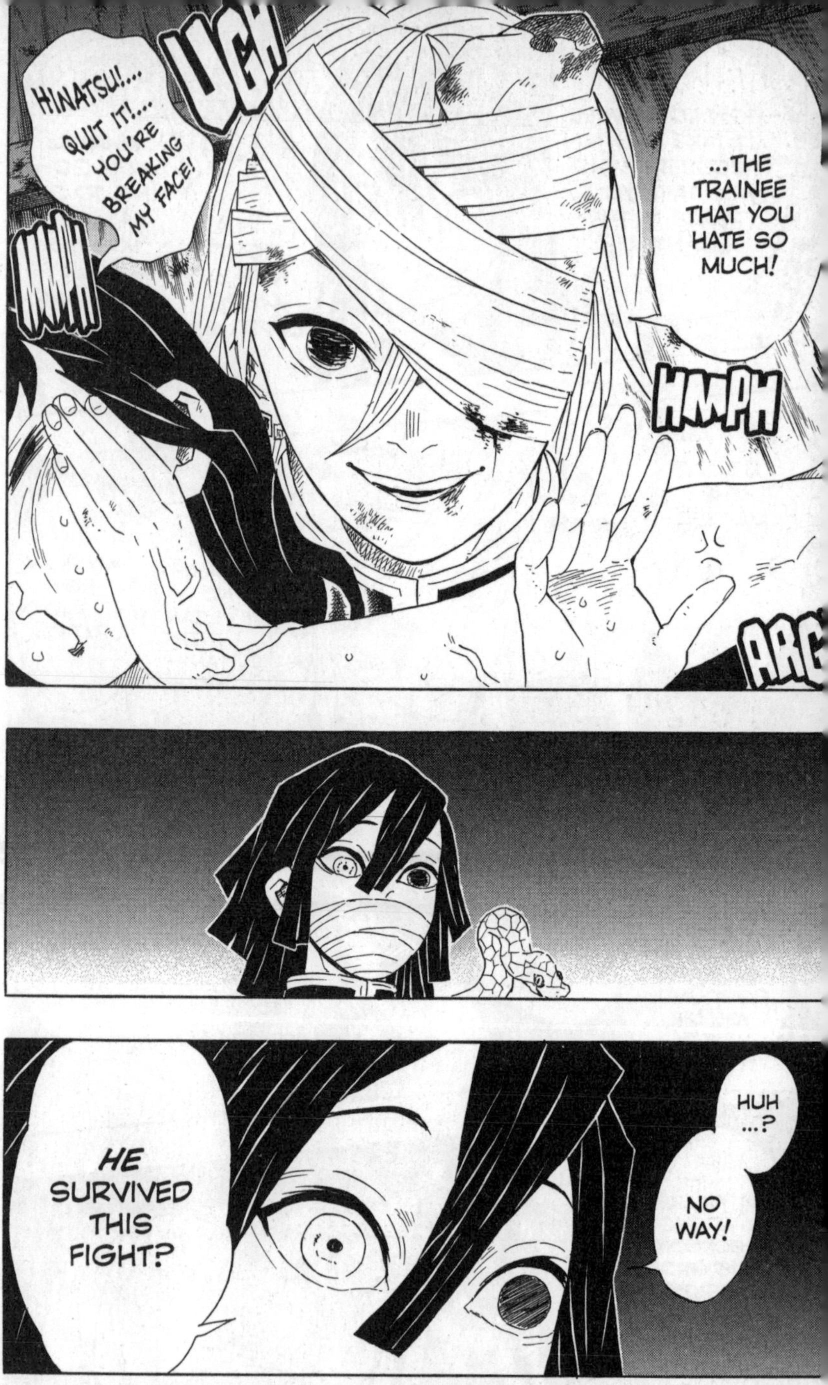
...THE TRAINEE THAT YOU HATE SO MUCH!
HMPH
ARG
UGH
HINATSU!... QUIT IT!... YOU'RE BREAKING MY FACE!
MMPH
HUH ...?
NO WAY!
HE SURVIVED THIS FIGHT?

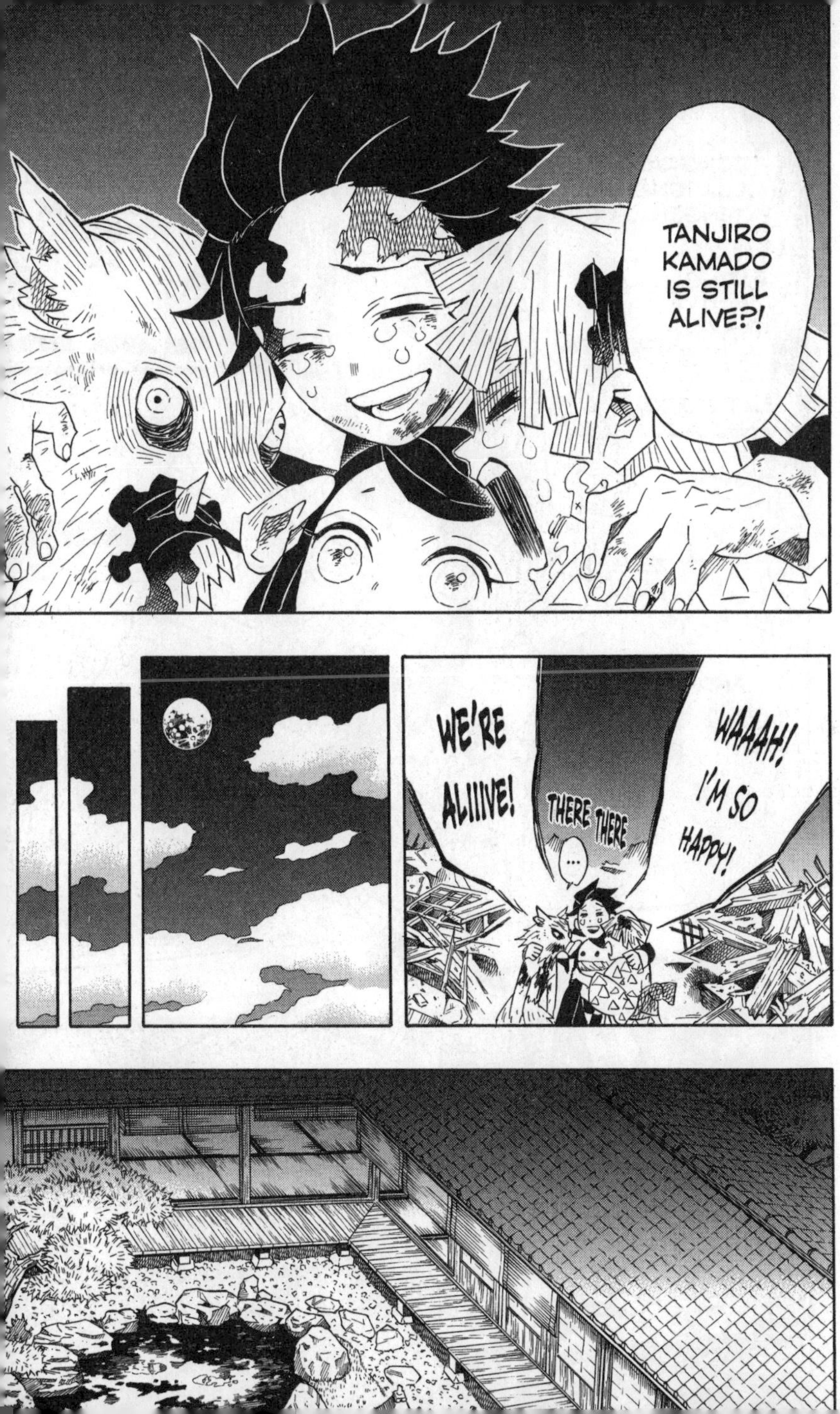
TANJIRO KAMADO IS STILL ALIVE?!
WAAAH! I'M SO HAPPY!
WE'RE ALIIIVE!
THERE THERE
...

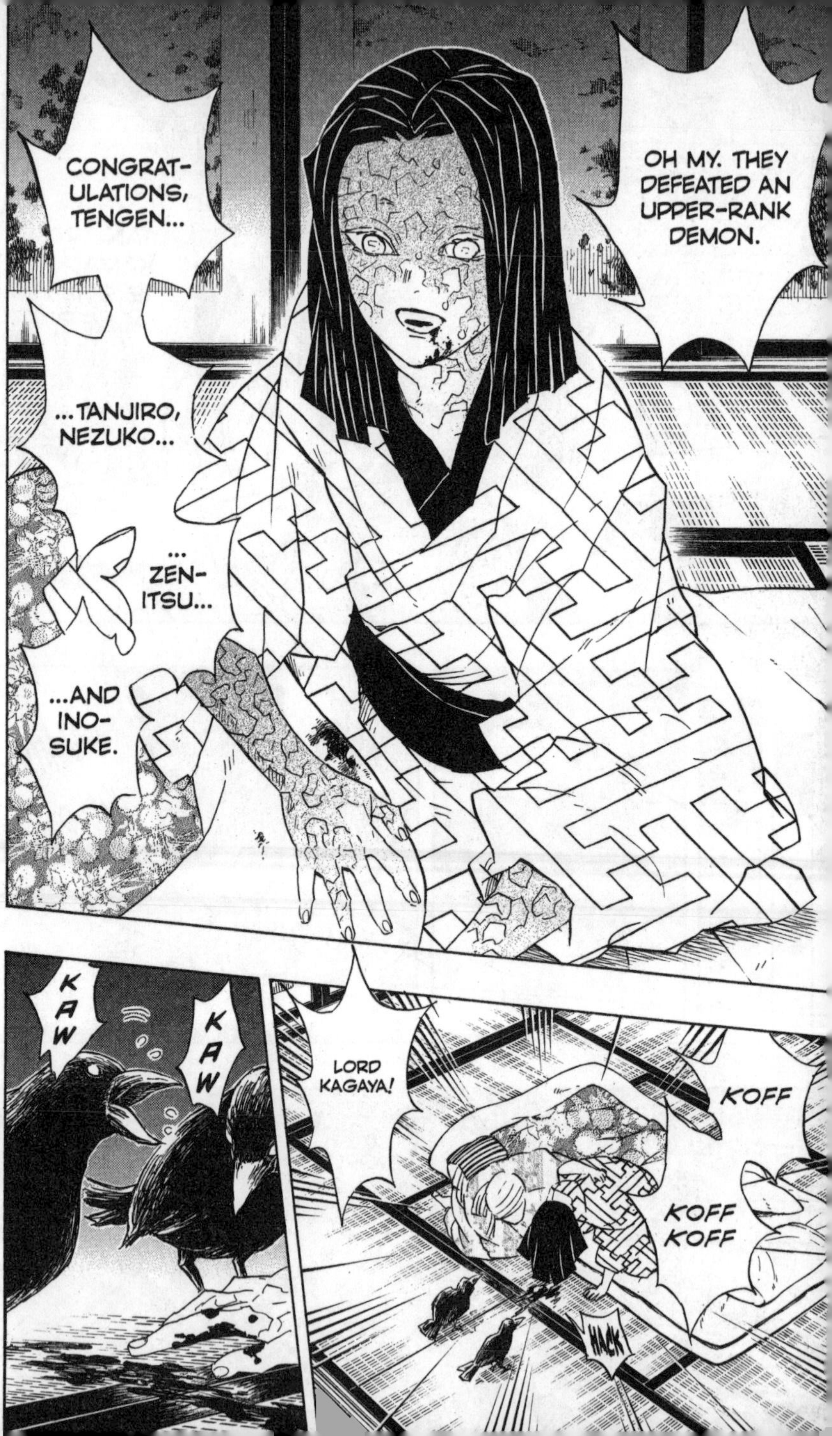
OH MY. THEY DEFEATED AN UPPER-RANK DEMON.
CONGRAT-ULATIONS, TENGEN...
...TANJIRO, NEZUKO...
...ZEN-ITSU...
...AND INO-SUKE.
KOFF
LORD KAGAYA!
KOFF KOFF
HACK
KAW
KAW

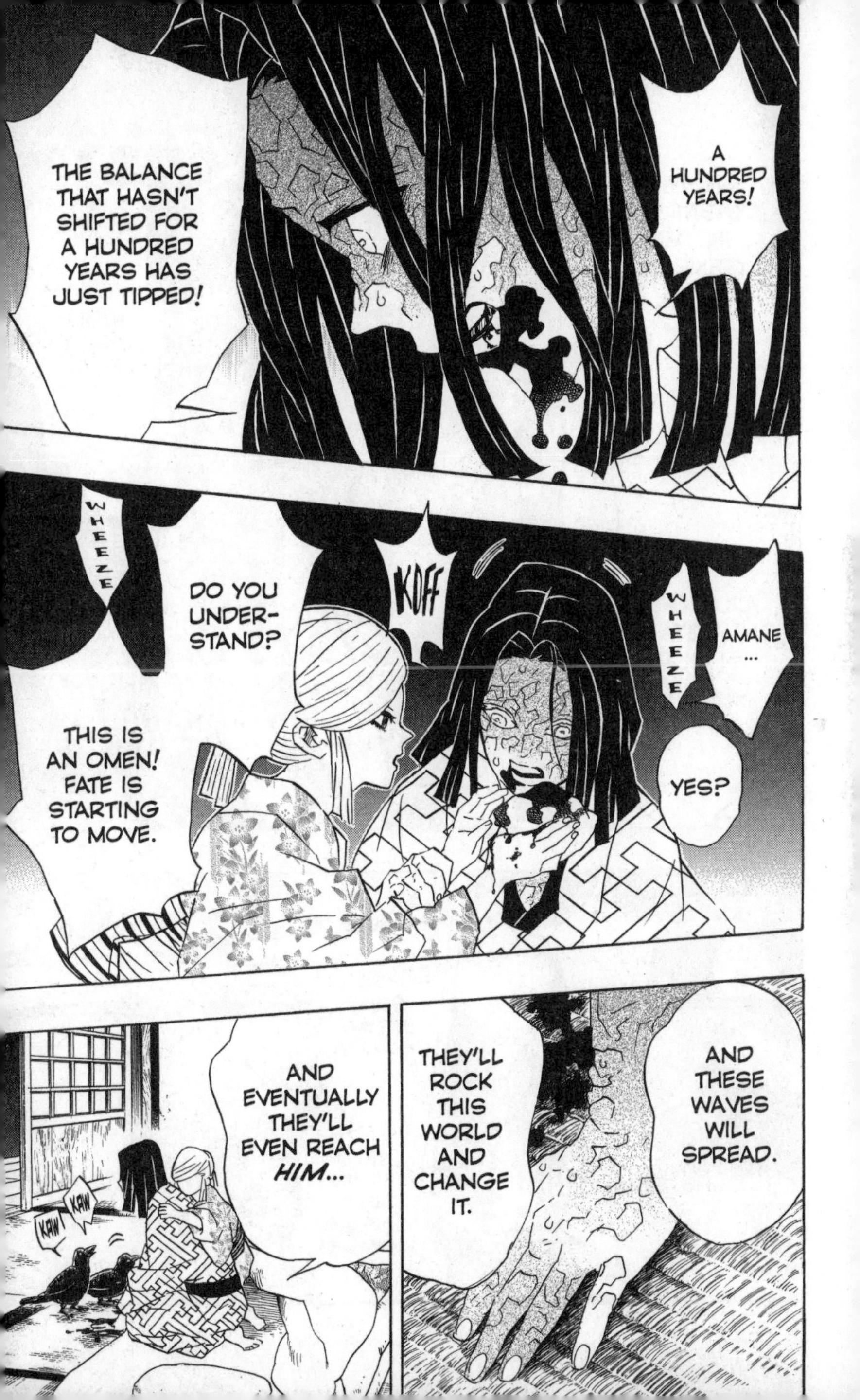
A HUNDRED YEARS!
THE BALANCE THAT HASN'T SHIFTED FOR A HUNDRED YEARS HAS JUST TIPPED!
AMANE...
WHEEZE
KOFF
YES?
WHEEZE
DO YOU UNDER-STAND?
THIS IS AN OMEN! FATE IS STARTING TO MOVE.
AND THESE WAVES WILL SPREAD.
THEY'LL ROCK THIS WORLD AND CHANGE IT.
AND EVENTUALLY THEY'LL EVEN REACH *HIM*...
KAW
KAW

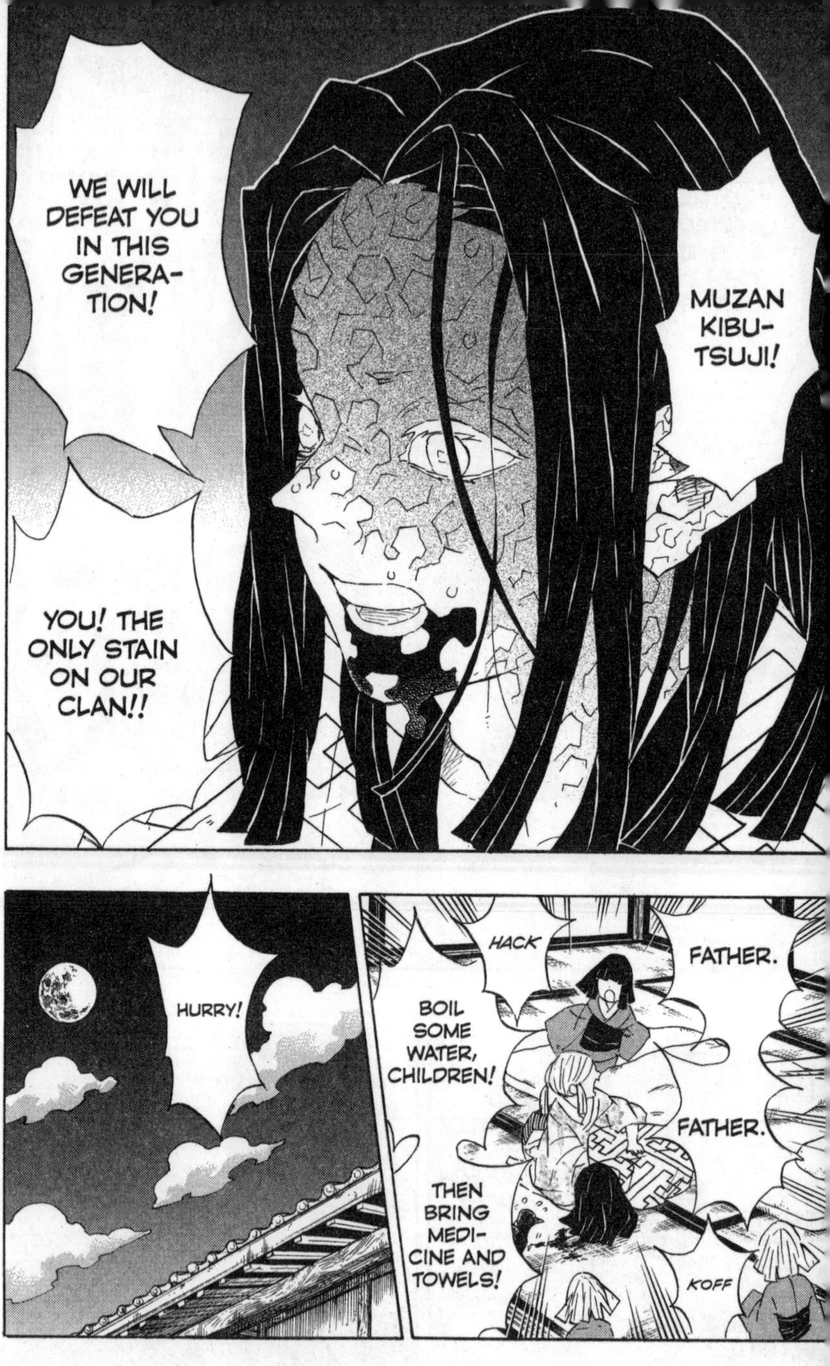
MUZAN KIBU-TSUJI!
WE WILL DEFEAT YOU IN THIS GENERA-TION!
YOU! THE ONLY STAIN ON OUR CLAN!!
FATHER.
HACK
BOIL SOME WATER, CHILDREN!
FATHER.
THEN BRING MEDI-CINE AND TOWELS!
KOFF
HURRY!

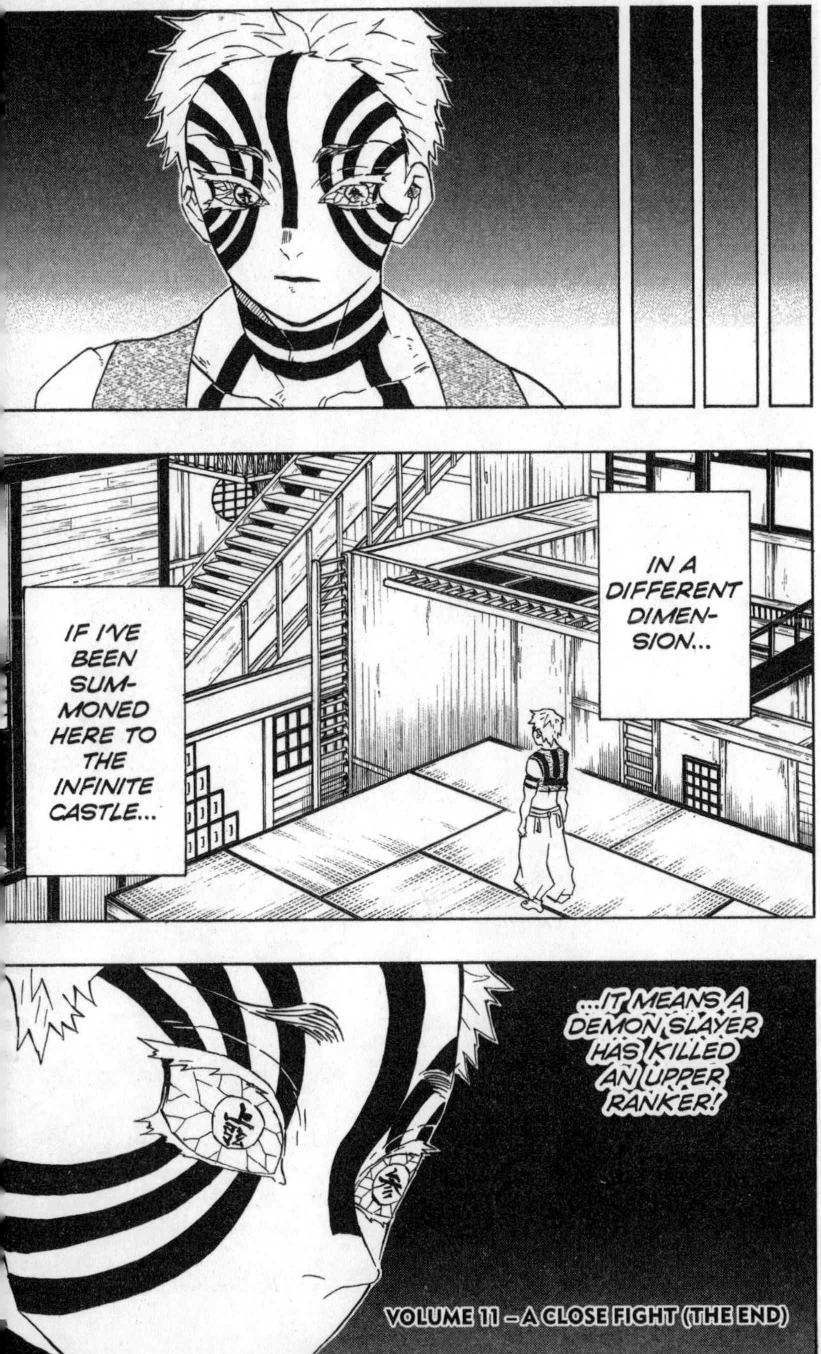
IN A DIFFERENT DIMENSION...
IF I'VE BEEN SUMMONED HERE TO THE INFINITE CASTLE...
...IT MEANS A DEMON SLAYER HAS KILLED AN UPPER RANKER!
VOLUME 11 – A CLOSE FIGHT (THE END)

Dr. STONE

STORY BY
RIICHIRO INAGAKI

ART BY
BOICHI

One fateful day, all of humanity turned to stone. Many millennia later, Taiju frees himself from petrification and finds himself surrounded by statues. The situation looks grim—until he runs into his science-loving friend Senku! Together they plan to restart civilization with the power of science!

 VIZ

YOU'RE READING THE
WRONG WAY!

142

DEMON SLAYER: KIMETSU NO YAIBA reads from right to left, starting in the upper-right corner. Japanese is read from right to left, meaning that action, sound effects and word-balloon order are completely reversed from English order.